T0234024

Lecture Notes in Computer Science   12599

More information about this subseries at http://www.springer.com/series/7407

Tomasz M. Gwizdałła ·
Luca Manzoni · Georgios Ch. Sirakoulis ·
Stefania Bandini · Krzysztof Podlaski (Eds.)

Cellular Automata

14th International Conference on Cellular Automata
for Research and Industry, ACRI 2020
Lodz, Poland, December 2–4, 2020
Proceedings

Springer

Editors
Tomasz M. Gwizdałła 🆔
University of Łódź
Lodz, Poland

Georgios Ch. Sirakoulis 🆔
Democritus University of Thrace
Xanthi, Greece

Krzysztof Podlaski 🆔
University of Łódź
Lodz, Poland

Luca Manzoni 🆔
Università degli Studi di Trieste
Trieste, Italy

Stefania Bandini 🆔
University of Milano-Bicocca
Milan, Italy

ISSN 0302-9743   ISSN 1611-3349 (electronic)
Lecture Notes in Computer Science
ISBN 978-3-030-69479-1   ISBN 978-3-030-69480-7 (eBook)
https://doi.org/10.1007/978-3-030-69480-7

LNCS Sublibrary: SL1 – Theoretical Computer Science and General Issues

This Springer imprint is published by the registered company Springer Nature Switzerland AG
The registered company address is: Gewerbestrasse 11, 6330 Cham, Switzerland

Preface

This volume contains a collection of original papers covering a variety of theoretical results and applications of cellular automata that were selected for presentation at the 14th International Conference on Cellular Automata for Research and Industry – ACRI 2020, held in Łódź, Poland, December 2–4, 2020. The conference was organized by the Faculty of Physics and Applied Informatics of the University of Łódź. Its primary goal was to provide a forum to enable researchers from a large variety of scientific fields based on the Cellular Automata approach to establish and strengthen international collaborations in their research and spread information about their achievements among the scientific community.

The ACRI conference series was first organized in Italy, namely, ACRI 1994 in Rende, ACRI 1996 in Milan, ACRI 1998 in Trieste and followed by ACRI 2000 in Karlsruhe (Germany), ACRI 2002 in Geneva (Switzerland), ACRI 2004 in Amsterdam (The Netherlands), ACRI 2006 in Perpignan (France), ACRI 2008 in Yokohama (Japan), ACRI 2010 in Ascoli Piceno (Italy), ACRI 2012 on Santorini (Greece), ACRI 2014 in Kraków (Poland), ACRI 2016 in Fez (Morocco), and ACRI 2018 in Como (Italy).

Cellular Automata offer a very powerful approach to the study of phenomena related to a large variety of problems. Initially presented as some form of counterpart or supplement to partial differential equations, they now enable us to study many real-world phenomena. Besides this practical significance, they often present behavior that is interesting from the theoretical point of view. For these reasons, CA became very popular for studying real applications. For many years researchers from academia and industry have used CA in many different fields dealing with theoretical as well as practical problems.

This 14th edition of ACRI was organized in an extraordinary situation caused by the COVID-19 pandemic, which strongly limited the possibilities of direct interaction between researchers knowledge between experts in several scientific areas: pure and applied mathematics, computer science, physics, biology, and mathematical systems theory.

This volume contains the papers accepted for presentation during the online sessions and online poster sessions of the 14th ACRI conference. Each submission was the subject of a detailed and careful review carried out by at least two Program Committee members. Finally, the selected papers were organized only in the form of the main track. Despite this homogeneity, a lot of different topics, corresponding to the typical areas covered by previous editions of the ACRI conference, were raised during the event.

First of all, let us express our thanks to Jarkko Kari, who kindly accepted our invitation to give a plenary lecture at ACRI 2020. The regular papers presented during the conference were often a wide and interesting outgrowth of papers from former ACRI conferences covering the problems of control, asynchronous CA, or traffic, thus corresponding strictly to previous meetings' special sessions. We decided, however, to divide the accepted submissions into three parts according to rather to the general idea of particular papers.

The first part, "Theory and Cryptography", contains studies of the dynamical properties of cellular automata and their application to cryptography as well as papers devoted to the classic problems of Cellular Automata or to the theory of control.

Part II, "Modeling and Simulation", collects papers related to various phenomena modeled by Cellular Automata. They address a lot of practical issues, such as economic, physical, or ecological problems. This part also covers the well-known problems of pedestrian simulation and the modeling of CA by nanoscale hardware.

We decided to reserve papers related to the modeling of one of the most important problems of 2020 – the COVID-19 pandemic – to the separate, third part of these proceedings.

We have to express our gratitude to many people who contributed, at different stages, to the organization of the conference. The members of the Steering Committee provided permanent support while preparing the meeting. We should say special words of thanks to the Program Committee members, whose work was invaluable in ensuring the quality of the accepted papers. We want to direct our warm thanks to all the authors of the accepted papers for their commitment, independent of the time difference encompassing twelve time zones. We would also like to emphasize the importance of many people from the local staff, like the remaining members of the Organizing Committee: Marcin Skulimowski, Alicja Miniak-Górecka, and Grzegorz Zgondek, and the organizational support from the Foundation of the University of Łódź. Finally, we acknowledge the excellent cooperation from the Lecture Notes in Computer Science team of Springer for their help in producing this volume.

December 2020

Tomasz M. Gwizdałła
Luca Manzoni
Georgios Ch. Sirakoulis
Stefania Bandini
Krzysztof Podlaski

Organization

Conference Chairs

Tomasz M. Gwizdałła	University of Łódź, Poland
Luca Manzoni	University of Trieste, Italy
Georgios Ch. Sirakoulis	Democritus University of Thrace, Greece

Organizing Committee

Tomasz M. Gwizdałła	University of Łódź, Poland
Krzysztof Podlaski	University of Łódź, Poland
Marcin Skulimowski	University of Łódź, Poland
Alicja Miniak-Górecka	University of Łódź, Poland

Steering Committee

Stefania Bandini	University of Milano-Bicocca, Italy
Bastien Chopard	University of Geneva, Switzerland
Samira El Yacoubi	University of Perpignan, France
Giancarlo Mauri	University of Milano-Bicocca, Italy
Katsuhiro Nishinari	University of Tokyo, Japan
Georgios Ch. Sirakoulis	Democritus University of Thrace, Greece
Hiroshi Umeo	Osaka Electro-Communication University, Japan
Thomas Worsch	University of Karlsruhe, Germany

Program Committee

Andy Adamatzky	University of the West of England, UK
Jan Baetens	Ghent University, Belgium
Stefania Bandini	University of Milano-Bicocca, Italy
Sukanta Das	Indian Institute of Engineering Science and Technology, Shibpur, India
Bernard De Baets	Ghent University, Belgium
Alberto Dennunzio	University of Milano-Bicocca, Italy
Andreas Deutsch	TU Dresden, Germany
Salvatore Di Gregorio	University of Calabria, Italy
Samira El Yacoubi	Université de Perpignan, France
Nazim Fates	LORIA - Inria Nancy, France
Allyx Fontaine	Université de Guyane, France
Enrico Formenti	Université Côte d'Azur, France
Ioakeim Georgoudas	Democritus University of Thrace, Greece
Tomasz Gwizdałła	University of Łódź, Poland

Contents

Disease Spreading Dynamics

Theory and Cryptography

A Cellular Automaton that Computes Shortest Paths in Grid Graph

Debopriya Barman$^{(\boxtimes)}$ and Sukanta Das$^{(\boxtimes)}$

Department of Information Technology, Indian Institute of Engineering Science and Technology, Shibpur, Howrah 711103, India
debopriyabarman@gmail.com, sukanta@it.iiests.ac.in

Abstract. This work develops a two-dimensional cellular automaton (CA) which solves single source shortest path problem for a grid graph. Grid graphs are represented as configurations of the CA, and maximum degree of a node is considered as four. Nodes and edges of the graph are modeled by cells with different state sets. The cells for nodes use a rule to update their states whereas the rest cells including the cells for edges use another rule. That is, two rules are used by the automaton which makes it a non-uniform CA. The worst case time complexity for the scheme is $\mathcal{O}(n)$ where n is the total number of nodes in the connected graph.

Keywords: Cellular Automata (CAs) · Grid graph · Shortest paths · Rule

Since 1980s, the graph theoretic problems, like Shortest Path Problem, Spanning Tree Problem (see [1]), etc. have been solved by Cellular Automata (CAs). Shortest Path Problem is a well known problem of graph theory, which asks to find shortest path from one node to another. In this work, we address the Single Source Shortest Path Problem for the grid graphs, and propose a cellular automaton (CA) that computes shortest paths of all nodes of a grid graph from a given source.

To solve the Shortest Path Problem for a given graph (Fig. 1(a)), we take a configuration that encodes the given graph as initial configuration. In the proposed CA, the nodes and edges of the given graph both are modelled by the cells of the CA. However, the roles of cells for these two entities are not the same. So two rules are used by the proposed CA- one for the cells modelling nodes and the other for the rest cells. Hence, the proposed CA is a *non-uniform CA*. As here we take 2D grid graphs, our lattice $\mathscr{L} = \mathbb{Z}^2$. Let our given grid graph has n rows and m columns where n and m are the maximum number of nodes present in a row and a column respectively. To place the grid graph on the cells of our lattice suitably, the cells are modeled for the nodes and the edges alternatively. We require $(2n - 1) \times (2m - 1)$ cells of $\mathscr{L}$ to represent the graph.

This work is supported by the SERB, Govt. of India sponsored project titled "Computational Problems and Cellular Automata" (File No: EMR/2017/001571).

T. M. Gwizdałła et al. (Eds.): ACRI 2020, LNCS 12599, pp. 3–7, 2021.
https://doi.org/10.1007/978-3-030-69480-7_1

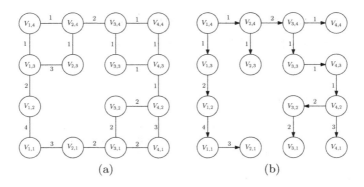

Fig. 1. (a) A 4 × 4 grid graph, and (b) The corresponding solution of (a)

We put the graph in the rectangle $(1,1), (2m-1,1), (2m-1,2n-1), (1,2n-1)$ in the first quadrant of $\mathscr{L}$. The cells inside the rectangle model the nodes and edges of the given graph, and take part in the computation. However, the cells of the rectangle are of three types:

1. Cell (i,j) models a node of the graph if i and j are both odd. A node $V_{i,j}$ is modeled by the cell $(2i-1, 2j-1)$. We call these cells as *Node Cell*.
2. Cell (i,j) models an edge if any one of i and j is odd and the other is even. These cells are labelled as *Edge Cell*.
3. Cell (i,j) is redundant if i and j are both even and is called *Blank Cell*.

The other cells of $\mathscr{L}$ remain unaffected throughout the computation. They are also treated as Blank Cells. Following are the steps of computation that are performed by each cell for a node.

1. We are given a source node. Initially it is assumed that no node is connected to the source i.e. they are *undiscovered*. The nodes systematically establish their connection to the source and then we call them as *discovered*.
2. The source node does nothing in the whole computation. However, the adjacent nodes to the source node change its state to connect themselves to the source node. These adjacent nodes store their distance from the source.
3. Consider that at least one neighbor node of an undiscovered node v connects itself to the source by changing its state. In the next step, the node v also updates its state to become discovered.
4. Whenever the node v connects itself to the source node through another node u and the weight of edge (u,v) is w, it notes down direction of u (up, down, left or right). Additionally, if the weight of u from the source is W, the node v stores its distance from the source as $W + w$.
5. Suppose that more than one neighbor node of v are discovered. Then it connects itself to that neighbor node which has minimum distance from the source node.
6. If the node v has more than one option to connect itself to the source, then to avoid confusion we make a preference list. Our first preference is to **left**

neighbor, second preference is to **upper** neighbor, third preference is to **right** neighbor, and fourth preference is to **lower** neighbor.

7. Whenever a node finds that it can reduce its distance from source through any of its neighbor nodes, it does so. The node also keeps track of the neighbor through which it has reduced its distance.

The CA runs and it reaches to a fixed point in finite time, we declare that the computation is over. We get Fig. 1(b) as the solution of Fig. 1(a). However, for some input graphs, the CA may not settle to a fixed point in finite time. If the graph contains a *negative weight cycle* (a cycle having total weight of its edges as negative), the CA does not reach to a fixed point in finite time. It is well known that single source shortest path problem cannot be solved if the graph contains a negative weight cycle.

According to our prescribed scheme, a node can *see* its adjacent nodes. But the cells, adjacent to the node cells, are used to represent the edges. Hence in each side, two consecutive cells are to be neighbors of the (node) cell. This makes the cell dependent on 9 neighbors (including itself). If (i, j) is the cell that models a node, then following set of cells are its neighbors: $\{(i - 2, j), (i - 1, j), (i, j + 2), (i, j + 1), (i, j), (i + 1, j), (i + 2, j), (i, j - 1), (i, j - 2)\}$.

States: It is clear from the steps of the computation stated before, a discovered Node Cell must be associated with two properties- say, A and B. That is, the state is an ordered pair - (A, B). To unify all the situations, we consider all the states as ordered pairs. If a state has only a single component, the first component of the pair is used to represent the state.

Property A: Consider at least one neighbor (say, node u) of a node v is connected to the source node. In order to get the path from the source node to the node v, v has to note that u is its previous node. So it stores the information that in which direction (left, right, up or down) of v, u is situated. Since we are using a 2-D CA, each node has degree at most four. For these four directions, we use four symbols- $\leftarrow, \rightarrow, \uparrow, \downarrow$. For the source node and an undiscovered node it is s and d respectively. We put b as property A if a Node Cell is absent.

For the Edge Cells property A denotes the presence of the edge. If an edge is present we put e as the property A of the cell. If a Node Cell or an Edge Cell is absent, it is b. For Blank Cells also it is b.

Property B: This property notes down the distance of a discovered node from the source node. Hence, this property assumes a real value. For the source node itself, the distance is always 0. For the Blank Cells and all other Node Cells this property is redundant. To denote that this property is not used, we put $-$ as second component of the state. For the Edge Cells property B is the weight of the edge if it exists.

Hence, the states are formally presented as the set $\{(s, 0), (d, -), (b, -), (e, w), (\leftarrow, \rho_1), (\rightarrow, \rho_2), (\uparrow, \rho_3), (\downarrow, \rho_4), \}$ where $\rho_1, \rho_2, \rho_3, \rho_4$ are distances from the source and w is the weight of an edge.

At this stage, we can classify the set of all possible initial configurations as *Valid* and *Invalid*. A configuration is called *Invalid* if one of the following conditions holds-

- If no cell or more than one cell is treated as source node, since we are dealing with Single Source Shortest Path Problem.
- If a cell, reserved for node (respectively edge), assigned a state of edges (respectively nodes), the configuration is invalid.
- If a cell (i, j), $i, j \in 2\mathbb{N}$ is used as either a Node Cell or a Edge Cell.

An initial configuration is *valid* if it is not *invalid*. That is, for a valid configuration, none of the above points is satisfied. These configurations can represent an input graph.

Local Rule: Let us now formally write down the rule for the Node Cells. We use algorithmic style to present the rule. We assume that the state of a cell (i, j) is $(\psi_{i,j}, \rho_{i,j})$. The rule is noted in Algorithm 1. Apart from the Node Cells, the rest cells use the *Identity Rule* as their local rule. These cells do not change their states during evolution.

Algorithm 1. The rule $\mathscr{R}_1$

---

begin
    if $\psi_{i,j} = s$ **or** b **then do nothing** and **return**
    if $\psi_{i-2,j} = \psi_{i,j+2} = \psi_{i+2,j} = \psi_{i,j-2} = d$ **or** b **then do nothing** and **return**
    if $\psi_{i-1,j} = \psi_{i,j+1} = \psi_{i+1,j} = \psi_{i,j-1} = b$ **then do nothing** and **return**
    Treat '-' as ∞, if '-' is the second component of a state
    Let c is $\min\{\rho_{i-2,j} + \rho_{i-1,j}, \rho_{i,j+2} + \rho_{i,j+1}, \rho_{i+2,j} + \rho_{i+1,j}, \rho_{i,j-2} + \rho_{i,j-1}\}$
    if $c = \rho_{i,j}$ **then do nothing** and **return**
    if $\rho_{i-2,j} + \rho_{i-1,j} = c$ **then**
        $\psi_{i,j} := \leftarrow$
    else if $\rho_{i,j+2} + \rho_{i,j+1} = c$ **then**
        $\psi_{i,j} := \uparrow$
    else if $\rho_{i+2,j} + \rho_{i+1,j} = c$ **then**
        $\psi_{i,j} := \rightarrow$
    else $\psi_{i,j} := \downarrow$
    $\rho_{i,j} := c$
end

The designed CA has the following properties.

Proposition 1. *Our prescribed CA computes the Shortest Path from a single source of a connected grid graph with n nodes.*

Proposition 2. *The worst case time complexity of the prescribed computation is $\mathcal{O}(n)$ where n is the total number of nodes in the connected graph.*

References

1. Roy, S., Ray, A., Das, S.: A cellular automaton that solves distributed spanning tree problem. J. Comput. Sci. **26**, 39–54 (2018)

Strengthening ACORN Authenticated Cipher with Cellular Automata

Jossy Joseph, Joseph Jacob, M. K. Abinshad, K. N. Ambili$^{(\boxtimes)}$ (iD),
and Jimmy Jose (iD)

Department of Computer Science and Engineering,
National Institute of Technology Calicut, Kozhikode, India
{jossy_b160072cs, joseph_b160515cs, abinshad_b140367cs,
ambili_p180002cs, jimmy}@nitc.ac.in

Abstract. The authenticated encryption (AE) scheme ACORN v3,
a CAESAR competition finalist, has been shown to be particularly
vulnerable against Differential Fault Attack (DFA), even more so than
its previous version ACORN v2. In this paper, we analyse how fault
attacks can be prevented in ACORN v3 by using cellular automata (CA).
The good pseudorandom properties of CA are exploited and renders the
ACORN v3 infeasible to perform fault attacks on. The Programmable
Cellular Automata (PCA) 90-150 is effectively deployed to make ACORN
cipher robust against DFA.

Keywords: ACORN · Differential Fault Attack · Cellular Automata ·
PCA 90-150 · Stream cipher · Authenticated encryption

1 Introduction

The rise in the use of technology in daily lives has made an increase in security
a necessity. The usual strategy of ensuring confidentiality and authenticity
separately may not be sufficient. In scenarios like the Internet of Things (IoT),
the authenticity of information passing through various sensors and servers is
very important.

The cryptographic algorithms which achieve confidentiality and authenticity
simultaneously are called authenticated encryption (AE) algorithms [1]. The
rising demand has triggered the cryptographic community to propose robust AE
designs based on stream ciphers, block ciphers or sponge functions. These are
evaluated in the CAESAR competition [2]. ACORN v3 [3], a CAESAR finalist,
is a stream cipher based AE scheme. In the current work, the inherent properties
of Cellular Automata (CA) [4] are exploited to improve the strength of ACORN.

The 1-dimensional CA structure [4] consists of a lattice of cells in a row
fashion, which can take value of 0 or 1. Each cell value evolves in every time step
depending on a function of values of itself and its neighbour cells. This is called
a two-state three-neighbourhood CA. The next state of a cell can be represented
as,

$$x_i(t+1) = f\{x_{i-1}(t), x_i(t), x_{i+1}(t)\} \tag{1}$$

© Springer Nature Switzerland AG 2021
T. M. Gwizdałła et al. (Eds.): ACRI 2020, LNCS 12599, pp. 8–17, 2021.
https://doi.org/10.1007/978-3-030-69480-7_2

where, $x_i(t)$ denotes the output state of the ith cell at the tth time step and f denotes the transition function of the particular cell realized with a combinational logic and is known as a rule of the CA.

When the rules used in the cells are different, the CA type is called a hybrid CA. Maximal length CA are those CA with specific rules which results in maximum cycle length. These cycle through every possible state (except all 0's) once before repeating the cycle of values. Wolfram's work in [5] proved that the patterns generated by the maximal-length CA are significantly better in randomness properties than other widely used methods like Linear Feedback Shift Registers (LFSRs).

The rules used in the design of CA in this paper are rules 90 and 150.

$$rule90 : x_i(t+1) = x_{i+1}(t) \oplus x_{i-1}(t) \qquad (2)$$

$$rule150 : x_i(t+1) = x_i(t) \oplus x_{i+1}(t) \oplus x_{i-1}(t) \qquad (3)$$

where $x_i(t)$ refers to the state bit of the ith cell at time t. These rules which only involve the logical XORs are called linear or additive rules. CA can also be divided into types based on the neighbors of the extreme cells (the first and last cells). Null boundary refers to the extreme cell's neighbors connected to logic '0'. The CA used in this paper will use null boundary, maximal length CA with rules 90 and 150.

2 Preliminaries

Programmable Cellular Automata (PCA) [6] are structures based on the elementary Cellular Automata but the rule structure is not fixed. The dynamic rule structure works based on control signal, each signifying a particular rule set on which the CA will perform iterations. Numerous hardware implementations have been made. However these control signals can be programmed in software to randomly select from a given set of rules. The PCA configuration used in this paper is based on the 90-150 configuration which signifies that each ruleset defines a hybrid null-boundary maximal length CA with rules 90 and 150. In Sect. 6, security analysis based on [7] has been provided to show the aptness of PCA 90-150 for use in ACORN.

The stream cipher ACORN v3 [3] is a finalist in the Caesar competition. One of the most significant attacks against ACORN v3 is the DFA. It is found that the modified version ACORN v3 is more vulnerable than ACORN v2 against the fault attack [8]. CA can be used as a good cryptographic primitive against fault attacks and in particular, the DFA. A brief description of the stream cipher ACORN v3 is provided in the next section.

3 Description of ACORN v3

ACORN v3 [3] uses a 128-bit key and a 128-bit initialization vector. The state size of ACORN v3 is 293 bits denoted by $S = (s_0, s_1, \ldots, s_{292})$. There are six

Fig. 1. The 6 LFSRs are concatenated to represent the state.

Linear Feedback Shift Registers (LFSRs) being concatenated in ACORN-128 as shown in Fig. 1.

Here, f_i indicates the feedback bit and m_i refers to the message bit that gets concatenated to the state at the last step of the State Update function which can be divided into 4 steps as outlined below:

1. Update the state:

$$S_{i,289} = S_{i,289} \oplus S_{i,235} \oplus S_{i,230} \tag{4}$$

$$S_{i,230} = S_{i,230} \oplus S_{i,196} \oplus S_{i,193} \tag{5}$$

$$S_{i,193} = S_{i,193} \oplus S_{i,160} \oplus S_{i,154} \tag{6}$$

$$S_{i,154} = S_{i,154} \oplus S_{i,111} \oplus S_{i,107} \tag{7}$$

$$S_{i,107} = S_{i,107} \oplus S_{i,66} \oplus S_{i,61} \tag{8}$$

$$S_{i,61} = S_{i,61} \oplus S_{i,23} \oplus S_{i,0} \tag{9}$$

2. Generate the keystream bit as

$$ks_i = S_{i,12} \oplus S_{i,154} \oplus maj(S_{i,235}, S_{i,61}, S_{i,193}) \oplus ch(S_{i,230}, S_{i,111}, S_{i,66}) \tag{10}$$

where
$maj(x, y, z) = (x \& y) \oplus (x \& z) \oplus (y \& z)$
$ch(x, y, z) = (x \& y) \oplus ((\neg x) \& z)$

3. Generate the nonlinear feedback bit using control bits and feedback function. The control bits ca_i and cb_i are set to either 0 or 1 in different iterations specified in [3]. The feedback function (FBK) computes the nonlinear feedback bit as

$$f_i = S_{i,0} \oplus (\neg S_{i,107}) \oplus maj(S_{i,244}, S_{i,23}, S_{i,160}) \oplus (ca_i \& S_{i,196}) \oplus (cb_i \& ks_i) \tag{11}$$

4. Shift the 293-bit register with the feedback bit f_i as

$$\text{for } j := 0 \text{ to } 291 \text{ do}$$

$$S_{i+1,j} = S_{i,j+1} \tag{12}$$

$$S_{i+1,292} = f_i \oplus m_i \tag{13}$$

The state update is run for 1792 iterations in the initialization step after loading the key and IV into the state. Similarly, the update function is used in a different number of iterations in the associated data processing, encryption and finalization stages [3].

The modified version ACORN v3 is different from ACORN v2 in the feedback function and the filter function. This resulted in a better balance between the feedback function and the output filtering function and larger security margin against guess-and-determine attack. However, these modifications resulted in an increase in the vulnerability against the Differential Fault Attack [8] and is described in the next section.

4   Differential Fault Attack on ACORN v3

The attack consists of two main parts: fault locating and equation solving [8]. If the fault locating step is achieved reliably, then the equation solving can be done by retrieving a system of equations with respect to the initial state of ACORN at which the fault was induced. At this step, fundamental methods to retrieve equations and some improvement strategies to get more linear equations are implemented. After obtaining the linear equations, the guess-and-determine method is used to obtain the initial state. After that, forgery attacks can be performed on the cipher.

The first algorithm of the fault locating step is explained briefly.

This algorithm returns two sets MQ_i and AQ_i. MQ_i contains positions where 1 occurs with a probability of less than 1. The AQ_i set contains positions where 1 always occurs. Firstly, 32 initial states are chosen randomly. In each state, a random state bit is flipped (from 0 to 1 or from 1 to 0). Now the encryption algorithm proceeds to output the fault-induced keystream (z^i) of size l (size of plaintext and hence the ciphertext). The same state is run without inducing any fault resulting in the correct keystream output (z).

The corresponding bits of z and z^i are logical XORed and put in a set Δz. Based on values of Δz, the positions are input into the sets AQ_i and MQ_i. These sets AQ_i and MQ_i are then used for further computations.

In [9], the prevention of fault attacks using the pseudorandomness and fast-diffusion properties of CA in stream ciphers is shown. Using PCA 90-150, we will prevent the first step of the attack, that is, the fault locating step, by rendering the first algorithm unreliable, thereby rendering the next steps unreliable and successfully preventing the attack. In the section below, we will describe the design of our PCA 90-150 enhanced ACORN in preventing this attack on ACORN.

5   Design of PCA Enhanced ACORN

The modified state update function using PCA 90-150 is shown in Fig. 2.

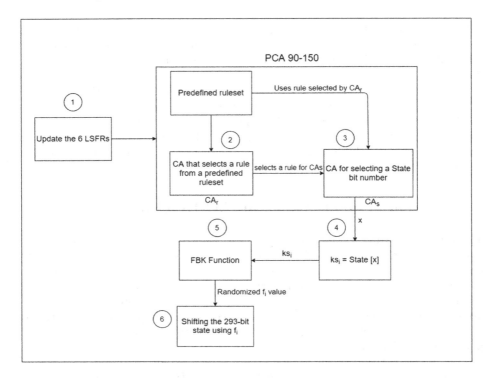

Fig. 2. The modified State Update Function (stepwise as per numbering) in the CA enhanced ACORN

Our novel approach uses two CAs to achieve randomization. This overcomes the uniqueness of state bits used in keystream generation function by randomizing the ks_i bit, described in step 2 of Sect. 3, earlier in the paper.

The modified keystream generation function uses PCA 90-150 as shown in Fig. 2. A predefined ruleset is used. CA random-rule (CA_r), a maximal length [1] null boundary hybrid CA which selects the rule from the ruleset for CA state (CA_s) to use in each call to the keystream bit generation function. CA_s is a 9-cell maximal length null boundary CA using PCA 90-150 configuration. Hence, a basic simulation of programmable CA is used here.

The keystream bit generation function in ACORN v3 is

$$ks_i = S_{i,12} \oplus S_{i,154} \oplus maj(S_{i,235}, S_{i,61}, S_{i,193}) \oplus ch(S_{i,230}, S_{i,111}, S_{i,66}) \quad (14)$$

In our modified cipher the keystream bit generation function is,
$CA_r();$
$ks_i = CA_s();$

ACORN v3 uses a polynomial function of degree 2. CA configuration in the current design can be represented as a polynomial [6] of degree 6, for n (number of cells) = 6 as

$$x(x + 1)(x^4 + x + 1) \quad (15)$$

For n = 8, we can achieve an even higher degree of 8 with polynomial

$$x(x+1)(x^6 + x + 1) \qquad (16)$$

Similarly for higher values of n, we obtain a higher degree expression.

The fault attacks which are successful on ACORN v3 are ineffective against this modified CA based ACORN cipher. This is due to the parallel transformation of the CA that spreads the fault very quickly into the state, which makes the fault difficult to track. The unpredictability of the nonlinear feedback bit, which is appended to the last bit of the state bit during every state update, is the key reason behind this.

6 Randomness Review of PCA 90-150

In this section, we try to show why the PCA 90-150 is apt for use as a good pseudorandom number generator in the feedback bit function to randomize both the state number as well as the cycle length to be run. It has been shown in countless references that fault attacks are easily prevented by randomization.

In [7], PCA 90-150 has been compared with Controllable Cellular Automata (CCA). In PCA, there are control bits for each cell to control the rules corresponding to each cell. In CCA, there are more control lines to control the neighbourhood relations between cells and updating of states to further improve the randomness of 1-dimensional CA. CCA0 refers to type of CCA which keeps the state of the cells constant during the CA computation process. CCA1 refers to type of CCA which complements the state of the cells during the CA computation process. More details can be found in [7].

Below are some of the tests that have been performed on PCA 90-150 to prove its quality of randomness [7].

6.1 DIEHARD Test on PCA 90-150

DIEHARD tests [10] are a set of statistical tests used to measure the quality of randomness of a random number generator. DIEHARD is seemingly the best test for general randomness measurement. Usually, a Pseudorandom Number Generator that passes DIEHARD is considered as good.

The results from Table 1 show that PCA 90-150 is potentially an excellent pseudo-random number generator passing 13 out of 18 tests which is significantly better than single ruleset hybrid cellular automata.

6.2 Entropy (ENT) Test

ENT [11] is a Pseudorandom Number Sequence Test Program, which applies specific tests to bytes of data in a given file and submits the results back. This test program is useful for evaluating pseudorandom number generators for encryption. ENT performs a variety of tests on the input stream and produces

Table 1. DIEHARD test result on PCA, p = 8-bit integer [7]

Test name	PCA 90-150 (p)
1. Overlapping sum	Pass
2. Runs up 1	Pass
Runs Down 1	Pass
Runs up 2	Pass
Runs Down 2	Pass
3. 3D sphere	Pass
4. A parking lot	Fail
5. Birthday Spacing	Pass
6. Count the ones 1	Pass
7. Binary Rank 6*8	Pass
8. Binary Rank 31*31	Pass
9. Binary Rank 32*32	Pass
10. Count the ones 2	Pass
11. Bitstream test	Pass
12. Craps wins	Pass
13. Minimum distance	Fail
14. Overlapping Perm	Fail
15. Squeeze	Pass
16. OPSO test	Fail
17. OQSO test	Fail
18. DNA test	Pass
Number of tests passed	*13*

Table 2. ENT values for PCA 90-150 [7]

	Chi-square (pass rate)	Entropy (average value)	SCC (average value)
PCA 90-150	70%	6.101210	0.121479

output based on various parameters, such as Entropy, Chi-square Test, and Serial Correlation Coefficient (SCC).

As shown in Table 2, the entropy values are very good with acceptable chi-square pass rate compared to Controllable Cellular Automata (CCA) given in [7].

6.3   Randomness Value Variance

The randomness value variance shown in Fig. 3 shows the randomness value variance, which is a good indicator of the randomness of the values generated by the CA. Here 15-cell PCA 90-150 is used. PCA 90-150 has higher variance values than both CCA0 and CCA1. This has 100% Chi-square pass rate, which is a very significant advantage. In addition, CCAs are much harder to implement, as well.

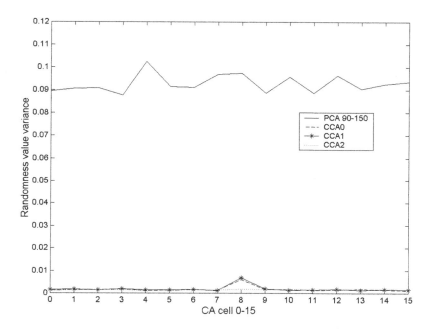

Fig. 3. Variance of randomness value [7]

7   DFA on PCA Enhanced ACORN

Differential Fault Attack is not possible on the modified ACORN. The fault locating cannot be executed reliably, since the keystream bit found in every state update function cannot be predicted accurately. This is because, in each state update iteration, a random state bit is assigned as feedback bit by running the CA_s, which has a dynamic rules defined by CA_r.

The minimum number of steps in encryption is 1279, excluding the 1792 steps in the initialization phase. Assuming that on average, the 32 random states selected for the fault locating step of the attack are near 1792/2 steps in the initialization step, on average, the minimum number of steps required is 1279 + (1792/2) = 2175. For each iteration, the attacker has to make on average 2175 accurate predictions about the keystream bit, which is to be XOR'ed to the state and added to the last bit of the updated state. So in total, 32 * 2175 = 69000 accurate predictions altogether must be made in order for the first algorithm of the fault locating step, to give the correct output. Assuming the probability of getting 1 or 0 as the keystream bit in each iteration is 50%, since the initial seed in the Cellular Automata is random, the attacker will have to choose one correct set of values from a permutation of 2^{69600}. Hence the probability of the attacker finding this correct combination is near 0 or negligible.

As shown in [8], let n be the number of fault experiments. We can get $11.26n$ equations, including $7.03n$ linear equations. We use the guess-and-determine method to solve the equations. The time complexity of obtaining the initial state equals to $c * 2^{146.5-3.52n}$ approximately, where c is the time complexity of solving linear equations and $26 < n < 43$. Assuming the attacker reaches the correct combination of keystream bits in half the total permutations, The total complexity of obtaining the initial state would equal to

$$c * 2^{146.5-3.52n} * 2^{(69600/2)}$$

which is a huge improvement. This shows that the attacker cannot brute-force the keystream bits feasibly in order to further continue with the attack algorithm in Sect. 4.

8   Conclusion

By utilizing the pseudorandom and fast-diffusion properties of cellular automata, we have shown that the DFA is ineffective against the PCA enhanced ACORN cipher by randomizing the state bits in each iteration and the number of cycles the CA runs for in each iteration. The degree of the keystream bit generation function would be greater than or equal to 8 which is much higher than previous degree of 2, effectively thwarting the fault attack. Also, we have shown that it is infeasible to obtain the keystream bits by brute-force due to such a large number of permutations.

References

1. Rogaway, P.: Authenticated-encryption with associated-data. In: Proceedings of the 9th ACM Conference on Computer and Communications Security, pp. 98–107 (2002)
2. Zhang, F., Liang, Z.-Y., Yang, B.-L., Zhao, X.-J., Guo, S.-Z., Ren, K.: Survey of design and security evaluation of authenticated encryption algorithms in the Caesar competition. Front. Inf. Technol. Electron. Eng. **19**(12), 1475–1499 (2018)
3. Wu, H.: Acorn: a lightweight authenticated cipher (v3). Candidate for the CAESAR Competition (2016). https://competitions.cr.yp.to/round3/acornv3.pdf. Accessed 04 Sept 2020
4. Wolfram, S.: Cellular automata as models of complexity. Nature **311**(5985), 419–424 (1984)
5. Wolfram, S.: Cryptography with cellular automata. In: Williams, H.C. (ed.) CRYPTO 1985. LNCS, vol. 218, pp. 429–432. Springer, Heidelberg (1986). https://doi.org/10.1007/3-540-39799-X_32

6. de la Guía Martínez, D., Peinado Domínguez, A.: On the sequences generated by 90-150 programmable cellular automata (2001)
7. Guan, S.-U., Zhang, S.: Pseudorandom number generation based on controllable cellular automata. Future Gener. Comput. Syst. **20**(4), 627–641 (2004)
8. Zhang, X., Feng, X., Lin, D.: Fault attack on acorn v3. Comput. J. **61**(8), 1166–1179 (2018)
9. Jose, J., Das, S., Chowdhury, D.R.: Prevention of fault attacks in cellular automata based stream ciphers. J. Cell. Automata **12**(1–2), 141–157 (2016)
10. Alani, M.M.: Testing randomness in ciphertext of block-ciphers using diehard tests. Int. J. Comput. Sci. Netw. Secur. **10**(4), 53–57 (2010)
11. ENT test suite. http://www.fourmilab.ch/random. Accessed 04 Sept 2020

Prevention of Fault Attacks in ASCON Authenticated Cipher Using Cellular Automata

Joseph Jacob, Jossy Joseph, M. K. Abinshad, K. N. Ambili$^{(\boxtimes)}$ (iD),
and Jimmy Jose (iD)

Department of Computer Science and Engineering,
National Institute of Technology Calicut, Kozhikode, India
{joseph_b160515cs,jossy_b160072cs,abinshad_b140367cs,
ambili_p180002cs,jimmy}@nitc.ac.in

Abstract. ASCON is a sponge function based authenticated encryption (AE) scheme chosen in CAESAR competition for lightweight applications. Its suitability for high performance applications make it desirable in environments like Internet of Things (IoT) where large number of very constrained devices communicate with high-end servers. The drawback is that fault analyses like Statistical Ineffective fault attack (SIFA) and Sub-Set Fault Analysis (SSFA) are possible. In this paper, we modify ASCON 128a exploiting the pseudo-random properties of Cellular Automata (CA) to prevent these attacks.

Keywords: ASCON · Fault analysis · Pseudorandom ·
Cryptography · Cellular Automata · Authenticated encryption ·
SSFA · SIFA

1 Introduction

The changing landscape of electronic devices and technologies involved has created new demands for security of devices and software. The conventional methods of providing privacy and authentication separately are not sufficient to address their simultaneous need.

Authentic Encryption schemes provide both privacy and integrity of the transmitted messages. Often, messages have associated data with them such as the receiver's IP address. Here, it is prudent to use Authentic Encryption with Associated Data (AEAD) [9] schemes. There are three types of AEAD processes which are Encrypt-and-MAC, Encrypt- then-MAC and MAC-then-Encrypt. ASCON [3] is an AEAD scheme which follows Encrypt-then-MAC.

ASCON is vulnerable to fault attack by double fault injection, wherein two faults are injected at two different locations. We propose to use CA to prevent fault attacks on ASCON and provide mathematical validation for the same.

Section 2 of the paper captures the details of ASCON 128a. Section 3 provides literature survey of fault attacks and the specific attacks under consideration,

© Springer Nature Switzerland AG 2021
T. M. Gwizdałła et al. (Eds.): ACRI 2020, LNCS 12599, pp. 18–25, 2021.
https://doi.org/10.1007/978-3-030-69480-7_3

namely, SIFA and SSFA. Section 4 describes the features of CA, its use in modified design of ASCON and the rationale for the same.

2   ASCON

ASCON [3] is a light-weight 320-bit state sponge cipher whose initial state S is given by concatenating the Initial Vector (IV) of 64 bits with key and nonce of 128 bits each. From hereon, unless otherwise stated, ASCON refers to ASCON 128a. ASCON has four stages as shown in Fig. 1, namely:

- Initialization: 12 rounds of the SPN transformation in which permutation p is applied to the initial state S followed by XORing of the key K to it.
- Processing Associated Data: The associated data are processed in blocks of length r (bitrate).
- Processing Plain-text: The plain-text is encrypted blockwise to give the ciphertext.
- Finalization: The state S passes through 12 rounds of transformation p, and the key K is XORed to the last 128 bits of S to get the tag T.

The SPN permutation p consists of three sub-transformations:

- p_c where a round specific constant is added to x_2 where $S = x_0\|x_1\|x_2\|x_3\|x_4$, x_i are part of the block
- p_s where the data is passed through 64 parallel 5-bit sliced S-boxes
- p_l where each x_i, $0 \leq i \leq 4$ is mixed within itself.

Since ASCON is inverse-free, the decryption can be done in the same way. The decrypted ciphertext is returned only if the tags match.

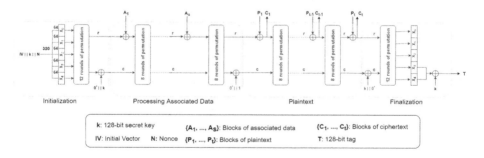

Fig. 1. ASCON block diagram

3   Fault Attacks

A fault attack is an attack on the physical device. It leads to errors, which causes failure of the placed security systems when exploited. Fault attack is done in two steps fault injection and fault exploitation [1]. Permanent and transient fault attacks are the two types. Fault attacks which cause the device to be permanently damaged are called permanent fault attacks. Transient fault attacks are those which are not permanent and there is negligible damage to the device [4].

3.1   Statistical Ineffective Fault Analysis (SIFA)

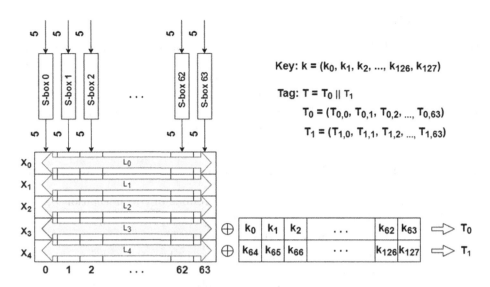

Fig. 2. SIFA attack on ASCON

SIFA [8] works by injecting double faults at the bits 3 and 4 (counting starts from zero) of the output of a pair of selected S-boxes during the last round of finalization. Let X be $x_0\|x_1\|x_2\|x_3\|x_4$ where each x_i represents consecutive 64 bits of input to the linear diffusion layer L_i. The L_3 and L_4 is XORed to key K to get tag T to form equations with key K. The key K is XORed with tag T, which is equal to the output of linear diffusion layer, as shown in Fig. 2. The output of linear diffusion layer is obtained by using a sparse matrix. The inverse of this output gives the input to the linear diffusion layer or the output of the substitution layer. The equation for bits 3 and 4 can be found for the selected pair of S-boxes, which is already known. Hence, the following Eqs. (1) are obtained in which the only unknown is the key [8].

$$s_3^j = \sum_{r=0}^{63}[(T_{0,r} \oplus k_r) \odot l_{j,r}^{(3)}] \bmod 2$$

$$s_4^j = \sum_{r=0}^{63}[(T_{1,r} \oplus k_{r+64}) \odot l_{j,r}^{(4)}] \bmod 2 \tag{1}$$

$$L_i^{-1} = [l_0^{(i)T}, l_1^{(i)T}, ..., l_{63}^{(i)T}]^T, \quad i = 0, 1, ..., 4$$

In Eqs. (1), s_3^j and s_4^j refers to the faulted bits 3 and 4 at the output of the selected S-boxes,

L_i^{-1} refers to the inverse of ith linear diffusion layer and $l_j^{(i)T}$ is the jth row of the inverse diffusion matrix corresponding to x_i. k_r, k_{r+64} refers to the rth bit and $r+64^{th}$ bit of the key K respectively. $T_{0,r}$ and $T_{1,r}$ are the rth bit of first and next consecutive 64 bits of the tag T.

The entire process from double fault injection to forming equations, is repeated M times. Using the key-dividing strategy to these equations, we find the secret key K.

3.2   Sub-Set Fault Analysis (SSFA)

SSFA [6] is done on the same path as SIFA. However, the fault is induced to the 64-bit input x_2 of the Substitution layer. It was observed that when the 3rd bit was set to zero in 10 out of 16 cases, taking the XOR of 4th and 5th bits results in zero. This is used here to perform the fault analysis. The analysis is done in two phases. The flowchart for phase 1 is shown in Fig. 3. Phase 2 is not relevant to this paper.

4   CA-Based ASCON

CA [10] is a lattice of cells that can take any number of values depending on its state, e.g., 2-state CA cells can take 0 or 1. Each cell value modifies in every iteration depending on a function whose parameters are the current values of the corresponding cell and its neighbor cells. In two-state three-neighbourhood CA, the neighbors are the two adjacent cells to it. The next state of a cell can be represented as the output of a function,

$$x_i(t+1) = f\{x_{i-1}(t), x_i(t), x_{i+1}(t)\} \tag{2}$$

where $x_i(t)$ denotes the output state of the ith cell at the tth time step or iteration. Here f denotes the transition function of the particular cell realized with a combination logic and is known as a rule of the CA [7].

When the rules used in the cells are different, then it is a hybrid CA. Those CA with specific rules which result in maximum cycle length, which cycles through every possible state (except 0) once before repeating the cycle of values is called maximal length CA. The rules 90 and 150 for CA are:

$$rule90 : q_i(t+1) = q_{i+1}(t) \oplus q_{i-1}(t)$$

$$rule150 : q_i(t+1) = q_i(t) \oplus q_{i+1}(t) \oplus qi_{i-1}(t)$$

where $q_i(t)$ refers to the state bit of the ith cell at time t.

The rules which only involve the logical XOR are called linear or additive rules. CA can also be divided into types based on the neighbors of the extreme cells (the first and last cells). Null boundary CA refers to the extreme cell's neighbors connected to logic '0'. In the current work, null boundary maximal length CA with rules 90 and 150 are used.

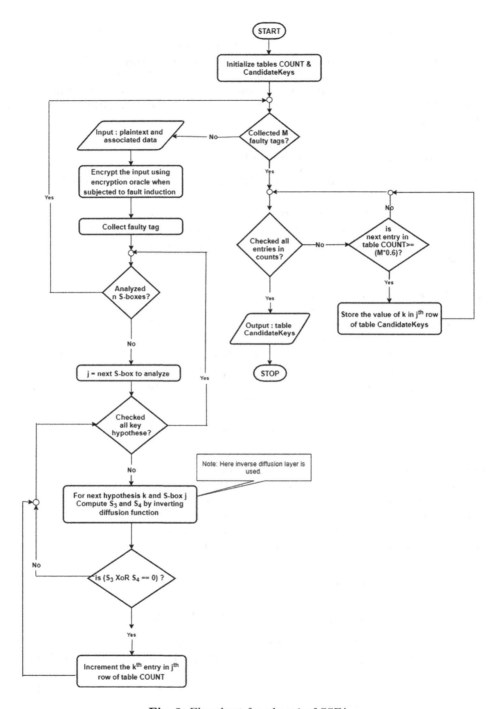

Fig. 3. Flowchart for phase1 of SSFA

4.1 Design

During the Initialization and Finalization rounds of ASCON, transformation p^a (12 rounds of permutation p) is done. Since the SIFA attack takes place during the final round of Finalization, the pseudorandom number generator is used in the linear diffusion layer of p^a only. The pseudorandom generator used here is a linear hybrid cellular automata [7]. The algorithm for permutation p^a for Initialization and Finalization stages of ASCON is given below. In the algorithm, prng() function calls two CAs: CA_s and CA_r to implement a PCA 90-150 [5]. The CA_s function uses a 6-cell, null boundary, maximal length [2] hybrid CA. This function returns the value between 1 and 63. The CA_r function is a 6-cell, maximal length, null boundary hybrid CA which selects a rule from a predefined ruleset for CA_r to use. Together this results in a simulation of PCA 90-150.

For n (number of cells) = 6, the PCA 90-150 configuration results in an expression of degree 6,

$$x(x+1)(x^4+x+1)$$

Algorithm 1: Permuatation(byte S[])

Result: Gives the modified permutation for p_a for given S

i=0;

x0,x1,x2,x3,x4 contains the progessive eight indexes of data in S;

while $i<12$ **do**

  Addition of round constants:(no changes)

  x2 $=x2 \oplus round - constant$;

  Substitution layer:(no changes);

  .....;

  Linear Diffusion layer:

  $x0 = x0 \oplus x0 >>> prng() \oplus x0 >>> prng()$;

  $x1 = x1 \oplus x1 >>> prng() \oplus x1 >>> prng()$;

  $x2 = x2 \oplus x2 >>> prng() \oplus x2 >>> prng()$;

  $x3 = x3 \oplus x3 >>> prng() \oplus x3 >>> prng()$;

  $x4 = x4 \oplus x4 >>> prng() \oplus x4 >>> prng()$;

  i++;

end

4.2 PRNG

The requirements of pseudorandom number generator are

- The function should generate numbers from 1 to 63 randomly (0 excluded because the first term of linear diffusion layer is x_i)
- The random numbers generated should be unequal so as to prevent cancellation.

Considering the above requirements, a maximal length CA which generates numbers from 1 to 63 [2] are chosen. The six options for the rule set so obtained are shown in Table 1. In option 1, 0 represents rule 90 and 1 represents rule 150.

Table 1. Table showing different rulesets possible for prng()

Option no.	Rule set
Option 1	000110
Option 2	101110
Option 3	011010
Option 4	100101
Option 5	101010
Option 6	100000

The security can be further enhanced by making the random number generated by prng() hard to predict by using an additional CA whose value determines which ruleset option to choose each time prng is called.

Design Rationale: The equations for SIFA (1) and the flowchart for SSFA show that L_3 and L_4 are of vital importance in forming the set of linear equations. In the current design, we use a PRNG in the linear diffusion layer. The attacker should find the correct positions across which it is rotated twice. Thus, 63×31 options are to be tried out of which only one is correct. To find L_3 and L_4, the attacker would have to guess the correct L_3 and L_4 out of $(63 \times 31)^2$ choices for each of the M cases. Out of the M cases, success probability is 1 out of $(63 \times 31)^{2M}$, which is negligible. Thus, SIFA attack is rendered useless on the modified ASCON.

Note: We get 63×31 for the two positions of L_i matrix for which the value is one. Combination is used instead of permutation because XOR is commutative, i.e., a XOR b = b XOR a. Hence, the attacker has to guess just the number generated and their order is not significant.

5   Conclusion

The proposed introduction of cellular automata based pseudorandom generator in the permutation p^a makes the calculation of L_i^{-1} infeasible, which is needed for the SIFA and phase-1 of SSFA thereby rendering SIFA and SSFA ineffective against the modified ASCON algorithm. Also, we noticed that the proposed change prevents any attack from the trivial path produced due to XORing the key for tag calculation mentioned in [6]. In the modified ASCON, it is also observed that if the attacker already has the key, nonce, and the ciphertext, she cannot decrypt the message without the sequence used in the linear diffusion layer. The number of iterations of permutations of p^a and p^b can be reduced without reducing the security of ASCON and thereby increasing the performance of the algorithm.

References

1. Benot, O.: Encyclopedia of Cryptography and Security, pp. 218–219. Springer, Boston (2011)
2. Bhaumik, J.: Synthesis of all maximum length cellular automata of cell size up to 12. arXiv preprint https://arxiv.org/pdf/1503.04006.pdf (2015). Accessed 04 Sept 2020
3. Dobraunig, C., Eichlseder, M., Mendel, F., Schläffer, M.: ASCON v1.2. submission to NIST (2019). https://csrc.nist.gov/CSRC/media/Projects/lightweight-cryptography/documents/round-2/spec-doc-rnd2/ascon-spec-round2.pdf. Accessed 04 Sept 2020
4. Giraud, C., Thiebeauld, H.: A survey on fault attacks. International Federation for Information Processing Digital Library; Smart Card Research and Advanced Applications VI, 153, January 2004
5. de la Guía Martínez, D., Peinado Domínguez, A., et al.: On the sequences generated by 90-150 programmable cellular automata. In: 5th World Multiconference on Systemics, Cybernetics and Informatics and 7th International Conference on Information System Analysis and Synthesis (SCI/ISAS), Orlando, Florida. International Institute of Informatics and Systemics, July 2001
6. Joshi, P., Mazumdar, B.: A sub-set fault analysis attack on ASCON (2019). https://eprint.iacr.org/2019/1370. Accessed 04 Sept (2020)
7. Nandi, S., Kar, B.K., Pal Chaudhuri, P.: Theory and applications of cellular automata in cryptography. IEEE Trans. Comput. $43(12)$, 1346–1357 (1994)
8. Ramezanpour, K., Ampadu, P., Diehl, W.: A statistical fault analysis methodology for the ASCON authenticated cipher. In: 2019 IEEE International Symposium on Hardware Oriented Security and Trust (HOST), pp. 41–50. IEEE (2019)
9. Rogaway, P.: Authenticated-encryption with associated-data. In: Proceedings of the 9th ACM Conference on Computer and Communications Security, pp. 98–107 (2002)
10. Wolfram, S.: Cellular automata as models of complexity. Nature $311(5985)$, 419–424 (1984)

Detection of Topology Changes in Dynamical System: An Information Theoretic Approach

Pierre-Alain Toupance[1,2], Bastien Chopard[1(✉)], and Laurent Lefèvre[2]

[1] University of Geneva, Geneva, Switzerland
Bastien.Chopard@unige.ch
[2] Univ. Grenoble Alpes, Grenoble INP, LCIS, Valence, France
pierre-alain.toupance@grenoble-inp.fr,
laurent.lefevre@lcis.grenoble-inp.fr

Abstract. In this paper, we show that the theory of information offers some tools to detect changes in the interaction topology of a dynamical system defined on a graph. As an illustrative example, the system we consider is a probabilistic voter model defined on a scale-free network. We show that, using time-delayed mutual-information, the interaction topology of an unknown graph can be reconstructed to some level. We apply this approach on a sliding time window to detect possible changes in the interaction topology over time.

Keywords: Dynamical systems · Complex network · Probabilistic models · Delayed mutual information · Interaction topology reconstruction · Online topology identification · Voter model

1 Introduction

The knowledge of the interconnection topology of a complex network is important in order to have results on structural observability and controllability, as discussed in [1,2].

In this paper we consider the concept of causality as a way to obtain the interaction topology among the variables of complex dynamical systems. For probabilistic models, the theory of information proposed by Shannon in 1948 ([3]) offers tools to define causality, for example the transfer entropy introduced by Schreiber [4], as a measure of directed (time-asymmetric) information transfer between joint processes.

In [5] we use the time-delayed mutual- and multi-information, defined in the Sect. 2.2, to analyze the most influential components of a complex system with no a priori knowledge of the interconnection topology. This approach is non-intrusive in the sense that it may be performed by a simple sampling of the system state, even if the underlying dynamics is unknown. We proved – on the example of the so-called voter model– that the nodes (voters) may be

© Springer Nature Switzerland AG 2021
T. M. Gwizdałła et al. (Eds.): ACRI 2020, LNCS 12599, pp. 26–35, 2021.
https://doi.org/10.1007/978-3-030-69480-7_4

ranked according to their influence (the impact of their opinion on the average opinion of the entire group) by monitoring the time-delayed multi-information. This ranking closely relates to controllability/observability Grammians singular values, as defined in classical system theory (see [6]). Furthermore, by sampling the state of the dynamical system, we showed [7] that time-delayed mutual- and multi-information can be used to reconstruct the interaction topology.

In this paper, the problem of a change of the interaction topology during time is investigated. The goal is to detect structural modifications in a dynamical system defined on a graph, by simply observing its state variables. To this end, we compute the delayed mutual-information on sliding time-windows and study whether this quantity can alert us of a change in the structure of the system.

The paper is organized as follows: Sect. 2 introduces the voter model which will be used throughout the paper as an example. The metrics from information theory that we will use are recalled. An overview of results previously obtained to measure the relative influence of the agents is presented. Then we present how we used our approach to reconstruct the interconnection topology of a complex system. Our main new contributions are presented in Sect. 4 where we discuss how the delayed mutual-information can be measured in a time sliding-window and how this leads to the identification of dynamical topology changes.

2 Dynamical System and Mutual Information

2.1 Voter Model

As an illustration of our approach we consider a voter model as a representative dynamical system on a graph. Various versions of voter models have been studied. For example Castellano et al. [8] have defined a q-voter model in which an agent votes like its neighbors if the opinion is unanimous; otherwise the vote is random. This model has been used by Nycska et al. [9]. Our model is closer to those used by Mobilia et al. [10], Masuda [11] or Galam [12]: it is a model where the vote of an agent depends on the average vote of its neighbors. The version we consider here is a time synchronous agent-based model defined on a graph of arbitrary topology, whether directed or not.

Our model can be described in the following way. Each node i of the network represents an agent whose opinion is either $s_i = 0$ or $s_i = 1$. The dynamics is specified by assuming that each agent i looks at every other agents in its neighborhood, and counts the fraction ρ_i of those neighbors which are in state $+1$. In case an agent is linked to itself, it belongs to its own neighborhood. A function f is specified such that $0 \leq f(\rho_i) \leq 1$ gives the probability for agent i to be in state $+1$ at the next iteration. For instance, if f would be chosen as $f(\rho) = \rho$, an agent for which all neighbors are in state $+1$ would turn into state $+1$ with certainty. The update is performed synchronously over all n agents.

Formally, the dynamics of our voter model can be express as

$$s_i(t+1) = \begin{cases} 1 & \text{with probability } f(\rho_i(t)) \\ 0 & \text{with probability } 1 - f(\rho_i(t)) \end{cases} \tag{1}$$

where $s_i(t) \in \{0, 1\}$ is the state of agent i at iteration t, and

$$\rho_i(t) = \frac{1}{|N_i|} \sum_{j \in N_i} s_j(t) \tag{2}$$

The set N_i is the set of agents j that are neighbors of agent i, as specified by the network topology.

The global density of all n agents with opinion 1 is

$$\rho(t) = \frac{1}{n} \sum_{i=1}^{n} s_i(t) \tag{3}$$

In the present case, we consider a voter model in which agent can vote differently than the majority of their neighbors. According to the total probability formula, the probability p_i that agent i votes $+1$ is

$$p_i(t+1) = (1 - \epsilon)p_{V_i}(t)) + \epsilon(1 - p_{V_i}(t))$$
$$= (1 - 2\epsilon)p_{V_i}(t) + \epsilon$$

where ϵ is the probability to take a decision different from that of the neighborhood and $p_{V_i}(t)$ is the probability that the majority of neighbors of agent i votes 1 at time t. Thus, we defined $f(\rho)$ as

$$f(\rho) = (1 - \epsilon)\rho + \epsilon(1 - \rho) = (1 - 2\epsilon)\rho + \epsilon \tag{4}$$

From now on, the quantity ϵ will be called the noise. We limit the noise in the range $0 \le \epsilon \le 1/2$. The upper value $\epsilon = 1/2$ corresponds to a blind vote, i.e a probability $1/2$ for each outcome.

To illustrate the behavior of this model, we consider a random scale-free graph G [13] which is considered as some instance of a social network [14]. In a scale-free network, a small number of particular nodes have many connections. These nodes, often referred to as hubs, are the leaders of the social network. Most other nodes have very few connections. The majority of voters are in this situation. The scale free graph structure is based on communities built around a leader, as discussed for instance in Wu et al. [15]. We use the algorithm of Bollobás and Riordan [16] to generate the random scale free graphs throughout this paper.

2.2   Delayed Mutual- and Multi-information

Let us consider a set of random variables $X_i(t)$ associated with each agent i, taking their values in a set A. For instance, $X_i(t) = s_i(t)$ would be the opinion of agent i at iteration t.

To measure the influence of an agents i on j, we define the τ-delayed mutual information $w_{i,j}$ as

$$w_{i,j}(t, \tau) = I(X_i(t), X_j(t + \tau)) \tag{5}$$

$$= \sum_{(x,y) \in A^2} p_{xy} \log\left(\frac{p_{xy}}{p_x p_y}\right) \tag{6}$$

with
$$p_{xy} = \mathbb{P}(X_i(t) = x, X_j(t + \tau) = y)$$
$$p_x = \mathbb{P}(X_i(t) = x) \text{ and } p_y = \mathbb{P}(X_j(t + \tau) = y)$$

We also defined the τ-delayed multi-information w_i to measure the influence of one agent i on all the others

$$w_i(t, \tau) = I(X_i(t), Y_i(t + \tau)) \tag{7}$$

$$Y_i(t + \tau) = \sum_{k \neq i} X_k(t + \tau) \tag{8}$$

2.3 Controllability and Information Theory

In our recent paper [5] entitled "Controllability of the Voter Model: an information theoretic approach", we define the influence of an agent in two different ways. The so-called *intrusive* approach consists in forcing (or controlling) the opinion of an agent and to measure the impact on the global density of opinions 1 in the system. More specifically we average ρ as given by Eq. (3) over a large number N of independent realizations (ensemble average). This gives a quantity $\langle \rho(t) \rangle_i$, where subscript i indicates which agent has been forced to 1. For large enough t, $\langle \rho \rangle_i$ no longer depends on t and provides a measure of the influence of agent i on the system.

A second way to define the influence of agent i is to use the delayed multi-information introduced in Eq. (7). The quantity $w_i(t, \tau)$ provides a non-intrusive measure (no forcing is required) of the influence of agent i. Here the time delay τ is taken as the diameter of the network, so that the influence of an agent can propagate to all the vertices of the graph.

We showed in [5] that the intrusive and non-intrusive measurements are very similar, as illustrated in Fig. 1. The gray scale representation for the nodes shows the intensities of the multi-information $w_i(t, \tau)$ or the influence $\langle \rho \rangle_i$ of the corresponding agent i. The multi-information gives also indication about the controllability of the system as it clearly identifies the agents that are best to control the system when their vote is forced.

3 Topology of the System

3.1 1-Delayed Mutual Information and Adjacency Matrix

After these first results about the controllability, we were interested in the topology of the system. The aim was to use information theory, to reconstruct the graph of interaction, assuming it was not known beforehand. In the following sections we present the results we have obtained in [7].

In Fig. 2, we can see the values of the $1-$delayed mutual information, $w_{i,j}(1)$, between one agent i and any other agent j in the system. These values were calculated by sampling the system when it has reached its steady state. The

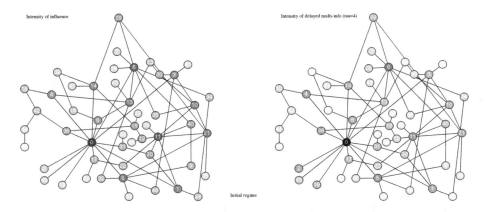

Fig. 1. Scale free graph colored as a function of the values of the influence (left) and the τ-delayed multi-information (right), for $\tau = 4$. In this case, the multi-information is computed in the transient initial regime.

peaks that we observe in $w_{i,j}(1)$ for some values of $j \in \{1, \ldots, 50\}$ suggest that node i is a direct neighbor of this node j, as there is a causal effect after one time step.

In order to infer the edges of the interaction graph and build its adjacency matrix M, we used the 1-delayed mutual-information in the following way. For each agent i, we fixed a threshold T_i on the value of $w_{i,j}(1)$ to decide whether or not i is a neighbor of j. The value of T_i was determined empirically as

$$T_i = \mu_i + a_i \sigma_i$$

where μ_i is the mean value of the 1-delayed mutual-information between agent i and the other agents, and σ_i its standard deviation. We chose two different values for the coefficient a_i, to reflect the different nature of the agents (influential agents have more neighbors). We propose the following values for a_i:

$$a_i = \begin{cases} 0.2 & \text{if } w_i(t, \tau) > \alpha + \frac{1}{2}\beta \text{ (then agent } i \text{ is considered as very influential)} \\ 0.7 & \text{otherwise} \end{cases}$$

$$(9)$$

where $w_i(t, \tau)$ is agent i's τ-delayed multi-information at time t, as defined in Eq. (7). The value of t is chosen to be in the initial regime and τ is taken large enough to capture the influence over the rest of the system. The values α and β are respectively the average and the standard deviation of $w_i(t, \tau)$ over i.

The elements of the adjacency matrix, $M = (m_{ij})_{1 \leq i,j \leq n}$, are computed as

$$m_{ij} = \begin{cases} 1 & \text{if } w_{ij}(1) > T_i \text{ or } w_{j,i}(1) > T_j \\ 0 & \text{otherwise} \end{cases} \qquad (10)$$

When $w_{ij}(1) > T_i$ or $w_{ji}(1) > T_j$ then it is assumed that agents i and j are neighbors and interact symmetrically. One could of course also defined a criterion for non-symmetrical graphs.

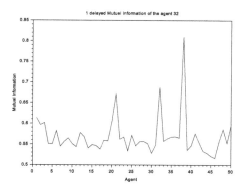

Fig. 2. 1-delayed mutual information of agent 32 with every other agent.

The values of a_i have been chosen in order to minimize the error rate r between the reconstructed matrix M and the actual graph adjacency matrix A. We have considered several scale-free graphs, by testing all values of a from 0 to 1 with a step of 0.1. The error rate is defined as $r = \frac{\Delta(M,A)}{n^2}$, where $\Delta(M,A)$ is the number of different values between M and A and n^2 the number of elements in M, n being the number of nodes.

The left panel of Fig. 3 shows the graph G_1 we obtain with an error rate $r = 1.3\%$. To have a better result, we computed the 1-delayed mutual information when the system is in its initial regime, as shown in the right side of Fig. 3 (graph G_2). There, the error rate dropped down to $r = 0.24\%$. This suggests that the results are better in a transient mode than in the steady state. Such a transient regime can be created artificially by disrupting the system temporarily by increasing the noise, when calculating the mutual information. This method has been tested by randomly generating 20 scale-free graphs. The average error rate was found to be $r = 0.9\%$ with a standard deviation 0.0026.

3.2 Comparison of System Behavior Between the Original and Reconstructed Graph

To compare the vote dynamics of the original system associated with graph G, with the one associated with graph G_1 (obtained with the 1-delayed mutual information computed in the steady state, see Fig. 3), we look at the evolution of the fraction of voters in state 1, starting with the same initial state and making use of the same noise history (i.e. same seed for the random generator). In the left side of Fig. 4, we can see that the behaviors of G and $G1$ are similar whereas the evolution of the fraction of vote 1 looks in general very different for another arbitrarily chosen graph, such as it is illustrated in the right side of Fig. 4. This suggests that our method of reconstructing the topology in the steady state

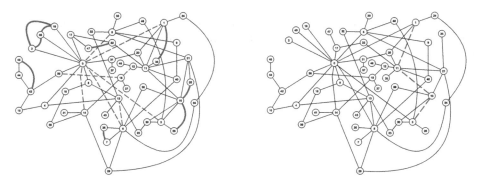

Fig. 3. (Left:) Graph G_1 built with the 1-delayed mutual information calculated when the system is in steady state. (Right:) Graph G_2 built with the 1-delayed mutual information computed when the system is in the initial transient regime. Red lines are the errors we got on the edges during reconstructions: the dashed line for the extra links and thick line for the missing links (Color figure online)

selects the most important edges from the point of view of their influence on the dynamical evolution.

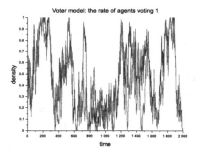
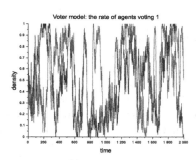

Fig. 4. Left: Plot of the time evolution of the density of opinion 1 with noise $\epsilon = 0.01$ for graph G (blue curve) and for the reconstructed graph G_1 (red curve). Right: the same quantity as produced by G (blue curve) and another, non-related graph (red curve). (Color figure online)

4   Delayed Mutual-Information to Detect Topology Changes

In this section, we assume that the topology of the dynamical system changes over time. Our goal is the real time detection of such changes through online analysis of the 1-delayed mutual information $w_{ij}(t, \tau)$ between the two corresponding vertices i and j.

Therefore, we compute $w_{ij}(t, \tau)$ at time $t = t_0$ by sampling $s_i(t - \tau)$ and $s_j(t)$ on a sliding window $t \in [t_0 - \Delta - 1, t_0]$ with width Δt. During this time interval, we record the pairs $(s_i(t - \tau), s_j(t))$ of the states of vertices i and j with a time delay $\tau = 1$. This leads to the following quantities:

$$N_{i,j}^{00}(t_0) = \sum_{k=0}^{\Delta t} \bar{s}_i(t_0 - k - 1) \times \bar{s}_j(t_0 - k) \qquad N_{i,j}^{01}(t_0) = \sum_{k=0}^{\Delta t} \bar{s}_i(t_0 - k - 1) \times s_j(t_0 - k)$$

$$N_{i,j}^{10}(t_0) = \sum_{k=0}^{\Delta t} s_i(t_0 - k - 1) \times \bar{s}_j(t_0 - k) \qquad N_{i,j}^{11}(t_0) = \sum_{k=0}^{\Delta t} s_i(t_0 - k - 1) \times s_j(t_0 - k)$$

with $\bar{s}_i(t) = 1 - s_i(t)$.

According to Eq. (6) the estimation of the mutual information on the time interval $[t_0 - \Delta - 1, t_0]$ is given by

$$w_{i,j} = \frac{N_{i,j}^{00}}{\Delta t} \log \left(\frac{(\Delta t) \times N_{i,j}^{00}}{(N_{i,j}^{00} + N_{i,j}^{01})(N_{i,j}^{00} + N_{i,j}^{10})} \right) + \frac{N_{i,j}^{01}}{\Delta t} \log \left(\frac{(\Delta t) \times N_{i,j}^{01}}{(N_{i,j}^{01} + N_{i,j}^{00})(N_{i,j}^{01} + N_{i,j}^{11})} \right)$$

$$+ \frac{N_{i,j}^{10}}{\Delta t} \log \left(\frac{(\Delta t) \times N_{i,j}^{10}}{(N_{i,j}^{10} + N_{i,j}^{11})(N_{i,j}^{10} + N_{i,j}^{00})} \right) + \frac{N_{i,j}^{11}}{\Delta t} \log \left(\frac{(\Delta t) \times N_{i,j}^{11}}{(N_{i,j}^{11} + N_{i,j}^{10})(N_{i,j}^{11} + N_{i,j}^{01})} \right)$$

We now consider a graph of size $n = 500$ whose topology is modified over time in a prescribed way. The 1-delayed mutual information was computed using a sliding-window with $\Delta = 300$. Figure 5 shows the time evolution of $w_{ij}(t)$ between two selected vertices of low degree on one side and between two selected hubs (vertices of high degree) on the other side. Between these pairs of vertices an edge was alternatively added and removed every 2000 time steps. In the case of low degree vertices, we see that the value of w_{ij} informs us of this change of topology. On the other hand, when the changes occur between the two hubs, $w_{ij}(t)$ does not detect them. However, in this case, it was found that the corresponding edge does not have a great influence on the system dynamics, using a similar analysis as the one reported in Sect. 3.2.

If the link is modified between a vertex i of low degree and a hub j, w_{ij} hardly detects this change, as seen in Fig. 6 (right). This is expected as a terminal node does not influence a hub. But this change can be detected by measuring the opposite delayed mutual-information, w_{ji}, (see Fig. 6, left panel), reflecting the fact that the hub does influence a neighboring vertex.

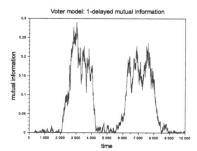
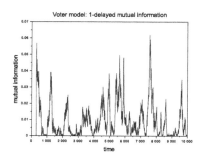

Fig. 5. Plots of the 1-delayed mutual information between two vertices of low degree (left) and between two hubs (right). The parameters of the simulation are $\epsilon = 0.01$, $n = 500$, $\Delta t = 300$.

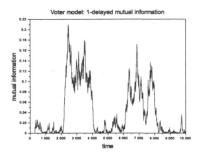
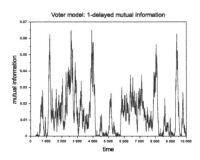

Fig. 6. Left: plot of the 1-delayed mutual information between a hub and a low degree vertex. Right: plot of the 1-delayed mutual information between the low degree vertex and the hub. The parameters of the simulation are $\epsilon = 0.01$, $n = 500$, $\Delta t = 300$.

As discussed above, the 1-delayed mutual information on a sliding window seems to be a good metric to detect when the link between 2 nodes appears or disappears. As a confirmation, we made simulations in which the topology of the graph changes randomly over time: at each iteration, a topology change is decided with probability p. In this case a pair of nodes is chosen randomly and an edge is either added or removed between them. For example, with a scale free graph of size $n = 500$ and with a probability of change $p = 0.01$ there was 54 changes during a simulation of 6000 steps. In this simulation all changes were detected because there was no changes between two hubs. For each pair of nodes i and j, the 1-delayed mutual information $w_{i,j}$ and $w_{j,i}$, were computed on a sliding window of size 100. When these two values exceed and remain above a threshold, we assume that a new edge has appeared. When these values become lower than another threshold, we assume that an edge has disappeared. With this method, the average time to detect changes is 160 with a standard deviation of 110.

5   Conclusions

In this paper, we have described a way to detect topology changes in a dynamical system on a graph, such as the voter model. Detecting structural changes is important as it can provide an early warning of tipping points. We expect that our approach can be applied to many other complex systems. The 1-delayed mutual information computed on a sliding-window was used to identify the possible changes of connectivity. We saw that this quantity allows us to detect whether an edge is added or removed between two vertices of low degree, or between a hub and a vertex of low degree. Between two hubs this method is not effective, but the actual presence or absence of a link between them does not affect much the global behavior of the system.

Delayed mutual- and multi-information can also be used to determine communities in a graph, as discussed in [7]. In a forthcoming study we will investigate, using the approach developed here, how a change of community can be detected in a dynamic system, thus indicating a possible loss of controllability.

References

1. Liu, Y.Y., Slotine, J.J., Barabasi, A.L.: Controllability of complex networks. Nature **473**, 167 (2011)
2. Liu, Y.Y., Slotine, J.J., Barabási, A.L.: Observability of complex systems. Proc. Natl. Acad. Sci. **110**(7), 2460–2465 (2013)
3. Shannon, C.E.: A mathematical theory of communication. Bell Syst. Tech. J. **27**(3), 379–423 (1948)
4. Schreiber, T.: Measuring information transfer. Phys. Rev. Lett. **85**(2), 461 (2000)
5. Toupance, P.A., Lefèvre, L., Chopard, B.: Influence measurement in a complex dynamical model: an information theoretic approach. J. Comput. Sci. **44**, 101115 (2020)
6. Antoulas, A.C.: Approximation of Large-Scale Dynamical Systems, vol. 6. SIAM, Philadelphia (2005)
7. Toupance, P.A., Chopard, B., Lefèvre, L.: Identification of complex network topologies through delayed mutual information. In: 21st IFAC World Congress, Berlin, Germany. arXiv:2003.08792 (2020, accepted)
8. Castellano, C., Muñoz, M.A., Pastor-Satorras, R.: Nonlinear q-voter model. Phys. Rev. E **80**(4), 041129 (2009)
9. Nyczka, P., Sznajd-Weron, K.: Anticonformity or independence?—Insights from statistical physics. J. Stat. Phys. **151**(1–2), 174–202 (2013). https://doi.org/10.1007/s10955-013-0701-4
10. Mobilia, M., Petersen, A., Redner, S.: On the role of zealotry in the voter model. J. Stat. Mech.: Theory Exp. **2007**(08), P08029 (2007)
11. Masuda, N.: Opinion control in complex networks. New J. Phys. **17**(3), 033031 (2015)
12. Galam, S., Chopard, B., Masselot, A., Droz, M.: Competing species dynamics: qualitative advantage versus geography. Eur. Phys. J. B **4**, 529–531 (1998). https://doi.org/10.1007/s100510050410
13. Barabási, A.L., Albert, R., Jeong, H.: Scale-free characteristics of random networks: the topology of the world-wide web. Phys. A: Stat. Mech. Appl. **281**(1–4), 69–77 (2000)
14. Newman, M.E., Watts, D.J., Strogatz, S.H.: Random graph models of social networks. Proc. Natl. Acad. Sci. **99**(suppl 1), 2566–2572 (2002)
15. Wu, A.Y., Garland, M., Han, J.: Mining scale-free networks using geodesic clustering. In: Proceedings of the Tenth ACM SIGKDD International Conference on Knowledge Discovery and Data Mining, pp. 719–724. ACM (2004)
16. Bollobás, B., Riordan, O.M.: Mathematical results on scale-free random graphs. In: Handbook of Graphs and Networks: From the Genome to the Internet, pp. 1–34 (2003)

Observability of Affine Cellular Automaton Through Mobile Sensors

Théo Plénet[1(✉)], Samira El Yacoubi[1], Clément Raïevsky[2],
and Laurent Lefèvre[2]

[1] Images UMR Espace-Dev, University of Perpignan Via Domitia, Perpignan, France
{theo.plenet,yacoubi}@univ-perp.fr
[2] Univ. Grenoble Alpes, Grenoble INP, LCIS, 26000 Valence, France
{clement.raievsky,laurent.lefevre}@lcis.grenoble-inp.fr

Abstract. In this paper, we define observability for cellular automaton. Then we extend the Kalman observability criterion to affine cellular automaton with a time-varying output operator. Finally, this observability characterisation is applied to the observation of affine cellular automaton through mobile sensors.

Keywords: Cellular automaton · Observability · Mobile sensors · Kalman criterion

1 Introduction

Sensors and actuators constitute an important link between a system and its environment. Their structures play an important role in Distributed Parameter Systems (DPS) analysis and control; particularly regarding the controllability and observability issues. These two major concepts in control theory were introduced by Kalman [11] for finite dimensional linear systems and developed the last fifty years, [13,14]. Their study through the concepts of sensors and actuators has also been of great interest in the automatic control community [8,9]. While the controllability focuses on the steering capabilities of the controlled evolution processes, observability is dealing with the ability to reconstruct the initial system state, given sufficient knowledge of the system dynamics through some output measurements.

This paper focuses on the observability problem and assumes that the system under investigation is autonomous. Motivated by some real distributed environmental phenomena (*e.g.* wildfires, weather, atmosphere or river pollution) we use a group of mobile robots equipped with different sensors [4]. Robots share information with each other and we simply call this group a *network of mobile sensors*. This network constitute a natural extension of sensors and offers more flexibility in collecting distributed information within its environment. A model-based approach through trajectory optimisation (for the mobile sensors) with partial differential equation constraints (PDE, for the environment dynamical

© Springer Nature Switzerland AG 2021
T. M. Gwizdałła et al. (Eds.): ACRI 2020, LNCS 12599, pp. 36–45, 2021.
https://doi.org/10.1007/978-3-030-69480-7_5

model) would lead to very complicated [1] - sometimes intractable - mathematical issues, particularly in the case of complex geometries and/or non linear dynamics.

Among other modelling approaches that have been developed to describe life phenomena which exhibit complex behaviours, cellular automaton (CA) provide powerful models usually viewed as a counterpart of PDEs for modelling spatio-temporal systems. A CA is a mathematical model which is perfectly suited to complex systems containing a large number of discrete elements with local interactions, for example Ising model, fluid dynamics, traffic flow, growth of crystal [2,3,16]. They were first introduced by [17], as a modelling tool to investigate self-organisation and self-reproduction phenomena and become increasingly attractive thanks to their ability to exhibit a wide variety of amazingly complex behaviours while offering an easiness of implementation.

The research activity regarding cellular automaton has been essentially focused, so far, on modelling and implementation problems. Recently, CA were presented as a distributed parameter system in relation with systems theory [10]. An interesting study of controllability of CA has been carried out in [7] that highlighted new ways to prove the controllability of complex systems. It mainly focused on regional controllability of Boolean CA that has been proved using Markov chains or graph theory tools [5,6]. The boundary regional controllability has also been investigated for linear (additive) Boolean CA for which some characterisation results using the Kalman condition were given.

Our interest in this paper is focused on observability as a dual notion of controllability. The purpose is to apply the above mentioned tools in order to prove the observability according to the choice of sensor structures, locations and types (mobile or fixed). We show for the 1D case, that observability of linear (affine) CA can be characterised using the observability matrix. A complete study of affine CA by means of mobile sensors is carried out in the last section. Some examples are given to illustrate the theoretic results.

2   Sensors and Observability for Cellular Automaton

Definitions for control and observation of cellular automaton has already been given in [10]. Throughout this article we will reuse these definitions but for the consistency of this article we will redefine some of these.

First, a cellular automaton is formulated as the quadruple $\mathcal{A} = \{\mathcal{L}, \mathcal{S}, \mathcal{N}, f\}$ where $\mathcal{L}$ represents the lattice of cells c; $\mathcal{S}$ represents the set of states; $\mathcal{N}$ represents the neighbourhood; and f represents the transition function. In this paper, we need $\mathcal{S}$ to be a finite field, thus the number of elements, k, must be prime.

The CA state or configuration at time t is defined by:

$$s: \mathcal{L} \to \mathcal{S}$$
$$c \mapsto s_t(c) \tag{1}$$

The global transition function F is then defined by:

$$F \colon \mathcal{S}^{\mathcal{L}} \to \mathcal{S}^{\mathcal{L}}$$
$$s_t \mapsto F(s_t) = s_{t+1} \tag{2}$$

In order to be able to study observability using mobile sensors, we need to define first the notion of mobile sensor, which will then allow us to define the notion of observability.

Definition 1. *We note q a set of Q sensors which observe a set $\mathcal{L}_q \subset \mathcal{L}$ of cells. Each sensor of this set is indexed by $i \in [\![1; Q]\!]$. So we have a sensor q_i observing a set of cell $\mathcal{L}_{q_i} \subset \mathcal{L}$ hence:*

$$\mathcal{L}_q = \bigcup_{i=1}^{Q} \mathcal{L}_{q_i} \tag{3}$$

Remark 1. The sensor set q can contain mobile sensors, i.e. the set of cells they observe varies over time. Thus, we note the mobile sensor set $q_{i,t}$ and the set of cells it observes $\mathcal{L}_{q_{i,t}}$. Therefore we note q_t the set of sensors and $\mathcal{L}_{q_t}$ the set of cells observed by the sensors at time t.

Remark 2. In the sensor set q, some sensors may be inactive at time t; because they are faulty, inadequate, or simply not in use. In this case, we add a parameter λ_i to the sensor q_i which describes whether this sensor is active or not. We then define the set of all observed cells as:

$$\mathcal{L}_{q_t} = \bigcup_{i=1}^{Q} (\lambda_{i,t} \diamond \mathcal{L}_{q_{i,t}}) \tag{4}$$

Where $\lambda_{i,t} \in \{0,1\}$ such that $\lambda_{i,t}$ equals 0 if the sensor q_i is inactive at time t and 1 if it is active. Using this definition, we then define the $\diamond$ operator, with $\mathcal{P}(\mathcal{L})$ the power set of $\mathcal{L}$:

$$\diamond \colon \{0,1\} \times \mathcal{P}(\mathcal{L}) \to \mathcal{P}(\mathcal{L})$$
$$\lambda_i \times \mathcal{L}_{q_i} \mapsto \begin{cases} \emptyset & \text{if } \lambda_i = 0 \\ \mathcal{L}_{q_i} & \text{else} \end{cases} \tag{5}$$

Based on these definitions, we will now define an output operator of the system, i.e. what the sensors are measuring. This definition will in turn be used to define the observability of a cellular automaton when it is observed by a mobile sensor network.

Definition 2. *The output operator H_t generates, at each time t, an output $\theta_t \in \mathcal{O}_t = l_2(\mathcal{L}_{q_t}, \mathbb{R})$ from the state s_t of the automaton $\mathcal{A}$.*

$$H_t \colon \mathcal{S}^{\mathcal{L}} \to \mathcal{O}_t$$
$$s_t \mapsto \theta_t \tag{6}$$

Where $\mathcal{O}_t = l_2(\mathcal{L}_{q_t}, \mathcal{S})$ *is a set of output functions such that their quadratic sum over all cells is finite [10, Sect. 2.3]:*

$$l_2(\mathcal{L}_{q_t}, \mathcal{S}) = \{\theta \colon \mathcal{L}_{q_t} \to \mathcal{S} \mid \sum_{c \in \mathcal{L}_{q_t}} \theta^2(c) < \infty\}$$

In order to illustrate the different theorems and propositions that are presented in the following sections, the same cellular automaton and the same output operators will be used in the different examples.

Example 1. Let us consider the following one-dimensional cellular automaton defined by:

- $\mathcal{L} = \{0, 1, 2, 3, 4\}$
- $\mathcal{S} = \{0, 1, 2\}$
- $\mathcal{N} \colon c_i \mapsto \{c_{i-1}, c_i, c_{i+1}\}$ with periodic boundaries so $c_{-1} = c_4$ and $c_5 = c_0$.
- $f \colon s_t(\mathcal{N}(c_i)) \mapsto s_t(c_{i-1}) + 2s_t(c_i) + s_t(c_{i+1}) + 1$

Then let us consider two output operators H and H'. Both of these will observe one cell at a time, but H represents a mobile sensor (i.e. $\mathcal{L}_q$ varying over time) while H' represents a stationary sensor.

- **Mobile Sensor:** $\mathcal{L}_{q_t} = \{c_{t \bmod 5}\}$ and $H \colon s_t \mapsto s_t(c_{t \bmod 5}) + 2$
- **Stationary Sensor:** $\mathcal{L}'_q = \{c_0\}$ and $H' \colon s_t \mapsto s_t(c_0) + 2$

The observability of a system has already been presented in numerous publications. The oldest definition goes back to the definition of observability for linear systems given by Kalman [11]. More recent definitions include discrete time systems [15]. We aim to extend the definition of observability to cellular automaton.

Definition 3 (State Observability). *A state $s_0 \in \mathcal{S}^{\mathcal{L}}$ of a cellular automaton $\mathcal{A}$ is observable by an output operator H if and only if it is possible to reconstruct this initial state from the corresponding output sequence $(\theta_t)_{t \in I}$ with $I = \{0, 1, \ldots, T - 1\}$.*

Definition 4 (Global Observability). *A cellular automaton $\mathcal{A}$ is observable by an output operator H if and only if all states $s \in \mathcal{S}^{\mathcal{L}}$ are observable by this output operator.*

Remark 3. Proving the global observability of a system is equivalent to proving the injectivity of the output sequence Θ [8].

$$\Theta \colon \mathcal{S}^{\mathcal{L}} \to \mathcal{O}^T$$

$$s_0 \mapsto \begin{bmatrix} \theta_0 \\ \theta_1 \\ \cdots \\ \theta_{T-1} \end{bmatrix} = \begin{bmatrix} H(s_0) \\ H \circ F(s_0) \\ \cdots \\ H \circ F^{T-1}(s_0) \end{bmatrix} \tag{7}$$

3   Observability Criterion for Affine Cellular Automaton

In this part, we present a definition for affine CAs. Then, we present the different observability properties of affine CAs.

Proposition 1. *If the cellular automaton is finite in size (i.e. $|\mathcal{L}| = N \in \mathbb{N}$) then there exists an isomorphism ξ that would allow the state s of the automaton to be written as a vector x. ξ is defined by:*

$$\xi \colon \mathcal{S}^{\mathcal{L}} \to \mathcal{S}^N$$

$$s_t \mapsto x_t = \begin{pmatrix} x_t^1 \\ x_t^2 \\ \dots \\ x_t^N \end{pmatrix} \tag{8}$$

where $N = |\mathcal{L}|$ and x_t^i represents the state of the cell c_i at time t.

This isomorphism makes it possible to switch from a state function s_t to a state vector x_t (which is the representation used in the study of linear systems) and also to reduce the lattice dimension to facilitate the study of multi-dimensional systems.

Remark 4. This isomorphism can be applied to the global transition function F to have another function $\tilde{F}$ which computes x_{t+1} from x_t.

Definition 5 (Affine). *A cellular automaton is* affine *if and only if its $\tilde{F}$ transition function is an affine map. Moreover, this affine map can be written in the form of a linear map and a constant, which can be written as a matrix A and a constant $\eta = F(0)$. The evolution of the cellular automaton can then be written as:*

$$\begin{cases} x_{t+1} = \tilde{F}(x_t) = Ax_t + \eta \\ x_0 \quad \in \mathcal{S}^N \end{cases} \tag{9}$$

Remark 5. If an affine CA has a null η constant, this CA is said linear. Then, its transition function $\tilde{F}$ can be written in the form $x_{t+1} = A(x_t)$. Where A is a linear map.

In the case of elementary CA [18], linear CA are called additive CA. Also, affine CA will be the complement of additive CA. For example, rule 90 and 150 will be considered linear rules, but their complementary rule (165 and 105) will be considered affine rules.

Remark 6. In the same way as for the CA definition, if the observation space is finite (i.e. $|\mathcal{L}_q| \in \mathbb{N}$) then there is an isomorphism χ which make it possible to write the output θ_t as a vector y_t, defined by:

$$\chi \colon \mathcal{O} \to \mathcal{S}^Q$$

$$\theta_t \mapsto y_t = \begin{pmatrix} y_t^1 \\ y_t^2 \\ \dots \\ y_t^Q \end{pmatrix} \tag{10}$$

where $Q = |\mathcal{L}_q|$ and y_t^i represents the ith output at time t.

Moreover, the output operator is linear (respectively affine) if and only if the $\tilde{H}$ function (i.e. the H function composed with the χ isomorphism) is linear (affine). The system can then be written as $y_t = Cx_t + \gamma$ where C is the matrix of the linear map and γ is the affine constant (which is 0 if the CA is linear).

The Kalman criterion [11,12] is derived from the control of linear dynamical systems and proves the controllability (resp. observability) of a dynamical system when the system is controlled (observed). It has been generalised to discrete-time systems [15] and in this paper we generalise it to cellular automaton.

Theorem 1 (Kalman Criterion). *Let $\mathcal{A}$ and H be an affine CA and affine output operator; A, C their matrix form; and η and γ their constants.*

The pair $(\mathcal{A}, H)$ (i.e. the automaton $\mathcal{A}$ with the output operator H) is observable if and only if there exists $T \in \mathbb{N}$ such that:

$$
rank \begin{bmatrix} C \\ CA \\ .. \\ CA^{T-1} \end{bmatrix} = N
$$

Remark 7. The Kalman criterion can also be used with mobile sensors. In this case, the H output operator and the C matrix will both be time-dependent. The Kalman criterion thus becomes:

$$
rank \begin{bmatrix} C_0 \\ C_1 A \\ \dots \\ C_{T-1} A^{T-1} \end{bmatrix} = N \tag{11}
$$

Remark 8. We call O the observability matrix and Γ the constant matrix, it represents the output vector using only the initial state x_0:

$$
Y_T = \begin{bmatrix} y_0 \\ y_1 \\ \dots \\ y_{T-1} \end{bmatrix} = \begin{bmatrix} C_0 \\ C_1 A \\ \dots \\ C_{T-1} A^{T-1} \end{bmatrix} x_0 + \begin{bmatrix} \gamma_0 \\ C_1 \eta + \gamma_1 \\ \dots \\ \sum_{k=0}^{T-2}(C_{k+1} A^k \eta) + \gamma_{T-1} \end{bmatrix} = Ox_0 + \Gamma
$$

In order to prove the Kalman criterion, we will demonstrate only for affine CAs because the linear case is a special case where the constants η and γ are zero.

Proof. Let $\mathcal{A}$ an affine CA and A and η its associated matrix and constant. Let H_t be a time dependant affine output operator associated to the matrix C_t and the constant γ_t. Then, let $x_0 \in \mathcal{S}^N$ be the initial state and $Y_T = \begin{bmatrix} y_0 \ y_1 \ \dots \ y_{T-1} \end{bmatrix}$ the output vector generated by the output operator.

To Prove the Sufficiency
Suppose that $rank\ O = N$, it means that it exists P such that $PO = I_N$ (not necessarily $OP = I_M$ because O can have more row than column).

$$Y_T = Ox_0 + \Gamma \tag{12}$$

$$P(Y_T - \Gamma) = x_0 \tag{13}$$

Since the initial state of the automaton can be recovered through its outputs, the pair $(\mathcal{A}, H)$ is observable.

To Prove the Necessity
Suppose that the pair $(\mathcal{A}, H)$ can be observed, it means that the initial state x_0 can be retrieved using the output Y_T, so it exists a mapping g such that $g(Y_T - \Gamma) = x_0$.

We note h, the linear map of O and as $Y_T - \Gamma = x_0 \iff g(Y_T - \Gamma) = g \circ h(x_0)$ we have:

$$g \circ h = id_{S^N} \tag{14}$$

Thus:

$$rank\ O \geq N \ (\text{because } g \circ h = id_{S^N}) \text{ and } rank\ O \leq \min(N, M) \tag{15}$$

where M is the row number of O. Finally we have:

$$rank\ O = N \tag{16}$$

Corollary 1. *If the Kalman criterion is verified, then it is possible to recover the initial state by inverting the observability matrix. Indeed, based on the formulation (8) we obtain:*

$$x_0 = O^\dagger(Y_T - \Gamma) \tag{17}$$

Proof. As $rank\ O = N$, it means that it exists P such that $PO = I$ (but not necessarily $OP \neq I$ because O is not necessarily a square matrix). We can find $P = O^\dagger$ by computing the pseudo-inverse of O. Using the Eq. (8) we find that:

$$Y_T = Ox_0 + \gamma \iff O^\dagger(Y_T - \gamma) = O^\dagger Ox_0 \iff O^\dagger(Y_T - \Gamma) = x_0 \tag{18}$$

As O is full column rank, $O^\dagger = (O^t O)^{-1} O^t$. If O is square then $O^\dagger = O^{-1}$.

4 Observation of an Affine Cellular Automaton Through Mobile Sensors

In this section, we will carry out a complete study on an affine cellular automaton that is observed by an affine mobile sensor. For ease of calculation, we will use a one-dimensional cellular automaton, but the study method applies to other kind of CA.

Let us consider the cellular automaton and the two output operators presented in Example 1. This CA is affine, so we can write its transition function in affine form with a square matrix A and a constant vector η, which leads to:

$$A = \begin{bmatrix} 2 & 1 & 0 & 0 & 1 \\ 1 & 2 & 1 & 0 & 0 \\ 0 & 1 & 2 & 1 & 0 \\ 0 & 0 & 1 & 2 & 1 \\ 1 & 0 & 0 & 1 & 2 \end{bmatrix} \quad \text{and} \quad \eta = \begin{bmatrix} 1 \\ 1 \\ 1 \\ 1 \\ 1 \end{bmatrix} \tag{19}$$

The two output operators being affine, we can write them in matrix form:

- **Stationary Sensor:** $C' = \begin{bmatrix} 1 & 0 & 0 & 0 & 0 \end{bmatrix}$ and $\gamma' = 2$
- **Mobile Sensor:**

$$C_0 = \begin{bmatrix} 1 & 0 & 0 & 0 & 0 \end{bmatrix} \text{ and } \gamma_0 = 2$$
$$C_1 = \begin{bmatrix} 0 & 1 & 0 & 0 & 0 \end{bmatrix} \text{ and } \gamma_1 = 2$$
$$\dots$$
$$C_4 = \begin{bmatrix} 0 & 0 & 0 & 0 & 1 \end{bmatrix} \text{ and } \gamma_4 = 2$$
$$C_5 = \begin{bmatrix} 1 & 0 & 0 & 0 & 0 \end{bmatrix} \text{ and } \gamma_5 = 2$$

So we can calculate the matrices O and Γ for both sensors and we get:

- **Stationary:** $O = \begin{bmatrix} C' \\ C'A \\ C'A^2 \\ C'A^3 \\ C'A^4 \end{bmatrix} = \begin{bmatrix} 1 & 0 & 0 & 0 & 0 \\ 2 & 1 & 0 & 0 & 1 \\ 0 & 1 & 1 & 1 & 1 \\ 2 & 0 & 1 & 1 & 0 \\ 1 & 0 & 0 & 0 & 0 \end{bmatrix}, \Gamma = \begin{bmatrix} 2 \\ 0 \\ 1 \\ 2 \\ 0 \end{bmatrix}$ and $rank\ O = 3$

- **Mobile:** $O = \begin{bmatrix} C_0 \\ C_1A \\ C_2A^2 \\ C_3A^3 \\ C_4A^4 \end{bmatrix} = \begin{bmatrix} 1 & 0 & 0 & 0 & 0 \\ 1 & 2 & 1 & 0 & 0 \\ 1 & 1 & 0 & 1 & 1 \\ 1 & 1 & 0 & 2 & 0 \\ 0 & 0 & 0 & 0 & 1 \end{bmatrix}, \Gamma = \begin{bmatrix} 2 \\ 0 \\ 1 \\ 2 \\ 0 \end{bmatrix}$ and $rank\ O = 5$

The CA is observable by the mobile sensor because the rank is 5 which is not the case for the static sensor which has a rank of 3.

In the mobile sensor case we know that the system is observable, we can thus reconstruct its initial state based on the measurements made by this sensor using the Corollary 1. We will reconstruct the initial state from the evolution of the CA presented on the Fig. 1, with this evolution we have $Y_T = \begin{bmatrix} 2 & 2 & 1 & 1 & 0 \end{bmatrix}^t$. We can thus start by finding $O^\dagger$ and then calculate x_0. We should find $x_0 = \begin{bmatrix} 0 & 1 & 0 & 2 & 0 \end{bmatrix}^t$.

As O is a square matrix we can compute the inverse instead of the pseudo-inverse. To calculate O^{-1}, we will use the inverse of the determinant of O, $det(O)$ and its adjugate matrix $adj(O)$.

	c_0	c_1	c_2	c_3	c_4
$t = 0$	0	1	0	2	0
$t = 1$	2	0	1	2	0
$t = 2$	2	1	2	0	2
$t = 3$	2	1	0	2	1
$t = 4$	1	2	1	0	1
$t = 5$	0	1	2	0	1

Fig. 1. Example of CA evolution for $x_0 = \begin{bmatrix} 0 & 1 & 0 & 2 & 0 \end{bmatrix}^t$. The time is along the vertical axis. Cells are numbered from left to right with c_0 on the left and c_4 on the right. Grey cells are those observed by the mobile sensor.

$$O^{-1} = det(O)^{-1}adj(O) = 2^{-1}\begin{bmatrix} 2&0&0&0&0 \\ 1&0&1&1&2 \\ 2&2&1&1&2 \\ 0&0&1&2&2 \\ 0&0&0&0&2 \end{bmatrix} = \begin{bmatrix} 1&0&0&0&0 \\ 2&0&2&2&1 \\ 1&1&2&2&1 \\ 0&0&2&1&1 \\ 0&0&0&0&1 \end{bmatrix} \tag{20}$$

In modular arithmetic base k, the inverse is obtained by finding b so that $ab \equiv 1 (\text{mod } k)$, yet in the field $\mathcal{S}$ that we have, $2^{-1} = 2$ because $2 \times 2 = 1$.

We can now find x_0 using Y_T, Γ and O^{-1}. We get:

$$x_0 = O^{-1}(Y_T - \Gamma) = \begin{bmatrix} 1&0&0&0&0 \\ 2&0&2&2&1 \\ 1&1&2&2&1 \\ 0&0&2&1&1 \\ 0&0&0&0&1 \end{bmatrix} \left(\begin{bmatrix} 2 \\ 2 \\ 1 \\ 1 \\ 0 \end{bmatrix} - \begin{bmatrix} 2 \\ 0 \\ 1 \\ 2 \\ 0 \end{bmatrix} \right) = \begin{bmatrix} 0 \\ 1 \\ 0 \\ 2 \\ 0 \end{bmatrix} \tag{21}$$

5   Conclusion and Perspectives

In this paper, we presented a method to prove the observability of affine cellular automaton with linear output operators, either time-varying or not. We started by presenting a formulation of cellular automaton observed by a mobile sensors network. Then we extended the Kalman criterion from discrete-time linear systems to affine cellular automaton and we studied the observability of a one-dimensional automaton with this method.

In an extended version of this paper, we will generalise our observability analysis to nonlinear cellular automaton and construct an associated state estimator. This estimator will make it possible to have an estimate of the state of the cellular automaton without having to wait for the time necessary for the inversion of the observability matrix. Such an observer would allow the use of cellular automaton for control, diagnosis or general supervision purposes, with many potential applications, for instance in wildfire, pollution, or traffic monitoring or tracking problems.

References

1. Armaou, A., Demetriou, M.A.: Optimal actuator/sensor placement for linear parabolic pdes using spatial H2 norm. Chem. Eng. Sci. **61**(22), 7351–7367 (2006)
2. Bagnoli, F., Boccara, N., Rechtman, R.: Nature of phase transitions in a probabilistic cellular automaton with two absorbing states. Phys. Rev. E **63**(4), 046116 (2001)
3. Chopard, B., Droz, M.: Cellular Automata Modeling of Physical Systems, pp. 122–137. Cambridge University Press, Cambridge (1998)
4. Demetriou, M.A.: Guidance of mobile actuator-plus-sensor networks for improved control and estimation of distributed parameter systems. IEEE Trans. Autom. Control **55**(7), 1570–1584 (2010)
5. Dridi, S., Bagnoli, F., Yacoubi, S.E.: Markov chains approach for regional controllability of deterministic cellular automata, via boundary actions. J. Cell. Autom. **14**(5/6), 479–498 (2019)
6. Dridi, S., Yacoubi, S.E., Bagnoli, F., Fontaine, A.: A graph theory approach for regional controllability of boolean cellular automata. Int. J. Parallel Emerg. Distrib. Syst. 1–15 (2019). https://doi.org/10.1080/17445760.2019.1608442
7. Dridi, S.: Recent advances in regional controllability of cellular automata. Theses, Université de Perpignan; Università degli studi (Florence, Italie), November 2019
8. El Jai, A.: Distributed systems analysis via sensors and actuators. Sens. Actuat. A **29**(1), 1–11 (1991)
9. El Jai, A., El Yacoubi, S.: On the relations between actuator structures and final-constraint minimum-energy problem. Sens. Actuat. A **33**(3), 175–182 (1992)
10. El Yacoubi, S.: A mathematical method for control problems on cellular automata models. Int. J. Syst. Sci. **39**(5), 529–538 (2008)
11. Kalman, R.E.: On the general theory of control systems. In: Proceedings First International Conference on Automatic Control, Moscow, USSR (1960)
12. Kalman, R.E.: Mathematical description of linear dynamical systems. J. Soc. Ind. Appl. Math. Ser. A: Control **1**(2), 152–192 (1963)
13. Lions, J.L.: Controlabilite exacte des systemes distribues: remarques sur la theorie generale et les applications. In: Bensoussan, A., Lions, J.L. (eds.) Analysis and Optimization of Systems. LNCIS, vol. 83, pp. 3–14. Springer, Heidelberg (1986). https://doi.org/10.1007/BFb0007542
14. Russell, D.L.: Controllability and stabilizability theory for linear partial differential equations: recent progress and open questions. Siam Rev. **20**(4), 639–739 (1978)
15. Sarachik, P., Kreindler, E.: Controllability and observability of linear discrete-time systems. Int. J. Control **1**(5), 419–432 (1965)
16. Toffoli, T.: CAM: a high-performance cellular-automaton machine. Phys. D: Nonlinear Phenom. **10**(1–2), 195–204 (1984). https://www.sciencedirect.com/science/article/abs/pii/0167278984902616
17. Von Neumann, J., Burks, A.W., et al.: Theory of self-reproducing automata. IEEE Trans. Neural Netw. **5**(1), 3–14 (1966)
18. Wolfram, S.: Statistical mechanics of cellular automata. Rev. Mod. Phys. **55**(3), 601 (1983)

One-Dimensional Pattern Generation by Cellular Automata

Martin Kutrib$^{(\boxtimes)}$ and Andreas Malcher

Institut für Informatik, Universität Giessen, Arndtstr. 2, 35392 Giessen, Germany
{kutrib,andreas.malcher}@informatik.uni-giessen.de

Abstract. To determine the computational capacity of cellular automata they are often investigated towards their ability to accept formal languages within certain time constraints. In this paper, we take up an opposite position and look at cellular automata towards their ability to *generate* formal languages, here called patterns, within certain time constraints. As an example we describe a construction of a cellular automaton that generates prefixes of the well-known Thue-Morse sequence within real time. Furthermore, we study the real-time generation of unary patterns in depth and obtain a characterization by time-constructible functions and their corresponding unary formal languages.

1 Introduction

Parallel computational models are appealing and widely used in order to describe, understand, and manage parallel processes occurring in real life. Cellular automata (CA) are a model which allows to describe massively parallel systems, since they are arrays of identical copies of deterministic finite automata. Furthermore, the single nodes are homogeneously connected to both their immediate neighbors, and they work synchronously at discrete time steps. In general, cellular automata work on a given input which is provided in a parallel way, that is, every cell is fed with an input symbol in a pre-initial step.

The computational power of cellular automata can be measured by their ability to accept formal languages. In this context, the given input is accepted if there is a time step at which the leftmost cell enters an accepting state. Usually studied models comprise the real-time one-way cellular automata [2], where every cell is connected with its right neighbor only which restricts the flow of information from right to left. Moreover, the available time for accepting an input is restricted to the length of the input. Other models studied are real-time two-way cellular automata and linear-time two-way cellular automata. A survey on results concerning the computational capacity, closure properties and decidability questions for these models and references to the literature may be found, for example, in [6,7].

Another point of view on computations with cellular automata is taken in [4,8], where cellular automata are used as transducers, that is, they transform an input into an output obeying time constraints such as real and linear

T. M. Gwizdałła et al. (Eds.): ACRI 2020, LNCS 12599, pp. 46–55, 2021.
https://doi.org/10.1007/978-3-030-69480-7_6

time. The paper [4] discusses for cellular automata several time constraints and inclusion relationships based on these constraints. Moreover, closure properties and relations to cellular automata considered as formal language acceptors are established. In [8] also cellular automata with sequential input mode, called iterative arrays, are considered as transducing devices and compared with the cellular automata counterpart with parallel input mode. Additionally, the cellular transducing models are compared with classical sequential transducing devices such as finite state transducers and pushdown transducers.

In this paper, we will take yet another view on computations with cellular automata. Namely, we will consider cellular automata not as devices processing an input and computing a yes or no answer as in the case of a language accepting device or computing an output as in the case of a transducing device, but we consider cellular automata as generating devices. This means that the cellular automaton starts with an arbitrary number of cells being all in a quiescent state. Subsequently, it works synchronously according to its transition function. Finally, if the configurations reach a fixpoint, we consider such configurations as the *patterns generated* by the automaton. Thus, cellular automata considered this way compute a (partial) function mapping an initial length n to a pattern of length n over the alphabet of the automaton. Here, we start to investigate the basic ability of cellular automata to compute such functions within real time.

It should be remarked that the notion of pattern generation is used for cellular automata also in other contexts, but with a different meaning. For example, in [11] the sequence of configurations produced by a cellular automaton starting with some input is considered as a two-dimensional pattern generated. In [5] a cellular automaton is studied as universal pattern generator in the sense that starting from a finite configuration all finite patterns over the state alphabet are generated. This means that these patterns occur as infixes in the sequence of configurations computed.

The paper is organized as follows. In Sect. 2 we provide a formal definition of cellular automata and describe how they accept formal languages as well as they generate patterns within time constraints, in particular, within real time and linear time. The section is concluded with an illustrating example generating prefixes of the Thue-Morse sequence. In Sect. 3, we study the ability of real-time cellular automata to generate unary patterns in depth. A given function $f : \mathbb{N} \to \mathbb{N}$ defines a unary pattern in a natural way, namely, the pattern consists of all strings a^n, where n is in the range of f, and is undefined otherwise. A first result is that such patterns can be generated in real time under the condition that the function f has some constructibility properties. If the pattern is modified so that strings b^n are generated if n is not in the range of f, then another result shows that the generation is still possible in real time, but the construction is much more involved, since the information whether or not n belongs to the range of f is locally computed, but has to be transported to all cells in due time. Finally, it can be shown that the notions of time-constructibility, real-time language acceptance, and real-time pattern generation are equivalent in the unary case.

2   Preliminaries

We denote the non-negative integers by $\mathbb{N}$. Let Σ denote a finite set of letters. Then we write Σ^* for the *set of all finite words* (strings) consisting of letters from Σ. The *empty word* is denoted by λ, and we set $\Sigma^+ = \Sigma^* \setminus \{\lambda\}$. A subset of Σ^* is called a *language* over Σ. For the *reversal of a word* w we write w^R and for its *length* we write $|w|$. In general, we use $\subseteq$ for *inclusions* and $\subset$ for *strict inclusions*. For convenience, we use $S_\#$ to denote $S \cup \{\#\}$.

A two-way cellular automaton is a linear array of identical finite automata, called cells, numbered $1, 2, \ldots, n$. Except for border cells each one is connected to its both nearest neighbors. The state transition depends on the current state of a cell itself and the current states of its two neighbors, where the outermost cells receive a permanent boundary symbol on their free input lines. The cells work synchronously at discrete time steps.

Formally, a *deterministic two-way cellular automaton* (CA, for short) is a system $M = \langle S, \Sigma, F, s_0, \#, \delta \rangle$, where S is the finite, nonempty set of *cell states*, $\Sigma \subseteq S$ is set of *input symbols*, $F \subseteq S$ is the set of *accepting states*, $s_0 \in S$ is the *quiescent state*, $\# \notin S$ is the permanent *boundary symbol*, and $\delta : S_\# \times S \times S_\# \to S$ is the *local transition function* satisfying $\delta(s_0, s_0, s_0) = s_0$.

A *configuration* c_t of M at time $t \geq 0$ is a mapping $c_t : \{1, 2, \ldots, n\} \to S$, for $n \geq 1$, occasionally represented as a word over S. Given a configuration c_t, $t \geq 0$, its successor configuration is computed according to the global transition function Δ, that is, $c_{t+1} = \Delta(c_t)$, as follows. For $2 \leq i \leq n-1$,

$$c_{t+1}(i) = \delta(c_t(i-1)), c_t(i), c_t(i+1)),$$

and for the outermost cells we set

$$c_{t+1}(1) = \delta(\#, c_t(1), c_t(2)) \text{ and } c_{t+1}(n) = \delta(c_t(n-1), c_t(n), \#).$$

Thus, the global transition function Δ is induced by δ.

Here, a cellular automaton M can operate as decider or generator of one-dimensional patterns (or words, or strings).

A cellular automaton *accepts* a word $a_1 a_2 \cdots a_n \in \Sigma^+$, if at some time step during the course of the computation starting in the *initial configuration* $c_0(i) = a_i$, $1 \leq i \leq n$, the leftmost cell enters an accepting state, that is, the leftmost symbol of some reachable configuration is an accepting state. If the leftmost cell never enters an accepting state, the input is *rejected*. The *language accepted by* M is denoted by $L(M) = \{w \in \Sigma^+ \mid w$ is accepted by $M\}$.

A cellular automaton *generates* a word $a_1 a_2 \cdots a_n$, if at some time step t during the computation on the initial configuration $c_0(i) = s_0$, $1 \leq i \leq n$, (i) the word appears as configuration (that is, $c_t(i) = a_i$, $1 \leq i \leq n$) and (ii) configuration c_t is a fixpoint of the global transition function Δ (that is, the configuration is stable from time t on). The *pattern generated by* M is

$$P(M) = \{w \in S^+ \mid w \text{ is generated by } M\}.$$

Since the set of input symbols and the set of accepting states are not used when a cellular automaton operates as generator, we may safely omit them from its definition.

Let $t\colon \mathbb{N} \to \mathbb{N}$ be a mapping. If all $w \in L(M)$ are accepted with at most $t(|w|)$ time steps, or if all $w \in P(M)$ are generated with at most $t(|w|)$ time steps, then M is said to be of time complexity t. If $t(n) = n$ then M operates in *real time*. If $t(n) = k \cdot n$ for a rational number $k \geq 1$ then M operates in *linear time*.

We illustrate the definitions with an example.

Example 1. The Thue-Morse sequence is an infinite sequence over the alphabet $\{0, 1\}$. The well-known sequence has applications in numerous fields of mathematics and its properties are non-trivial. There are several ways of generating the Thue-Morse sequence one of which is given by a Lindenmayer system with axiom 0 and rewriting rules $0 \to 01$ and $1 \to 10$. The generation of words can be described as follows: starting with the axiom every symbol 0 (symbol 1) is in parallel replaced by the string 01 (10). This procedure is iteratively applied to the resulting strings and yields the prefixes $p_0 = 0$, $p_1 = 01$, $p_2 = 0110$, $p_3 = 01101001$, $p_4 = 0110100110010110$, and so on. We remark that the length of the prefix p_i is 2^i.

Next, we want to construct a real-time CA that will generate the pattern $P_{Thue} = \{p_i \mid i \geq 0\}$. The basic idea is to work with a real-time version of the FSSP based on the time optimal solution of Waksman [10]. The latter solution starts with one general at the left end of the array and it takes $n - 1$ time steps (n being the length of the array) to reach the right end. If we start instead with two generals at both ends, where the left general symmetrically behaves as the right general, we save $n - 1$ time steps. Since we need one additional time step to initialize the generals at both ends, we can realize the FSSP within $2n - 2 - (n - 1) + 1 = n$ time steps, that is, within real time.

Let us assume for a moment that the initial length is a power of two. In the further construction of the FSSP, the initial length is iteratively divided into halves, whereby two middle points and thus two new generals are generated. To generate the Thue-Morse sequence we consider the time steps at which two such middle cells are generated. Initially, at time $n/2 + 1$, the left new middle cell obtains the information 0 and the right new middle cell obtains the information 1. The signals sent out from the new middle cells to the left and right, respectively, are attached with this information. If these signals meet some other signal so that another two new middle cells are generated, the left cell gets the information 0 and the right cell gets the information 1 if the signal carried the information 0. Otherwise, the left cell gets the information 1 and the right cell gets the information 0. This behavior is iterated up to the last but one time step in which all cells have become a general. In the last time step, in which all cells are synchronized, a left signal 0 (1) in cell i at time $n - 1$ leads to 0 (1) in cell $i - 1$ and 1 (0) in cell i at time n. Analogously, a right signal 0 (1) in cell i at time $n - 1$ leads to 0 (1) in cell i and 1 (0) in cell $i + 1$ at time n. The states 0 and 1 are never changed so that the last configuration is a fixpoint and, hence, the pattern p_m is generated if the initial length has been 2^m.

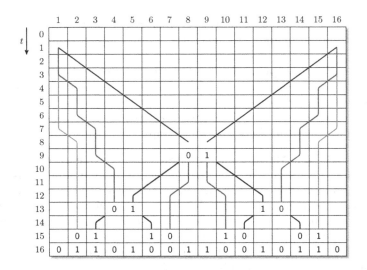

Fig. 1. Generation of $p_4 = 0110100110010110$. (Color figure online)

If the initial length is not a power of two, then in the procedure of iteratively dividing into halves there occurs at least one situation in which only one new middle point (and thus only one general) is generated. This situation can be identified and the corresponding cell is subsequently forced to oscillate between two states. Hence, the generated configurations are never a fixpoint which means that no pattern is generated in these cases.

The construction on input length $n = 16$ is illustrated in Fig. 1. The left signals starting from time 10 and 14 carry information 0 which leads to 01 in cells 4 and 5 and 2 and 3, respectively. The right signal starting from time 14 carries information 1 which leads to 10 in cells 6 and 7. In time step $n = 16$ the permanent states 0 and 1 are generated which are written in green. ∎

3   Pattern Generation, Languages Acceptance, and Time Constructibility

In order to explore the capabilities and properties of real-time cellular pattern generators, we start with unary words. At a first glance, to generate a unary pattern is trivial. In fact, this is true for patterns of the form $\{a^n \mid n \geq 1\}$. In such cases it is sufficient that any cell enters state a in its first step and remains in this state. However, these patterns are total which means that the pattern contains a word for any $n \geq 1$. So, let us make the task a little harder. Now we define the pattern to be generated as a partial function on n. More precisely, we impose a condition on n such that the pattern a^n is to be generated if and only if n meets the condition. Let, for example, $\varphi\colon \mathbb{N} \to \mathbb{N}$ be some function. Then pattern P_φ is defined to be a^n if there is some m such that $n = \varphi(m)$, and undefined otherwise. Clearly, such a pattern can only be generated by a cellular automaton in real time if the function φ is constructible in some sense. If it is uncomputable, trivially P_φ cannot be generated. In order to fix the notion of constructibility the notion of time-constructibility is widely used.

In particular, a strictly increasing function $\varphi \colon \mathbb{N} \to \mathbb{N}$ is *time-constructible* if there is a semi-infinite cellular automaton $M = \langle S, \Sigma, F, s_0, \#, \delta \rangle$, that is, n is infinite, whose leftmost cell is in some state of F at time $t \geq 0$ if and only if $t = \varphi(i)$ for some $i \geq 0$. The initial configuration of M is quiescent, that is, $c_0(i) = s_0$, $1 \leq i$.

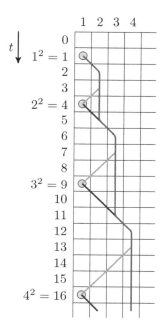

The investigation of time-constructible functions in cellular automata originates in [3], where a cellular automaton is constructed that time-constructs the function $i \mapsto p_i$ where p_i denotes the ith prime number. In [1] a time-constructor for the function $i \mapsto 2^i$ is given. The systematic study of this concept was started in [9]. The family of time-constructible functions is denoted by $\mathscr{F}(\mathrm{CA})$.

As a simple example, in Fig. 2 the time-construction of the function $i \mapsto i^2$ is given. Basically, the necessary signals can be derived from $(i+1)^2 = i^2 + 2i + 1$. In particular, after being designated at time i^2, the leftmost cell has to wait for $2i$ time steps before it is designated again at time $i^2 + 2i + 1$. This delay is exactly the time needed by an auxiliary signal α that moves from the leftmost cell 1 to cell $i+1$, stays there for one time step, and moves back to the leftmost cell. To this end, another auxiliary signal β is used that stays in cell i until it is hit by α and moves to cell $i+1$.

Fig. 2. Time construction of the function i^2. Signal α is depicted in blue and green, signal β is depicted in red. (Color figure online)

Let us come back to the pattern P_φ, where φ is a time-constructible function. Since the pattern is undefined for lengths n that are not in the range of φ, the pattern is easily generated by a CA.

Proposition 2. *Let $\varphi \colon \mathbb{N} \to \mathbb{N}$ be a time-constructible function. Then the pattern $P_\varphi = \{a^n \mid \text{there is an } m \text{ with } n = \varphi(m)\}$ is generated by some real-time CA.*

Proof. A real-time CA that generates P_φ essentially simulates a time constructor for φ. In addition, its rightmost cell initially sends a signal with maximal speed to the left. Each cell passed through by this signal enters state a and remains in it. The signal arrives at the leftmost cell at time n. If this cell is simultaneously distinguished by the time construction, the number of cells n is in the range of φ. In this case the leftmost cell enters state a and remains in it. This means that the pattern a^n is generated in real time. If at arrival of the signal the leftmost cell is not distinguished by the time construction, it starts to enter alternating some states b and c. So, the configuration will never be stable and no pattern is generated in this case. □

The simple construction of the generator of P_φ works fine since, in principle, only the leftmost cell decides whether a pattern has to be generated or not. Moreover, the other cells can safely enter the pattern states in advance without violating the overall result. So, let us make the task again a little harder. Now we define the pattern to be generated as a total function on n and impose a condition on n such that the pattern a^n is to be generated if n meets the condition, but the pattern b^n otherwise. In this case, the leftmost cell can still decide which pattern has to be generated, but all the other cells cannot enter the pattern state in advance. Instead, they have to know whether the condition is met or not. Since an FSSP synchronization of the array (starting at both ends simultaneously) cannot be done in less than $n - 1$ steps, for a real-time generation there is not enough time for the leftmost cell to inform the other cells about whether or not the condition is met. For a time-constructible function $\varphi : \mathbb{N} \to \mathbb{N}$, we define the pattern $\hat{P}_\varphi$ to be a^n if there is some m such that $n = \varphi(m)$, and b^n otherwise. The next theorem shows that even these unary patterns are generated in real time.

Theorem 3. Let $\varphi : \mathbb{N} \to \mathbb{N}$ be a time-constructible function. Then the pattern $\hat{P}_\varphi = \{ x^n \mid x = a$ if there is an m with $n = \varphi(m)$ and $x = b$ otherwise$\}$ is generated by some real-time CA.

Proof. The basic idea of a real-time CA M that generates $\hat{P}_\varphi$ is as follows. In order to check the condition on the length of the input, a time-constructor for φ is simulated. In order to gain enough time to synchronize the cells, it is sped-up by a factor of two. This is done by grouping two cells of the time-construction into one cell. So, the leftmost cell now simulates cell 1 and cell 2 of the original time-constructor. More precisely, if originally the leftmost cell is distinguished at an even time step i, now it is distinguished at time step $i/2$ by the simulation of the original cell 1. If originally the leftmost cell is distinguished at an odd time step i, now it is distinguished at time step $(i - 1)/2$ by the simulation of the original cell 2.

Note that all computations apart from the compressed simulation of the time-constructor are done without grouping the cells.

Next, the compressed simulation of the time-constructor is expanded again (see Fig. 3). To this end, a signal α with speed $1/3$ is initially sent to the right by the leftmost cell.

Case 1: Whenever the leftmost cell of the compressed simulation is distinguished at time step $i/2$ by the simulation of the original cell 1, that is, i is even, then it sends a signal β to the right. When this signal meets α, it follows α for one time step and runs back to the left. It arrives at the leftmost cell at time i again. This is inductively seen as follows.

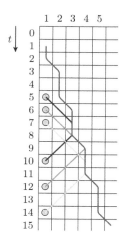
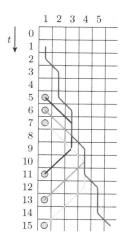

Fig. 3. Principles of designating time $2i$ (left) and $2i+1$ (right) starting at time i. The signal α with speed $1/3$ is depicted in red. The three computations starting at time steps 5, 6, and 7 are depicted in blue, green, and yellow. (Color figure online)

Case 1.a: Let $j = i/2$ be even. Then β meets α in cell $j/2$ at time $j + j/2 - 1$. This is true for $j = 2$ in cell 1 at time 2. Now assume it is true for some even j. Since j is even, $j + j/2 - 1$ is congruent 2 modulo 3. That is, signal α moves to cell $j/2 + 1$ at time $j + j/2$ and stays there until time $j + j/2 + 2$. Signal β is sent by the leftmost cell at time $j + 2$ and arrives in cell $j/2 + 1 = (j + 2)/2$ at time $j + 2 + j/2 + 1 - 1 = j + j/2 + 2 = (j + 2) + (j + 2)/2 - 1$.

Next, when signal β meets α it follows α for one time step, that is, when sent at time j it enters cell $j/2 + 1$ at time $j + j/2$, and moves back to the leftmost cell, where it arrives at time $j + j/2 + j/2 = 2j = i$ as claimed.

Case 1.b: Now let $j = i/2$ be odd. Then β meets α in cell $(j + 1)/2$ at time $j + (j - 1)/2$. This is true for $j = 1$ in cell 1 at time 1. Now assume it is true for some odd j. Since j is odd, $j + (j - 1)/2$ is congruent 1 modulo 3. That is, signal α moves to cell $(j + 1)/2 + 1$ at time $j + (j - 1)/2 + 2$ and stays there until time $j + (j - 1)/2 + 4$. Signal β sent by the leftmost cell at time $j + 2$ arrives in cell $(j + 1)/2 + 1 = (j + 2 + 1)/2$ at time $j + 2 + (j + 2 + 1)/2 - 1 = (j + 2) + (j + 1)/2$.

Next, when signal β meets α it follows α for one time step, that is, stays in cell $(j + 1)/2$ at time $j + (j - 1)/2 + 1$, and moves back to the leftmost cell, where it arrives at time $j + (j - 1)/2 + 1 + (j + 1)/2 - 1 = 2j = i$ as claimed.

Case 2: Whenever the leftmost cell of the compressed simulation is distinguished at time step $(i - 1)/2$ by the simulation of the original cell 2, that is, i is odd, then it sends a signal γ to the right. When this signal meets α, it follows α for one time step, stays in that cell for another time step, and runs back to the left. Case 2 is basically the same as Case 1 with the exception that the signal which bounces at α is delayed for one time step. So, it arrives at the leftmost cell one time step later than in Case 1, that is, at time $2(i - 1)/2 + 1 = i$.

Now we continue the construction of the real-time CA that generates $\hat{P}_\varphi$ (see Fig. 4 for an example). In addition to the simulation of the time-constructor, the rightmost cell initially sends a signal τ with maximal speed to the left. If the number of cells n is not congruent 3 modulo 4, this signal meets signal α of the time constructor in cell $\lfloor n/4 \rfloor + 1$. At this point it can be determined if some signal β or γ of the time constructor joins τ on its way to the leftmost cell. Since τ arrives at the leftmost cell at time n and β or γ distinguishes the leftmost cell, exactly in this case the pattern a^n has to be generated, and b^n otherwise. So, cell $\lfloor n/4 \rfloor + 1$ can send this information to the right and to the left to cause all cells reached to enter the correct pattern state. In this way, the cells 1 to $2\lfloor n/4 \rfloor + 1$ are reached in the remaining $\lfloor n/4 \rfloor$ time steps. Since n is not congruent 3 modulo 4 we have $2\lfloor n/4 \rfloor + 1 \geq \lceil n/2 \rceil$. So, the left half of the array generates the correct pattern. In order to achieve the same for the right half it is sufficient, additionally to implement the whole procedure symmetrically on the right end of the array.

Finally, the case where n is congruent 3 modulo 4 has to be considered. In this case, the signals α and τ meet in the adjacent cells $\lfloor n/4 \rfloor + 1$ and $\lfloor n/4 \rfloor + 2$. So, these cells can send the information which pattern is to be generated one time step after the meeting, for which then $\lfloor n/4 \rfloor$ time steps are left. This means that also in this case the cells 1 to $2\lfloor n/4 \rfloor + 2 \geq \lceil n/2 \rceil$ will receive this information in due time. $\square$

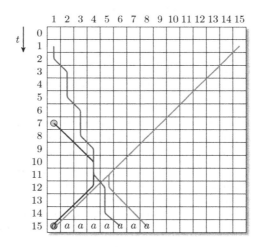

Fig. 4. Example of a $\hat{P}_\varphi$ generator, where $a^{15} \in \hat{P}_\varphi$. The signal α with speed $1/3$ is depicted in red, signal γ that designates time 15 is depicted in blue, and signal τ is depicted in gray. Since $15 \equiv 3 \pmod 4$, the signals α and τ meet in the adjacent cells 4 and 5. (Color figure online)

The family of time-constructible functions $\mathscr{F}(\mathrm{CA})$ is very rich. Several examples and the closure of the family under a bunch of operations are shown in [9]. This fact transfers immediately to the family of unary patterns of the form $\hat{P}_\varphi$ generated by cellular automata in real time. Moreover, in [9] the following relation between time-constructible functions and unary languages is shown: A function $\varphi \colon \mathbb{N} \to \mathbb{N}$ is time constructible if and only if the language $L_\varphi = \{a^{\varphi(m)} \mid m \geq 1\}$ is accepted by a real-time cellular automaton.

Proposition 4. *Let $\varphi \colon \mathbb{N} \to \mathbb{N}$ be a function and $\hat{P}_\varphi$ be generated by some cellular automaton in real time. Then language $L_\varphi = \{a^{\varphi(m)} \mid m \geq 1\}$ is accepted by a real-time cellular automaton.*

Now by Theorem 3, Proposition 4, and the result from [9], we have shown that for unary languages/patterns the three different notions of language acceptance, time-constructibility, and pattern generation, in fact, coincide.

Theorem 5. *A function $\varphi \colon \mathbb{N} \to \mathbb{N}$ is time constructible if and only if the language L_φ is accepted by a real-time cellular automaton if and only if the pattern $\hat{P}_\varphi$ can be generated by a cellular automaton in real time.*

References

1. Choffrut, C., Čulik II, K.: On real-time cellular automata and trellis automata. Acta Inform. **21**, 393–407 (1984)
2. Dyer, C.R.: One-way bounded cellular automata. Inform. Control **44**(3), 261–281 (1980)
3. Fischer, P.C.: Generation of primes by a one-dimensional real-time iterative array. J. ACM **12**, 388–394 (1965)
4. Grandjean, A., Richard, G., Terrier, V.: Linear functional classes over cellular automata. In: Formenti, E. (ed.) International workshop on Cellular Automata and Discrete Complex Systems and Journées Automates Cellulaires (AUTOMATA & JAC 2012). EPTCS, vol. 90, pp. 177–193 (2012)
5. Kari, J.: Universal pattern generation by cellular automata. Theor. Comput. Sci. **429**, 180–184 (2012)
6. Kutrib, M.: Cellular automata - a computational point of view. In: Bel-Enguix, G., Jiménez-López, M.D., Martín-Vide, C. (eds.) New Developments in Formal Languages and Applications. SCI, pp. 183–227. Springer, Heidelberg (2008). https://doi.org/10.1007/978-3-540-78291-9_6
7. Kutrib, M.: Cellular automata and language theory. In: Meyers, R.A. (ed.) Encyclopedia of Complexity and Systems Science, pp. 800–823. Springer, Heidelberg (2009). https://doi.org/10.1007/978-0-387-30440-3_54
8. Kutrib, M., Malcher, A.: One-dimensional cellular automaton transducers. Fundam. Inform. **126**(2–3), 201–224 (2013)
9. Mazoyer, J., Terrier, V.: Signals in one-dimensional cellular automata. Theor. Comput. Sci. **217**, 53–80 (1999)
10. Waksman, A.: An optimum solution to the firing squad synchronization problem. Inform. Control **9**, 66–78 (1966)
11. Wolfram, S.: Random sequence generation by cellular automata. Adv. Appl. Math. **7**, 123–169 (1986)

Exploring Semi-bent Boolean Functions Arising from Cellular Automata

Luca Mariot[1]([✉]), Martina Saletta[2], Alberto Leporati[2], and Luca Manzoni[3]

[1] Cyber Security Research Group, Delft University of Technology,
Mekelweg 2, Delft, The Netherlands
l.mariot@tudelft.nl
[2] DISCo, Università degli Studi di Milano-Bicocca,
Viale Sarca 336/14, 20126 Milan, Italy
m.saletta1@campus.unimib.it, alberto.leporati@unimib.it
[3] Dipartimento di Matematica e Geoscienze, Università degli Studi di Trieste,
Via Valerio 12/1, 34127 Trieste, Italy
lmanzoni@units.it

Abstract. Semi-bent Boolean functions are interesting from a cryptographic standpoint, since they possess several desirable properties such as having a low and flat Walsh spectrum, which is useful to resist linear cryptanalysis. In this paper, we consider the search of semi-bent functions through a construction based on cellular automata (CA). In particular, the construction defines a Boolean function by computing the XOR of all output cells in the CA. Since the resulting Boolean functions have the same algebraic degree of the CA local rule, we devise a combinatorial algorithm to enumerate all quadratic Boolean functions. We then apply this algorithm to exhaustively explore the space of quadratic rules of up to 6 variables, selecting only those for which our CA-based construction always yields semi-bent functions of up to 20 variables. Finally, we filter the obtained rules with respect to their balancedness, and remark that the semi-bent functions generated through our construction by the remaining rules have a constant number of linear structures.

Keywords: Cellular automata · Stream ciphers · Semi-bent functions · Nonlinearity · Combinatorial search · Balancedness · Linear structures

1 Introduction

Cellular Automata (CA) represent an appealing approach to the design of cryptographic primitives. Indeed, starting from the 80s, CA have been extensively investigated for designing *Pseudo-Random Number Generators* (PRNGs) [6,14,16], *S-boxes* [4,11,15] and *secret sharing schemes* [8,9,12], among other things.

In this work, we consider the use of CA for the construction of *Boolean functions* with interesting cryptographic properties. Boolean functions are cryptographic primitives that play an important role in the design of *stream ciphers*,

© Springer Nature Switzerland AG 2021
T. M. Gwizdałła et al. (Eds.): ACRI 2020, LNCS 12599, pp. 56–66, 2021.
https://doi.org/10.1007/978-3-030-69480-7_7

where they may be used to combine or filter the output of linear feedback shift registers (LFSR) to construct a keystream, and in *block ciphers*, where they constitute the coordinates of S-boxes. Previous research [3,5] focused on the investigation of CA local rules as Boolean functions, selecting those with the best cryptographic properties to withstand particular attacks when used in a CA-based PRNG. In this work we adopt a different viewpoint, which spawns from the following question: given a Boolean function of m variables with good cryptographic properties, is it possible to derive new functions from it with a larger number of variables and analogous properties by using a CA?

More specifically, the construction that we investigate in this paper employs an initial m-variable Boolean function as the local rule of a CA of $n \geq m$ cells. Then, a new function of n variables is constructed by applying the CA global rule and by computing the XOR of the CA cells in the output configuration. In this way, one can generate an infinite family of Boolean functions starting from the initial local rule by simply adding more cells to the CA. Techniques for generating new Boolean functions from existing ones are also called *secondary* (or *recursive*) *constructions*, and only few of them are known in the related literature, none of which are based on CA (see e.g. [2] for a survey). Our analysis focuses on the particular case of *semi-bent* Boolean functions, which have interesting cryptographic properties such as high nonlinearity. In particular, we are interested in finding semi-bent functions which generate larger semi-bent functions when plugged as local rules in our CA-based construction. As a first basic result, we show that our construction preserves the algebraic degree of the local rule. We thus design a combinatorial algorithm based on the *Algebraic Normal Form* representation to enumerate all Boolean functions of a fixed degree. For our experiments, we use our algorithm to enumerate all *quadratic* functions of $3 \leq m \leq 6$ variables, and among them we select only those that generate semi-bent functions of up to $n = 20$ variables through our CA construction. The first remarkable finding is that for $m = 4$ variables our construction always fails, i.e. no quadratic rule of 4 variables is able to generate semi-bent functions of up to $n = 20$ variables. By focusing on the balanced rules of 3, 5 and 6 variables over which the construction works, we finally remark that they all have a constant number of non-trivial *linear structures*, namely 1 when the number of variables is odd, and 3 when it is even.

The rest of this paper is organized as follows. Section 2 covers the basic definitions concerning Boolean functions and their cryptographic properties. Section 3 introduces the CA model considered in this work and defines our CA-based construction of Boolean functions, while Sect. 4 describes the search algorithm used to enumerate functions of a fixed degree. Section 5 presents the results of our exhaustive search experiments on the spaces of quadratic local rules. Finally, Sect. 6 concludes the paper and points out some open problems concerning our construction for future research.

2   Background on Boolean Functions

In what follows, let $\mathbb{F}_2 = \{0,1\}$ denote the finite field of two elements and let $\mathbb{F}_2^n$ be the n-dimensional vector space over $\mathbb{F}_2$. The *support* of $x \in \mathbb{F}_2^n$ is defined as $supp(x) = \{i : x_i \neq 0\}$, while the *Hamming weight* of x is $w_H(x) = |supp(x)|$, i.e. the number of 1s in x.

A *Boolean function* of $n \in \mathbb{N}$ variables is a mapping $f : \mathbb{F}_2^n \to \mathbb{F}_2$, with its *truth table* being the 2^n-bit string Ω_f that specifies the output value of f for each of the vectors in $\mathbb{F}_2^n$, in lexicographic order. A function f is called *balanced* if its truth table is composed of an equal number of 0s and 1s, i.e. if $w_H(\Omega_f) = 2^{n-1}$. Balancedness is a fundamental cryptographic property that Boolean functions used in stream and block ciphers should satisfy to resist statistical attacks.

Besides the truth table, a second unique representation of a Boolean function $f : \mathbb{F}_2^n \to \mathbb{F}_2$ commonly used in cryptography is the *Algebraic Normal Form* (ANF), which is defined as the following multivariate polynomial over the quotient ring $\mathbb{F}_2[x_1, \cdots, x_n]/(x_1^2 \oplus x_1, \cdots, x_n^2 \oplus x_n)$:

$$P_f(x) = \bigoplus_{I \in 2^{[n]}} a_I \left(\prod_{i \in I} x_i \right), \tag{1}$$

where $2^{[n]}$ is the power set of $[n] = \{1, \cdots, n\}$. The *algebraic degree* of f is the cardinality of the largest subset $I \in 2^{[n]}$ in its ANF such that $a_I \neq 0$. In particular, *affine functions* are defined as those Boolean functions with degree at most 1. As a cryptographic criterion, the algebraic degree should be as high as possible. The vector of the ANF coefficients a_I and the truth table of f are related by the *Möbius transform*:

$$f(x) = \bigoplus_{I \in 2^{[n]} : I \subseteq supp(x)} a_I, \tag{2}$$

Another representation used to characterize several cryptographic properties of Boolean functions is the Walsh transform. Formally, the *Walsh transform* of a Boolean function $f : \mathbb{F}_2^n \to \mathbb{F}_2$ is defined for all $a \in \mathbb{F}_2^n$ as:

$$W_f(a) = \sum_{x \in \mathbb{F}_2^n} (-1)^{f(x) \oplus a \cdot x}, \tag{3}$$

where $a \cdot x = \bigoplus_{i=1}^n a_i x_i$ is the *scalar product* of the vectors a and x. A function f is balanced if and only if the Walsh coefficient over the null vector is zero, i.e. $W_f(0) = 0$. More in general, the coefficient $W_f(a)$ measures the *correlation* between f and the linear function $a \cdot x$. Thus, the Walsh transform can be used to compute the *nonlinearity* of a Boolean function f, which is defined as the minimum Hamming distance of f from the set of all affine functions. In particular, the nonlinearity of f equals

$$N_f = 2^{n-1} - \frac{1}{2} \cdot \max_{a \in \mathbb{F}_2^n} \{|W_f(a)|\}. \tag{4}$$

For cryptographic applications, the nonlinearity of the involved Boolean functions should be as high as possible. From Eq. (4), this means that the maximum absolute value of the Walsh transform should be as low as possible. By *Parseval relation*, this can happen only when all Walsh coefficients have the same absolute value $2^{\frac{n}{2}}$, yielding the *covering radius bound*: $N_f \leq 2^{n-1} - 2^{\frac{n}{2}-1}$. Functions satisfying this bound are called *bent*, and they exist only when n is even. Unfortunately such functions are not balanced, since $W_f(0) = \pm 2^{\frac{n}{2}}$, and thus they cannot be used directly in the design of stream and block ciphers. For n odd, the *quadratic bound* is given by $N_f \leq 2^{n-1} - 2^{\frac{n+1}{2}-1}$, and it can be always achieved by functions of algebraic degree 2.

Plateaued functions represent an interesting generalization of bent functions, since they can also be balanced while still retaining high nonlinearity. Formally, a Boolean function $f : \mathbb{F}_2^n \to \mathbb{F}_2$ is *plateaued* if its Walsh transform takes only three values, i.e. if $W_f(a) \in \{-\lambda, 0, +\lambda\}$ for all $a \in \mathbb{F}_2^n$. In particular, a plateaued function is *semi-bent* if $\lambda = 2^{\frac{n+1}{2}}$ for n odd and $\lambda = 2^{\frac{n+2}{2}}$ for n even. This means that the nonlinearity of a semi-bent function equals $2^{n-1} - 2^{\frac{n-1}{2}}$ when n is odd and $2^{n-1} - 2^{\frac{n}{2}}$ when n is even. Hence, semi-bent functions reach the quadratic bound for nonlinearity when n is odd.

We conclude this section by recalling the concept of *linear structures*. Given a Boolean function $f : \mathbb{F}_2^n \to \mathbb{F}_2$, the *derivative* of f with respect to $b \in \mathbb{F}_2^n$ is defined as $D_b f(x) = f(x) \oplus f(x \oplus b)$. Then, b is called a *linear structure* for f if the derivative is a constant function, that is, if $D_b f(x) = 0$ for all $x \in \mathbb{F}_2^n$ or $D_b f(x) = 1$ for all $x \in \mathbb{F}_2^n$. Remark that the null vector is a trivial linear structure, since $D_0 f(x) = f(x) \oplus f(x \oplus 0) = 0$ for any Boolean function f. Ideally, the number of linear structures in Boolean functions used for stream and block ciphers should be as low as possible.

3   Our Construction

We start by introducing the CA model considered in this work.

Definition 1. *Let* $f : \mathbb{F}_2^m \to \mathbb{F}_2$ *be a Boolean function of* m *variables, and* $n \geq m$. *A* Cellular Automaton *(CA) of* n *cells and* local rule f *is a vectorial function* $F : \mathbb{F}_2^n \to \mathbb{F}_2^{n-m+1}$ *defined for all* $x \in \mathbb{F}_2^n$ *as:*

$$F(x_1, x_2, \cdots, x_n) = (f(x_1, \cdots, x_m), \cdots, f(x_{n-m+1}, \cdots, x_n)).$$

A CA can thus be seen as a vectorial Boolean function where each coordinate function $f_i : \mathbb{F}_2^m \to \mathbb{F}_2$ corresponds to the local rule f applied to the *neighborhood* $(x_i, \cdots, x_{i+m-1})$. This rule is applied just up to the coordinate $n-m+1$, meaning that the size of the input array shrinks by $m-1$ cells. Definition 1 corresponds to the *No Boundary CA* model studied in [7,11]. In particular, the fact that the CA array shrinks is not an issue in our work, since we are not interested in the long-term dynamical behavior of the CA over multiple time steps, but rather only the one-shot application of the global rule on the input array. Since the local rule $f : \mathbb{F}_2^m \to \mathbb{F}_2$ is a Boolean function, it can be defined by a truth table

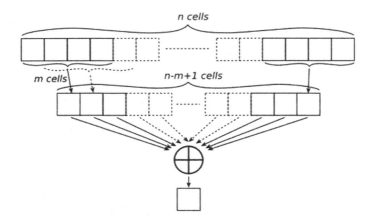

Fig. 1. Representation of our CA-based construction for Boolean functions.

Ω_f of 2^m bits. In the CA literature, the truth table of a local rule is usually represented by its *Wolfram code*, which amounts to the decimal value of Ω_f seen as a binary number.

We can now define our construction of Boolean functions based on the no-boundary CA model discussed above.

Definition 2. *Let* $F : \mathbb{F}_2^n \to \mathbb{F}_2^{n-m+1}$ *be a CA of length* $n \geq m$ *equipped with the local rule* $f : \mathbb{F}_2^m \to \mathbb{F}_2$. *Then, the Boolean function induced by* f *through the CA* F *is the* n-*variable function* $f^* : \mathbb{F}_2^n \to \mathbb{F}_2$ *defined for all* $x \in \mathbb{F}_2^n$ *as:*

$$f^*(x) = \bigoplus_{i=1}^{n-m+1} f(x_i, \cdots, x_{i+m-1}) = f(x_1, \cdots, x_m) \oplus \cdots \oplus f(x_{n-m+1}, \cdots, x_n).$$

$$(5)$$

In other words, the construction consists in first applying the CA vectorial function F induced by the local rule f to the input vector $x \in \mathbb{F}_2^n$; then, the value of the constructed function f^* is obtained by computing the XOR of all the output cells of the CA. Figure 1 gives a schematic depiction of how the construction works. Using the terminology of the Boolean functions literature [2], the construction of Definition 2 may be classified as a *secondary construction*, since it starts from a known function f of m variables used as a CA local rule, and generates a new function f^* of n variables from it. In particular, our construction gives rise to an *infinite family* of Boolean functions, since f^* can be defined for any number of variables $n \geq m$ by simply adding n cells to the CA.

Secondary constructions are mainly employed to generate new Boolean functions from old ones with analogous cryptographic properties. For example, Rothaus's construction [13] starts from three bent functions of n variables, whose sum is also bent, and produces a new bent function of $n + 2$ variables. We thus need to analyze which properties are preserved by our construction. The next lemma shows that the algebraic degree is one such property:

Lemma 1. *Let $f : \mathbb{F}_2^m \to \mathbb{F}_2$ be a Boolean function of m variables. For any $n \geq m$, the function f^* defined by the CA construction of Eq. (5) has the same algebraic degree of f.*

Proof. The result is clearly true when $n = m$, since in that case $f \equiv f^*$. We thus only consider the case where $n > m$.

Let d be the algebraic degree of f. Each summand in Eq. (5) has degree d, since it always corresponds to the local rule f applied on a different neighborhood. We thus have to show that not all terms of degree d cancel each other out. Consider the first summand $f(x_1, \cdots, x_m)$, and let $S_d = \{I \subseteq 2^{[m]} : |I| = d, a_I \neq 0\}$ be the set of monomials of degree d in the ANF of f. Further, denote by $I_{min} \in S_d$ the minimum element of S_d with respect to the lexicographic order, that is, if $I_{min} = \{i_1, \cdots, i_d\}$ and $J = \{j_1, \cdots, j_d\}$ is any other set of S_d, it holds $i_k < j_k$ for some $k \in [d]$ and $i_h = j_h$ for all $h \in [k-1]$. This monomial cannot be cancelled by any other monomial in the ANF of the subsequent summands, since by Eq. (5) their neighborhoods are shifted by at least one coordinate with respect to that of the first summand. Indeed, if we take the l-th summand $f(x_l, \cdots, x_{l+m-1})$ for $l \in \{2, \cdots, n - m + 1\}$, and we denote by I_{min}^l its minimum monomial of degree d in lexicographic order, we have that $I_{min}^l = (i_1 + l, \cdots, i_d + l)$, which is distinct from $(i_1, \cdots, i_d) = I_{min}$. Hence, the variables in the monomial I_{min}^l cannot overlap completely those of I_{min}, which means that the two terms do not cancel each other out. Similarly, the monomial I_{min} cannot be canceled by any non-minimal monomial of degree d in the l-th summand. Hence, the monomial corresponding to I_{min} appears in the ANF of (5), which proves that the algebraic degree of f^* is also d.   □

4   Search Algorithm

Lemma 1 gives us a first basic insight on the nature of the functions resulting from our construction. However, the fact that the algebraic degree of the original function is preserved is not sufficient from the cryptographic point of view, since as we saw in Sect. 2 there are other properties to take into account, such as balancedness and nonlinearity. Considering that semi-bent functions offer a good trade-off of these criteria, we turn our attention to the following question: what are the semi-bent Boolean functions that give rise to an infinite family of semi-bent functions when used as local rules of our CA-based construction? In other words, we are interested in finding a subset of semi-bent Boolean functions of m variables such that they generate semi-bent functions for any number of variables $n \geq m$ when plugged in Eq. (5). In this section and in the next one, we address this question by adopting an *experimental approach*. More precisely, we devise a combinatorial search algorithm to efficiently explore the search space of local rules, and retain only those semi-bent rules over which our construction yields semi-bent functions up to a specified number of variables. Clearly, we cannot prove that the rules obtained in this way indeed generate infinite families of semi-bent functions. However, this experimental search is useful to isolate at least a subset of candidate rules, to be investigated in future research.

SEARCH-ANF(m, n, d)
Initialization: For $1 \le k \le d$, build the family $\mathcal{I}_k = \{I \subseteq [d] : |I| = k\}$ of monomials
  of degree k, set all 2^m ANF coefficients of f to 0 and initialize $\mathcal{L}$ as the empty list
Outer Loop: For all subsets $\mathcal{T} \subseteq \mathcal{I}_d$ (except the empty set), do:
  ANF Initialization: Reset all d-degree terms in the ANF to 0
  Instantiation: For all $T \in \mathcal{T}$, set the ANF coefficient a_T to 1, i.e. include in the
    ANF the combination of d-degree monomials defined by $\mathcal{T}$
  Inner Loop: For all subsets $\mathcal{P} \subseteq \bigcup_{k=1}^{d-1} \mathcal{I}_k$ do:
    1. Reset all terms of degree less than d in the ANF to 0
    2. For all $P \in \mathcal{P}$, set the ANF coefficient a_P to 1, i.e. include in the ANF the
       combination of monomials of degree at most $d - 1$ defined by $\mathcal{P}$
    3. Apply the Möbius Transform (Equation (2)) to the ANF coefficients vector
       to obtain the truth table of the function f
    4. Compute the Walsh transform (Equation (3)) on the truth table of f
    5. If f is semi-bent, then for all $d < i \le n$ apply the CA construction of
       Equation (5) with i cells, and compute the Walsh transform of f^*
    6. If for all $d < i \le n$ the function f^* is semi-bent, then add f to $\mathcal{L}$
Output: return $\mathcal{L}$

Fig. 2. Pseudocode of the SEARCH-ANF algorithm.

A trivial algorithm to search for semi-bent functions simply consists in enumerating all possible truth tables of m-variables functions, which are 2^{2^m} in total.
However, this brute-force procedure is extremely inefficient: most Boolean functions are not semi-bent, and searching through all of them is feasible only up to
$m = 5$ variables. We thus designed a combinatorial algorithm to exhaustively
enumerate only the Boolean functions having a fixed algebraic degree. In this
way, by Lemma 1 we know that these functions will all generate Boolean functions of the same degree through our construction. This remark is especially
useful when considering the case of *quadratic functions*, i.e. functions of degree
2. As a matter of fact, quadratic functions are a subclass of *plateaued functions* [2], which in turn include semi-bent functions, as mentioned in Sect. 2.
Hence, focusing on the intersection of quadratic and semi-bent functions is a
reasonable trade-off between obtaining an interesting enough class of functions
to investigate with respect to our construction and enumerating it in a limited
amount of time.

Our search algorithm is based on the ANF representation. Given a target
algebraic degree d, the 2^m-bit vector of the ANF coefficients can be easily constrained to yield only Boolean functions of degree d: it suffices to set *at least one*
of the coefficients a_I such that $|I| = d$ to 1, while all coefficients a_J with $|J| > d$
must be set to 0. The other coefficients related to monomials of lower degree can
be freely chosen. Then, by using the *Möbius Transform* recalled in Eq. (2), one
can recover the truth table starting from its ANF coefficients, and check if the
corresponding quadratic function is semi-bent by computing its Walsh spectrum.
In this case, we can finally test if our construction generates quadratic semi-bent
functions up to a specified number of variables. The pseudocode of our search
algorithm is reported in Fig. 2.

Table 1. Results obtained with the SEARCH-ANF algorithm and by filtering only the rules that produce balanced functions.

m	2^{2^m}	$S_{m,2}$	QSB	Bal
3	256	56	24	8
4	65 536	1 008	0	0
5	$\approx 4.3 \cdot 10^9$	32 736	2 208	280
6	$\approx 1.84 \cdot 10^{19}$	$2.1 \cdot 10^6$	12 208	1937

5 Complexity and Search Experiments

Let us analyze the time complexity of the search algorithm described in the previous section for the case of quadratic functions, i.e. when $d = 2$. The outer loop is applied over all subsets of monomials of degree 2, except the empty set which of course does not give a quadratic function. Since the number of quadratic terms in the ANF of a m-variable function is $\binom{m}{2}$, it means that the outer loop is executed $2^{\binom{m}{2}} - 1$ times. The inner loop iterates only through all combinations of *linear terms*, hence it is executed for $2^{\binom{m}{1}}$ steps. The search space $\mathcal{S}_{m,2}$ visited by our algorithm is thus composed of the following number of ANF vectors:

$$S_{m,2} = \left(2^{\binom{m}{2}} - 1 \right) \cdot 2^{\binom{m}{1}} = \left(2^{\frac{m(m-1)}{2}} - 1 \right) \cdot 2^m. \qquad (6)$$

It follows that $S_{m,2} = 2^{\mathcal{O}(m^2)}$, which is asymptotically better than the $\mathcal{O}(2^{2^m})$ bound given by the brute-force search approach.

We thus applied our algorithm SEARCH-ANF on the sets of quadratic functions of $3 \leq m \leq 6$ variables, testing the CA construction up to $n = 20$ variables. Table 1 reports the results of our search. In particular, for each considered m we give the corresponding number 2^{2^m} of m-variable Boolean functions which would be searched by a brute-force algorithm, the number $S_{m,2}$ of quadratic functions actually explored by our algorithm and the number QSB of quadratic semi-bent functions found over which our construction works. A first remarkable finding that one can draw from Table 1 is that our construction does not work on *any* quadratic function of 4 variables. In particular, the largest number of CA cells for which our construction produced semi-bent functions for $m = 4$ variables was $n = 8$. Contrarily, for all other values of m our algorithm found semi-bent functions over which our construction worked up to the target value $n = 20$. For this reason, we excluded the case $m = 4$ in our subsequent experiments.

To further investigate the functions produced by our construction, we considered two additional cryptographic properties: balancedness and number of non-trivial linear structures. Among the functions found by the SEARCH-ANF algorithm for which our CA-based construction always produced semi-bent functions of up to 20 variables, we filtered only those local rules that always produce balanced functions, as reported in the last column of Table 1. For each of the remaining functions, we observed that the number of linear structures of every function obtained with the application of our construction is constant. In particular our experiments show that, regardless of the number of variables of the initial local rule, the number of linear structures of each constructed function is equal to 1 when the number of cells n is odd, and 3 when n is even.

6   Conclusions and Open Problems

As we observed in Sect. 4, our experimental results do not rule out the possibility that our CA-based construction fails for $n > 20$ over the semi-bent rules found by our algorithm. However, we believe that at least for a subset of these rules this construction indeed generates semi-bent functions for any $n \in \mathbb{N}$, and the preliminary filtering operation performed in this paper greatly reduces the number of possible candidates, thus easing their theoretical analysis for future research. The first interesting open question to address is understanding why our construction always failed only for $m = 4$ variables, and to assess whether this is the case also for other numbers of variables not considered in this work. Then, the next step would be to investigate the rules filtered by our combinatorial search experiments, and try to formally characterize the family of quadratic rules for which our CA-based construction always yields semi-bent functions. A possible idea towards this direction would be to study more in depth the regularity of the number of linear structures of these functions, and assess whether this could be a necessary or sufficient condition for our construction to work.

From an applicative point of view, we remark that the 8 balanced rules of $m = 3$ variables found in our experiments include the elementary rules 30 and 210, which have been extensively adopted for designing CA-based cryptographic primitives [1,16]. It could thus be interesting to investigate whether our construction could enhance these primitives, such as the CA pseudorandom generator in [16], which samples only one cell of a CA with rule 30 to produce a pseudorandom keystream. Since rule 30 seems to produce semi-bent functions for any $n \in \mathbb{N}$, one idea could be to modify the pseudorandom generator by taking the value of *all* cells in the CA instead of only the central one, and then compute their XOR as the next pseudorandom bit.

More in general, a very interesting research direction would be to investigate our construction with respect to semi-bent functions of higher algebraic degree. Indeed, even though quadratic functions can reach high levels of nonlinearity, their degree is too low and this can be exploited in *algebraic attacks* [2]. In this regard, it would be interesting to apply our algorithm to search for cubic semi-bent functions over which our construction works.

Finally, another avenue for further research not related to cryptography is to investigate whether our construction can give any insight about the periods of *spatially periodic preimages* in surjective CA, which have been characterized in [10] only for the case of linear bipermutive rules. In this case, our construction could possibly give further information on the least periods of preimages of quadratic bipermutive CA.

Acknowledgements. The authors wish to thank Claude Carlet and Stjepan Picek for useful comments on a preliminary version of this work. This research was partially supported by FRA 2020 - UNITS.

Appendix: Source Code and Experimental Data

The source code of the search algorithm and the experimental data are available at https://github.com/rymoah/ca-boolfun-construction.

References

1. Bertoni, G., Daemen, J., Peeters, M., Assche, G.V.: The Keccak reference, January 2011. http://keccak.noekeon.org/
2. Carlet, C.: Boolean functions for cryptography and error correcting codes. In: Crama, Y., Hammer, P. (eds.) Boolean Models and Methods in Mathematics, Computer Science, and Engineering, pp. 257–397. Cambridge University Press (2010)
3. Formenti, E., Imai, K., Martin, B., Yunès, J.-B.: Advances on random sequence generation by uniform cellular automata. In: Calude, C.S., Freivalds, R., Kazuo, I. (eds.) Computing with New Resources. LNCS, vol. 8808, pp. 56–70. Springer, Cham (2014). https://doi.org/10.1007/978-3-319-13350-8_5
4. Ghoshal, A., Sadhukhan, R., Patranabis, S., Datta, N., Picek, S., Mukhopadhyay, D.: Lightweight and side-channel secure 4×4 s-boxes from cellular automata rules. IACR Trans. Symmetric Cryptol. **2018**(3), 311–334 (2018)
5. Leporati, A., Mariot, L.: Cryptographic properties of bipermutive cellular automata rules. J. Cell. Autom. **9**(5–6), 437–475 (2014)
6. Manzoni, L., Mariot, L.: Cellular automata pseudo-random number generators and their resistance to asynchrony. In: Mauri, G., El Yacoubi, S., Dennunzio, A., Nishinari, K., Manzoni, L. (eds.) ACRI 2018. LNCS, vol. 11115, pp. 428–437. Springer, Cham (2018). https://doi.org/10.1007/978-3-319-99813-8_39
7. Mariot, L., Gadouleau, M., Formenti, E., Leporati, A.: Mutually orthogonal Latin squares based on cellular automata. Des. Codes Cryptogr. **88**(2), 391–411 (2019). https://doi.org/10.1007/s10623-019-00689-8
8. Mariot, L., Leporati, A.: Sharing secrets by computing preimages of bipermutive cellular automata. In: Wąs, J., Sirakoulis, G.C., Bandini, S. (eds.) ACRI 2014. LNCS, vol. 8751, pp. 417–426. Springer, Cham (2014). https://doi.org/10.1007/978-3-319-11520-7_43
9. Mariot, L., Leporati, A.: Inversion of mutually orthogonal cellular automata. In: Mauri, G., El Yacoubi, S., Dennunzio, A., Nishinari, K., Manzoni, L. (eds.) ACRI 2018. LNCS, vol. 11115, pp. 364–376. Springer, Cham (2018). https://doi.org/10.1007/978-3-319-99813-8_33
10. Mariot, L., Leporati, A., Dennunzio, A., Formenti, E.: Computing the periods of preimages in surjective cellular automata. Nat. Comput. **16**(3), 367–381 (2016). https://doi.org/10.1007/s11047-016-9586-x
11. Mariot, L., Picek, S., Leporati, A., Jakobovic, D.: Cellular automata based s-boxes. Cryptogr. Commun. **11**(1), 41–62 (2019)
12. del Rey, Á.M., Mateus, J.P., Sánchez, G.R.: A secret sharing scheme based on cellular automata. Appl. Math. Comput. **170**(2), 1356–1364 (2005)
13. Rothaus, O.S.: On "bent" functions. J. Comb. Theory Ser. A **20**(3), 300–305 (1976)

14. Seredynski, F., Bouvry, P., Zomaya, A.Y.: Cellular automata computations and secret key cryptography. Parallel Comput. **30**(5–6), 753–766 (2004)
15. Szaban, M., Seredynski, F.: Cryptographically strong s-boxes based on cellular automata. In: Umeo, H., Morishita, S., Nishinari, K., Komatsuzaki, T., Bandini, S. (eds.) ACRI 2008. LNCS, vol. 5191, pp. 478–485. Springer, Heidelberg (2008). https://doi.org/10.1007/978-3-540-79992-4_62
16. Wolfram, S.: Cryptography with cellular automata. In: Williams, H.C. (ed.) CRYPTO 1985. LNCS, vol. 218, pp. 429–432. Springer, Heidelberg (1986). https://doi.org/10.1007/3-540-39799-X_32

EnCash: an Authenticated Encryption scheme using Cellular Automata

Tapadyoti Banerjee[(⊠)] and Dipanwita Roy Chowdhury

Crypto Research Lab, Department of Computer Science and Engineering,
Indian Institute of Technology Kharagpur, Kharagpur, India
tapadyoti@gmail.com, drc@cse.iitkgp.ac.in

Abstract. In this paper, we present a new Cellular Automata (CA) based authenticated encryption scheme, named as EnCash. Both for encryption and authentication, it proposes a CA-based cost-effective design structure. Encryption follows the substitution-permutation-network (SPN) where, at the substitution layer, randomized mapping is introduced and cellular automata, both linear and non-linear are used for the permutation. We perform the cryptanalysis of the substitution table and also the Strict Avalanche Criterion test for the encryption function. The results assure the security of EnCash.

Keywords: Authenticated encryption · Cellular automata · Substitution–permutation network

1 Introduction

Over the network, maybe an insecure channel, two parties always want to communicate securely for the confidential messages. So they need confidentiality or privacy and authenticity, together with integrity. Traditionally, privacy and authenticity have been formalized in separate notions and studied separately. However, they can be used together and produce the two fundamental goals with guaranteed security; but, the implementation of both these algorithms individually means additional implementation effort for each algorithm, as well as becomes costly for both software and hardware. This situation brings researchers to the classical trade-off scenario where both these goals furnish simultaneously in a single communication between the sender and the receiver and dream up Authenticated Encryption (AE). Now a days, AE is widely used in Marine Navigation, Vehicle tracking, Mapping and Geodetic data capture, etc. I.e., whenever need to provide restricted service, i.e., an encrypted service provided only to the authorised users, authenticated encryption is needed. In our current work, the main aim is to design a new AE scheme by exploiting the cellular automata, which can provide a similar level of security concerning most of the other existing AE schemes.

Since the introduction of the AE scheme by Bellare and Rogaway [3] in 2000, a lot of research has been done to date. Although recently, the CAESAR-competition (Competition for Authenticated Encryption: Security, Applicability, and Robustness) has completed and has been presented many fruitful products [18, 19] which reflect a

© Springer Nature Switzerland AG 2021
T. M. Gwizdałła et al. (Eds.): ACRI 2020, LNCS 12599, pp. 67–79, 2021.
https://doi.org/10.1007/978-3-030-69480-7_8

significant role in the world of authenticated encryption, until now among all the AE schemes, AES-GCM [10] is considered to be the most efficient NIST standard high throughput AE mode [4, 12]. Parallelly, there is a great demand for a low-cost highspeed scheme for the generation of Message Authentication Code (MAC). Therefore, there exists another wave of research based on Cellular Automata (CA) due to its simple, elegant, and faster design approach [13]. Until now, there are so many research works have been done for CA-based AE schemes [1, 11]. Here, in our proposed scheme EnCash, the center of concentration is to design a fully CA-based design approach instead of any complex architecture. To the best of our knowledge, it is the first time where encryption function has been constructed by only exploiting the randomness property of the CA [9].

In this paper, we propose a CA-based authenticated encryption scheme, called EnCash. For the encryption portion, it follows the substitution-permutation network, implemented by using only the linear and non-linear cellular automata and a random mapping. Conventional encryption scheme uses a fixed substitution box, whereas, our scheme is flexible in choosing the random mapping of substitution table. The authentication tag has also been generated by the CA-based construction. We perform the cryptanalysis of the substitution table and also the strict avalanche criterion test for the encryption function.

Our Contributions:

- A new authenticated encryption scheme EnCash, based on Cellular Automata, is proposed, which follows the construction of substitution-permutation-network.
- In encryption, the substitution layer uses a randomized mapping function.
- For the authentication tag generation, it uses a simple and elegant construction made by CA, and this design has successfully passed the NIST test.
- EnCash provides good security against the Strict Avalanche Criterion (SAC) Test.
- Finally, the Linear and Differential Cryptanalysis of the substitution table have done.

The rest of the paper is organized as follows. In Sect. 2, the overall design of EnCash is introduced and described in detail. Section 3 claims that EnCash provides high-security bounds concerning the Strict Avalanche Criterion Test and can resist the Linear and Differential attacks. Finally, we conclude our work in Sect. 4.

2   EnCash

The underlying primitive of our proposed work is Cellular Automata (CA). Before going to the design of EnCash, the fundamentals of CA are provided. CA are a discrete lattice of cells arranged in a specific geometry and build with memory element (i.e., flip-flop) with combinational logic function [13]. The cells are updated concurrently at each clock pulse by using the rule or transition function, where the decimal equivalent of the truth table of the function is defined as a rule. To update the value of a cell, they take the present values of the cell itself and its neighborhood cells and perform some logical operations. For one-dimensional three-neighborhood cellular automata, the next state of the ith cell is:

$$S_i^{t+1} = f(S_{i-1}^t, S_i^t, S_{i+1}^t) \tag{1}$$

where S_i^t is the state of the ith cell at time t. In the construction of EnCash, maximum length hybrid cellular automata are used with rule 90 ($S_i^{t+1} = S_{i-1}^t \oplus S_{i+1}^t$) and rule 150 ($S_i^{t+1} = S_{i-1}^t \oplus S_i^t \oplus S_{i+1}^t$). In maximum length CA, all the states except one (all 0's state) lie in one cycle. Whereas, for hybrid CA, the cells evolve with rules, both linear and non-linear generating Linear Hybrid CA (LHCA) and Non-Linear Hybrid CA (NHCA), respectively. For linear CA, only linear functions such as XOR are used, and Non-linear CA contains linear rules along with some non-linear functions such as AND/OR. The linear CA can be turned into non-linear one by injecting the non-linear function at one/more cells [7].

The architecture of the proposed scheme is described from here. Our scheme uses two different keys for encryption and authentication purposes. The hash key is generated from the encryption key/private key by using NHCA. For ciphertext generation and also for the authentication, a CA-based elegant and straightforward construction has introduced. Consider the following notations, those are used throughout this paper.

$len(X)$: Denotes the length of the vector X

$\mathcal{P}$: Plaintext, which can be represented block-wise as $p_1||p_2||\cdots||p_{n-1}||p_n^*$: $p_i \in \{0,1\}^{128}$ and $|p_i| = 128$, for $i = 1,2,3,\ldots,n-1$ and $0 < |p_n^*| \leq 128$

$\mathcal{AAD}$: Additional Authenticated Data, which can be represented block-wise as $\mathcal{A}_1||\mathcal{A}_2||\cdots||\mathcal{A}_{m-1}||\mathcal{A}_m^*$ and $|\mathcal{A}_i| = 128$, for $i = 1,2,3,\ldots,m-1$, and $0 < |\mathcal{A}_m^*| \leq 128$

C: Ciphertext, which can be represented block-wise as $c_1||c_2||\cdots||c_{n-1}||c_n^*$: $c_i \in \{0,1\}^{128}$ and $len(c_i) = len(p_i)$ for $i = 1,2,3,\ldots,n-1$ and also for $len(c_n^*) = len(p_n^*)$

$\mathcal{T}$: Authentication Tag, and $len(\mathcal{T}) = 128$

$\mathcal{K}_e$: 128-bit encryption key

$\mathcal{K}_h$: 128-bit hash key

$LHCA(X)$: State of the maximum length 128-bit linear CA after evolving '63' number of clock pulses with the initial value X.

$NHCA(X)$: State of the maximum length 128-bit non-linear CA after evolving '63' number of clock pulses with the initial value X.

$X \oplus \mathcal{Y}$: The addition of two bit strings X and $\mathcal{Y}$

$X \parallel \mathcal{Y}$: The concatenation of two bit strings X and $\mathcal{Y}$

$\mathcal{F}_E$: The sub-function for the encryption operation

$\mathcal{F}_A$: The sub-function for the authentication operation

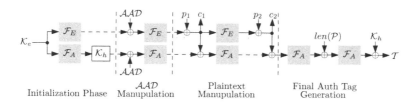

Fig. 1. Design architecture of the encryption function of EnCash.

2.1 Design of EnCash

Before describing the detail design of the proposed AE scheme, the outline of the block diagram of the encryption function is illustrated in Fig. 1. For simplicity, only one block of Additional Authenticated Data ($\mathcal{AAD}$) and two blocks of plaintext message (p_1 and p_2) are shown here. The private key $\mathcal{K}_e$ produces the hash key $\mathcal{K}_h$ by using the subfunction of authentication operation $\mathcal{F}_A$. To generate the final authentication tag $\mathcal{T}$, the length of the plaintext plays an important role in this design. The ciphertext blocks c_1 and c_2 are produced from the message blocks p_1 and p_2 respectively through the subfunction for the encryption operation $\mathcal{F}_E$. The mode of operation of our proposed design is described as follows.

Initialization Phase: In this phase of work, the private key is fed into the subfunctions $\mathcal{F}_E$ and $\mathcal{F}_A$. In AE, the use of the same key for both authentication and encryption is error-prone. Specifically, the same block cipher key for both encrypt the data and to generate the hash key leads to produce wider classes of weak-keys [15]. To avoid this issue, EnCash uses two different keys, one is for encryption, and another is for authentication. The authentication key $\mathcal{K}_h$ is computed as follows:

$$\mathcal{K}_e \xleftarrow{R} \{0,1\}^{128}$$
$$\mathcal{K}_h = \mathcal{F}_A(\mathcal{K}_E)$$

where $\mathcal{F}_A$ is the sub-function to generate the authentication tag (the detail description of $\mathcal{F}_A$ is described later).

Additional Authentication Data Manupulation: During encryption and decryption processes, the bit strings $\mathcal{P}$, $\mathcal{C}$ and $\mathcal{AAD}$ are divided into 128-bit blocks. Pretend the pair $\langle n, s \rangle |\ \forall n, s \in \mathbb{Z}^+ : len(\mathcal{P}) = (n-1) \times 128 + s$ *and* $0 < s \leq 128$. The sequence of these plaintext blocks are $p_1, p_2, \ldots, p_{n-1}, p_n^*$. The corresponding sequence of ciphertext blocks are $c_1, c_2, \ldots, c_{n-1}, c_n^*$, where $len(p_i) = len(c_i)|\ \forall i \in \mathbb{Z}_{n+1}$. Similarly, The $\mathcal{AAD}$ is denoted as $\mathcal{A}_1||\mathcal{A}_2||\ldots||\mathcal{A}_{m-1}||\mathcal{A}_m^*$, and pretend the pair $\langle m, t \rangle |\ \forall m, t \in \mathbb{Z}^+ : len(\mathcal{AAD}) = (m-1) \times 128 + t$ *and* $0 < t \leq 128$. Now the $\mathcal{AAD}$ is manupulated by using the following procedures:

$$\mathcal{F}_{E_i} = \mathcal{F}_E(\mathcal{F}_{E_{i-1}} \oplus \mathcal{A}_{i-1}), \qquad \text{for } i = 1,2,3,\ldots,m-1$$
$$\mathcal{F}_{E_i} = \mathcal{F}_E(\mathcal{F}_{E_{i-1}} \oplus \mathcal{A}_m^*||10^{127-t}), \text{for } i = m, t = len(\mathcal{A}_m^*)$$

where $\mathcal{F}_E$ denotes the sub-function of encryption, that will be described later.

Plaintext Manupulation: The ciphertext generation phase is described as follows:

$$c_i \leftarrow p_i \oplus \mathcal{F}_{E_i} \qquad \text{for } i = 1,2,3,\ldots,n-1$$
$$c_n^* \leftarrow p_n^* \oplus MSB_s(\mathcal{F}_{E_n}), \ MSB_s \text{ is most significant s bit}$$

Here, $\mathcal{F}_{E_i}$ and $\mathcal{F}_{E_n}$ is the ith and n^{th} sub-function of encryption respectively.

Authentication Tag Generation: In the authentication phase, the tag is generated by the following method:

$$\mathcal{K}_e \xleftarrow{R} \{0,1\}^{128}, \quad \text{where } \mathcal{K}_e \text{ is the shared private key}$$
$$\mathcal{K}_h = \mathcal{F}_A(\mathcal{K}_E), \quad \text{where } \mathcal{K}_h \text{ denotes the derived hash key}$$
$$\mathcal{F}_{A_i} \leftarrow \mathcal{F}_A(\mathcal{F}_{A_{i-1}} \oplus c_i), \quad \text{for } i = 2,3,\ldots,n-1$$
$$\mathcal{F}_{A_i} \leftarrow \mathcal{F}_A(\mathcal{F}_{A_{i-1}} \oplus c_n^* || 10^{127-s}), \text{ for } i = n, s = len(p_n^*)$$
$$\mathcal{T} \leftarrow \mathcal{K}_h \oplus \mathcal{F}_A(\mathcal{F}_{A_n} \oplus len(\mathcal{P}))$$

Here $\mathcal{F}_A$ denotes the sub-function of the Authentication phase. It will be described in the next section.

2.2   The Encryption and Authentication Function

The main components of the EnCash are encryption and authentication. Both are designed based on a simple cellular automata-based structure. Those are described here.

Encryption Function: The encryption function follows the iterative structure of the substitution-permutation-network. It avoids the AES Encryption scheme for the encryption purpose to make the function cost-efficient. The ith iteration of the Encryption function $\mathcal{F}_E$ is depicted in Fig. 2. The previous output is fed into the NHCA for getting 63 number of pulses and then goes through a padding scheme. Here, '10' is padded with the output of the NHCA to make the length of the output as 130-bit. Thenceforth, this will become the input of the substitution layer. This input of the substitution layer is depicted in Fig. 3. Here, 26 parallel applications of the 5-bit substitution/mapping $M(x)$ are performed on the 130-bit state. Here, we have introduced a randomized mapping concept instead of a fixed mapping, which is described in the next subsection. As illustrated in Fig. 3, the mapping is applied to each bit-slice of the five registers x_0, x_1, x_2, x_3, x_4. Here, x_0 is the MSB (Most Significant Bit), and x_4 is the LSB (Least Significant Bit) of the mapping. Hereafter, the output of the mapping (the last two bits are truncated from the output to make it 128-bit) is fed into the LHCA for the diffusion. After 63 number of pulses, the output has been totally diffused.

Fig. 2. Design architecture of Encryption Function.

Authentication Function: Very recently, a double-block-length hash function, named NCASH [2] has been proposed that has produced a $2n$ length tag from an n-bit key. But, in the case of the authenticated encryption, it is not cost-effective with respect to the software, as well as hardware also. This limitation is removed in the proposed scheme. The single iteration of the authentication function is depicted in Fig. 4. To generate the

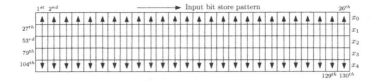

Fig. 3. The substitution layer of EnCash applies a 5-bit mapping to the state.

authentication tag, in each iteration the states are traversed through a linear and non-linear CA-chain. This construction has successfully passed the NIST Statistical Test Suite for Random and Pseudorandom Number Generators (NIST SP 800-22) [14]. For this test, we have generated one crore of hashtags by using EnCash and apply the test to that data-set. This test signifies the construction of this CA-chain provides a high diffusion and excellent random output.

Fig. 4. Design architecture of a single iteration of $\mathcal{F}_A$.

2.3   The Randomized Mapping

In this newly proposed Authenticated Encryption scheme, EnCash, we have introduced a new concept of the randomized mapping function. To the best of our knowledge, until now, most of the construction uses a fixed substitution stored in memory. But, in our case, our scheme is flexible in choosing the random mapping of substitution table. The evolution of non-linear cellular automata is used to produce these sets of mappings. The creation procedure of these mappings is stated here.

Initialisation Vector Selection: As discussed earlier, here, a 5-bit substitution/mapping $M(x)$ is used for the substitution layer. Therefore, a 5-bit NHCA has been used to generate the values of the mapping. Mathematically:

$$IV_{Map} \xleftarrow{R} \{0,1\}^5$$
$$IV_{Map} \leftarrow IV_{Map} \oplus 00001$$

The initialization vector (IV_{Map}) of the NHCA is a publicly known nonce value and should be decided by the sender and receiver before the communication. After that, '00001' is XORed with IV_{Map} to get the new IV_{Map}.

CA-Based Mapping: The states of the mapping are created by evolving the NHCA with the IV_{Map}. Here the rule vector of the CA is used such that it provides the maximum length cycle. The example of a mapping is given in Table 1. Here $IV_{Map} =$ '10110', and the updated $IV_{Map} =$ '10111', after XORing '00001'. The rule vector

Table 1. The 5-bit mapping of EnCash.

x	0	1	2	3	4	5	6	7
$M(x)$	17	19	08	1C	0A	1F	01	02
x	8	9	A	B	C	D	E	F
$M(x)$	07	0B	1D	06	09	1E	0D	10
x	10	11	12	13	14	15	16	17
$M(x)$	18	04	0E	11	14	16	15	00
x	18	19	1A	1B	1C	1D	1E	1F
$M(x)$	1A	03	05	0C	12	1B	0F	13

Table 2. Another mapping of EnCash.

x	0	1	2	3	4	5	6	7
$M(x)$	19	08	1C	0A	1F	01	02	07
x	8	9	A	B	C	D	E	F
$M(x)$	0B	1D	06	09	1E	0D	10	18
x	10	11	12	13	14	15	16	17
$M(x)$	04	0E	11	14	16	15	1A	03
x	18	19	1A	1B	1C	1D	1E	1F
$M(x)$	05	00	0C	12	1B	0F	13	17

is $<150, 150, 150, 150, 90>$, and the values are written in hexadecimal format. Thenceforth, another example of the mapping is depicted in Table 2. Here, the updated IV_{Map} = '11001'. In this way, several mappings can be designed. Moreover, for a fixed CA rule vector, 31 number of mappings can be generated. The most exciting fact is that, if we consider the different CA rule vector for this CA, and if there are 'r' number of rule vectors that can generate the maximum length CA, then the number of possible mappings become $r \times 31$.

3 Security Analysis

The choice of operations and parameters in the design of EnCash have a strong theoretical background. As cellular automata is a good random number generator [9], the maximum-length linear hybrid CA is used here. They make the correlation between the two subsequent states as complex and intricate as possible. Parallelly, for NHCA, it is difficult to find the previous state from the current state. So, we use this NHCA to prevent for finding inverse from any particular state. Therefore, both the NHCA and LHCA are used in encryption and authentication functions. The security analysis of the proposed CA-based authenticated encryption scheme, EnCash, is performed based on the standard model of concrete security. The linear and differential cryptanalysis is considered here. Moreover, the Strict Avalanche Criterion test has also been performed for this AE scheme.

3.1 Strict Avalanche Criterion Test

The Strict Avalanche Criterion (SAC) was formerly presented by Forré [6], as a ratiocination of the avalanche effect by Webster et al. [17]. In the field of cryptography, these concepts somehow already exist [5], but not defined in concrete terms. The intuitive idea behind this concept is aimed at analyzing the diffusion characteristics of the underlying cipher, i.e., minimal changes in the input cause a tremendous difference in the output, thus an avalanche of changes. Mathematically it can be defined as:

$$\forall a, b | H(a,b) = 1 : Mean(H(Av(a), Av(b))) = n/2 \qquad (2)$$

In Eq. 2, the Hamming distance, H for two random input vectors (a, b) is 1. Hamming distance for two vectors is defined as the number of positions where the vectors differ. Therefore, here one of them is a random input vector, and another is generated by randomly flipping one of its bits. So, if Av is the avalanche effect, the Mean of the hamming distance between the outputs of those two vectors should be, on average, $n/2$, where n is the length of the vectors. It denotes, a minimum input change (only one single bit is considered in Eq. 2) produces a maximum output change (half of the bits) on average. In fact, strict avalanche criterion or SAC is even more demanding property than the avalanche criterion. Mathematically it is described as:

$$\forall a, b | H(a,b) = 1 : Mean(H(Av(a), Av(b))) \approx B(1/2, n) \tag{3}$$

In Eq. 3, it is an interesting fact that this implies the avalanche effect, as the average of a binomial distribution with parameters $1/2$ and n is $n/2$.

To perform the SAC test for EnCash, we have considered a randomly chosen 128-bit plaintext block $(A61B51BD3621EF42E0CC74001B4BF3AA)_{16}$, and three types of private keys; dense, sparse and random key. For each of the key types, we consider hundred number of different keys. Initially we have generated the ciphertext with respect to the plaintext p and the corresponding encryption key $\mathcal{K}_E$, i.e., $c \leftarrow p \oplus \mathcal{F}_E$. Therefore, generate $\mathcal{K}_E' : \forall \mathcal{K}_E, \mathcal{K}_E' | H(\mathcal{K}_E, \mathcal{K}_E') = 1$ and calculate c' with respect to the corresponding $\mathcal{K}_E'$. Thenceforth, compute the $Mean(H(Av(c), Av(c'))), \forall \mathcal{K}_E'$. Finally compute the Coefficient of Variance, that is a standardized measure of dispersion of a probability distribution or frequency distribution. It measures the amount of deviation of data points about the mean, and it is computed as follows:

$$Coefficient\ of\ Variance = \frac{Standard\ Deviation}{Mean}\%$$

A summary of the results of the SAC test obtained for EnCash is given in Table 3. In each case of the measures, the average values for the hundred keys of each key types are mentioned here. The results show the encryption function posses good confusion.

Table 3. Experimental result of SAC test for EnCash.

Measure	Random	Dense	Sparse
Expected mean	64	64	64
Observed mean	64.3203	64.2109	63.1016
Std. deviation	5.5353	5.5066	5.2289
Variance	30.6395	30.3226	27.3412
Coeff. of variance	8.6058	8.5758	8.2865

3.2   Linear Cryptanalysis

Linear cryptanalysis posits a linear relationship between the elements of plaintext, the ciphertext, and the key. It, therefore, tries to find a linear approximation to the action of a cipher [8, 16]. Consider Table 1, which is defined by a permutation $\pi_M : \{0,1\}^5 \rightarrow \{0,1\}^5$. The possible binary values of the input-end (x) and output-end $(M(x))$ are denoted by the ten random variables $X_1, X_2, ..., X_5$ and $Y_1, Y_2, ..., Y_5$ respectively. Consider the following equation:

$$\Psi = \left(\bigoplus_{i=1}^{5} a_i X_i \right) \oplus \left(\bigoplus_{i=1}^{5} b_i Y_i \right) \tag{4}$$

where the each binary vectors $(a_1, a_2, a_3, a_4, a_5)$ and $(b_1, b_2, b_3, b_4, b_5)$ are the hexadecimal digit, or the *input sum* and the *output sum* respectively, and $a_i, b_i \in \{0,1\}, \forall i = 1, 2, ..., 5$. Now, for a random variable having hexadecimal input sum a and output sum b, let $\Upsilon_L(a,b)$ denote the number of binary ten-tuples $(x_1, x_2, x_3, x_4, x_5, y_1, y_2, y_3, y_4, y_5)$ such that $(y_1, y_2, y_3, y_4, y_5) = \pi(x_1, x_2, x_3, x_4, x_5)$ and

$$\psi_L = \left(\bigoplus_{i=1}^{5} a_i x_i \right) \oplus \left(\bigoplus_{i=1}^{5} b_i y_i \right) = 0 \tag{5}$$

We are interested in linear relations for the mapping, i.e., relations of the Eq. 4. Now assume, there are $2^5 = 32$ different equally likely values for $x_1 x_2 x_3 x_4 x_5$. Hence, the probability that such a linear relation holds can be determined by counting the number of input-output pairs satisfy the Eq. 5, divided by 32. Moreover, for independent X and Y, a linear relation holds the probability $1/2$. We describe the probability bias for all possible relations in the linear profile at Table 4. It's uppermost row and leftmost column describe the possible input sums and output sums respectively. The each cell of the table contains the number of matches between the sum of input bits and the sum of output bits minus half the number of possible input values (i.e., for a 5-bit mapping, $\frac{1}{2} \times 2^5 = 16$). Thus, we compute $\Upsilon_L(a,b) = \psi_L - 16$. The linear distribution table of the mapping shown in Table 1 is given in Table 4, which consists of all the values of Υ_L. Therefore, the probability bias for any relation can be found by searching the corresponding number in the linear profile and divide that by 32.

3.3 Differential Cryptanalysis

Differential cryptanalysis aims to map bitwise differences in inputs to differences in the outputs in order to reverse the action of the encryption algorithm [8, 16]. Again, consider Table 1, which is defined by a permutation $\pi_M : \{0,1\}^5 \rightarrow \{0,1\}^5$ with possible binary values of the input-end (x) and output-end $(M(x))$. Consider an ordered pair of bitstrings of length 5, say (x, x'). Therefore, the input XOR and the output XOR of the mapping is $x \oplus x'$ and $\pi_M(x) \oplus \pi_M(x')$ respectively. Now, we will define the set $\Delta(x') : x' \in \{0,1\}^5$ to consist of all the ordered pairs (x, x') having input XOR equal to x'. Mathematically it is written as:

$$\Delta(x') = \{(x, x \oplus x') : x, x' \in \{0,1\}^5\} \tag{6}$$

Moreover, it is obvious that $\Delta(x')$ contains 2^5 pairs that satisfy the condition explained in Eq. 6. Thus, for each pair in $\Delta(x')$, we can compute output XOR of the mapping

Table 4. The linear profile of the EnCash mapping of Table 1.

	0	1	2	3	4	5	6	7	8	9	A	B	C	D	E	F	10	11	12	13	14	15	16	17	18	19	1A	1B	1C	1D	1E	1F
0	16	0	0	0	0	0	0	0	0	0	0	0	0	0	0	0	0	0	0	0	0	0	0	0	0	0	0	0	0	0	0	0
1	0	2	-4	2	0	6	0	-6	0	2	-4	-2	4	-2	4	2	-2	0	2	0	2	0	2	-4	-2	-4	2	-4	-2	0	-2	-4
2	0	-2	2	0	0	6	-2	4	4	-2	2	4	4	-2	-2	0	4	6	-2	0	0	2	-2	0	0	-2	-2	4	-4	2	-2	-4
3	0	0	-2	2	4	0	2	2	-4	4	-2	2	-4	0	-2	-2	-2	2	-4	-4	2	2	0	-4	2	-2	-4	-4	-6	2	4	0
4	0	2	-2	4	-2	-4	-4	-2	2	-4	-4	2	0	-2	2	-4	0	2	-6	0	-2	-4	0	2	2	4	0	-2	0	6	-2	0
5	0	-4	2	-2	-2	2	-4	0	-2	-2	-4	4	0	8	2	2	-2	2	4	0	0	4	2	-2	4	4	-2	-2	2	2	0	0
6	0	-4	-4	-4	2	-6	2	-2	2	2	-2	2	4	0	-4	-4	0	0	4	-2	2	2	-6	2	-2	2	2	0	0	0	-4	0
7	0	-2	0	-2	-2	4	-2	4	6	4	-2	-4	0	-2	0	-2	2	-4	-2	0	0	2	4	-2	0	2	4	-2	2	4	6	0
8	0	-4	-2	2	2	2	-8	0	-6	2	0	0	0	-4	-2	2	0	-4	2	-2	-2	-2	0	0	2	2	4	4	-4	0	-2	2
9	0	2	-2	-4	-2	0	0	-2	-2	0	4	2	4	-2	-2	4	-6	4	-4	2	0	2	6	4	0	2	2	0	-2	0	4	2
A	0	-2	0	-2	-6	-4	-2	0	2	0	-2	4	0	-6	0	2	0	2	4	-2	2	0	-6	0	2	-4	2	-4	0	-2	4	2
B	0	-4	0	0	2	-2	2	2	-2	-2	2	-2	0	0	4	0	-2	6	2	2	-4	-4	0	-4	-4	0	4	4	2	6	2	2
C	0	2	4	2	4	-2	0	6	0	-2	0	2	0	-2	0	2	-4	-2	0	6	4	-2	0	-2	4	2	4	-2	0	-2	0	-6
D	0	0	4	-4	0	-4	0	4	0	0	0	0	0	-4	4	0	-2	-2	2	-6	-2	2	6	2	-2	-2	-2	-2	-2	2	-6	-2
E	0	0	2	6	0	0	-2	2	4	4	-2	2	0	0	-2	2	0	4	2	2	0	-4	6	-2	-4	0	-2	-2	0	-4	-2	6
F	0	-2	2	0	0	2	2	4	-4	-2	-2	0	4	2	-2	-4	-2	0	0	2	-6	0	-4	2	-6	0	4	-6	-2	0	0	2
10	0	2	-2	-4	-2	0	-4	2	2	0	0	2	0	6	-2	0	-2	-4	-4	-2	8	-2	-2	0	-4	-2	2	0	-2	0	-4	2
11	0	4	2	-2	2	2	0	0	2	6	-4	0	0	0	6	-2	-4	4	-2	-2	-2	2	-4	0	2	2	4	4	0	-4	-2	2
12	0	0	0	-4	2	2	-2	2	-2	-2	2	2	-2	0	0	0	4	2	2	-6	-2	-4	-4	0	-4	4	-4	0	-4	6	-2	2
13	0	2	4	-2	2	0	-2	-4	-2	4	6	4	4	-2	4	-2	4	-2	0	2	2	0	-2	-4	-2	4	-2	-4	0	2	0	2
14	0	-4	0	4	0	0	0	-4	4	0	0	4	0	0	4	2	2	-2	-2	2	6	2	2	-2	2	6	2	-2	2	-2	-2	-2
15	0	-2	4	-2	-4	2	4	-2	0	-2	0	-6	2	-2	-4	-2	0	2	0	-2	4	-2	0	-2	4	6	0	-2	-4	-2	-4	2
16	0	6	-2	-4	0	2	2	4	-4	2	-6	0	4	-2	-2	0	2	0	4	2	2	-4	0	2	2	0	-4	2	2	4	0	2
17	0	0	2	-2	0	0	-6	-2	0	4	2	-6	-4	0	-2	-2	-4	4	2	6	0	0	-2	2	0	-4	-2	-2	0	4	-2	-2
18	0	-2	4	-2	4	-2	0	-2	0	-2	-4	-2	0	2	4	2	6	0	-2	4	2	0	2	4	2	-4	2	0	-6	0	2	4
19	0	4	4	0	-4	0	-4	0	-4	-4	0	0	0	0	-8	0	0	0	0	0	0	0	4	-4	0	-4	0	4	0	-4	4	0
1A	0	0	-2	2	0	4	2	2	0	-4	2	2	-4	-4	2	-2	-2	-2	0	4	2	6	0	0	2	-2	0	0	2	2	-4	8
1B	0	-2	-2	-4	-4	2	2	0	-4	2	-2	4	-8	-2	2	0	4	2	-2	4	0	-2	2	0	-4	2	2	0	0	-2	-2	-4
1C	0	-4	-2	2	-6	-2	0	4	-2	2	0	-4	4	0	6	2	-2	-2	-4	4	0	0	-2	-2	0	0	-6	2	-2	-2	0	0
1D	0	2	6	4	-6	0	4	-2	-2	4	0	2	0	2	-2	4	0	-2	-2	0	-2	0	0	-2	2	-4	4	2	0	6	-2	0
1E	0	-6	4	-2	2	4	2	-4	2	0	-2	4	0	-2	0	-2	-6	-4	-2	0	0	-6	0	2	0	-2	-4	2	2	0	2	0
1F	0	0	-4	0	-2	2	2	2	2	2	6	2	0	4	4	-4	0	0	4	0	-2	-6	2	2	6	-2	2	-2	-4	0	0	0

π_M. Clearly, there are 2^5 output XORs, which are distributed among 2^5 possible values. Whereas, if the output distribution seems non-uniform, it will become the basis for a successful differential attack. This distribution can be mathematically written as:

$$\Upsilon_D(x',y') = |\{(x,x') \in \Delta(x') : \pi_M(x) \oplus \pi_M(x') = y'\}| \tag{7}$$

All the values of $\Upsilon_D(x',y')$ for the mapping shown in Table 1 are stated in Table 5. It's uppermost row and leftmost column describe the possible input difference and output difference respectively. The each cell of the table contains the number of matches between the input difference and output difference, i.e., the count of inputs for which the corresponding differential characteristic holds. From Table 5, it is visible that it has a uniform output distribution, which can resist differential attacks.

Table 5. The differential profile of the EnCash mapping of Table 1.

	0	1	2	3	4	5	6	7	8	9	A	B	C	D	E	F	10	11	12	13	14	15	16	17	18	19	1A	1B	1C	1D	1E	1F
0	32	0	0	0	0	0	0	0	0	0	0	0	0	0	0	0	0	0	0	0	0	0	0	0	0	0	0	0	0	0	0	0
1	0	0	0	0	0	2	2	4	2	0	0	0	0	0	2	0	0	4	2	0	4	0	2	2	0	0	2	0	2	0	2	
2	0	0	2	0	2	0	0	0	0	0	0	2	0	4	2	0	2	0	0	0	2	2	2	4	0	0	2	0	0	0	2	4
3	0	0	2	0	0	4	0	0	0	0	2	0	2	4	0	2	4	2	2	2	0	0	0	0	2	2	2	0	0	0	0	0
4	0	2	2	2	0	0	2	0	0	2	2	0	2	2	2	2	0	2	2	0	0	2	0	2	0	0	0	2	0	0	0	2
5	0	2	2	0	2	0	0	0	2	0	2	0	0	2	4	0	2	2	0	2	0	0	2	2	2	2	2	0	0	0	0	0
6	0	2	0	2	2	2	0	0	2	0	2	2	0	2	0	0	0	0	0	0	2	2	0	2	0	0	4	2	4	0	0	0
7	0	0	0	6	0	0	2	0	0	0	0	0	2	2	0	4	0	2	2	0	2	0	0	2	0	0	0	0	4	2	0	
8	0	2	0	0	0	0	2	0	2	4	0	4	2	0	0	0	2	0	0	0	0	2	2	2	2	2	2	0	2	0	0	0
9	0	0	0	0	2	4	0	2	2	0	0	0	2	2	2	4	2	2	0	0	0	0	0	0	0	0	2	0	0	6	0	
A	0	0	4	0	0	2	0	2	0	2	2	0	0	0	0	0	0	0	0	2	0	0	2	0	0	0	4	4	2	4	2	
B	0	0	0	0	2	2	0	0	0	4	0	2	0	0	2	0	2	2	0	2	0	0	2	0	2	0	4	2	2	0	0	2
C	0	2	0	0	2	2	4	2	2	0	2	0	0	0	2	2	2	0	0	0	2	2	2	0	0	0	0	0	2	0	0	2
D	0	2	0	4	0	0	2	0	0	0	0	0	0	2	0	2	2	2	2	2	2	0	0	2	2	0	0	0	2	2	0	2
E	0	0	0	0	0	0	0	2	2	0	2	4	2	0	0	0	2	2	4	2	0	0	0	0	2	0	0	0	0	6	2	0
F	0	0	0	2	0	2	2	0	2	0	2	2	0	4	0	0	0	0	0	2	4	0	0	2	2	4	0	2	0	0	0	
10	0	0	2	2	0	2	0	0	4	0	2	0	2	0	0	2	0	0	2	0	2	0	2	4	2	0	0	2	0	0	2	0
11	0	0	0	0	2	0	2	2	0	4	0	0	0	0	2	4	4	0	2	0	0	0	0	2	2	2	0	0	2	0	2	
12	0	2	2	2	0	2	0	0	2	0	0	0	2	0	0	0	0	0	2	2	2	2	0	0	2	0	4	0	0	6		
13	0	0	0	2	0	2	2	2	0	4	2	2	4	2	2	0	2	0	0	0	0	0	0	0	2	0	0	4	0	0		
14	0	2	2	0	0	0	0	4	0	4	0	0	0	0	0	0	0	4	0	4	2	4	0	2	0	0	4	0				
15	0	2	2	0	2	0	2	2	0	0	2	0	0	0	4	0	4	0	4	2	0	2	2	0	0	0	2	0	0			
16	0	0	2	2	2	0	2	2	2	2	0	2	0	2	0	0	0	4	0	0	0	2	0	2	0	0	0	2	2	0		
17	0	0	2	0	2	4	2	0	0	0	2	2	2	0	2	2	0	2	0	0	4	0	0	0	0	0	4	0	2	0	0	
18	0	4	2	4	2	0	0	0	0	0	0	2	0	0	2	0	0	2	0	0	0	4	2	0	2	0	0	0	2	2	2	
19	0	0	2	0	2	2	2	0	0	2	2	0	0	0	0	0	2	0	2	2	0	6	0	4	2	0	0	0	0	0	2	
1A	0	0	0	0	0	0	2	2	2	4	0	2	2	0	0	2	0	0	2	4	4	2	0	0	0	2	0	0	0	0	0	2
1B	0	4	0	0	2	0	0	2	0	0	0	2	2	2	0	2	0	0	2	4	2	0	0	0	0	4	4	0	0	0	0	
1C	0	2	2	0	2	0	0	2	2	0	0	2	2	0	2	0	2	2	0	0	2	0	0	2	2	2	0	0	2	0	2	0
1D	0	0	0	0	0	0	2	2	0	0	0	2	0	0	2	0	2	2	0	2	0	4	2	0	4	2	2	2	0	0	2	
1E	0	2	0	2	0	2	0	0	0	2	2	2	0	0	0	2	0	2	0	0	2	0	0	0	2	2	2	4	0	4	0	
1F	0	2	2	4	2	0	0	0	2	2	0	2	2	2	2	2	0	0	2	0	0	0	0	0	2	2	0	2	0	0	0	

4   Conclusion

This paper presents a new cellular automata-based authenticated encryption scheme, named as EnCash. To generate the ciphertext, it proposes an encryption function, which follows the strategy of substitution-permutation-network (SPN) and designed by linear and non-linear CA. Moreover, a randomized mapping has been introduced at the substitution layer. Our encryption function achieves good security with respect to the SAC test. A CA-based construction also produces the authentication tag, which has successfully passed the NIST Statistical Test Suite for Random and Pseudorandom Number Generators (NIST SP 800-22) [14]. Moreover, the linear and differential cryptanalysis of this scheme have also been done. Finally, EnCash can boost researchers to concentrate on the cellular automata-based design approaches for enhancing simple, faster, and cost-effective design aspects.

References

1. Banerjee, T., Das, B., Mehta, D., RoyChowdhury, D.: RACE: randomized counter mode of authenticated encryption using cellular automata. In: Obaidat, M.S., Samarati, P. (eds.) Proceedings of the 16th International Joint Conference on e-Business and Telecommunications, ICETE 2019 - Volume 2: SECRYPT, Prague, Czech Republic, 26–28 July 2019, pp. 504–509. SciTePress (2019). https://doi.org/10.5220/0007971505040509
2. Banerjee, T., Chowdhury, D.R.: On the security of the double-block-length hash function NCASH. In: Shankar Sriram, V.S., Subramaniyaswamy, V., Sasikaladevi, N., Zhang, L., Batten, L., Li, G. (eds.) ATIS 2019. CCIS, vol. 1116, pp. 266–278. Springer, Singapore (2019). https://doi.org/10.1007/978-981-15-0871-4_21
3. Bellare, M., Rogaway, P.: Encode-then-encipher encryption: how to exploit nonces or redundancy in plaintexts for efficient cryptography. In: Okamoto, T. (ed.) ASIACRYPT 2000. LNCS, vol. 1976, pp. 317–330. Springer, Heidelberg (2000). https://doi.org/10.1007/3-540-44448-3_24
4. Dworkin, M.J.: Recommendation for block cipher modes of operation: Galois/Counter Mode (GCM) and GMAC. Technical report (2007)
5. Feistel, H.: Cryptography and computer privacy. Sci. Am. **228**(5), 15–23 (1973)
6. Forrié, R.: The strict avalanche criterion: spectral properties of boolean functions and an extended definition. In: Goldwasser, S. (ed.) CRYPTO 1988. LNCS, vol. 403, pp. 450–468. Springer, New York (1990). https://doi.org/10.1007/0-387-34799-2_31
7. Ghosh, S., Sengupta, A., Saha, D., Chowdhury, D.R.: A scalable method for constructing non-linear cellular automata with period $2^n - 1$. In: Wąs, J., Sirakoulis, G.C., Bandini, S. (eds.) ACRI 2014. LNCS, vol. 8751, pp. 65–74. Springer, Cham (2014). https://doi.org/10.1007/978-3-319-11520-7_8
8. Heys, H.M.: A tutorial on linear and differential cryptanalysis. Cryptologia **26**(3), 189–221 (2002)
9. Hortensius, P.D., McLeod, R.D., Pries, W., Miller, D.M., Card, H.C.: Cellular automata-based pseudorandom number generators for built-in self-test. IEEE Trans. Comput. Aided Des. Integr. Circuits Syst. **8**(8), 842–859 (1989)
10. McGrew, D., Viega, J.: The Galois/Counter Mode of operation (GCM). Submission to NIST Modes of Operation Process, vol. 20 (2004)
11. Mukherjee, M., Ganguly, N., Chaudhuri, P.P.: Cellular automata based authentication (CAA). In: Bandini, S., Chopard, B., Tomassini, M. (eds.) ACRI 2002. LNCS, vol. 2493, pp. 259–269. Springer, Heidelberg (2002). https://doi.org/10.1007/3-540-45830-1_25
12. NIST: Information Technology Laboratory: CSRC, Block Cipher Techniques: Current Modes (2020). https://csrc.nist.gov/projects/block-cipher-techniques/bcm/current-modes. (Created 04 January 2017, Updated 22 June 2020)
13. Chaudhuri, P.P., Chowdhury, D.R., Nandi, S., Chattopadhyay, S.: Additive Cellular Automata: Theory and Applications, vol. 1. Wiley, Hoboken (1997)
14. Rukhin, A., Soto, J., Nechvatal, J., Smid, M., Barker, E.: A statistical test suite for random and pseudorandom number generators for cryptographic applications, NIST Special Publication 800–22. Technical report, Booz-Allen and Hamilton Inc Mclean Va (2001)
15. Saarinen, M.O.: GCM, GHASH and weak keys. IACR Cryptology ePrint Archive. 2011, 202 (2011). http://eprint.iacr.org/2011/202
16. Stinson, D.R.: Cryptography: Theory and Practice. CRC Press, Boca Raton (2005)
17. Webster, A.F., Tavares, S.E.: On the design of S-boxes. In: Williams, H.C. (ed.) CRYPTO 1985. LNCS, vol. 218, pp. 523–534. Springer, Heidelberg (1986). https://doi.org/10.1007/3-540-39799-X_41

18. Wu, H.: ACORN: a lightweight authenticated cipher (v3). Candidate for the CAESAR Competition (2016). https://competitions.cr.yp.to/round3/acornv3.pdf
19. Wu, H., Preneel, B.: AEGIS: a fast authenticated encryption algorithm. In: Lange, T., Lauter, K., Lisoněk, P. (eds.) SAC 2013. LNCS, vol. 8282, pp. 185–201. Springer, Heidelberg (2014). https://doi.org/10.1007/978-3-662-43414-7_10

High Order Cellular Automata for Edge Detection: A Preliminary Study

Enrico Formenti[1]([✉]) [iD] and Jean-Louis Paquelin[2] [iD]

[1] Université Côte d'Azur, CNRS, I3S, Nice, France
enrico.formenti@univ-cotedazur.fr
[2] Université Côte d'Azur, Villa Arson, Nice, France
jean-louis.paquelin@univ-cotedazur.fr

Abstract. In this paper we explore the possibility of using high-order cellular automata to perform edge detection. Experiments are conducted to show how to find optimal values for the model. Using these optimal values, the model is compared to common methods for edge detection. The obtained results are encouraging since they are very close to the best performing commonly used methods.

Keywords: Cellular automata · Edge detection · Image processing

1 Introduction

Cellular automata (CA) are a well-known formal model used in a host of applications both at a scientific and at an industrial level. This is essentially due to the main characteristics of the model: uniformity, locality and massive parallelism which allow to conceive simple and effective applications. In particular, locality and uniformity are well-adapted in some fundamental domains of image processing, namely, edge detection and boundary detection [10]. Edge detection by cellular automata received a great attention over the last half century producing hundreds of papers and methods applied in highly specialized fields such as brain tumor detection [5] or cell detection and identification in images [6]. For more details and for an historical perspective of edge detection by cellular automata we refer the reader to the excellent survey of Rosin and Sun [11].

A cellular automaton is an arrangement of finite state automata placed on a regular grid. All automata are identical and can take a state s chosen from a finite set S called the *set of states*. A *local* rule $h \colon S^N \to S$ updated the state of the current automaton on the basis of the data it has access to. In our experiments, these data are those located on the grid at the position of the automaton and in its direct vicinity N. All automata are updated synchronously. This simple definition contrasts with the huge variety of the dynamical behaviors. High-order CA (HOCA) are a variant of CA in which each automaton can memorize a certain (finite) number of its past states. This additional feature allows many further applications, for example, in secret sharing schemes [9] or in data encryption [2].

© Springer Nature Switzerland AG 2021
T. M. Gwizdałła et al. (Eds.): ACRI 2020, LNCS 12599, pp. 80–89, 2021.
https://doi.org/10.1007/978-3-030-69480-7_9

For more details about the formal definition of HOCA and their dynamical behavior we refer to [3,4].

In this paper, we explore the possibility of performing edge detection. The advantage of using HOCA over the previous models based on CA is that exploiting memory should bring to better performing algorithms (from the image processing point of view). Our method is somewhat similar to the one (based on CA) proposed by Popovici and Popovici [8]. We look for a difference in intensity on the image between neighboring pixels and we suitably modify the intensity if the difference is large enough or we leave everything unchanged. Moreover, we use the memory of the HOCA to have informations about the previously visited sites and hence we can try to make wiser decisions. From this preliminary exploration, we obtained a simple model which has performances close to the most common methods used in edge detection.

The paper is structured as follows. The next section precisely defines our model and its parameters. Section 3 contains a series of experiments in which we try to optimize two of the parameters of the model, namely, the number of iterations $\#I$ and the number of agents $\#A$. After fixing those parameters, in Sect. 4, we compare the results of our model with classical methods. In the last section we draw some conclusions and provide perspectives for future work.

2   Edge Detection by 2D HOCA

In this section we are going to illustrate our HOCA algorithm. First of all, remark that in order to gain in efficiency, we implemented an agent based approach of 2D HOCA. The idea is that the state set S can be seen as splitted into two parts: a background (B) which holds the image informations (color intensity) and a foreground (F) which contains the agents information. Indeed, B (resp., F) is further divided into three planes B^r, B^g, B^b (resp., F^r, F^g, F^b) one per color plane of the input image. At each iteration t, the automaton produces a new image. Denote $B(t)_{x,y}$ the content of the background at iteration t. Similarly, $B^i(t)$ for $i \in \{r, g, b\}$ denotes the image content at iteration t according to the color plane i. For any pair of integers a, b with $a < b$, let $[a, b[$ be the set of integer between a and $b - 1$ (a and $b - 1$ included).

The information contained in the foreground $F^c_{x,y}(t)$ is a stack of (at most 8) quadruples of the type $(dy, dx, life, val)$ where $(dy, dx) \in \{-1, 0, +1\}^2 \setminus \{(0,0)\}$, $life \in [0, \lambda]$ and $val \in [0, 1]$. The quadruple indicates the presence of an agent if $life > 0$. This value roughly (see the precise definition below) quantifies the number of iterations that the agent will go through before disappearing. The values dy and dx represent the direction in which the agent is moving and val is a value which stores the value of the intensity of the pixel seen at the previous iteration so that the agent can compare it with the intensity of the current pixel.

Initialization. Assume that $I^c_{x,y}$ is the pixel of the input image at coordinates (x, y) in the color plane $c \in \{r, g, b\}$ and that I has $w \times h$ pixels per plane. We consider that the input image has been rescaled so that $I^c_{x,y}$ is an IEEE-754 float in [0,1]. Then, $\forall c \in \{r,g,b\} \, \forall x \in [0, w[\, \forall y \in [0, h[$:

$$B^c_{x,y}(0) = I^c_{x,y}$$

$$F^c_{x,y}(0) = \begin{cases} (dy, dx, life, val) & \text{if } X_p = 1 \\ (0,0,0,0) & \text{if } X_p = 0 \end{cases}$$

where X_p is a Bernoulli random variable with parameter $p = \frac{\#A}{3wh}$ (of course we assume $\#A < 3wh$), the direction (dx, dy) is chosen uniformly at random in $\{-1, 0, +1\}^2 \setminus \{(0,0)\}$. The parameter $life = \lambda \cdot B^c_{x,y}(0)$ is hence proportional to the intensity of the pixel on which the agent spawn. Of course, at time 0 we set $val = 0$ since the agent has not seen any other pixel yet. We fixed λ at 64. This is chosen so that the agent does not live too long when going through a rapidly changing zone and, conversely, allow a long range exploration when no variations of intensity is encountered.

Iteration. At each time step $t > 0$, agents update their state according to their own state and the one of the background point at their position. More formally, assume that $F^c_{x-dx,y-dy}(t) = (dx, dy, life, val)$ for some direction $(dx, dy) \in \{-1, 0, +1\}^2 \setminus \{(0,0)\}$, then

$$B^c_{x,y}(t+1) = \begin{cases} \max(B^c_{x,y}(t), \min(2 \cdot edge, 1)), & \text{if } edge > \theta \text{ and } life > 0 \\ B^c_{x,y}(t) & \text{otherwise} \end{cases}$$

and

$$F^c_{x,y}(t+1) = \begin{cases} (dy, dx, life/2, b) & edge > \theta \text{ and } life > 0 \\ (dy, dx, life\text{-}1, b) & \text{if } edge \leq \theta \text{ and } life > 0 \\ (0,0,0,0) & \text{if } life \leq 0 \text{ or } (x + dx, y + dy) \notin [0, w] \times [0, h] \\ & \quad \text{or } B^c_{x,y}(t) = 1 \end{cases}$$

where $edge = val - B^c_{x,y}(t)$, $b = B^c_{x,y}(t+1)$ and $\theta = 0.05$. On the other hand, if there is no direction (dx, dy) such that $F^c_{x-dx,y-dy}(t) = (dx, dy, life, val)$, then $B^c_{x,y}(t+1) = B^c_{x,y}(t)$ and $F^c_{x,y}(t+1) = F^c_{x,y}(t)$.

In other words, first the edge value e is computed. If we consider the image as a height field, the edge value may be interpreted as how high the agent has climbed from its previous position. If the edge value exceeds 0.05 (i.e. 5% of the maximum difference of height between the two points), the agent just climbed an edge and it updates the corresponding point $B^c_{x,y}(t)$ in the background image. The new value $B^c_{x,y}(t+1)$ is twice the edge value, so the brightness of the drawn edge will be proportional to the edge height.

On top of the general behavior described, an agent will die (and will be stopped and reinitialized) when at least one of the following condition occurs:

– $life < 0$,
– $(x + dx, y + dy)$ falls outside of the image,
– $B^c_{x,y}(t)$ has reached 1, the maximum value.

In order to keep the number of agents constant along iterations, when an agent dies, a new one is created (see initialization step).

Finally, remark that it is clear from the above definitions that upon iterations, at each position (x, y) there might be up to 8 agents (one coming from each direction). In this case, the only maximum value of $B^c_{x,y}(t)$ is kept and all agents are "superposed".

3   Experiments

As pointed out by Rosin and Sun [11], determining the number of iterations necessary to converge towards an acceptable solution is an issue in edge detection by CA since many authors provide no clear indications. In the HOCA case, we have also one more parameter to work with, namely, the number of agents and their spatial distribution. It is clear that both parameters: number of iterations $\#I$ and number of agents $\#A$ are a function of the image quality and size. In order to have an idea of the values taken by these parameters we first consider the following experimental setting. Consider the image in Fig. 1. It has a size of 840×460 for a total of 386400 pixels.

Fig. 1. Edward Hopper - *Night hawks*, 1942.

If we fix $\#I$ to $10K$, then in the worst case, if we let the $\#A = 10K$ and the agents are initially uniformly distributed over the pixels, $\#A = 10K$ means that each agent has approximatively an empty Moore neighborhood around him which would make HOCA solution very similar to a classical approach by convolution operators. The optimal value of $\#A$ will be the one for which MSE and PSNR stabilize.

Recall that MSE (*Mean Square Error*) and PSNR (*Peak Signal to Noise Ratio*) are two quantities commonly used to evaluate the distance between the original image O and the image G generated by an image processing algorithm. MSE is given by

$$\mathsf{MSE} = \frac{\sum_{i=1}^{w} \sum_{j=1}^{h} (O_{i,j} - G_{i,j})^2}{w \cdot h}$$

where w and h are the width and the height of the image, respectively. The PSNR is defined as

$$\mathsf{PSNR} = 10 \log_{10} \frac{M^2}{\mathsf{MSE}}$$

where M is the maximum possible pixel value in the images, $M = 255$ in our case. Both values are stabilized for $\#A \approx 3800$ (see Fig. 2).

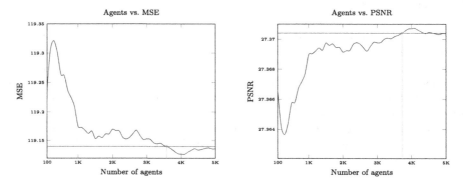

Fig. 2. Running edge detection for 10000 iterations and varying the number of agents.

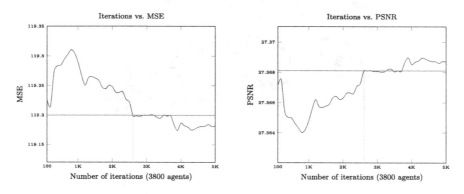

Fig. 3. Running edge detection with a fixed number of agents (3800) and varying the number of iterations.

The second batch of experiments consisted in fixing $\#A$ at 3800 and search for the value of $\#I$ which stabilizes both MSE and PSNR. We found $\#I \approx 2700$ (see Fig. 3). Remark that if one looks at our HOCA as a dynamical system, then one can consider that the system stabilizes when the variation of MSE and PSNR

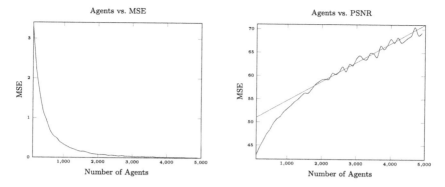

Fig. 4. Running edge detection for a fixed number of iterations (10K) and increasing the number of agents. MSE and PSNR are computed $w.r.t$ the previously generated image.

between two generated images become small enough. As in the previous cases, we started the new series of experiments by fixing the number of iterations to $10K$ and varying the number of agents between 100 and $5K$ with increments of 100. This provided a sequence of images $X_1, \ldots, X_n$. In Fig. 4, we plotted both MSE and PSNR for successive images X_i, X_{i+1}. As we can see, MSE decreases rapidly and it is almost zero when $\#A$ becomes bigger than $2K$ and at the same value the PSNR starts increasing almost linearly. In Fig. 5, we remark similar results when $\#A$ is fixed at 3800 and $\#I$ varies between 100 and $5K$.

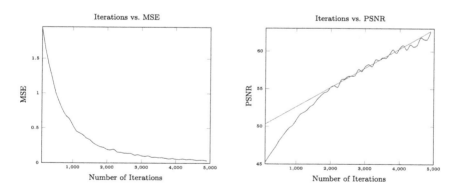

Fig. 5. Running edge detection with 3800 agents and varying the number of iterations but accounting values $w.r.t$ the previous generated image.

4   Comparing with the Classics

In this section we briefly review some classical edge detection algorithm widely used in practical applications. More informations can be found in classical image processing books, for instance, see [7].

4.1 Simple Thresholding

A thresholding algorithm aims at classifying the pixels of an image into *edges* and *non-edges* according to their intensity. An initial threshold is chosen θ_0 (0.2 in our experiments), then all pixels are divided into two sets $A_{<=\theta_0}$ and $A_{>\theta_0}$. Let $\mu_\le$ (resp. $\mu_>$) be the average intensity value of $A_{\le\theta_0}$ (resp. $A_{>\theta_0}$), then $\theta_1 = \frac{\mu_\le + \mu_>}{2}$ and another iteration of the previous step is performed until $|\theta_{i+1} - \theta_i| < \epsilon$ ($\epsilon = 10^{-2}$). Assume $\theta_{\tilde{i}}$ is the threshold found when exiting the loop, then all values in $A_{>\theta_{\tilde{i}}}$ (resp., $A_{\le\theta_{\tilde{i}}}$) are set to maximal (resp., minimal) intensity.

4.2 Kernel Methods

Consider an image $I_{x,y}$ as 2D arrays of color intensity (only gray color maps are considered here), where (x, y) are the spatial coordinates of the pixels of the image. Points belonging to an edge are characterized by rapid changes in intensity in their close neighborhood. These rapid changes can be analytically detected using the first derivative (gradient) $\nabla = (\nabla_x, \nabla_y)$ of $I_{x,y}$ where $|\nabla| = \sqrt{\nabla_x^2 + \nabla_y^2}$ is the magnitude and $\theta = \arctan\left(\frac{\nabla_y}{\nabla_x}\right)$ of ∇ is its direction. Recall that $\theta = 0$ for a vertical edge with lighter intensity on its right side. X and Y are the usual orthogonal coordinates axis. In most of the following algorithms, ∇ is approximated by a pair of kernels which are convoluted over the original image, generating a new image $B_{x,y}$. We considered the Roberts cross, Prewitt and Sobel kernels (see Fig. 6).

$$\nabla_x = \begin{bmatrix} +1 & 0 \\ 0 & -1 \end{bmatrix} \quad \nabla_y = \begin{bmatrix} 0 & +1 \\ -1 & 0 \end{bmatrix}$$

(a) Roberts kernels.

$$\nabla_x = \begin{bmatrix} -1 & 0 & +1 \\ -1 & 0 & +1 \\ -1 & 0 & +1 \end{bmatrix} \quad \nabla_y = \begin{bmatrix} +1 & +1 & +1 \\ 0 & 0 & 0 \\ -1 & -1 & -1 \end{bmatrix}$$

(b) Prewitt kernels.

$$\nabla_x = \begin{bmatrix} -1 & 0 & +1 \\ -2 & 0 & +2 \\ -1 & 0 & +1 \end{bmatrix} \quad \nabla_y = \begin{bmatrix} +1 & +2 & +1 \\ 0 & 0 & 0 \\ -1 & -2 & -1 \end{bmatrix}$$

(c) Sobel kernels.

$$L = \begin{bmatrix} 0 & 1 & 0 \\ 1 & -4 & 1 \\ 0 & 1 & 0 \end{bmatrix}$$

(d) The LoG kernel.

Fig. 6. Kernels used in edge detection methods.

Another possibility is to consider the second derivative. Indeed, we have seen that a rapid change in intensity determines a steep increase (resp., decrease) followed by a steep decrease (resp., increase) of the first derivative. Finally, this last fact implies a zero crossing of the second derivative. Approximating the

Laplacian by finite differences (as previously done for the gradient) brings to the Laplacian of the Gaussian method. The kernel used in this case is reported in Fig. 6(d).

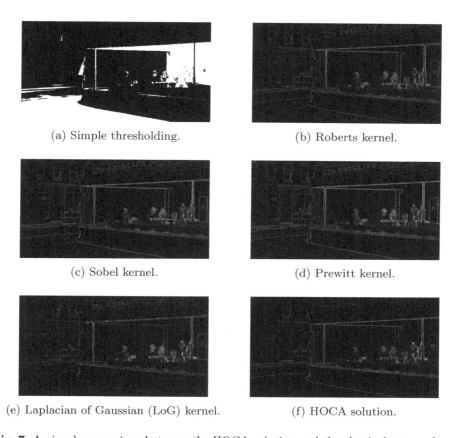

(a) Simple thresholding.   (b) Roberts kernel.

(c) Sobel kernel.   (d) Prewitt kernel.

(e) Laplacian of Gaussian (LoG) kernel.   (f) HOCA solution.

Fig. 7. A visual comparison between the HOCA solution and the classical approaches.

In Table 1, we report the values of MSE and PSNR between the image of Hopper's painting and the image obtained by applying one the considered methods. The table shows that our method performs worse than the others. Anyway, remark that the difference between the best performing (LoG) and the worst one is about 1.76%. Similar considerations can be made for the PSNR.

In order to confirm the results of the first two batches of experiments, we used the BSDS500 (Berkeley Segmentation Data Set, [1]) data set which consists of 500 images and compared the results of our model with the values of $\#A$ and $\#I$ found in the previous experiments against the best performing competitor considered here, namely LoG algorithm. The results are reported in Table 2. As we can see the difference for MSE is less than 1% and for the PSNR the difference

Table 1. Quantitative comparison between HOCA and classic methods.

Method	MSE	PSNR
Simple thresholding	118.79269409937888	27.382906290602115
Roberts	117.56277950310559	27.42810515445974
Prewitt	117.37082556935817	27.435202015100963
Sobel	117.62519151138716	27.425800173357132
LoG	117.13097826086957	27.444085904026085
HOCA	119.19873188405798	27.36808725754679

Table 2. Quantitative comparison between HOCA and LoG method over the BSDS500 data set.

Method	MSE	PSNR
LoG	99.5655254013899	27.828705300879
HOCA	100.474360485575	27.852131472538

is practically negligible since it is less than 0.01%. These facts convinced us that we are in the good path towards a competitive solution (Fig. 7).

5   Conclusions and Perspectives

In this paper we proposed an edge detection method based on HOCA. The experiments confirmed that the method provides results comparable with the most common competitors. Our algorithm is based on four main parameters: $\#A$ (number of agents), $\#I$ (number of iterations), θ (edge threshold) and λ (agents life coefficient).

The computational complexity of the method is $O(\#A \cdot \#I)$ (for fixed λ and θ). Hence, the method becomes more interesting a standard kernel method when $\#A \cdot \#I < 3wh$ (recall that w and h are width and the height of the image). Hence, it is important to find optimal values of $\#A$ and $\#I$.

We showed a methodology to find those optimal values according to a given image but a more general formula (or at least tight bounds) depending only on the image size would be desirable. More experiments are needed also to find the optimal value of the edge threshold parameter since it can affect performances both from an image quality point of view and not only the computational performances of the method.

Another interesting research direction would consider the agents *life* parameter. Remark that if λ is quite small then agents keep dieing and respawning over the image with a global effect of becoming similar to the asynchronous application of a kernel method. If λ is too high (comparable with the size of the image) the risk is to visit too few regions of the image. Here also a formula linking λ to the other parameters of the model is of major interest.

However, these are not the only parts we need to explore in order to evaluate the interest or effectiveness of this approach. We would like to assess the subjective quality of the result HOCA by comparing it with perception based models and against ground truth images. And of course, there is room to improve the local rule of the HOCA method for edge detection, edge thinning and extension, antialiasing and other image quality enhancements.

References

1. Arbelaez, P., Maire, M., Fowlkes, C., Malik, J.: Contour detection and hierarchical image segmentation. IEEE Trans. Pattern Anal. Mach. Intell. **33**(5), 898–916 (2011)
2. Chai, Z., Cao, Z., Zhou, Y.: Encryption based on reversible second-order cellular automata. In: Chen, G., Pan, Y., Guo, M., Lu, J. (eds.) ISPA 2005. LNCS, vol. 3759, pp. 350–358. Springer, Heidelberg (2005). https://doi.org/10.1007/11576259_39
3. Dennunzio, A., Formenti, E., Manzoni, L., Margara, L., Porreca, A.E.: Decidability of sensitivity and equicontinuity for linear higher-order cellular automata. In: Martín-Vide, C., Okhotin, A., Shapira, D. (eds.) LATA 2019. LNCS, vol. 11417, pp. 95–107. Springer, Cham (2019). https://doi.org/10.1007/978-3-030-13435-8_7
4. Dennunzio, A., Formenti, E., Manzoni, L., Margara, L., Porreca, A.E.: On the dynamical behaviour of linear higher-order cellular automata and its decidability. Inf. Sci. **486**, 73–87 (2019)
5. Diwakar, M., Patel, P.K., Gupta, K.: Cellular automata based edge-detection for brain tumor. In: 2013 International Conference on Advances in Computing, Communications and Informatics (ICACCI), pp. 53–59 (2013)
6. Girault, M., et al.: Algorithm for the precise detection of single and cluster cells in microfluidic applications. Cytometry Part A **89**(8), 731–741 (2016)
7. Gonzalez, R.C., Woods, R.E.: Digital Image Processing, 3rd edn. Prentice Hall, Upper Saddle River (2008)
8. Popovici, A., Popovici, D.: Cellular automata in image processing. In: International Symposium on the Mathematical Theory of Networks and Systems (2002)
9. del Rey, A.M., Mateus, J.P., Sánchez, G.R.: A secret sharing scheme based on cellular automata. Appl. Math. Comput. **170**(2), 1356–1364 (2005)
10. Rosin, P., Adamatzky, A., Sun, X.: Cellular Automata in Image Processing andGeometry, 1st edn. Springer, Heidelberg (2016). https://doi.org/10.1007/978-3-319-06431-4
11. Rosin, P.L., Sun, X.: Edge detection using cellular automata. In: Rosin, P., Adamatzky, A., Sun, X. (eds.) Cellular Automata in Image Processing and Geometry. ECC, vol. 10, pp. 85–103. Springer, Cham (2014). https://doi.org/10.1007/978-3-319-06431-4_5. Chap. 5

PENTAVIUM: Potent Trivium-Like Stream Cipher Using Higher Radii Cellular Automata

Anita John$^{(\boxtimes)}$ (iD), B. C. Nandu(iD), Athul Ajesh, and Jimmy Jose(iD)

Department of Computer Science and Engineering,
National Institute of Technology Calicut, Kozhikode, India
{anita_p170007cs,jimmy}@nitc.ac.in

Abstract. Cellular Automata (CA) have recently evolved as a good cryptographic primitive. CA have been used as pseudorandom number generators in stream ciphers, block ciphers and hash functions. The eSTREAM cipher Trivium, though secure in its complete rounds, was cryptanalyzed in its reduced rounds. Trivium has a simple internal structure and a very long key setup phase that consists of 1152 rounds. This paper emphasizes the advantage of using CA of higher radii in Trivium. Here, we have proposed a 5-neighbourhood CA to be used in Trivium which helps the cipher to attain better cryptographic properties at a faster rate. The diffusion and randomness of the cipher also increases with the use of higher radii, but at the cost of increased computational complexity. The new cipher is named Pentavium.

Keywords: Stream cipher · Cellular automata · 5-neighbourhood CA · Cryptography · Trivium

1 Introduction

In cryptography, encryption techniques are categorized as symmetric-key encryption and asymmetric-key encryption. Symmetric-key encryption has a common shared key between the sender and the receiver and this shared key is used to perform encryption and decryption. In asymmetric key encryption, the sender and receiver make use of public and private keys. In symmetric encryption, the encryption can be done either on blocks of plaintext or one bit at a time. A block cipher encrypts a fixed size of n-bit block of data at a time. A stream cipher encrypts one bit or byte of data at a time and hence they use a long stream of pseudo-random bits as the key. A secure stream cipher should generate the keystream bits in an unpredictable manner and the reuse of the key should never happen. This implies that the keystream generator should also be a good pseudorandom generator. Stream ciphers are in general faster than block ciphers.

The eSTREAM project [16], part of ECRYPT [5], aimed to promote the design of efficient and compact stream ciphers that can be widely adopted. The

© Springer Nature Switzerland AG 2021
T. M. Gwizdałła et al. (Eds.): ACRI 2020, LNCS 12599, pp. 90–100, 2021.
https://doi.org/10.1007/978-3-030-69480-7_10

finalists of the project were classified into two profiles, profile-1 and profile-2. The ciphers in profile-1 were intended to give excellent throughput when implemented in software whereas the ciphers in profile-2 were intended to be efficient in terms of hardware resources. One such widely studied cipher is Trivium [7], which belongs to profile-2. Trivium has a simple design and is secure in its full round (1152 clocks).

Cellular Automata (CA) have evolved as a good pseudorandom generator. So CA is used in many applications like pattern recognition, VLSI design, error correcting code and cryptography. The properties of CA vary with the CA rules. The non-linear Rule 30 exhibits very good statistical properties like non-linearity and higher algebraic degree [17]. Several studies have been made on CA rules of higher radii. From further experimentation, it was found that 5-neighbourhood rules, i.e., rules having radius - 2 showed better performance than 3-neighbourhood rules in lesser clock cycles. Among the 5-neighbourhood rules, the rules 1721342310 and 2523490710 have been considered to be good pseudorandom sequence generators [11].

In this paper, we exploit the strength of higher radii CA in designing robust stream ciphers. We propose Pentavium, a 5-neighbourhood CA based stream cipher inspired by the designs of Trivium and its 3-neighbourhood CA based alternative, CAvium [12]. The rest of the paper is organized as follows. Section 2 discusses some basic concepts about CA and also about the stream ciphers - Trivium and CAvium. Section 3 provides the proposed design of the stream cipher followed by design rationale in Sect. 4. The security analysis based on the test results is done in Sects. 5 and 6 followed by conclusion.

2 Preliminaries

2.1 Trivium

Trivium [7] is a hardware oriented stream cipher developed as part of the eSTREAM cipher project. The cipher generates upto 2^{64} keystream bits from an 80 - bit key and an 80 - bit Initialization Vector (IV). Here the cipher makes use of three linear shift registers which together constitutes 288 - bit internal state registers. The cipher executes the initialization phase for 1152 rounds. Once the initialization phase is over, the keystream generation begins. Both initialization and key generation phases execute the same algorithm.

2.2 Cellular Automata

A Cellular Automaton is a collection of cells and each cell is capable of storing a value and a next state computation function (CA rule). Rules determine the behaviour of CA. The state of each cell of a CA together at any instant t defines the current state of the CA. In 3-neighbourhood CA, the value of the cell after one clock cycle depends on one left neighbour, itself and one right neighbour. The next state of the ith cell of a 3-neighbourhood CA at any instant t is given by

$$S_i^{t+1} = f(S_{i-1}^t, S_i^t, S_{i+1}^t)$$

In 5-neighbourhood CA, the change in cell value depends on two left neighbours, itself and two right neighbours. The next state of the ith cell of a five neighbourhood CA at any instant t is given by

$$S_i^{t+1} = f(S_{i-2}^t, S_{i-1}^t, S_i^t, S_{i+1}^t, S_{i+2}^t)$$

where f is the next state function or rule, S_i^{t+1} denotes the next state of the ith cell, S_{i-2}^t is the current state of second left-neighbour, S_{i-1}^t is the current state of first left-neighbour, S_i^t is the current state of the cell to be updated, S_{i+1}^t is the current state of first right-neighbour and S_{i+2}^t is the current state of second right-neighbour. In general, the number of cells n that participate in a CA cell update is given by $n = 2r + 1$, where r is the radius of the neighbourhood [8]. From the above CA transition rules, we can see that as the neighbourhood radii increases, the number of cells that participate in a CA cell update also increases.

2.3   CAvium

CAvium is a modification of Trivium stream cipher by introducing 3 - neighbourhood CA into it [12]. CAvium uses a hybrid null boundary CA to replace the shift registers of Trivium. Like Trivium, CAvium contains 288-bit internal state registers. The cells in the CA update itself based on the 3 - neighbourhood rule set <30, 60, 90, 120, 150, 180, 210, 240> in that order one after the other. CAvium executes the initialization phase for 144 rounds without generating any output. At the end of this phase, the keystream generation phase starts producing the bits of the keystream. Both these phases execute the same algorithm.

3   Proposed Methodology

In this section, we discuss the methodology used to design the new stream cipher Pentavium.

Pentavium is a Trivium-like stream cipher which makes use of higher radii CA. Pentavium makes use of 5-neighbourhood rules in its design. The intention of our design is to affirm the fact that as the neighbourhood radii of a cell increases, the strength of the cipher also increases and that too in less number of cycles. Pentavium uses three hybrid null boundary CAs which make use of a set of 5-neighbourhood CA rules that showed good cryptographic properties. The rule set used in our cipher is <1452976485, 1721342310, 2523490710, 1520018790, 1721342310, 1452976485, 1520018790, 2523490710>. The rule set contains 5-neighbourhood linear and nonlinear rules which showed good cryptographic properties. The rules 1721342310, 2523490710 are linear rules and the rules 1452976485, 1520018790 are nonlinear rules.

The internal structure of this new cipher exactly resembles Trivium since we wish to retain the simplicity of its design while reducing the time taken for initialization phase by reducing the number of clock cycles. Through our proposed cipher, we show that the use of higher radii CA (5-neighbourhood) helps to reduce the number of iterations to 32 without any compromise in its security properties.

Pentavium cipher contains 288-bit internal state registers $(s_1, s_2, ..., s_{288})$ which are implemented as three hybrid CAs of lengths 93, 84 and 111 respectively. The first two registers are used to store the key $\{k_1, k_2, ..., k_{80}\}$ and Initialization Vector $\{iv_1, iv_2, ..., iv_{80}\}$ respectively. The third register is filled with zeros except for the last 3 cells which are filled with ones.

$$(s_1, s_2, ..., s_{93}) \leftarrow (k_1, k_2, ..., k_{80}, 0, ..., 0)$$
$$(s_{94}, s_{95}, ..., s_{177}) \leftarrow (iv_1, iv_2, ..., iv_{80}, 0, ..., 0)$$
$$(s_{178}, s_{179}, ..., s_{288}) \leftarrow (0, 0, ..., 0, 1, 1, 1)$$

After loading the bits, the initialization phase begins where the CA will be evolved through 32 cycles by suppressing the output bit. In each cycle the rule set <1452976485, 1721342310, 2523490710, 1520018790, 1721342310, 1452976485, 1520018790, 2523490710> is applied consecutively through all the 288 cells. i.e., rule 1 is applied on 1st cell, rule 2 on 2nd cell and so on, again rule 1 on 9th cell, rule 2 on 10th cell. This order is followed for all the 288 cells. After 32 cycles, the keystream generation begins. Both these phases execute the same algorithm which is discussed in Algorithm 1. The function $CA_5(s)$ in the algorithm refers to the Boolean value obtained after applying the 5-neighbourhood CA rule on a cell s during a single cycle and $+$ indicates xor operation. The registers t_1, t_2 and t_3 are the temporary registers and z_i is the ith output of the keystream bit.

4   Design Rationale

4.1   Selection of Linear and Nonlinear 5-Neighbourhood Rules

The selection of rules in the rule set is an important factor that affects the cryptographic properties of the generated keystream bits. Rule 30 was extensively studied by Stephen Wolfram and was considered as a good pseudorandom number generator. But it was later cryptanalyzed by Meier and Staffelbach [15]. So, a combination of linear and nonlinear CA rules was used to enhance the properties of CA than using them separately. CAvium had selected a combination of cryptographically secure linear and nonlinear 3-neighbourhood rules which enhanced the cryptographic properties of the cipher.

Algorithm 1: Pentavium Keystream Generation Algorithm

---

for $i \leftarrow 1$ **to** N **do**
$\quad t_1 \leftarrow s_{66} + s_{93}$
$\quad t_2 \leftarrow s_{162} + s_{177}$
$\quad t_3 \leftarrow s_{243} + s_{288}$
$\quad z_i \leftarrow t_1 + t_2 + t_3$
$\quad t_1 \leftarrow t_1 + s_{91}.s_{92} + s_{171}$
$\quad t_2 \leftarrow t_2 + s_{175}.s_{176} + s_{264}$
$\quad t_3 \leftarrow t_3 + s_{286}.s_{287} + s_{69}$
$\quad (s_1, s_2, ..., s_{93}) \leftarrow (t_3, CA_5(s_1), ..., CA_5(s_{92}))$
$\quad (s_{94}, s_{95}, ..., s_{177}) \leftarrow (t_1, CA_5(s_{94}), ..., CA_5(s_{176}))$
$\quad (s_{178}, s_{179}, ..., s_{288}) \leftarrow (t_2, CA_5(s_{178}), ..., CA_5(s_{287}))$

Later, Leporati and Mariot [13] did an extensive research on bipermutive CA rules of a given radius and some of the 5-neighbourhood nonlinear rules of radius 2 were investigated for their cryptographic suitability. They had taken Rule 30 as the base rule for all the benchmarking during the study. They analyzed the 5-neighbourhood rules using NIST [1] and ENT [2] and concluded that the rules 1452976485, 1520018790 and 2778290790 exhibited good properties among other 5-neighbourhood nonlinear rules.

The rule vector for 5-neighbourhood Linear Hybrid CA was selected based on [14]. It was found that the combination of rules 2523490710 and 1721342310 gives the largest number of rule vectors for 5-bit maximum length 5-neighbourhood CA [14]. The linear rules ensure maximum period, while the nonlinear rules prevent linear cryptanalysis and hence for better cryptographic properties we have selected both of them. Therefore the rule set <1452976485, 1721342310, 2523490710, 1520018790, 1721342310, 1452976485, 1520018790, 2523490710> is chosen for the implementation of this cipher.

The hybrid design ensures that balancedness and maximum length property of the linear rules and higher algebraic degree and nonlinearity properties of the nonlinear rules are achieved.

4.2   Choice of the Number of Cycles

Pentavium makes use of only 32 cycles during the initialization phase, reducing the number of cycles without loss of cryptographic properties. This reduction is appreciable when compared to 1152 rounds of Trivium and 144 cycles of CAvium, but with the same or even more strength than both the ciphers. This asserts the fact that as the neighbourhood radii increases, the cryptographic properties of the cipher increases in less number of cycles as compared to smaller radii CA. The choice of taking 32 cycles for initialization phase was made by observing the growth of cryptographic properties of Pentavium compared to Trivium. An analysis of the generated keystream bit shows that the cryptographic properties required for the cipher are achieved by Pentavium in 22 iterations. We give a brief explanation for the observation.

In the first iteration, the output register value is given by

$$z_1 = t_1 \oplus t_2 \oplus t_3 = s[66] \oplus s[93] \oplus s[162] \oplus s[177] \oplus s[243] \oplus s[288].$$

The left most bit in the equation is the register value at 66th position. In order to decide the number of cycles, we need to find the minimum number of iterations such that the output bit depends on all the cell values which marks the completion of the initialization process. Hence, we need to iterate until we include $s[1]$ in the Boolean expression, which ensures that the output bit is dependent on all the input bits.

In the second iteration,

$$z_2 = CA_5(s[65]) \oplus CA_5(s[92]) \oplus CA_5(s[161]) \oplus CA_5(s[176])$$
$$\oplus CA_5(s[242]) \oplus CA_5(s[287])$$

the left most value being $CA_5(s[65])$ will depend on s[63] to s[67]. Hence the left most value is s[63] for the second iteration. Similarly, in the 3rd iteration, the leftmost value will be $CA_5(s[63])$ which is s[60]. This dependency continues for each iteration and by the end of 22 iterations, $s[1]$ will be covered. In the same manner, the neighbours on the right side of s[66] will also be included in the output bit. However, to make sure that the output generated is secure against existing attacks on reduced round versions of Trivium, the number of rounds in the initialization phase is set to the nearest power of 2, i.e., 32.

5   Software Implementation and Results

Pentavium, CAvium and Trivium were coded in C and compiled using GCC 7.5.0. The code was run on on an IBM Lenovo Thinkpad E431 laptop with Intel Core-i5 3320m CPU@2.60 GHz. The time taken for computing 1 million and 100 million keystream bits using the three ciphers have been computed and used for analysing their relative performance.

A bitstream obtained using a random secret key

0x00002EC0657D0DCD2F655C99

and Initialization Vector (IV)

0x00004F557DD6AF2D0C417B20

was used for testing. After generating 100 million streams, we anlayzed the randomness of the keystream using NIST statistical test suite [1] and DIEHARD battery of tests of randomness. Here, we check whether the cipher passes all tests to qualify as a random generator.

Wolfram's Mathematica 12 [3] was used to obtain the Boolean expression of the output bits during the first and second iterations. Sage Ver.8.6 [4] was used to find the properties of these Boolean expressions. The number of Boolean variables involved during the first three iterations were respectively 6, 26 and 47

Table 1. Pentavium NIST Test results

Sl. No.	Test name	P-value	Status
1	Frequency	0.554420	Pass
2	Block frequency	0.946308	Pass
3	Cumulative sums	0.137282	Pass
4	Runs	0.851383	Pass
5	Longest Run	0.554420	Pass
6	Rank	0.032923	Pass
7	FFT	0.699313	Pass
8	Non overlapping template	0.202268	Pass
9	Overlapping template	0.595549	Pass
10	Universal	0.275709	Pass
11	Approximate entropy	0.723129	Pass
12	Random excursions	0.875539	Pass
13	Random excursions variant	0.517442	Pass
14	Serial	0.897763	Pass
15	Linear complexity	0.637119	Pass

which shows the exponential growth in the number of input variables. The NIST and DIEHARD test results obtained are shown in Tables 1 and 2 respectively. The results show that the proposed cipher passes all the tests in both NIST and DIEHARD with successful P-values.

Table 3 shows the values for nonlinearity, algebraic degree and resiliency which are crucial in deciding the strength of any stream cipher. The table also shows the values for Trivium and CAvium. It can be seen that the proposed cipher achieves a higher algebraic degree, nonlinearity and resiliency at a faster rate than both CAvium and Trivium. While Trivium takes about 70 rounds to gain algebraic degree of 2, nonlinearity 16 and resiliency order 3, CAvium which uses 3 neighbourhood CA rules reaches algebraic degree 2 in 3 rounds with nonlinearity 384 and resiliency order 5. Pentavium achieves better values in just 2 rounds.

An analysis of Pentavium shows that at the second iteration itself the cipher gains algebraic degree 2 with very high nonlinearity 31457280 and resiliency order 17. These features of CA rules were studied by Formenti et al. in [10]. They had proposed the idea of extending good updating CA rules and thereby increasing the number of Boolean variables. The fast growth rate of algebraic degree, resiliency and nonlinearity of Pentavium shows its resistance to algebraic attacks and correlation attacks.

The use of higher radii CA had its effects on the running time of the cipher. The software efficiency of the cipher was compared with that of CAvium and Trivium. The use of CA has incurred some additional time when compared to

Table 2. Pentavium DIEHARD test results

Sl. No.	Test name	P-value	Status
1	Birthday Spacings	0.969021	Pass
2	Overlapping 5-Permutations	0.456966	Pass
3	Binary Ranks	0.347940	Pass
4	Bitstream	0.40552	Pass
5	Count the 1's (successive)	0.735036	Pass
6	Count the 1's (specific)	0.218799	Pass
7	Craps	0.565967	Pass
8	Runs	0.511294	Pass
9	Overlapping Sums	0.796271	Pass
10	Squeeze	0.216076	Pass
11	3D Spheres	0.371883	Pass
12	Minimum Distance	0.963800	Pass
13	Parking Lot	0.199364	Pass
14	DNA	0.9463	Pass
15	OQSO	0.7758	Pass
16	OPSO	0.5544	Pass

Table 3. Comparison of cryptographic properties

Iteration	Balancedness	Nonlinearity	Algebraic degree	Resiliency
Trivium				
1	Balanced	0	1	1
70	Balanced	16	2	3
71	Balanced	32	2	3
83	Balanced	384	3	4
98	Balanced	1792	3	5
CAvium				
1	Balanced	0	1	1
2	Balanced	0	1	3
3	Balanced	384	2	5
4	Balanced	1792	3	6
Pentavium				
1	Balanced	0	1	1
2	Balanced	31457280	2	17

the feedback shift registers used in Trivium. Pentavium takes 1.34 times the run time of CAvium and 4.44 that of Trivium when implemented in C. With more optimizations in the code, we hope to reduce the running time even more. The statistical properties of Pentavium have shown significant improvements even during the initial iterations of the cipher which definitely makes the cipher highly resistant to the known attacks against stream ciphers.

Table 4 shows the comparison of parameters of Pentavium with that of Trivium and CAvium.

Table 4. Comparison of Pentavium with Trivium and CAvium

Cipher	Keysize	IV size	State size	Initialization cycles	Time Taken in seconds		
					Initialization time	KeyGeneration time	
						10^6 bits	10^8 bits
Trivium	80	80	288	1152	0.00132	0.738	72.29
CAvium	80	80	288	144	0.00034	2.387	235.734
Pentavium	80	80	288	32	0.00010	3.245	316.369

6   Security Analysis and Resistance to Known Attacks

The cipher exhibits good cryptographic properties like balancedness, nonlinearity and algebraic degree which are necessary for a good cipher. Since Pentavium makes use of 5-neighbourhood CA, each variable changes the value based on its five neighbours. So during each iteration, the number of variables involved increases at a very fast rate. As the number of variables increase, the strength of the cipher also increases at the cost of high computation. The additional advantage with our cipher is that we can get the required properties at a very high level with limited number of cycles. We have substantially reduced the number of iterations from 1152 of Trivium and 144 of CAvium to 32 in our cipher. From Table 3, we can see the fast growth rate of algebraic degree, nonlinearity and resiliency also. This clearly indicates the resistance of the cipher to algebraic attacks, linear cryptanalysis and correlation attacks.

6.1   Resistance Against Known Attacks

We discuss some of the attacks against stream ciphers and how Pentavium resists them based on its cryptographic properties.

(i) **Linear cryptanalysis:** This attack occurs as a result of the linear relation between the input and output bits. From Table 3, we can see the growth in nonlinearity during the second iteration. This clearly establishes the resistance of Pentavium against linear cryptanlaysis at the end of initialization phase.

(ii) **Differential Cryptanalysis:** The idea of differential cryptanalysis is that a known small difference in the key or plaintext or the internal state of the cipher is likely to introduce predictable changes in the keystream or internal state [6]. In Pentavium, the keystream generation starts only after 32 cycles of CA operations during which the key and IV bits are diffused between themselves. Moreover, each bit is dependent on itself and its 4 neighbours, 2 from left and 2 from right. So, even a small change in the input will bring out unpredictable keystream bits. The NIST and DIEHARD results also proves the randomness of the keystream generated which affirms the resistance of Pentavium to differential cryptanalysis.

(iii) **Algebraic attacks:** This attack exploits the low algebraic degree of the cipher. Pentavium will be resistant to algebraic attacks since the algebraic degree increases at a faster rate when compared to Trivium and CAvium.

(iv) **Cube Attacks:** Cube attacks are a class of attacks that come under algebraic cryptanalysis [9]. In cube attack, the attacker tries to obtain linear equations in the unknown key bits by combining the equations for an output bit of the cipher for a set of IVs. This attack exploits ciphers that can be represented using low degree multivariate polynomial. The high algebraic degree of Pentavium as well as its fast growth rate definitely prevents cube attacks on the proposed cipher.

(v) **Correlation attacks:** The property that measures the resistance of a cipher to correlation attacks is resiliency. Pentavium has good resiliency characteristics even at small iterations. Hence, the cipher will be resistant to correlation attacks.

7   Conclusion

This paper proposes a new stream cipher based on 5-neighbourhood hybrid CA. The initialization phase of Pentavium has considerably lesser number of cycles when compared to Trivium and CAvium, without any compromise in the strength of the cipher. The use of higher radii CA rules have played a vital role in the strength of the cipher owing to the exponential growth of its cryptographic properties even in lesser number of iterations. The generated keystream has higher algebraic degree, nonlinearity and resiliency which makes it resistant to attacks against stream ciphers. This cipher also proclaims the advantage of using 5-neighbourhood CA as a cryptographic primitive in the design of secure stream ciphers.

References

1. NIST Statistical Test Suite. https://csrc.nist.gov/projects/random-bit-generati on/documentation-and-software. Accessed 1 Sept 2020
2. Walker, J.: ENT - A pseudorandom number sequence test program (1993). http://www.fourmilab.ch/random/. Accessed 1 Sept 2020

3. Wolfram Mathematica: Modern Technical Computing. https://www.wolfram.com/mathematica/. Accessed 1 Sept 2020
4. SageMath - Open-Source Mathematical Sotware System. http://www.sagemath.org. Accessed 1 Sept 2020
5. estream: the ecrypt stream cipher project. www.ecrypt.eu.org/stream
6. Biham, E., Dunkelman, O.: Differential cryptanalysis in stream ciphers. IACR Cryptology ePrint Archive **2007**, 218 (2007)
7. De Cannière, C., Preneel, B.: Trivium. In: Robshaw, M., Billet, O. (eds.) New Stream Cipher Designs. LNCS, vol. 4986, pp. 244–266. Springer, Heidelberg (2008). https://doi.org/10.1007/978-3-540-68351-3_18
8. Cattell, K., Muzio, J.C.: Synthesis of one-dimensional linear hybrid cellular automata. IEEE Trans. Comput. Aided Des. Integr. Circ. Syst. **15**(3), 325–335 (1996)
9. Dinur, I., Shamir, A.: Cube attacks on tweakable black box polynomials. In: Joux, A. (ed.) EUROCRYPT 2009. LNCS, vol. 5479, pp. 278–299. Springer, Heidelberg (2009). https://doi.org/10.1007/978-3-642-01001-9_16
10. Formenti, E., Imai, K., Martin, B., Yunès, J.-B.: Advances on random sequence generation by uniform cellular automata. In: Calude, C.S., Freivalds, R., Kazuo, I. (eds.) Computing with New Resources. LNCS, vol. 8808, pp. 56–70. Springer, Cham (2014). https://doi.org/10.1007/978-3-319-13350-8_5
11. Gayathri, P.P., Jose, J.: Design and analysis of maximum length cellular automata. M. Tech. thesis, National Institute of Technology Calicut (2016)
12. Karmakar, S., Mukhopadhyay, D., RoyChowdhury, D.: CAvium - strengthening trivium stream cipher using cellular automata. J. Cell. Automata **7**(2), 179–197 (2012)
13. Leporati, A., Mariot, L.: Cryptographic properties of bipermutive cellular automata rules. J. Cell. Autom. **9**, 437–475 (2014)
14. Maiti, S., Roy Chowdhury, D.: Study of five-neighborhood linear hybrid cellular automata and their synthesis. In: Giri, D., Mohapatra, R.N., Begehr, H., Obaidat, M.S. (eds.) ICMC 2017. CCIS, vol. 655, pp. 68–83. Springer, Singapore (2017). https://doi.org/10.1007/978-981-10-4642-1_7
15. Meier, W., Staffelbach, O.: Analysis of pseudo random sequences generated by cellular automata. In: Davies, D.W. (ed.) EUROCRYPT 1991. LNCS, vol. 547, pp. 186–199. Springer, Heidelberg (1991). https://doi.org/10.1007/3-540-46416-6_17
16. Robshaw, M.: The eSTREAM project. In: Robshaw, M., Billet, O. (eds.) New Stream Cipher Designs. LNCS, vol. 4986, pp. 1–6. Springer, Heidelberg (2008). https://doi.org/10.1007/978-3-540-68351-3_1
17. Wolfram, S.: Random sequence generation by cellular automata. Adv. Appl. Math. **7**(2), 123–169 (1986). https://doi.org/10.1016/0196-8858(86)90028-X

Modeling and Simulation

Blockchain Smart Contract for Cellular Automata-Based Energy Sharing

Iliasse Abdennour[1]([✉]), Mustapha Ouardouz[1], and Abdes Samed Bernoussi[2]

[1] MMC Team, Abdelmalek-Essaadi University, B.P. 416, Tangier, Morocco
iliasseabdennour@gmail.com, ouardouz@gmail.com
[2] GAT Team, Abdelmalek-Essaadi University, B.P. 416, Tangier, Morocco
a.samed.bernoussi@gmail.com

Abstract. This paper deals with energy management in a microgrid through peer-to-peer (P2P) energy exchange method. The P2P process is executed on the basis of cellular automaton (CA) approach and implemented by smart contracts blockchain over a time horizon, enabling consensus to be recorded between consumers in a secure and fully automated transaction. The CA proposed model identifies the end-user state in a set of five possible states and supports the convergence of supply and demand decisions, thus ensuring the decentralization of energy distribution.

Keywords: Cellular automata · Smart contract · Blockchain · Microgrid · Prosumer · Energy sharing

1 Introduction

Over the last few years the energy systems in most developed countries have been undergoing a process of "vertical integration". These changes are the result of the increase of renewable energies in the energy mix, their share in the electricity sector is expected to increase from 25% in 2017 to 85% in 2050 [8]. Renewable technologies are now a cost-effective solution for small-scale power generation in households. However, due to the intermittent nature of Renewable Generation (RG), there could be a significant gap between electricity supply and demand. The concept of peer-to-peer (P2P) energy sharing offers possible solutions for these issues. The purpose of P2P sharing is to connect the households (node) to each other, each node operating autonomously while being able to intelligently share power with the entire micro-grid. The node functions both as an energy producer and consumer, more commonly known as a prosumer. This allows consumers who have an energy deficit to buy renewable energy at a cheaper price from a neighbor with excess energy. The emerging blockchain technology can fulfill exactly this requirement by developing self-consumption and to meet the expectations of consumers looking for more transparency and understanding regarding the origin and price of electricity. The register of this technology traces

T. M. Gwizdałła et al. (Eds.): ACRI 2020, LNCS 12599, pp. 103–112, 2021.
https://doi.org/10.1007/978-3-030-69480-7_11

the complete history of transactions and is accessible to all users in a decentralized manner. As for smarts contracts (automated contracts via the blockchain), they cover another major expectation of prosumers: the sale of energy adapted to local production and consumption. The smart contract allows asset transfers based on pre-established rules between several users without going through a trusted third party. A significant amount of decentralized applications based on blockchain technology related to energy sharing has been done [4,5,17].

In this work, we studied the blockchain technology related to energy sharing from the perspective of the consensus algorithm. Consensus protocol is configured to determine the amount and price of energy shared between peers. In Ref. [9], a localized Practical Byzantine Fault-Tolerant based-Consortium is proposed as the consensus mechanism for P2P trading. Besides, by combining the PoS (Proof of Stakes) consensus with the TOPSIS (Technique for Order Preference by Similarity to an Ideal Solution) comprehensive evaluation method, a new credibility-based equity proof consensus was designid [18]. In Ref. [16], Manuel Utz propose a smart contract ecosystem based on the Proof-of-Authority (PoA) consensus mechanism. An interesting analysis is carried in [3] on factors relevant to the implementation of block chain use cases and consensus mechanisms in the energy sector. In contrast with the existing literature, a new consensus algorithm for P2P energy sharing is proposed. The P2P process is executed on the basis of cellular automaton (CA) approach and implemented by smart contracts blockchain over a time horizon, enabling consensus to be recorded between consumers in a secure and fully automated transaction. We consider CA transition rules as the consensus algorithms of the smart contract shared in the blockchain which automatically executes predefined conditions to apply the logic of the transactions and to check their relevance [10]. The main advantages of CA modeling over existing energy sharing methods are the rapid convergence of supply and demand decisions as well as the spatial aspect in terms of an adaptive lattice. It should also be noted that this is the first time that a cellular automaton is proposed for energy sharing in micro-grids. Our CA model allows us to identify the user's state from a set of five possible states and ensures convergence of supply and demand decisions. The excess energy is automatically shared with users without intermediaries (distribution system operators or market operators). In fact, the combination of the two approaches (CA and blockchains) ensures that the system is entirely decentralized.

The rest of the document is organized as follows. In Sect. 2 we describe the CA model for P2P sharing . In Sect. 3, we present how we can implement the proposed CA on smart contract blockchain. The case study and simulation results are then presented in Sect. 4.

2   CA Model Formulation

Our CA model is based on our previous one reported in [2] that we will recall in this paper. We consider an electrical grid consisting of connected members exchanging energy with one another. Members can be consumers or prosumers and can represent residential users (homes, apartments or villas). They are equipped with a RG (e.g., solar panels or wind turbines) with batteries.

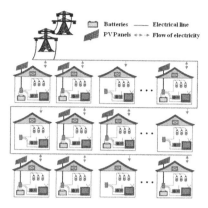

Fig. 1. CA lattice

The cells are energy consumers and prosumers arranged in a two-dimensional lattice as illustrated in Fig. 1. All cells are interconnected to their nearest neighbours via the power lines, either by conventional lines or universal interfaces.

$$\mathcal{L} = \{C_{ij}; \, i, j \in \mathbb{N}; \, i = 1, 2.., n \text{ and } j = 1, 2.., m\} \tag{1}$$

with n and m are the number of nodes cells along vertical and horizontal axis respectively.

The energy balance between supply and demand is based on the determination of the state of the cell.

The state of a cell C_{ij} is determined by a combination of three parameters, namely the amount of energy produced P_{rg}^t, consumed P_c^t and stored Q^t. In addition, the model allows us to identify the state of the participants according to five defined states:

$$\mathcal{S} = \{1, 2, 3, 4, 5\} \tag{2}$$

with

> **State 1** : *Demand satisfied$^+$*,
>
> **State 2** : *Demand satisfied$^-$*,
>
> **State 3** : *Surplus power*,
>
> **State 4** : *Power deficit*,
>
> **State 5** : *Grid connexion*.

- **Demand satisfied$^+$:** The energy produced by RG is sufficient and the excess energy is used to charge the batteries.

- **Demand satisfied⁻:** The energy produced by RG is not sufficient to meet the requested load. The priority is to use the energy stored in the batteries.
- **Surplus power:** Same as case 1, but the excess energy generated by the renewable generation is greater than the need for the load and batteries. Therefore, in this case, the surplus power is transmitted to the neighbors.
- **Power Deficit:** The energy produced by RG is not sufficient to meet the requested load and the battery bank is also exhausted. In this case the charge and the batteries are powered by the surplus power of other houses.
- **Grid connexion:** Same as case 4 but the surplus power of other houses is not sufficient to meet the requested load. Power is drawn from the grid in this case.

The state of each cell depends on a set of attributes as summarized in Table 1. The configuration of the proposed CA state is defined by Eq. 3.

$$
\mathcal{S}\left(c_{ij}, t\right) : \begin{cases}
① & \text{if } Nl^t\left(i,j\right) > 0 \quad \text{and} \quad Soc^t\left(i,j\right) \leq \alpha Soc^t_{max}\left(i,j\right) \\[2mm]
② & \text{if } Nl^t\left(i,j\right) < 0 \quad \text{and} \quad \alpha Soc^t_{max}\left(i,j\right) < Soc^t\left(i,j\right) \leq Soc^t_{max}\left(i,j\right) \\[2mm]
③ & \text{if } Nl^t\left(i,j\right) > 0 \quad \text{and} \quad \alpha Soc^t_{max}\left(i,j\right) < Soc^t\left(i,j\right) \leq Soc^t_{max}\left(i,j\right) \\[2mm]
④ & \text{if } Nl^t\left(i,j\right) < 0 \quad \text{and} \quad Soc^t\left(i,j\right) \leq \alpha Soc^t_{max}\left(i,j\right) \\[2mm]
⑤ & \text{if } Nl^t\left(i,j\right) < 0 \quad \text{and} \quad Soc^t\left(i,j\right) \leq \beta Soc^t_{max}\left(i,j\right)
\end{cases}
$$

$$(3)$$

where

$Nl^t\left(i,j\right)$ is the net load of the (i,j) cell at the time t, defined as the difference between the RG power $P^t_{rg}\left(i,j\right)$ and the power consumption $P^t_c\left(i,j\right)$ (Eq. 5).

$Soc^t\left(i,j\right)$ is the state of charge of the (i,j) battery at time t, $Soc^t_{max}\left(i,j\right)$ and $Soc^t_{min}\left(i,j\right)$ are respectively the maximum and minimum allowable state of charge.

α and β are two specified coefficients, which guarantee battery storage balancing and safety.

Table 1. Dynamic parameters of a C_{ij}

At time t	Between t and $t+1$
$P^t_{rg}\left(i,j\right)$: Renewable generation power	$P^{[t]}_{la}\left(i,j\right)$: Surplus power
$P^t_c\left(i,j\right)$: Power consumption by electrical load	$P^{[t]}_{sr}\left(i,j\right)$: Deficit power
$Q^t\left(i,j\right)$: Batteries energy storage	$P^{[t]}_c\left(i,j\right)$: Charging battery power
	$P^{[t]}_d\left(i,j\right)$: Discharging battery power
	$P^{[t]}_{im}\left(i,j\right)$: Power imported from the neighborhood
	$P^{[t]}_{tr}\left(i,j\right)$: Power exported to the neighborhood

According to the Eq. 3 the main loop of the model consist of the identified transition function $\mathcal{F}$, between instants t and $t+1$:

- State of charge (Soc) expressed by Eq. 4;
- Net load power (Nl) expressed by Eq. 5.

$$Soc^t(i,j) = \frac{Q^t(i,j)}{C_n(i,j)} \times 100 \tag{4}$$

$$Nl^t(i,j) = P_{rg}^t(i,j) - P_c^t(i,j) \tag{5}$$

Where $Q^t(i,j)$ is the stored energy by the battery at the time of interest t and $C_n(i,j)$ is the battery nominal capacity.

We consider the cost function defined by [12]. For each residential household n, the electricity cost for time interval $[t, t+\Delta t)$ during the planning horizon starting at time t_0 is defined by Eq. 6, where $C_{low} < C_{high}$ reflects the lower cost of Solar generation. The electricity cost is an increasing function of load [11].

$$C_{e,r}^t(i,j) : \begin{cases} \gamma_n^{t_0}(i,j)\left[C_{low}\left(L^t\right)^2\right] & \text{if } L^t \le l_{gen}^t \\ \\ \gamma_n^{t_0}(i,j)\left[C_{low}\left(l_{gen}^t\right)^2 + C_{high}\left(L^t - l_{gen}^t\right)^2\right] & \text{otherwise} \end{cases} \tag{6}$$

Where l_{gen}^t is the total energy obtained from solar PV generation, L^t is total electricity requirement for all consumers and $\gamma_n^{t_0}$ is the the share of electricity consumption for user n starting at time t_0, given by Eq. 7

$$\gamma_n^{t_0}(i,j) = \frac{\sum_{i=0}^{N-1} l_{gen}^{t_0+i\Delta t}}{\sum_{i=0}^{N-1} L^{t_0+i\Delta t}} \tag{7}$$

3   CA Modeling for Smart Contract

The smart contract are a set of executable functions resides at a specific address on the Ethereum blockchain [10], first proposed in 1996 by Szabo [15]. The smart contract also called blockchain contracts is written as code in programming language Solidity or Serpent [1] and compiled on the Ethereum Virtual Machine (EVM) [6]. The implementation of the CA on the smart contract is possible by considering the configuration of our CA model expressed by Eq. 3 as the collection of the smart contract code and data.

In the P2P energy sharing of our model, participants are free to participate or not in the consensus algorithm. Each participant has its own numerical identity called Decentralized Identifier (DID) which can be integrated on the blockchain as a identity service [14]. The use of a DID with a user interface is necessary to set up a decentralized identity network based on Ethereum and to prove access to the microgrid and the P2P system.

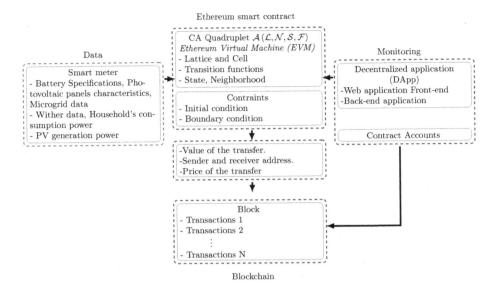

Ethereum smart contract

Fig. 2. Principle of the proposed Blockchain-based CA approach

The blockchain network is public, any user wishing to benefit from an energy exchange and who has the evidence and conditions of a valid prosumer can join it and obtain an identity. The execution of the AC algorithm (smart contract code in our case) provides information on the power to be imported and exported in the neighborhoods for each participant, called P_{im} and P_{tr} respectively. We also consider these amounts of Ether energy transfer from one account to another as the blockchain transactions between participants executed in Ethereum.

At each stage of the simulation, the participant receives a message consisting of the sender and receiver address, the value and the price of the transfer. The smart contract code is executed again at step $t + \Delta t$. If a participant no longer needs to participate in the P2P energy system, he is free to deactivate his account, in this case the network of our CA model is reformulated and the smart contract code is automatically modified. The Fig. 2 gives an overview of the system described above.

4   Simulation

4.1   Case Study

In order to test our P2P energy exchange model in a micro-grid, an application case based on Dubai in the Mohammed bin Rashid Al Maktoum solar park is studied. 15 solar energy houses are considered. The houses are the 15 teams that participated in the Solar Decathlon Middle East (SDME) competition, held in Dubai from 14 to 29 November 2018.

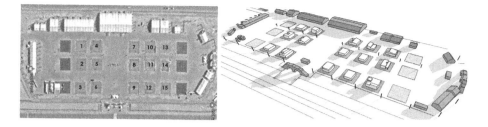

Fig. 3. Arrangement of the 15 houses in the SDME Microgrid

Solar decathlon is the world's largest green building competition, created by the US Department of Energy, that challenges college teams to design, build and assemble solar-powered homes [13]. Two reasons explain the choice of the SDME as the application case:

– The 15 teams are arranged in a 2D lattice in the form of a micro-grid connected to the grid which is similar to the configuration of our AC model (Fig. 3)
– the electrical data collected during the two weeks of the competition are available free on the SDME website [7]. The data comprises: PV output power, energy consumption, grid consumption and injection of excess power into the grid as shown in Fig. 4.

4.2   Evaluation of Energy Sharing Results

We consider the data of a contest period "18-9-2018" for 24 h (Fig. 4). According to these data we run our CA model as shown in Fig. 5. The following color connotation are consedired to represent the state set of houses given by Eq. 2: ■ State 1 ■ State 2   State 3 ■ State 4, ■ State 5.

At Iteration 0 (12:00 am) it is seen from Fig. 4a and Fig. 4c that the power produced by the PV panels and the power sent to the grid are both null. The load is powered by batteries, except for houses that are not equipped with them (2, 5 and 10), in which case the charge is drawn from the grid as illustrated in Fig. 4d. This situation is confirmed by the simulation as is shown in Fig. 5a, in which all cells are in state 2 ■, except for the three houses with no storage banks (state 5 ■). The cells maintain the same states for the next iterations until iteration 6 (3:00 am), when two houses change their state. House number 5 reports a lack of energy (state 4 ■) and house number 10 changes to state 1 ■, meaning that team HW's batteries are down to less than 40% and that team VT's house has started producing its own energy. The experimental data confirms this state change; team VT generated a cumulative power equal to 5 kWh in that period (Fig. 4a). Due to the early sunrise in Dubai (06:05 am), houses with east-facing solar panels such as VT, VQ and USI started producing electricity at 06:00 am. These three houses are shown in blue in the simulation

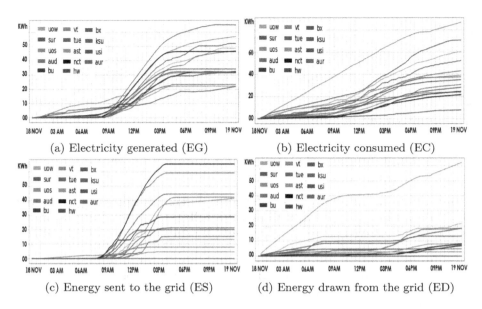

(a) Electricity generated (EG)

(b) Electricity consumed (EC)

(c) Energy sent to the grid (ES)

(d) Energy drawn from the grid (ED)

Fig. 4. Electrical data collected by the 15 houses on a typical day during the contest period (September 18, 2018) (Color figure online)

(Fig. 5e). The other teams covered their power deficit either through the grid (BXN, CT, HW and UOW) or using batteries (all the remaining teams). For the next four hours (from 4:00 am to 8:00 am), the loading profile is generally stable. The supply and demand for battery-equipped teams is well balanced. The total power consumed during the night is 85 kWh and the total storage capacity of the battery banks is 102 kWh. The loads of the houses is therefore satisfied. Additionally, for the three houses without batteries (BX, UOW, VT), electricity is drawn from the grid. P2P sharing of electricity up to iteration 18 does not yet work, no energy exchange takes place between neighbors due to general lack of excess energy in the microgrid. At iteration 22 (11:00 am), the solar radiation on site is greater than 700 w/m^2, the cumulative power produced (EG) varies between 4.5 kWh (AUD team) and 15 kWh (VT team). The power produced by PV systems is greater than the consumption, so all houses have a surplus of energy. 8 teams have used this surplus to recharge their batteries and the rest have fed it into the grid. 60 min later, due to significant variations in the load, house number 4 (UOS) declares its energy needs as shown in Fig. 5m. Here we see the CA in action, also according to smart contract conditions a neighbors with excess energy (NCT) automatically meet these needs and begin to exchange the requested energy to balance the energy flows. The block is created after validation of the trasaction. These simulation results are validated by the actual data presented in Fig. 4a, Fig. 4c and Fig. 4d, in which there is a significant increase in the amount of electricity produced by photovoltaic panels and the electrical energy sent to the grid, but the electrical energy drawn from

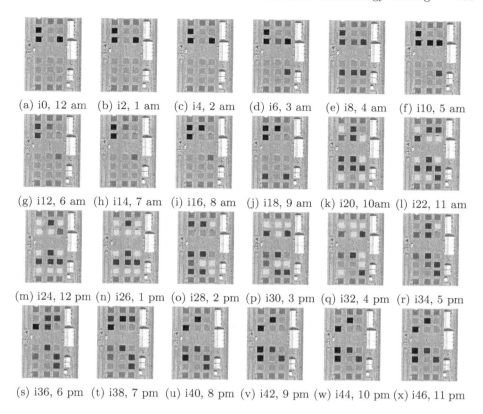

(a) i0, 12 am   (b) i2, 1 am   (c) i4, 2 am   (d) i6, 3 am   (e) i8, 4 am   (f) i10, 5 am

(g) i12, 6 am (h) i14, 7 am (i) i16, 8 am (j) i18, 9 am (k) i20, 10am (l) i22, 11 am

(m) i24, 12 pm (n) i26, 1 pm (o) i28, 2 pm (p) i30, 3 pm (q) i32, 4 pm (r) i34, 5 pm

(s) i36, 6 pm (t) i38, 7 pm (u) i40, 8 pm (v) i42, 9 pm (w) i44, 10 pm (x) i46, 11 pm

Fig. 5. Evolution of the state of cells in the 15 houses on a typical day during the contest period (September 18, 2018) (Color figure online)

the grid plateaus. The principle of cellular automaton also appears clearly in the next iterations, in which energy exchange between teams is possible due to the excess energy available in the microgrid.

5   Conclusion

In this paper, a new model for P2P energy sharing in microgrid is proposed. The model is based on a cellular automaton approach with a blockchain contracts. The necessary consensus algorithm between users is obtained by executing the CA transition function. Simulations illustrating our approach are presented by an application case. In summary, the model presented in this paper demonstrates the potential of implementing the CA with Smart Contract to solve energy management applications. The comparison between simulation results and experimental data has shown a convergence of supply and demand decisions towards a state of energy equilibrium.

Acknowledgments. This work has been supported by MESRSFC and CNRST under the project PPR2-OGI-Env, reference PPR2/2016/79.

References

1. Ethereum Revision 8dda9521. Solidity, v0.6.3. https://solidity.readthedocs.io/en/v0.6.3/. 2016–2020
2. Abdennour, I., Ouardouz, M., Bernoussi, A.S.: Peer-to-peer energy sharing using cellular automata approach. In: Ezziyyani, M. (ed.) AI2SD 2019. LNEE, vol. 624, pp. 221–228. Springer, Cham (2020). https://doi.org/10.1007/978-3-030-36475-5_21
3. Albrecht, S.. Reichert, S., Schmid, J., Strüker, J., Neumann, D., Fridgen, G.: Dynamics of blockchain implementation-a case study from the energy sector. In: Proceedings of the 51st Hawaii International Conference on System Sciences (2018)
4. Andoni, M., et al.: Blockchain technology in the energy sector: a systematic review of challenges and opportunities. Renew. Sustain. Energy Rev. **100**, 143–174 (2019)
5. Brilliantova, V., Thurner, T.W.: Blockchain and the future of energy. Technol. Soc. **57**, 38–45 (2019)
6. Dannen, C.: Introducing Ethereum and Solidity, vol. 1. Springer, Heidelberg (2017). https://doi.org/10.1007/978-1-4842-2535-6
7. Dubai Electricity Dubai Supreme Council of Energy, Water Authority, and the U.S. Department of Energy. Solar decathlon middle east competition (2018). https://sdme-contest.com
8. IRENA: Global energy transformation: a roadmap to 2050 (2018)
9. Jiang, Y., Zhou, K., Xinhui, L., Yang, S.: Electricity trading pricing among prosumers with game theory-based model in energy blockchain environment. Appl. Energy **271**, 115239 (2020)
10. Karamitsos, I., Papadaki, M., Barghuthi, N.B.A.: Design of the blockchain smart contract: a use case for real estate. J. Inf. Secur. **9**(3), 177–190 (2018)
11. Li, Y., Yang, W., He, P., Chen, C., Wang, X.: Design and management of a distributed hybrid energy system through smart contract and blockchain. Appl. Energy **248**, 390–405 (2019)
12. Mohsenian-Rad, A.-H., Wong, V.W.S., Jatskevich, J., Schober, R., Leon-Garcia, A.: Autonomous demand-side management based on game-theoretic energy consumption scheduling for the future smart grid. IEEE Trans. Smart Grid **1**(3), 320–331 (2010)
13. U.S. Department of Energy. Solar decathlon (2020). https://www.solardecathlon.gov/about.html
14. Reed, D., Sporny, M., Longley, D., Allen, C., Grant, R., Sabadello, M.: Decentralized identifiers (dids) v0. 11. W3C, Draft Community Group Report, 9 (2018)
15. Szabo, N.: Smart contracts: building blocks for digital markets. EXTROPY: J. Transhumanist Thought (16) **18**(2) (1996)
16. Utz, M., Albrecht, S., Zoerner, T., Strüker, J.: Blockchain-based management of shared energy assets using a smart contract ecosystem. In: Abramowicz, W., Paschke, A. (eds.) BIS 2018. LNBIP, vol. 339, pp. 217–222. Springer, Cham (2019). https://doi.org/10.1007/978-3-030-04849-5_19
17. Wang, N., et al.: When energy trading meets blockchain in electrical power system: the state of the art. Appl. Sci. **9**(8), 1561 (2019)
18. Zhang, H., Wang, J., Ding, Y.: Blockchain-based decentralized and secure keyless signature scheme for smart grid. Energy **180**, 955–967 (2019)

Influence of Topology on the Dynamics of in Silico Ecosystems with Non-hierarchical Competition

Gisele H. B. Miranda[1,2,3]([envelope]) [ID], Jan M. Baetens[2] [ID], Aisling J. Daly[2] [ID],
Odemir M. Bruno[3] [ID], and Bernard De Baets[2] [ID]

[1] School of Electrical Engineering and Computer Science,
KTH Royal Institute of Technology, Lindstedtsvägen 3, 10044 Stockholm, Sweden
gmirand@kth.se
[2] KERMIT, Department of Data Analysis and Mathematical Modelling,
Faculty of Bioscience Engineering, Ghent University, Gent, Belgium
[3] Scientific Computing Group, São Carlos Institute of Physics,
University of São Paulo, São Carlos, SP, Brazil

Abstract. The extinction of ecosystems and the mechanisms that support or limit species coexistence have long been studied by scientists. It has been shown that competition and cyclic dominance among species promote species coexistence, such as in the classic Rock-Paper-Scissors (RPS) game. However, individuals' mobility and the underlying topology that defines the neighbourhood relations between individuals also play an important role in maintaining biodiversity. Typically, square grids are used for simulating such interactions. However, these constrain the individuals' spatial degrees of freedom. In this work, we investigate the effect of the underlying topology on the RPS dynamics. For that purpose, we considered networks with varying node degree distributions and generated according to different theoretical models. We analyzed the time to the first extinction and the patchiness of the *in silico* ecosystem over time. In general, we observed a distinct large effect of the network topology on the RPS dynamics. Moreover, leaving regular networks aside, the probability of extinction is very high for some network models due to their inherent long-range connections. On the other hand, spatial arrangements characterized by nearest neighbors interactions have fewer long-range correlations, which is essential for biodiversity.

Keywords: Non-hierarchical competition · Biodiversity maintenance · Network topology

1 Introduction

One of the most intriguing questions for ecologists relates to whether biodiversity can be maintained in an ecosystem. The mechanisms that support or limit species coexistence have long been investigated [11,12]. Extinction is related to the loss

© Springer Nature Switzerland AG 2021
T. M. Gwizdałła et al. (Eds.): ACRI 2020, LNCS 12599, pp. 113–122, 2021.
https://doi.org/10.1007/978-3-030-69480-7_12

of biodiversity, while it has been shown that competition is one of the mechanisms that supports biodiversity, particularly when it is intransitive [10], as the case of cyclic competition. Previous works show that cyclic dominance among species is one of the factors that promotes their coexistence and contributes to maintaining biodiversity. Different mathematical models incorporate such cyclic dominance, among which the rock-paper-scissors (RPS) game is a classic example. The RPS has a strong background in evolutionary game theory and is widely used as a model to describe species diversity [8,14,16]. In this model, three species interact in a non-hierarchical way, so that each species has one predator, and, at the same time, it preys on another species. Examples of such behavior in nature include bacterial species [9], coral reefs [3], vertebrates [2], some human decision-making processes [20], amongst others.

Although very important for maintaining biodiversity, coexistence is not only supported by cyclic competition. Other mechanisms should also be taken into account [8,16]. Community evenness and the individuals' mobility also play important roles when modeling evolutionary systems. The first is related to the species distribution, which is often assumed to be uniform [5]. Mobility, on the other hand, is crucial in different ecosystems and can be driven by demographic processes that are resource-dependent. For instance, the coexistence of species can be mediated by their dispersal, but there might exist a critical threshold mobility above which biodiversity is lost [14,15]. The most common topologies used to simulate the interactions among species are square grids, which strongly limit the individuals' spatial degrees of freedom. To a much lesser extent, graphs have been considered [11,18,19]. Given that studies show that system dynamics can be affected by the underlying topology [4,13], we investigate how the structural properties of networks influence the RPS dynamics. For this purpose, we generated networks using different theoretical models, e.g., random, small-world, scale-free, and others. We will first introduce the RPS model proposed by Reichenbach et al. [14], after which we will present some related work concerning RPS on small-world networks. Finally, we will describe our experiments and present our results.

2   Spatially Explicit Rock-Paper-Scissors Game

The RPS game mimics cyclic competition in which species A (rock) outcompetes species B (scissors), species B outcompetes species C (paper), and, species C, in turn, outcompetes species A. A regular grid is mostly used to simulate the RPS game in space, where it is assumed that local interactions are taking place only between the nearest neighbors. However, other irregular topologies can, as well, be used for modeling the RPS game. Figure 1(a) illustrates a network with N sites that can be either unoccupied or occupied by an individual from one of three species. Figure 1(b) illustrates the possible interactions between individuals according to the grid RPS game. Reproduction occurs at a rate μ when an empty site is occupied by an individual from a neighboring species, while selection happens at rate α occurs according to the cyclic competition

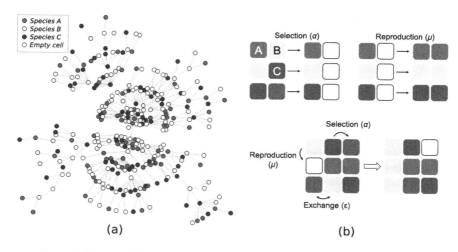

Fig. 1. The RPS game. (a) Irregular topology illustrating a possible configuration with three species and empty sites. (b) RPS transition rules: Selection, reproduction and exchange occur at rates α, μ and ε, respectively.

scheme. Finally, neighbouring individuals can exchange positions at rate ε. In this way, local interactions of reproduction and selection take place along with the migration of individuals. The above interactions can be described by rate equations that account for the population densities of each species through time. As such, RPS is a frequency-dependent model [11]. Alternatively, in the continuum limit, the interactions can also be described by partial differential equations (PDEs) [5,6]. Reichenbach *et al.* [14,15] describe the same rate equations as complex PDEs, which can give rise to spiral waves. The authors show that the spiral wavelengths can be associated with critical mobility values, above which the species co-existence is not possible. For low mobility values, species diversity is maintained for a longer time due to the fact that reproduction and selection will occur relatively more frequently. However, when mobility is high, biodiversity is lost due to the spatial homogenisation.

2.1   Individual-Based Modeling

Individual-based models allow the study of a system by explicitly tracking the interactions among individuals instead of doing this at population level. Here, we present a computational method that uses a stochastic individual-based approach for simulating the RPS dynamics. This method was proposed in [14] and was already employed using regular grids [5,6].

Given a regular grid of size $L \times L = N$, reproduction, selection and mobility occur at rates μ, α and ε. These processes are implemented according to a modified version of the Gillespie algorithm [7], which is frequently used for modeling biological and chemical systems. Initially, individuals of the three species and empty sites are randomly assigned following a uniform distribution. Then,

---

Algorithm 1. Gillespie algorithm for simulating RPS dynamics.

1: **procedure** GILLESPIE(L, t_{end})
2:     *set*: μ, α, ε
3:     $N = L \times L$
4:     $t = 0$
5:     $r = \mu + \alpha + \varepsilon$
6:
7:     **while** $t \neq t_{end}$ **do**
8:         *select site* s_i ▷ randomly draw a site of the grid
9:         *select a neighboring site* s_j ▷ randomly draw a neighbor site of s_i
10:        *select interaction:*
11:            *reproduction, with probability* μ/r
12:            *selection, with probability* α/r
13:            *exchange, with probability* ε/r
14:
15:        **if** *interaction is possible* **then**
16:            *update* s_i *and* s_j *accordingly*
17:
18:        $t = t + 1$

---

subsequent steps are carried out according to Algorithm 1. In this algorithm, t is the time step and r is a normalization factor for drawing the probability of each interaction. At each time step, a site s_i of the grid (focal site) and one of its neighbors s_j are drawn at random. Next, an interaction is chosen by drawing a random number from the interval $[0, r]$, given the following probabilities: μ/r (reproduction), α/r (selection) and ε/r (migration). If the selected interaction can occur among individuals in s_i and s_j, then their states are updated in accordance with the RPS rules. This procedure is repeated for t time steps. Due to the asynchronous update scheme, updates are clustered into generations, which define the Monte Carlo (MC) steps. One MC step corresponds to the number of time steps for which, on average, each individual will be selected once for an interaction event. Here, we chose the grid size ($N = L \times L$) as an MC step. Reichenbach *et al.* found that the area explored by one individual per time unit is $M \sim 2\varepsilon N^{-1}$, which is also referred to as the *mobility rate*.

2.2   From Regular Grids to Irregular Tessellations

RPS dynamics can be affected by the structure on which the underlying processes are taking place [11]. Spatial constraints are relevant to real-world problems, such as biological systems restricted to two-dimensional substrates (e.g. biofilms), since spatial structures favor the interaction with nearest neighbors and can be used for modeling different coexistence strategies. However, using graphs for modeling interactions is more realistic for many real-world systems [11]. Several works address how small-world topologies can be used for evolving competition dynamics. Between the uniformity of the regular grids and the randomness of stochastic networks [21], small-world networks have been used to simulate many real-world phenomena. Szabó *et al.* investigated RPS dynamics on topologies ranging from regular grids to random graphs [18,19]. They discuss how the species distribution is affected by the system dynamics using a modified grid for which connections are rewired but the degree of each site is kept constant, using a procedure very similar to the transition of a regular to a random network. The resulting spatio-temporal RPS patterns remain stable when only a few rewiring steps occur, but species coexistence might be lost. Other works discuss how coexistence is maintained as a function of structural changes, individuals' mobility or the dispersal rate [1,11,17,22]. Motivated by these works, we investigated the influence of the network topology on the coexistence of species governed by the RPS rules.

3   RPS on Networks

When resorting to networks, RPS defines cyclic competition among species A, B and C that now occupy the nodes of a network. We performed extensive simulations and analyses to assess how the structural characteristics of the network affect species coexistence, and hence biodiversity, of *in silico* communities governed by cyclic relations.

3.1   Experimental Design

We evaluated synthetic networks that were generated according to five theoretical network models: random, small-world, scale-free and regular networks. Similarly to regular grids, the regular networks also have a uniform degree distribution, but the node arrangement is different. Besides structural differences, we also consider networks from the same family with a different mean degree $\langle k \rangle$ and number of nodes N. The networks considered in our study have $\langle k \rangle$ equal to 4, 6, 8 or 10 and N equal to 400, 900, 1600 or 10000. The species interactions were implemented according to Algorithm 1. The number of Monte Carlo generations for each simulation is proportional to N. For all simulations we set $\mu = \alpha = 1$, while mobility M was varied between 10^{-12} and 10^{-2}. The mobility is calculated as a function of the exchange rate ε and N, in the same way as for regular grids ($M \sim 2\varepsilon N^{-1}$). We carried out 50 simulations for each combination of network model, $\langle k \rangle$ and, N, with different initial configurations, which were defined according to a uniform distribution involving the three species and the empty sites.

3.2   Results

Probability of Extinction. The probability of extinction reflects the chance that two species go extinct after a certain time t and is proportional to the grid size $t(N) \propto N$. The number of simulations in which the species went extinct after a certain time t versus the total number of simulations is the probability of extinction. In order to calculate this probability, we considered 50 simulations

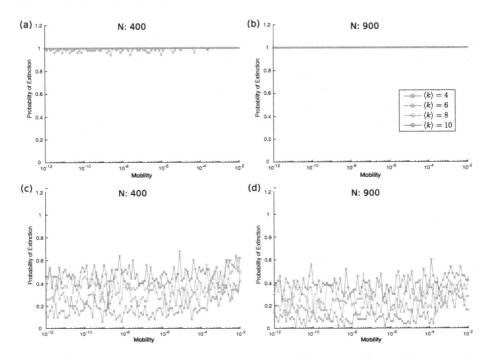

Fig. 2. Probability of extinction as a function of mobility for scale-free networks with $N = 400$ and $N = 1600$. Each curve corresponds to a different average degree, $\langle k \rangle$.

for each combination of network model, $\langle k \rangle$ and N. Figures 2(a) and (b) show the probability of extinction as a function of mobility M for scale-free networks with $N = 400$ and $N = 900$ for different values of $\langle k \rangle$. Irrespective of the average degree or the network size, we observe that the probability of extinction is always high, which is in contrast to the regular grid case. This is largely due to the existence of a few nodes with long range connections in networks with scale-free degree distributions. A few exceptions occur for networks with low $\langle k \rangle$, which is related to the fact that there are fewer connections in such networks. This implies a longer time to extinction. Figures 2(c) and (d) show the same plots for regular networks with the same connectivity and size as the analyzed scale-free networks. In this case, the probability of extinction is much smaller for all values of N. Due to the absence of long-range connections, the clustering coefficient [21] of the network is higher and there are many local interactions, which is similar as when considering grids. Additionally, as $\langle k \rangle$ increases, the probability of extinction also increases, due to a larger number of connections that can favor species selection. This is observed for all values of N. RPS on random, small-world and geographical networks leads to a similar behavior as on scale-free networks, even when considering very low mobility values. The probability of extinction is very high in almost all situations.

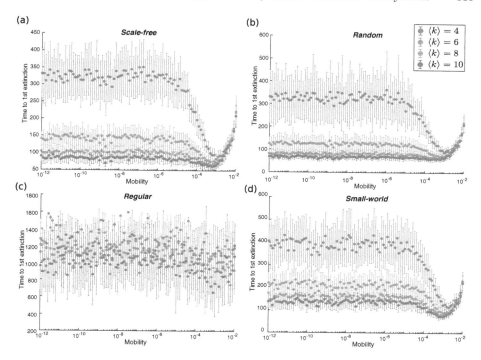

Fig. 3. Average time to the first extinction as a function of mobility for scale-free, random, regular and small-world networks, with $N = 1600$ and different $\langle k \rangle$ values.

Time to the First Extinction. We also analyzed the average time to the first species extinction. The obtained results are shown in Fig. 3 for different network models with $N = 1600$. For computing the average time to the first extinction, only the simulations in which at least one species went extinct are taken into account. We can observe in Fig. 3 that the species go extinct faster than one MC step (N updates), irrespective of N or $\langle k \rangle$ for scale-free, random and small-world networks. In addition, the lower the average node degree, the longer the time to the first extinction irrespective of the number of nodes and mobility. However, as N increases, the average time to the first extinction also increases. For higher mobility values, there is a steep increase of the time to the first extinction, especially for larger N. This can be explained by the fact that as mobility increases, exchange events will happen more frequently as compared to competition and selection events. In the case of small-world networks, the rewiring process from which they are constructed creates enough long-range connections that speed up extinction, though they have many short-range connections (high clustering coefficient). Regarding regular networks (Fig. 3(c)), the effect of the average degree on the time to the first extinction is smaller as compared to the other network families. Networks with $\langle k \rangle = 4$ also require more time to the first extinction, since their connectivity is lower. Since regular networks had the lowest probabil-

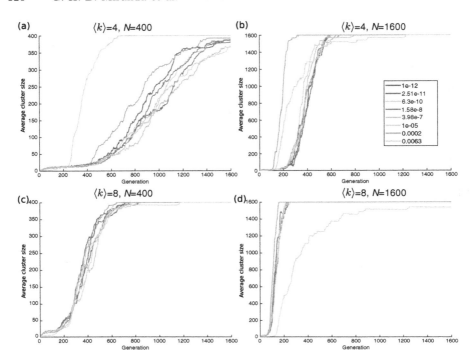

Fig. 4. Average cluster size per MC step for scale-free networks with different N and $\langle k \rangle$. Each curve corresponds to a fixed mobility value.

ities of extinction (Figs. 2(c) and (d)), the time to the first extinction for these networks was averaged over a smaller number of simulations, thereby increasing the standard deviation.

Patchiness. We also analyzed the patchiness of the evolved patterns. This measures how closely individuals from the same species are clustered. For this purpose, we calculated the average cluster size per time step. A cluster is a series of connected nodes occupied by individuals of the same species. At the beginning of the simulation, the species are uniformly distributed, so there are many small clusters. The average cluster size will increase during simulation and how fast this happens depends on the network family, $\langle k \rangle$ and N. Figure 4 shows the average cluster size as a function of the MC steps for scale-free networks with $N = 400$ and $N = 1600$, and $\langle k \rangle = 4$ and $\langle k \rangle = 8$. Each curve in Fig. 4 corresponds to a fixed mobility value. The higher the value of $\langle k \rangle$, the more similar the curves are across the range of mobility values. Note that the system is already a monoculture when the average cluster size is equal to N. In addition, when extinction occurs faster, the maximum cluster size is also reached faster. We also observe that the time to monoculture is proportional to the system size, N, and, for a very high mobility, it takes a longer time to extinction (Fig. 3), so more time is required for the system to reach the maximum cluster size. In conclusion, for the scale-free networks, the lower the number of nodes and the lower the values of $\langle k \rangle$, the lower the extinction at the highest mobility values (Fig. 4). Moreover, increasing $\langle k \rangle$ and/or increasing N will result in a faster increase of the cluster size. The same experiments were carried out for scale-free networks with different sizes ($N = 900$ and $N = 10000$) and different network families. For $N = 10000$ the effect of high mobility is even more pronounced. The same conclusions also hold for random and small-world networks. For regular networks, the average cluster size increases smoothly. In this case, the probability of extinction is very low and although the average cluster size increases over time, in most of the simulations, it does not reach the maximum size. Consequently, the clusters grow in size which means that individuals belonging to the same species tend to group together more. This situation corresponds to an increase of the spiral wavelengths for the grid case, as discussed in Sect. 2.1.

4   Conclusion

In general, for the different network families analyzed in this work, we observed a considerable influence of the topology on the RPS dynamics. Likewise, except for regular networks, the probability of extinction is very high for the different network families and network configurations, due to their long-range connections. In most experiments the time to the first extinction is shorter than one MC step. As in the grid-based RPS, we observed a similar spatial clustering of species before extinction. As the system evolves, the species are arranged in larger clusters. Additionally, based on these extensive simulations and corroborating preliminary studies, we conclude that not only the mobility of the species has an important impact on the evolved dynamics, but also their connectedness. Spatial arrangements restricted to nearest neighbors interactions have fewer long-range correlations, and therefore favor biodiversity. Meanwhile, random or scale-free networks did not promote species diversity, with a short time to first extinction. For small-world networks, biodiversity depends on the rewiring probability used to generate such networks. Still, rewiring just a few links is enough to introduce long-range connections and therefore threaten biodiversity. Regular networks are closer to the grid case. The probability of extinction for regular networks is lower than on a grid, even for higher mobility. In general, for random, scale-free and small-world networks, the lower the degree ($\langle k \rangle$), the longer the time to first extinction, irrespective of the number of nodes and mobility. In addition, the higher the number of nodes, the longer the time to the first extinction at high mobility.

References

1. Bastolla, U., Lässig, M., Manrubia, S.C., Valleriani, A.: Biodiversity in model ecosystems, I: coexistence conditions for competing species. J. Theor. Biol. **235**(4), 521–530 (2005)

2. Bleay, C., Comendant, T., Sinervo, B.: An experimental test of frequency-dependent selection on male mating strategy in the field. Proc. R. Soc. London B: Biol. Sci. **274**(1621), 2019–2025 (2007)
3. Buss, L., Jackson, J.: Competitive networks: nontransitive competitive relationships in cryptic coral reef environments. Am. Nat. **113**(2), 223–234 (1979)
4. Costa, L.F., et al.: Analyzing and modeling real-world phenomena with complex networks: a survey of applications. Adv. Phys. **60**(3), 329–412 (2011)
5. Daly, A.J., Baetens, J.M., De Baets, B.: The impact of initial evenness on biodiversity maintenance for a four-species in silico bacterial community. J. Theor. Biol. **387**, 189–205 (2015)
6. Daly, A.J., Baetens, J.M., De Baets, B.: In silico substrate dependence increases community productivity but threatens biodiversity. Phys. Rev. E **93**(4), 042414 (2016)
7. Gillespie, D.T.: A general method for numerically simulating the stochastic time evolution of coupled chemical reactions. J. Comput. Phys. **22**(4), 403–434 (1976)
8. Kerr, B., Riley, M.A., Feldman, M.W., Bohannan, B.J.: Local dispersal promotes biodiversity in a real-life game of rock-paper-scissors. Nature **418**(6894), 171 (2002)
9. Kirkup, B.C., Riley, M.A.: Antibiotic-mediated antagonism leads to a bacterial game of rock-paper-scissors in vivo. Nature **428**(6981), 412 (2004)
10. Laird, R.A., Schamp, B.S.: Competitive intransitivity promotes species coexistence. Am. Nat. **168**(2), 182–193 (2006)
11. Laird, R.A., Schamp, B.S.: Competitive intransitivity, population interaction structure, and strategy coexistence. J. Theor. Biol. **365**, 149–158 (2015)
12. Mendes, R.S., Evangelista, L.R., Thomaz, S.M., Agostinho, A.A., Gomes, L.C.: A unified index to measure ecological diversity and species rarity. Ecography **31**(4), 450–456 (2008)
13. Newmann, M., Barabási, A.L., Watts, D.: The Structure and Dynamics of Networks. Princeton Studies in Complexity (2006)
14. Reichenbach, T., Mobilia, M., Frey, E.: Mobility promotes and jeopardizes biodiversity in rock-paper-scissors games. Nature **448**(7157), 1046 (2007)
15. Reichenbach, T., Mobilia, M., Frey, E.: Self-organization of mobile populations in cyclic competition. J. Theor. Biol. **254**(2), 368–383 (2008)
16. Rulquin, C., Arenzon, J.J.: Globally synchronized oscillations in complex cyclic games. Phys. Rev. E **89**(3), 032133 (2014)
17. Schreiber, S.J., Killingback, T.P.: Spatial heterogeneity promotes coexistence of rock-paper-scissors metacommunities. Theor. Popul. Biol. **86**, 1–11 (2013)
18. Szabó, G., Szolnoki, A., Izsák, R.: Rock-scissors-paper game on regular small-world networks. J. Phys. A: Math. Gen. **37**(7), 2599 (2004)
19. Szolnoki, A., Szabó, G.: Phase transitions for rock-scissors-paper game on different networks. Phys. Rev. E **70**(3), 037102 (2004)
20. Tversky, A.: Intransitivity of preferences. Psychol. Rev. **76**(1), 31 (1969)
21. Watts, D.J.: Small Worlds: The Dynamics of Networks Between Order and Randomness. Princeton University Press, Princeton (1999)
22. Zhang, G.Y., Chen, Y., Qi, W.K., Qing, S.M.: Four-state rock-paper-scissors games in constrained Newman-Watts networks. Phys. Rev. E **79**(6), 062901 (2009)

Control of 3D Cellular Automata via Actuator and Space Attributes: Application to Fires Forest

Mohamed Byari[1]([✉]), Abdes Samed Bernoussi[1], Mustapha Ouardouz[2], and Mina Amharref[1]

[1] Faculty of Sciences and Techniques, Geoinformation et Aménagement du Territoire, GAT, Tangier, Morocco
mohamedbyari@gmail.com, a.samed.bernoussi@gmail.com, amharrefm@yahoo.fr
[2] Faculty of Sciences and Techniques, Mathematic Modeling and Control, MMC, Tangier, Morocco
ouardouz@gmail.com

Abstract. In this work, we consider the control problem for a phenomenon modeled by Cellular Automata (CA) through actuators and attributes. To achieve this, we introduce what we called attributes and the adaptation of the definition of actuators to the CA in connection with attributes. The proposed control is then given through the attributes and not directly on the state of the system, as was the case in previous works like for the additive (elementary) CA. To illustrate our approach, we consider the fire forest control problem in the 3D cellular automata.

Keywords: Actuators · Attributes · Controllability · 3D Cellular automata · Fire forest

1 Introduction

Environmental problems have attracted the attention of the scientific community in recent decades. Among these problems are those of forest fires. Various studies and models have been carried out, mainly by ecologists or biologists to understand the nature of these phenomena and to highlight the factors involved.

To better understand these dynamic systems and their evolution, above all to better control them, some concepts have been introduced in the framework of systems theory. Among these concepts, those of controllability and observability have been widely studied [1,2]. To link these abstract concepts to the application, the notions of sensors, actuators and strategic actuators have been introduced [3,4].

In recent decades, systems theory has contributed to the development of Cellular Automata (CA) as a particular discrete system [5–7]. Since then, their computational efficiency, simplicity of implementation and relevance to the realities of complex macroscopic systems have made them attractive modeling tools. CA

© Springer Nature Switzerland AG 2021
T. M. Gwizdałła et al. (Eds.): ACRI 2020, LNCS 12599, pp. 123–133, 2021.
https://doi.org/10.1007/978-3-030-69480-7_13

are becoming increasingly popular and represent a good alternative to PDE for modeling, analysis, and control of complex and heterogeneous systems, including natural behavioral systems described in terms of the local interactions of their components [8]. The work of El Yacoubi and El Jai [9, 10] in early 2000 considers the basis for the controllability of CA. They deal with the cases of particular CA such as additive CA or boolean one in 1D and 2D [11, 12].

In this work we propose an approach to control CA-modelled dynamic systems using actuators and attributes. Specifically, we defined an attribute as a spatial characteristic that influences the dynamic behavior of the system. While actuators are the intermediaries between a system and its environment, they serve to excite the system, which leads us to study the notion of controllability via its structures. We propose a control function that aims to minimize the normalized Hamming distance between the end state and the desired state of the CA by using actuators to excite the attributes of space. Moreover, we consider as an application case the control of local forest fires, modeled by a 3D AC, and we simulate two different control strategies: one in which the actuators support is chosen arbitrarily, while in the second, it is defined only in the burning cells and their neighborhood. The results are then compared to an uncontrolled simulation of the same system, where no actuator is applied and the forest fire evolves without constraint. For the simulations, we use a 3D LIDAR scanner for spatial data. This document is organized as follows. We start with a recall of the CA description in the 3D case and we define the attributes. We present, then the adaptation of the control and actuator definition via attributes. Simulations results are given later to illustrate our approach using a developed simulator.

2   3D Cellular Automata (3D-CA): Generalities

A cellular automaton is defined by the quadruple

$$\mathcal{A} = (\mathcal{L}, \mathcal{N}, \mathcal{S}, f). \tag{1}$$

Where

- $\mathcal{L}$ is the lattice. In the three-dimensional case $\mathcal{L} = \{c_{i,j,k}; \; i, j, k \in \mathbb{Z}\}$.
- $\mathcal{N}(c)$ is the neighborhood. The $D_n Q_m$ model is used to classify the different choices of lattice and neighborhood. Where n is the dimension of lattice and m is the number of neighborhood cells (Fig. 1).
- $\mathcal{S}$ is the states set : $\mathcal{S} = \{s_1, s_2, \ldots, s_n\}; \quad n \in \mathbb{N}$.
- f is the local transition rule. f calculates the state of a c cell based on the state of its neighborhood.

In the following section we define the attribute structure and its relationship with the local transition rules.

3   The Attributes

The quality of a model depends closely on how accurately this later describes the observed phenomena. Hence the interest of CA, not only in describing the system's evolution through a local view but also in their capacity to consider space heterogeneity, in relation to the properties or attributes that character-ize the space. Here an attribute represents a static or dynamic property that characterizes a cell according to the considered phenomenon.

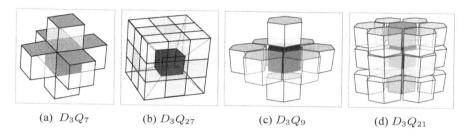

(a) D_3Q_7 (b) D_3Q_{27} (c) D_3Q_9 (d) D_3Q_{21}

Fig. 1. Neighborhoods examples in cubic and hexagonal 3D geometry cells

Definition 1 (Attribute)

- *For a given phenomenon the set attributes is the set of all space characteris-tics, σ_i, that influence the system's evolution.*

$$\mathbb{A} = \{\sigma_1, \cdots, \sigma_m\} \tag{2}$$

- *The Attribute function is a map that associates to each cell of the lattice at an instant t_τ, a value in a bounded set F_σ that constitutes the value of the property.*

$$\begin{aligned}\sigma : \mathcal{L} \times I &\to \quad F_\sigma \\ (c, t_\tau) &\mapsto \sigma^{t_\tau}(c)\end{aligned} \cdot \tag{3}$$

with $I = \{t_0, \cdots, t_N\}$.
- *The attribute set values associated to $\mathcal{L}$ at time t_τ is defined by:*

$$\mathbb{A}_{t_\tau}(\mathcal{L}) = \bigcup_{c \in \mathcal{L}} \mathbb{A}_{t_\tau}(c). \tag{4}$$

Internal transformations are defined as the change in values between attributes and state.

Definition 2 (Internal transformations)
Configuration and attributes have a mutual influence on the cell. Φ is the map that represents the interaction between the configuration and attributes in c at the time t_τ defined by:

$$\begin{aligned}\Phi : \mathcal{S} \times \mathbb{A}_{t_\tau}(\mathcal{L}) &\to \mathcal{S} \times \mathbb{A}_{t_\tau}(\mathcal{L}) \\ (s_{t_\tau}, \mathbb{A}_{t_\tau}) &\mapsto \Phi(s_{t_\tau}, \mathbb{A}_{t_\tau})\end{aligned} \cdot \tag{5}$$

During the evolution, the values of the attributes, in a given cell, can change depending on the state of the cell and the neighboring cells states and attributes. For example, in the case of forest fire modeling, the air humidity in the cell depends on the air humidity and the state of the neighborhood.

Definition 3
The local transition function determines the state and attribute values at instant $t_{\tau+1}$ of the cell from the state and values of the neighborhood attributes at instant t_τ.

$$f\left(s_{t_\tau} \circ \mathcal{N}, \mathbb{A}_{t_\tau} \circ \mathcal{N}\right)(c) = (s_{t_{\tau+1}}, \mathbb{A}_{t_{\tau+1}})(c). \tag{6}$$

This leads to the following representation of the global dynamics:

$$\begin{cases} (s_{t_{\tau+1}}, \mathbb{A}_{t_{\tau+1}}) = F(s_{t_\tau}, \mathbb{A}_{t_\tau}) \\ (s_{t_0}, \mathbb{A}_{t_0}) \end{cases} \tag{7}$$

4   Controllability via Actuators

Controllability of a given systems consists in being able to bring the system from each initial state to any desired state at the end of a given time horizon. For a CA $\mathcal{A}$ and a given configuration defined on a non-empty region ω of $\mathcal{L}$ ($\mathcal{L}$ is finite), we define a normalized Hamming distance d_ω on the configuration space $\mathcal{S}^\omega$ by:

$$d_\omega(s_1, s_2) = \frac{card\{c \in \omega : s_1(c) \neq s_2(c)\}}{card(\omega)}. \tag{8}$$

For a CA $\mathcal{A}$, the control u is a function defined by:

$$\begin{aligned} u : \mathcal{L} \times I &\to \quad U \\ (c, t_\tau) &\to u_{t_\tau}(c) \end{aligned} \tag{9}$$

where U is the set of values taken by the control u.

Definition 4
During an interval of time $I = \{t_0, \cdots, t_N\}$, for any initial configuration s_{t_0} and for any desired configuration s_d. Let's be a control u and a tolerance $\varepsilon > 0$:
It is said that $\mathcal{A}$ is controllable   if $d_\mathcal{L}(s_{t_N}, s_d) = 0$.
It is said that $\mathcal{A}$ is weakly controllable   if $d_\mathcal{L}(s_{t_N}, s_d) < \varepsilon$.
It is said that $\mathcal{A}$ is ω-controllable   if $d_\omega(s_{t_N}, s_d) = 0$.
It is said that $\mathcal{A}$ is weakly ω-controllable if $d_\omega(s_{t_N}, s_d) < \varepsilon$.

4.1   Controllability and Actuators

The introduction of the actuators forms an important link between a system and its environment. They have an active role and are used to control the system. Their structure depends on the geometry, the location of the support, and the spatial distribution of the action. The notion of controllability can be then studied through actuators [13]. Indeed, in our environmental phenomenon case, we suit the actuators definition to the CA systems considering the attributes of each cell. For example, in the case of forest fires, the fire spread can be controlled by removing fuel or increase the vegetation humidity.

Definition 5 (Actuator)
We call zone actuator for a CA $\mathcal{A}$ with a set of attributes $\mathbb{A}$, the couple (D, g) where:

- $D = \bigcup\limits_{i=1}^{p} c_i$ *is the actuator support such that $c_i \in \mathcal{L}$*
- g *defines the spatial distribution and intensity of the action on the cell attributes c in D*

$$g : \mathbb{A}_{t_\tau}(D) \to \mathbb{A}(D)$$
$$\mathbb{A}_{t_\tau}(c) \to g\left(\mathbb{A}_{t_\tau}(c)\right) = (g_1(\sigma_1^{t_\tau}(c)), \cdots, g_m(\sigma_m^{t_\tau}(c)))$$

with g_i being the intensity applied to the attribute $\sigma_i^{t_\tau}$.

Remark 1

- A uni-cell actuator is the actuator applied on a single cell, it is defined by a couple (c, g_c)
- A boundary zone actuator (D, g) is the actuator applied on a boundary of $\mathcal{L}$ $(\partial\mathcal{L})$, such that $D \subset \partial\mathcal{L}$.
- For multiple actuators, we denote $(D_i, g_i)_{1 \leqslant i \leqslant q}$ the sequence of q actuators exciting the system.

Definition 6
Let $\mathcal{A}$ be a CA with a set of attributes $\mathbb{A}$ and (D, g) a zone actuator. We consider that the control as the function u which represents the actions that excite the cell attributes c in D.

$$u : D \times I \to \mathbb{A}(D)$$
$$(c, t_\tau) \to u_{t_\tau}(c) = (\sigma_1^{u_{t_\tau}}(c), \cdots, \sigma_m^{u_{t_\tau}}(c)) \cdot \tag{10}$$

with $\sigma_i^{u_{t_\tau}}$ is the function-attribute σ_i excited by the action u at instant t_τ.

The action on the attributes of the cell at a given instant has implications on the configuration and attributes of its neighborhood at the next instant.

Notation 1

- A controlled CA can be defined locally by :

$$\mathcal{A}_u = \left((\mathcal{L}, \mathcal{N}, \mathcal{S}, f), (D, g, u)\right). \tag{11}$$

- A controlled CA can be globally defined by the following state equation :

$$\begin{cases} s_{t_{\tau+1}} = F(s_{t_\tau}, \mathbb{A}_{t_\tau}^u) & \text{with } \mathbb{A}_{t_\tau}^u = \{\mathbb{1}_D g_i(\sigma_i^{u_{t_\tau}}) + \mathbb{1}_{\mathcal{L} \backslash D} \sigma_i^{t_\tau}\}_{1 \leqslant i \leqslant m} \\ s_0 \in \mathcal{S} \end{cases} \tag{12}$$

with $\mathbb{1}_D(c) = \begin{cases} 1 & if \ \ c \in D \\ 0 \ else \end{cases}$.

Figure 2 summarizes our approach of controllability through actuators and attributes. It illustrates how the application of an actuator to the support D influences the AC configuration in the following moments.

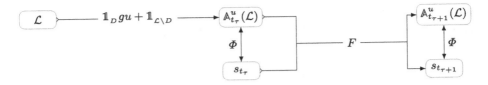

<figure>Fig. 2. Illustration of CA controllability based on attributes</figure>

5   Case Study: Forest Fire Control

We propose at the local scale a 3D model of forest fires distributed over a given area. The area can contain a heterogeneous set of spatial characteristics. We are mainly interested in studying the influence of these characteristics on fire evolution. The input data comes from the segmentation of 3D LIDAR scanner of an area in the Faculty of Science and Technology of Tangier, Morocco. The cell space contains three classes of cells representing vegetation, air, and subsoil. Below is a description of our model.

5.1   Lattice and Neighborhood

The lattice consists of 3D hexagonal cells $c_{i,j,k}$ with centered coordinates i, j, k representing a portion of the soil, vegetation or air (Fig. 3). For the neighborhood we consider the model D_3Q_{21} shown in Fig. 1d.

Fig. 3. Illustration of the cell lattice of the study area with a 3D hexagonal cell type

5.2   State Set

At a time t_τ, the cell state is given by the absence or existence of fire in the cell. The state set considered is:

$$State0 \equiv \text{unflamable cell}$$
$$State1 \equiv \text{cell without fire}$$
$$State2 \equiv \text{cell on fire}$$

5.3 Attributes

Each cell is associated with a set of attributes that can be static or dynamic.
$\mathbb{A}_{t_\tau} = \{\delta, \beta_{t_\tau}, \mathcal{H}_{t_\tau}, \mathcal{H}_{t_\tau}^{in}, \Theta, \lambda_{t_\tau}, \Gamma_{t_\tau}, \varrho_{t_\tau}, \phi_{t_\tau}, P_{t_\tau}, b_{t_\tau}\}$. In Table 1 are shown the
attributes details:

Table 1. Attribute-Function considered in this model

Cell classification	$\delta: \quad \mathcal{L} \mapsto \{0, 1, 2\}$	{air, fuel, soil}
Packing Ratio of the plant species	$\beta_{t_\tau}: \mathcal{L} \mapsto [0, 1]$	
Air humidity	$\mathcal{H}_{t_\tau}: \mathcal{L} \mapsto [0, 1]$	
Vegetation humidity	$\mathcal{H}_{t_\tau}^{in}: \mathcal{L} \mapsto [0, 1]$	
The topographic slope	$\Theta: \quad \mathcal{L} \mapsto \left[-\frac{\pi}{2}, \frac{\pi}{2}\right]^n$	$\Theta(c) = (\theta^{[1]}(c), \cdots, \theta^{[n]}(c))$
Thermal conductivity	$\lambda_{t_\tau}: \mathcal{L} \mapsto [0, 1]$	
Inflammation rate	$\Gamma_{t_\tau}: \mathcal{L} \mapsto [0, 1]$	
Ignition catalyst	$\varrho_{t_\tau}: \mathcal{L} \mapsto \{0, 1\}$	{without catalyst, with catalyst}
Porosity	$\phi_{t_\tau}: \mathcal{L} \mapsto [0, 1]$	$\phi_{t_\tau}(c) = 1 - \beta_{t_\tau}(c)$
Slope factor	$P_{t_\tau}: \mathcal{L} \mapsto \mathbb{R}^n$	$P_{t_\tau}^{[i]}(c) = 5.275\beta_{t_\tau}(c)^{-3}\tan^2(\theta_i(c))$
Radiative conductivity	$b_{t_\tau}: \mathcal{L} \mapsto \mathbb{R}^+$	$\sigma_n \varepsilon_{r,t_\tau} \varphi$

5.4 Local Transition Rules

We consider three processes for the local transition rules: the first defines the
neighborhood effect on a cell, while the second represents the cell feedback and
the third is the cell effect on its neighborhood. The evolution of $\mathcal{A}$ is identified
as the mutual action between three processes:

$$f \equiv \textbf{reception} \oplus \textbf{feedback} \oplus \textbf{exportation} \qquad (13)$$

where the symbol $\oplus$ refers to mutual action.

Fire Reception:

$$F_{t_{\tau+1}}^{[i]}(c) = \left(P_{t_\tau}^{[i]}(c)\nu_{t_\tau}^{[\kappa_i]}(c_i) + \lambda_{t_\tau}(c_i) + b_{t_\tau}(c_i)\right) \mathbb{1}_{\{s_{t_\tau}(c_i)=2\}} \qquad (14)$$

with c_i in $\mathcal{N}(c)$ at direction i, κ_i the opposite direction of i, $\nu_{t_\tau}^{[\kappa_i]}(c_i)$ the wind
speed at direction κ_i.

Inflammation Rate: $\Gamma_{t_{\tau+1}} = \Gamma_{t_\tau}\left(1 - \phi_{t_\tau}\mathbb{1}_{\{\sum_{i=1}^n F_{t_\tau}^{[i]}(c)>0\}}\right)$

Conditions for State Evolution:

$$
s_{t_\tau}(c) = \begin{cases} 0 \; if & \delta(c) = 0 \\[2mm] 1 \; if & \left[\sum\limits_{i=1}^{n} F_{t_\tau}^{[i]}(c) = 0\right] or \left[\sum\limits_{i=1}^{n} F_{t_\tau}^{[i]}(c) > 0 \; and \; R_{t_\tau}(c) > 0.5\right] \\ & or \; [\varrho_{t_\tau} = 1 \; and \; R_{t_\tau}(c) > 0.1] \\[4mm] 2 \; else \; if & \left[\sum\limits_{i=1}^{n} F_{t_\tau}^{[i]}(c) > 0\right] \; and \; [\Gamma_{t_\tau}(c) > 0 \;] \end{cases}
$$

(15)

where $R_{t_\tau}(c)$ represents the fire resistance of a cell c at instant t_τ, defined by:

$$
R_{t_\tau}(c) = \beta_{t_\tau} \min((\mathcal{H}_{t_\tau}(c) + \mathcal{H}_{t_\tau}^{int}(c)), 1).
$$

(16)

5.5   Simulation of the Autonomous System

In the initial configuration, we consider the burning cells in red (Fig. 4a). For the cells representing air ($\delta(c) = 0$) the humidity is 60%. For the cells representing vegetation ($\delta(c) = 1$), the humidity depends on the color and type of vegetation. Boundary conditions are fixed. At every instant t, the air cells at the boundaries of the space receive wind. The time step is $t = 5$ min. Figure 2 shows an uncontrolled simulation.

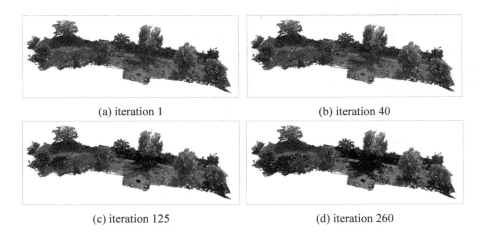

(a) iteration 1   (b) iteration 40

(c) iteration 125   (d) iteration 260

Fig. 4. Uncontrolled fire spread simulation. (Color figure online)

5.6   Simulation of the Controlled System

Control is one of the best strategies to fight forest fires as Canadair to discharge water and fire retardants. In our case, they are represented by the control u. D is the set of cells subject to u and g the intensity of humidity in each cell c in D.

For the dynamics of water discharges, we add rules defining the water propagation taking into account the effects of wind and space obstacles. The aim is to increase the air humidity values and the vegetation humidity values.

To apply the control, we look to modify the value of the fire resistance $R_{t_\tau}(c)$ of the cell c in relation 16 to avoid the ignition conditions quoted in relation 15. Indeed, the increase of air humidity $\mathcal{H}$ and vegetation humidity $\mathcal{H}^{int}$ makes $R_{t_\tau}(c)$ greater. We simulated, in the same time conditions, two choices of zone actuators to control the fire spread. In the first actuator we choose the support D_1 as a set of cells arbitrarily distributed in the lattice with a density 50%. With an intensity g_1 represents the increase of humidity by 75%. For the second actuator the support D_2 is chosen as a set of cells in fire or in the neighborhood of fire. With an intensity g_2 represents the increase of humidity by 95% (Fig. 6).

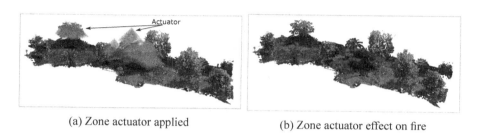

(a) Zone actuator applied   (b) Zone actuator effect on fire

Fig. 5. Application example of the zone actuator represented by the water discharge.

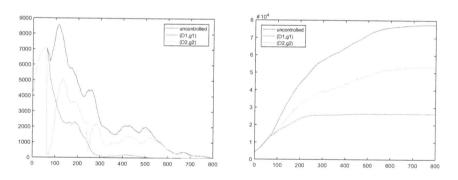

(a) Number of cells on fire with two actuators (b) Number of cells on fire or burned with the
choices   same case

Fig. 6. Example of application of different zone actuator choices represented by the water discharge.

Figure 6 shows the impact of actuator choice on the controllability of the system. It clear is that the choice of the support and the intensity of the action impacts considerably the number of burned cells. Each graph illustrates the impact of actuator choice on the evolution of the burning or burned cells.

We can see from (Fig. 6) that the strategy where the control is chosen arbitrarily is more effective than the strategy where it is defined according to the location of the fire. This result is due to the number of cells to which we add humidity (50% of the lattice). In fact, the first control strategy makes it difficult to transfer the flames from a cell to another. Meanwhile, in the second strategy of control that is applied to the fireplace, the number of burnt cells decreases very strongly and immediately. However, it is later increased because the cells that are not extinguished spread the fire to the others that remain vulnerable.

6   Conclusion

In this paper, we have considered the controllability of dynamic systems modeled by a 3D CA via the structure of actuators and attributes. We focused on CA models where space is heterogeneous. The developed control acts by modifying the structure of the space to reach the desired state of the system. To illustrate our approach we applied these control to simulate forest fire spreadability using 3D CA. A software framework was developed to simulate the forest fire dynamics between cells. The physical data of the study area were collected from a 3D LIDAR scanner. In perspective, this model will be coupled with other CA models of near-ground wind flows at different modeling scales. We plan also to apply the optimization procedure proposed in [14] to calibrate the availability of fire process information and the optimization of a large number of attributes. We will also study and apply systems theory concepts such that spreadability and vulnerability based on attributes to optimally manage forest areas.

Acknowledgments. This work has been supported by MESRSFC and CNRST under the project PPR2-OGI-Env, reference PPR2/2016/79.

References

1. Curtain, R.F., Pritchard, A.J.: Functional Analysis in Modern Applied Mathematics. Academic Press, Cambridge (1977)
2. Lions, J.L.: Contrôle optimal de systèmes gouvernés par des équations aux dérivées partielles (1968)
3. El Jai, A., Pritchard, A.J.: Distributed parameter systems analysis via sensors and actuators. Texts in Applied Mathe (1988)
4. El Jai, A., Pritchard, A.J.: Sensors and actuators in distributed systems. Int. J. Control **46**(4), 1139–1153 (1987)
5. Slimi, R., El Yacoubi, S.: Spreadable cellular automata: modelling and simulations. Int. J. Syst. Sci. **40**(5), 507–520 (2009)
6. Dennunzio, A., Formenti, E., Manzoni, L., Margara, L., Porreca, A.E.: On the dynamical behaviour of linear higher-order cellular automata and its decidability. Inf. Sci. **486**, 73–87 (2019)

7. Dennunzio, A., Formenti, E., Grinberg, D., Margara, L.: Chaos and ergodicity are decidable for linear cellular automata over (Z/mZ) n. Inf. Sci. **539**, 136–144 (2020)
8. Di Gregorio, S., Serra, R.: An empirical method for modelling and simulating some complex macroscopic phenomena by cellular automata. Future Gener. Comput. Syst. **16**(2–3), 259–271 (1999)
9. El Yacoubi, S., El Jai, A., Ammor, N.: Regional controllability with cellular automata models. In: Bandini, S., Chopard, B., Tomassini, M. (eds.) ACRI 2002. LNCS, vol. 2493, pp. 357–367. Springer, Heidelberg (2002). https://doi.org/10.1007/3-540-45830-1_34
10. El Yacoubi, S., Jacewicz, P.: Cellular automata and controllability problem. In: CD-Rom Proceeding of the 14th International Symposium on Mathematical Theory of Networks and Systems, pp. 19–23 (2000)
11. El Yacoubi, S., El Jai, A.: Cellular automata modelling and spreadability. Math. Comput. Modell. **36**(9–10), 1059–1074 (2002)
12. El Yacoubi, S.: A mathematical method for control problems on cellular automata models. Int. J. Syst. Sci. **39**(5), 529–538 (2008)
13. El Jai, A.: Distributed systems analysis via sensors and actuators. Sens. Actuators, A **29**(1), 1–11 (1991)
14. García-Duro, J., et al.: Hidden costs of modelling post-fire plant community assembly using cellular automata. In: Mauri, G., El Yacoubi, S., Dennunzio, A., Nishinari, K., Manzoni, L. (eds.) ACRI 2018. LNCS, vol. 11115, pp. 68–79. Springer, Cham (2018). https://doi.org/10.1007/978-3-319-99813-8_6

The Second Order CA-Based Multi-agent Systems with Income Sharing

Franciszek Seredyński[1], Jakub Gąsior[1(✉)], and Rolf Hoffmann[2]

[1] Department of Mathematics and Natural Sciences, Cardinal Stefan Wyszyński University, Warsaw, Poland
{f.seredynski,j.gasior}@uksw.edu.pl
[2] Technische Universität Darmstadt, Darmstadt, Germany
hoffmann@ra.informatik.tu-darmstadt.de

Abstract. We consider a multi-agent system composed of the second-order nonuniform Cellular Automata (CA)–based agents, where a spatial Prisoner's Dilemma (PD) game describes the interaction between agents. Each agent has some strategy that can change in time and acts in such a way to maximize its income. We intend to study conditions of emergence of collective behavior in such systems measured by the average total payoff of a team of agents in the game or by an equivalent measure – the total number of cooperating players. While the emergence of collective behavior depends on many parameters, we introduce to the game an income sharing mechanism, giving a possibility to share incomes locally by agents wishing to do it. We present results showing that under some conditions, the introduced mechanism can significantly increase the level of collective behavior.

Keywords: Collective behavior · Income sharing · Multi-agent systems · Spatial Prisoner's Dilemma game · Second–order cellular automata

1 Introduction

Cellular Automata (CA) (see, e.g., [16]) and Learning Automata (LA) [15] are two prominent classes of abstract machines which have features of collective behavior. Closer analysis of this notion in the context of these machines reveals that it is understood differently. According to the classification [2,9] of types of collective behavior in the context of multi-agent systems, CA can be described as spatially-organizing systems, where agents have a little interaction with an environment but they coordinate themselves to achieve a desired spatial formation, while LA is characterized by collective exploration, where agents interact a little between themselves but interact with an environment to achieve some goal.

In other words, one of the main differences is that LA is able to learn and adapt in an environment while CA is typically oriented on the other types of

© Springer Nature Switzerland AG 2021
T. M. Gwizdałła et al. (Eds.): ACRI 2020, LNCS 12599, pp. 134–145, 2021.
https://doi.org/10.1007/978-3-030-69480-7_14

activities. Only recently, the question of potential adaptability of CA by changing CA rules while running the system has appeared in the context of the so-called "the second-order CA" [5].

Their idea assumes that a rule for a given cell can be selected and copied from a neighborhood and then executed determining this way the next cell state. (Note that this notion appeared first [14] in the context of reversible CA with another definition, saying that the next state of a cell depends on the current and the previous states).

In this paper, we will consider a multi-agent nonuniform the second-order CA-based system where interaction between players is described in terms of non-cooperative game theory [7] with use of the Spatial Prisoner's Dilemma (SPD) game. We will expect a global collective behavior measured by a total number of cooperating players, i.e., an ability to maximize the average total payoff of all agents of the system.

The phenomenon of emerging cooperation in systems described by the SPD game has been a subject of current studies [3,4,8,11] which show that it depends on many factors such as payoff parameters, the type of learning agent, the way of interaction between agents. In this paper, we introduce a new mechanism of interaction between players, based on a possibility of a local income sharing by agents participating in the game, and we show a significant influence of this mechanism on emerging global cooperation. To our knowledge, it is the first attempt to apply this mechanism in CA-based SPD games. It is worth noting that the SPD game belongs to a class of game-theoretic models that include the Public Goods Game [1] and the Ultimatum Game [13].

The structure of the paper is the following. In the next section SPD game is presented. Section 3 contains a description of the CA-based multi-agent system acting in the SPD game environment. Section 4 presents a basic mechanism of the game, including income sharing. Section 5 presents some results of the experimental study, and the last section concludes the paper.

2   Iterated Spatial Prisoner's Dilemma Game

We consider a 2D spatial array of size $n \times m$. We assume that a cell (i, j) will be considered as an agent–player participating in the SPD game [5,6]. We assume that a neighborhood of a given player is defined in some way. Players from this neighborhood will be considered as his opponents in the game. At a given discrete moment of time, each cell can be in one of two states: C or D. The state of a given cell will be considered as an action C (cooperate) or D (defect) of the corresponding player against an opponent player from his neighborhood. The payoff function of the game is given in Table 1.

Each player playing a game with an opponent in a single round (iteration) receives a payoff equal to R, T, S or P, where $T > R > P > S$. We assume that $R = 1$, $S = 0$, $T = b$ and $P = a$ ($b > 1 > a > 0$). In experiments we will use $b = 1.2$ and values of a will vary depending on the purpose of an experiment.

If a player takes action C and the opponent also takes action C, then the player receives payoff $R = 1$. If a player takes action D and the opponent player

Table 1. Payoff function of a row player participating in SPD game.

Player's Action	Opponent's Action	
	Cooperate (C)	Defect (D)
Cooperate (C)	$R = 1$	$S = 0$
Defect (D)	$T = b$	$P = a$

keeps the action C, the defecting player receives payoff $T = b$. If a player takes action C while the opponent takes action D, the cooperating player receives payoff $S = 0$. When both players use the action D, then both of them receive payoff $P = a$.

It is worth to notice that choosing by all players the action D corresponds to the Nash equilibrium point [7] and it is considered as a solution of the one–shot game. Indeed, if all players select the action D, each of them receives a payoff equal to a, and there is no reason for any of them to change the action to C while the others keep their actions unchanged, what would result in decreasing his payoff to value 0.

The average total payoff (ATP) of all players in the Nash equilibrium point is also equal to a. Looking from the point of view of players' global collective behavior, this ATP of all players is low. We would instead expect to choose by all players the action C, which provides the highest value of ATP of all players equal to 1. For this instance of the game, it is the maximal value of a possible average total payoff of all players, and it will be achieved when all players decide to select the action C. We are interested in studying conditions when such behavior of players in iterated games is possible.

3   CA–Based Players

Cells (i, j) of the 2D array are considered as CA–based players. It is assumed that at a given discrete moment of time t, each cell is either in state D or C. The value of the state is used by CA–based player as an action with an opponent player. For each cell, a local neighborhood is defined. We apply a cyclic boundary condition in order to avoid irregular behavior at the borders. We will assume the Moore neighborhood with eight immediate neighbors. It means that each player has eight opponents in the game.

In discrete moments, CA–based players will select new actions according to local rules (also called strategies or transition functions) assigned to them, which will change the states of the corresponding cells. We will be using some number of rules among which one of them will be initially randomly assigned to each CA cell, so we deal with nonuniform CA.

To each cell one of the following rules: *all–C* (always cooperate), *all–D* (always defect), *k–D* (cooperate until the number of defecting neighbors does not exceed the value of k, defect otherwise), and *pC* (cooperate with probability

p_C) can be assigned. If we use only the first three strategies, we will call it the basic set. We will refer to an extended set of strategies if we use all four of them.

4   Competition and Income Sharing Mechanisms

To study the possibility of the emergence of the global collective behavior of CA-based players, we will introduce some local mechanisms of interaction between players.

The first mechanism is a competition that is based on the idea proposed in [6]. Each player associated with a given cell plays in a single round a game with each of his neighbors, and this way collects some total score. If the competition mechanism is turned *on*, after a q number of rounds (iterations), each agent compares its total payoff with the total payoffs of its neighbors. If a more successful player exists in the neighborhood, it replaces their own rule by the most successful one. This mechanism converts a classical CA into the *second–order* CA, which can adapt in time.

The second mechanism, called *income sharing mechanism* (ISM), which we propose, provides a possibility of sharing payoffs by players. Some hard local sharing was successfully used [10] in the context of LA games. Here we will be using a soft version of sharing, where a player decides to use it or not. It is assumed that each player has a tag indicating whether he wishes (*on*) or not (*off*) to share his payoff with players from the neighborhood who also wish to share. The sharing works in such a way that if two players both wish to share, they receive half of the payoff from the sum. Before starting the iterated game, each player turns on its tag with a predefined probability p_{shar}. Due to the competition mechanism, rules with tags containing information about willing to share incomes can be potentially spread or dismissed during the system's evolution.

5   Experimental Results

A 2D array of the size 50×50 was used, with an initial state C or D (player actions) of each cell set with a probability of 0.5. In experiments with the basic set of strategies, each of them was assigned initially to CA cells with probability 0.333, and when the extended set of strategies was used, each of them was assigned with probability 0.25. To an agent with the rule $k–D$, a value k randomly selected from the range (0 .. 7) was assigned. Updating rules assigned to agents by the competition mechanism was conducted after each iteration ($q = 1$). The results presented below were averaged on the base of 10 runs. Each run lasted from 50 to 200 iterations, depending on the experiment. The experiments have been conducted with a recently developed simulator presented in [12].

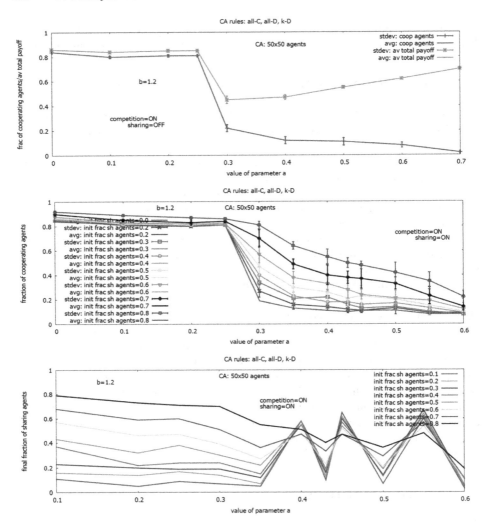

Fig. 1. The behavior of players with the basic set of strategies: the fraction of cooperating agents/average payoff of players in games without ISM (upper), the fraction of cooperating agents in games with ISM (middle), and the final fraction of agents wishing to share income in games with ISM (lower). (Color figure online)

5.1 Experiments with the Basic Set of Strategies

Figure 1 shows the results of the first set of experiments with the basic set of strategies. Figure 1 (upper) presents results for games without ISM. One can see that for the range of $0 \leq a \leq 0.25$ the number of cooperating agents (in red) is close to 82%. It drops to 22% for $a = 0.3$ and continues decreasing to 0 with the increase of a. Corresponding ATP (in blue) behaves similarly for $0 \leq a \leq 0.3$ but for greater values of a it starts to increase. At first glance, this behavior seems to be unexpected. We can see that a high level of agent cooperation observed for small values of a results in a high ATP level. However, a high level of defection observed for increasing values of a also provides relatively good ATP. Closer analysis shows that players' behavior depends on a relation between the value of b and the value of a, which defines ATP in a Nash equilibrium point. When the difference between b and a is relatively high (for $a \leq 0.25$), cooperation brings a much higher payoff for a single player than defecting. However, when the value of a increases and becomes closer to the value of b (for $a > 0.3$), defecting becomes more attractive for a single player. When they all defect being in the Nash equilibrium point, their payoff becomes equal to a. When a is relatively large, this equilibrium becomes some trap from which it is difficult to jump out. While the level of cooperation and ATP are closely related issues, we will focus in this study on this first issue.

Figure 1 (middle) shows averaged results for games with ISM. It shows how the level of cooperation depends on an initial fraction of *agents wishing to share* (AWS) their incomes with neighbors. This fraction changes from 0 (sharing is *off*, reference plot in red) to 0.8 and is set by the value of parameter p_{shar}. One can see that for small values of $a \leq 0.25$, ISM can improve the level of cooperation only slightly, a few percent. However, the situation significantly changes for values of $a \geq 0.3$. We can see that the increase in the level of cooperation under a given value of a depends proportionally on the value of p_{shar}. For $a = 0.3$ the level of cooperation is equal to 0.22 when sharing is *off*. However, when it is *on*, the cooperation level increases to 0.26 for $p_{shar} = 0.2$ (in violet) and reaches 0.81 (increase on 59%) for $p_{shar} = 0.8$ (in blue). We can observe also the significant improving of the cooperation level under ISM for a wide spectrum of larger values of a.

Figure 1 (lower) gives some insight into the process of changing final fractions of AWS as a function of an initial fraction of AWS and a. One can see that for the range $0 \leq a \leq 0.35$, the final fraction of AWS slightly decreases for a given initial fraction of AWS. Let us see, e.g., the plot (in green) corresponding to $p_{shar} = 0.4$, i.e., when around 40% of players start to share income at the beginning of the game. For $a = 0.1$, the game ends with the average final fraction of AWS equal to 0.37, and for values of a equal to 0.2 and 0.3, the corresponding values of final fractions of AWS are equal to 0.17 and 0.24, respectively. However, for $a = 0.4$ the final fraction of AWS jumps to 0.58 to fall down again when $a = 0.43$. We can see that for $a > 0.3$, some dynamic process starts and is related to taking local decisions by players to choose either cooperation or defecting and staying at the Nash equilibrium point. We can notice some specific values of a where the number of agents sharing income strongly increases (see, $a = 0.4, 0.45, 0.55$) or strongly decreases (see, $a = 0.43, 0.5$) to a narrow area of values, independently on an initial value of p_{shar}. These are specific phase transition points that visually look like some "convex lense".

Figures 2 and 3 inspect behavior of players in one of these specific points corresponding to $a = 0.43$ showing spatial diagrams for a single run of the game

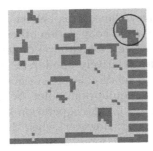 

Fig. 2. Spatial diagrams for the game with basic set of strategies and ISM ($a = 0.43$): distribution of agents wishing to share income (in red) (left), and distribution of agents with strategies $all - C$ (in red), $all - D$ (in blue) and $k - D$ (in green) (right). (Color figure online)

Fig. 3. Spatial diagrams for the game with basic set of strategies and ISM ($a = 0.43$): distribution of agents with variants of $k - D$ strategy (spectrum of yellow) (left), and distribution of CA cell states C (in red), D (in blue) (right). (Color figure online)

in the iteration 147. Figure 2 (left) shows spatial distribution of AWS and Fig. 2 (right) spatial distribution of agents' strategies. Figure 3 (left) presents spatial distribution of k–D strategies only, and Fig. 3 (right) the spatial distribution of the cells' states. This spatial distribution of cells' states is formed already in the iteration 10 and remains unchanged during the next iterations. The spatial distribution shown in Figs. 2 (left) partially stabilizes at the iteration 24, and the remaining two spatial distributions partially stabilize at the iteration 36. It means that in some regions of these distributions, some dynamic activities start, which can be described in terms of Artificial Life. Starting from the iteration 24 the group of AWS (see, (Fig. 2 (left)) located at upper-right corner behaves as a gun (in the circle) sending after each four iteration-steps rectangular "blocks of AW" to "the block of AW" located at the bottom-right corner of the diagram. Starting from the iteration, 36 five groups of agents' applying all–D strategy (in blue) and located on the right side of the diagram behave as guns (in circles) sending after every 4 iterations rectangular or quadratic blocks of all–D strategies. We can notice a similar behavior in the diagram with a spatial distribution of k–D strategies.

5.2   Experiments with the Extended Set of Strategies

Figure 4 shows the results of experiments with the extended set of strategies when the strategy pC was added to the basic set of available strategies. Figure 4 (upper) shows how a number of cooperating players depend on parameters a and the probability p_C of cooperation of a player acting as a stochastic automaton in games without ISM. The figure shows several plots presenting fractions of cooperating players for different values of p_C. The plot with $p_C = 0$ (in blue) serves as a reference for the results. We can see two regions related to values of a for the behavior of players: the first one for $a \leq 0.3$ and the second one for $a > 0.3$. The behavior of players under a given value of p_C depends on the region of a, except for the value of $p_C = 0.5$ (in orange).

When $p_C \geq 0.5$, all players quickly accept the strategy pC as the most profitable at the whole range of a, and the strategy eliminates all remaining strategies. The frequency of cooperating agents becomes equal to the value of p_C. Values of p_C lower than 0.5 results for $a \leq 0.3$ in establishing some equilibrium between all strategies and corresponding values of fractions of cooperating agents are greater than 0.5. We can observe the maximum number of cooperating agents for $p_C = 0.1$ (in red) with the fraction of cooperation in the range (0.83,...,0.88) and this value is slightly greater than in the case when $p_C = 0$ (see, reference plot in blue) with the fraction of cooperation in the range (0.82,...,0.84). It is also worth to notice that the border of the phenomenon of cooperation is shifted from $a = 0.25$ (in games without pC) to $a = 0.3$ in games with pC.

In games for $a > 0.3$ we can observe the process of elimination by the strategy pC remaining strategies used by the population of agents. This process depends on the value of a. For games with $p_C = 0.4$ this process takes place starting from $a = 0.35$ (in black), for $p_C = 0.3$ from $a = 0.4$ (in green) and with $p_C = 0.1$ from $a = 0.7$. Only the strategy pC with $p_C = 0.1$ is not aggressive in the relation to other strategies for the whole range of a and is an efficient component of building high level of cooperation, therefore it will be used in the next experiments.

Figure 4 (middle) shows results of experiments when both the strategy pC with $p_C = 0.1$ and ISM are used. We can see two reference plots: a plot showing the level of cooperation of the game without ISM and with the strategy pC with $p_C = 0$ (in blue) and the level of cooperation without ISM but with the strategy pC with $p_C = 0.1$ (in red). The experiments were conducted for the range $0.1 \leq p_{shar} \leq 0.8$. We can see that for $a \leq 0.3$ the fraction of cooperation achieves the highest values seen until now from the range (0.85,...,0.92). These values do not significantly depend on p_{shar} and also are close to the reference values up to $a = 0.25$. The increasing of the fraction of cooperation of agents starts from $a = 0.3$ and at this point reaches near 72%. For larger value of a the increase is lower and proportional to p_{shar}. For subsequent values of $a = 0.35, 0.4, 0.45$ and $p_{shar} = 0.8$ the increase of cooperation is measured by 59%, 46% and 24%, respectively.

Figure 4 (lower) shows how the final fraction of AWS depends on the value of a. We can notice some similarities with results presented for the basic set of strategies (see, Fig. 1 (lower)) for values $a \leq 0.4$. At $a = 0.4$, the final

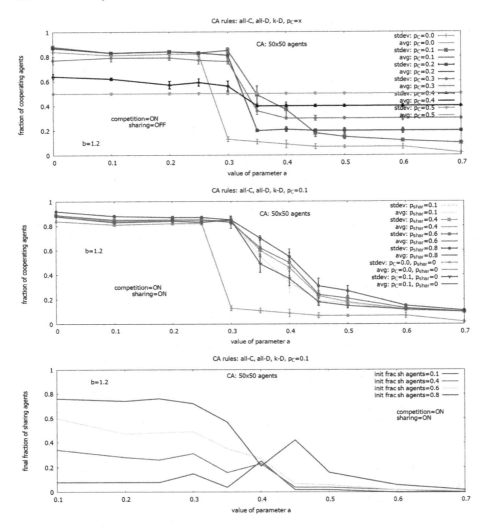

Fig. 4. Games with the extended set of strategies: the fraction of cooperating agents in games without ISM (upper), the fraction of cooperating agents in games with ISM (middle), and the final fraction of agents wishing to share income in games with ISM (lower). (Color figure online)

fraction of AWS is reduced to the fraction from the narrow range $(0.21,...,0.27)$ independently on the value of the initial fraction of AWS. There is only one such "lens", after which the final fractions of AWS approach 0 when a is increasing.

Figure 5 (upper) presents some details of the game conducted during 200 iterations with parameters corresponding to the "lens" with the initial value of AWS equal to 0.4. One can see changes during the game of frequencies of strategies *all–C* (in red), *all–D* (in blue), *k–D* (in green), *pC* (in orange) and

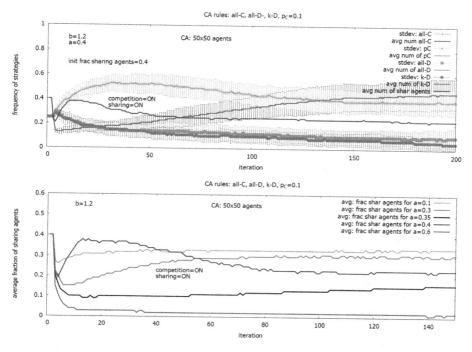

Fig. 5. Games with the extended set of strategies and ISM ($b = 1.2, a = 0.4$): frequency of strategies during the iterated game (upper), fractions of players wishing to share income during the iterated game (lower). (Color figure online)

the fraction of AWS (in violet). We can see that two strategies $all-C$ and pC are dominating in the game. At the beginning of the game, the strategy pC increases its frequency. The strategy $all-C$ is strongly suppressed, but after some iterations, it starts to increase its frequency slowly to overcome the frequency of pC finally. Finally, we can see some equilibrium between both strategies with some slight domination of $all-C$. The value close to $a = 0.4$ is a border value where both strategies achieve near the equal frequency. For values of a below this border, the dominating strategy becomes $all-C$, and for values of a higher this border, the dominating strategy becomes pC. Figure 5 (lower) shows the behavior of the fraction of AWS for the initial value of AWS equal to 0.4 for values of a below and above its border value.

Figures 6 and 7 show diagrams of spatial distributions of AWS, all strategies, strategies $k-D$ and CA states for a typical experiment presented in Fig. 5 (upper). In particular one can see (Fig. 6 (right)) how looks a spatial equilibrium between strategies $all-C$ (in red) and pC (in orange).

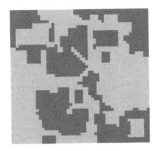 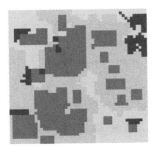

Fig. 6. Spatial diagrams for the game with extended set of strategies and ISM ($a = 0.40$): distribution of agents wishing to share income (in red) (left), and distribution of agents with strategies $all - C$ (in red), $all - D$ (in blue), $k - D$ (in green) and pC (in orange) (right). (Color figure online)

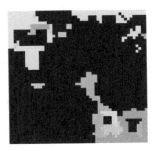 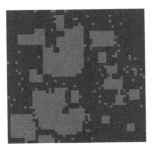

Fig. 7. Spatial diagrams for the game with extended set of strategies and ISM ($a = 0.40$): distribution of agents with variants of $k - D$ strategy (spectrum of orange) (left), and distribution of CA cell states C (in red), D (in blue) (right). (Color figure online)

6   Conclusions

In this paper, we have studied the conditions of emerging cooperation in a CA-based multi-agent system with agents interacting according to principles of a spatial PD game. Agents competed in the game for their incomes what was leading to reaching by them a Nash equilibrium. We have shown that despite the selfish behavior of players, the proposed mechanism of income sharing provided a high degree of global cooperation resulted in maximizing the average total payoff of players without their clear intention to do that. We believe that this result can be useful for solving distributed optimization problems in emerging computer-communication technologies by organizing large teams' collective behavior.

Our future work will be oriented on extending the set of currently used game strategies of behavior, including other mechanisms of social interactions between agents already verified in the context of game-theoretical models (see, e.g., [1,13]), such as signaling, hierarchy, and bribery.

References

1. Bazzan, A.L., Dahmen, S.R.: Bribe and punishment: effects of signaling, gossiping, and bribery in public goods games. Adv. Complex Syst. **13**(6), 755–771 (2010)
2. Brambilla, M., Ferrante, E., Birattari, M., Dorigo, M.: Swarm robotics: a review from the swarm engineering perspective. Swarm Intell. **7**(1), 1–41 (2013)
3. Fernández Domingos, E., et al.: Emerging cooperation in N-person iterated prisoner's dilemma over dynamic complex networks. Comput. Inform. **36**, 493–516 (2017)
4. Ishibuchi, H., Namikawa, N.: Evolution of iterated prisoner's dilemma game strategies in structured demes under random pairing in game playing. IEEE Trans. Evol. Comput. **9**(6), 552–561 (2005)
5. Katsumata, Y., Ishida, Y.: On a membrane formation in a spatio-temporally generalized prisoner's dilemma. In: Umeo, H., Morishita, S., Nishinari, K., Komatsuzaki, T., Bandini, S. (eds.) Cellular Automata, pp. 60–66. Springer, Heidelberg (2008)
6. Nowak, M.A., May, R.M.: Evolutionary games and spatial chaos. Nature **359**, 826 (1992)
7. Osborne, M.: An Introduction to Game Theory. Oxford University Press, New York (2009)
8. Peleteiro, A., Burguillo, J.C., Bazzan, A.L.: Emerging cooperation in the spatial IPD with reinforcement learning and coalitions. In: Bouvry, P., González-Vélez, H., Kołodziej, J. (eds.) Intelligent Decision Systems in Large-Scale Distributed Environments. Studies in Computational Intelligence, pp. 187–206. Springer, Heidelberg (2011). https://doi.org/10.1007/978-3-642-21271-0_9
9. Rossi, F., Bandyopadhyay, S., Wolf, M., Pavone, M.: Review of multi-agent algorithms for collective behavior: a structural taxonomy. IFAC-PapersOnLine **51**(12), 112–117 (2018). IFAC Workshop on Networked & Autonomous Air & Space Systems NAASS 2018
10. Seredyński, F.: Competitive coevolutionary multi-agent systems: the application to mapping and scheduling problems. J. Parallel Distrib. Comput. **47**(1), 39–57 (1997)
11. Seredyński, F., Gąsior, J.: Collective behavior of large teams of multi-agent systems. In: De La Prieta, F., et al. (eds.) PAAMS 2019. CCIS, vol. 1047, pp. 152–163. Springer, Cham (2019). https://doi.org/10.1007/978-3-030-24299-2_13
12. Seredyński, F., Gąsior, J., Hoffmann, R., Désérable, D.: Experiments with heterogenous automata-based multi-agent systems. In: Wyrzykowski, R., Deelman, E., Dongarra, J., Karczewski, K. (eds.) PPAM 2019. LNCS, vol. 12044, pp. 433–444. Springer, Cham (2020). https://doi.org/10.1007/978-3-030-43222-5_38
13. Stewart, I.: A puzzle for pirates. Sci. Am. **280**(5), 98–99 (1999)
14. Toffoli, T., Margolous, N.H.: Invertible cellular automata: a review. Phys. D **45**(1–3), 229–253 (1990)
15. Tsetlin, M.L.: Automaton Theory and Modeling of Biological Systems. Academic Press, Cambridge (1973)
16. Wolfram, S.: A New Kind of Science. Wolfram Media, Champaign (2002)

Parameter Adjustment of a Bio-Inspired Coordination Model for Swarm Robotics Using Evolutionary Optimisation

Claudiney R. Tinoco[1(✉)], Giuseppe Vizzari[2], and Gina M. B. Oliveira[1]

[1] Federal University of Uberlândia, Uberlândia, MG, Brazil
claudineyrt@gmail.com, {claudineyrt,gina}@ufu.br
[2] University of Milano-Bicocca, Milan, MI, Italy
giuseppe.vizzari@unimib.it

Abstract. This work proposed the application of an evolutionary technique to optimise the parameters of a coordination model for swarms of robots. A genetic algorithm with standard characteristics was applied in order to find suitable parameters for the IACA-DI model (Inverted Ant Cellular Automata with Discrete pheromone diffusion and Inertial motion), which, in turn, was proposed in previous works. The IACA-DI is a model to coordinate swarms of robots based on the combination of two bio-inspired techniques: cellular automata and inverted ant system. The main purpose of the model is to carry out surveillance, exploration and foraging tasks. Experiments were performed in different configurations of environments and with different movement strategies to validate this application. Results have shown significant improvements in the model performance compared with previous empirical calibrations, granting a better understanding of the IACA-DI parameters, and allowing significant improvements to be investigated in future works.

Keywords: Cellular automata · Genetic algorithms · Optimisation · Swarm robotics · Evolutionary computation · Repulsive pheromone

1 Introduction

The rise of swarm robotics has led to a large body of researches in associated fields, e.g., aggregation, self-assembly, path-planning, collective exploration, task allocation and others [2]. Bio-inspired computing has been an important area for the proposition of coordination models for swarms of robots, like ant-inspired models [1] and models based on Cellular Automata (CA) [6,16]. Other important models reproduce physical phenomena, such as potential fields [9] and fluid dynamics [21]. A relevant task in swarm robotics is surveillance [14]. It consists of monitoring the presence of other entities, their behaviours, activities, or other environmental changing information, with the aim of protecting people or objects [5]. This task involves environmental exploration where an area must be covered by the robots and a continuous updating of the involved relevant

© Springer Nature Switzerland AG 2021
T. M. Gwizdałła et al. (Eds.): ACRI 2020, LNCS 12599, pp. 146–155, 2021.
https://doi.org/10.1007/978-3-030-69480-7_15

local information. Cooperation and communication strategies are used among the swarm to assure a cyclical coverage of the environment in a reasonable period of time, without requiring spatial knowledge owned a-priori by the robots, and granting a degree of robustness to changes in the environmental structure.

Swarm robotics approaches require a proper calibration of specific working parameters to achieve the above desirable properties, and optimisation techniques have often been considered to perform this task. In particular, an investigation of the state-of-the-art applications of Genetic Algorithms (GA) in the field of aggregation in swarm robotics was made by [15]. In the same line, [10] proposed a GA-based method to track centroids in swarms of drones to minimise the travelled distance and the distance from the drones to the centroid. Seeking to optimise the evolution speed of a GA for collision avoidance in robots, [13] evaluated the individuals in a parallel and distributed manner. Both experiments have presented promising results, showing that GAs can naturally deal with parallelism and are very suitable for swarm robotics. Further investigations with GA in robotics are linked to locomotion [12] and coordination, e.g., navigation under formation control [11]. Decentralised controllers for swarm-based locomotion tasks in two- and three-dimensional environments were analysed by [3]. Since robots must overcome obstacles and attach to other robots, GA was used to assist the model development. More recently, a path-planning and formation control method was proposed by [8]. The model mimics the main features of a GA. Also in the path-planning task, [19] have investigated an application of GA for the coordination of underwater swarms of robots.

The goal of this work is to investigate and evaluate an application of an evolutionary technique to optimise the parameters of an environment mediated coordination model for swarm robotics. Previous work has proposed a coordination model for swarms of robots to perform the surveillance task (IACA-DI [16]). The coordination model is environment mediated, where the acceptation of the term environment is the one introduced in [20]: the environment is defined as a first-class abstraction in multi-agent system models, that provides exploitable mechanisms, such as a pheromone infrastructure (employed by our model), supporting agent interaction and coordination. In prior works, however, its parameters were calibrated through empirical experiments, supporting a visual analysis of the results of different runs. Any change in the model requires a new calibration to be performed, as the swarm's performance is directly linked to the values of these parameters [7,16–18]. This makes the approach costly and inadequate to real-world applications, requiring both mass testing and, especially, human evaluation for every application in real environments (including dynamic changes in the environment). Taking this into account, this work explores the application of an evolutionary strategy to optimise the parameters of the IACA-DI model. These parameters will be analysed and applied to a GA, seeking to improve its configuration and, consequently, its performance.

The organisation of this paper is as follows: Sect. 2 presents the IACA-DI model [16] and Sect. 3 the structure of the GA applied in the optimisation of the IACA-DI's parameters. Experimental results are discussed in Sect. 4. Finally, Sect. 5 presents the main conclusions and future works.

2   Coordination Model for Swarm Robotics (IACA-DI)

The IACA-DI is a model to coordinate swarms of robots that employs two bio-inspired approaches: CA and Inverted Ant System (IAS) [4]. It was proposed to perform tasks like exploration, foraging and, mainly, surveillance.

Environments are discretised into two-dimensional CA lattices. The first one (Fig. 1b) describes physical objects through 3 states: free, robot and obstacle {F, R, O}. The second one (Fig. 1c) describes the pheromone concentration, characteristic of models based on IAS. In this case, cells have continuous states that range between 0.0 and 1.0, where, the pheromone concentration is lower when values tend to zero and the concentration is higher otherwise. The pheromone grid evolves over time through the interactions of the robots. This temporal evolution, which occurs discretely, characterises the CA application.

Individual behaviour of the robots is defined using the Finite State Machine (FSM) illustrated in Fig. 1a. The FSM models the decision-making process of each robot, and how/when they will share information with other robots of the swarm. Combining these two features, which have local scope, it is possible to generate a complex global behaviour capable of performing the proposed task.

The FSM is composed of five states: four are cyclically executed (for T time steps), representing the interactions with the pheromone/environment to perform the decision-making process related to the individual actions (*Detection-1*, *Decision-2*, *Diffusion-3*, and *Movement-4*), and a final state (*End-5*). Each time a robot goes through all four states of the FSM's main cycle, a discrete CA time step is computed. The five states can be briefly detailed as follows:

- Pheromone Detection (State 1): each robot reads the pheromone concentration within its neighbourhood (Moore's neighbourhood [16]);
- Next position decision (State 2): choice of which cell will be the destination of the next movement. Previous works have evaluated five different movement strategies: 1.Random, 2.Deterministic, 3.Simple Probabilistic, 4.Elitist Probabilistic and 5.Inertial Probabilistic [16–18];
- Pheromone Diffusion (State 3): deposition of pheromone in the environment within the robots' neighbourhood (Eq. 1 [16]). Constants α, δ and η represent, respectively, the maximum amount of pheromone deposited, the rate of pheromone deposition and the influence of the rate of evaporation;

$$\Delta_{ij}^{k} = (\psi_{max} - \psi_{ij}^{t}) \cdot \left[\alpha \cdot (\delta \cdot e)^{\eta \cdot \frac{r}{\pi}} \right] \tag{1}$$

- Movement (State 4): represents the robot's transition from an origin cell x_{ij} to a target cell $x_{(i+a)(j+b)}$ in its neighbourhood, such that $\{a, b \in \mathbb{Z}\}$;
- Final state (State 5): activated when the robot completes the proposed task or reaches a limit of T time steps.

As a result of the local behaviour of individual robots, the global behaviour of the swarm emerges, making the collectivity capable of performing the complex task proposed. Global behaviour is related to the self-coordination of robots

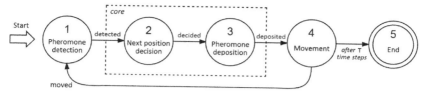

(a) Robot control mechanism represented by a FSM. [Adapted from [17]]

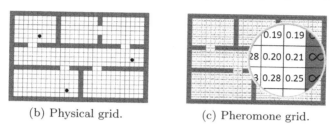

(b) Physical grid.   (c) Pheromone grid.

Fig. 1. Figure (a) describes the individual behaviour of each robot through a FSM with 5 states. Figures (b) and (c) show examples of virtual grids/maps on which the FSM operates (grids with six rooms and size (20×30) cells).

when they spread throughout the environment, with trajectories almost free of conflicts (since the pheromone is repulsive), pursuing and covering areas that have not been visited for a long time or that have not been visited at all.

In the surveillance task, the environment must be monitored cyclically, i.e., the robots must revisit areas that have already been visited in the past, to update dated information about their state. To allow a cyclical exploration process, an evaporation constant is added to the pheromone dynamics. Thus, decreasing pheromone concentration in a given area, proportionally increases the probability of that area being revisited. In the IACA-DI model, the pheromone present in the environment evaporates in a predefined rate at each time step of the CA. Evaporation rate is represented by the constant β (Eq. 2 [16]).

$$\psi_{ij}^{t+1} = \left[\psi_{ij}^t - (\beta \cdot \psi_{ij}^t)\right] + \sum_{k=1}^{N} \Delta_k \tag{2}$$

Therefore, it is possible to define that the pheromone concentration in a cell x_{ij} at time step $(t + 1)$, will be the pheromone concentration at time step t subtracting the amount of pheromone evaporated and adding the deposit contributions of all robots to that cell. It is noteworthy that a robot will contribute to the pheromone concentration of a cell iff that cell is within its neighbourhood [16]. When it comes to the surveillance, β constant is defined with values greater than zero $\{\beta \in \mathbb{R} \mid 0.0 < \beta \leq 1.0\}$. This is due to the fact that the pheromone needs to evaporate in order to allow cyclical visits. On the other hand, if it is an exploration task, for example, β would be set to zero.

3   Genetic Algorithm Structure

In previous works [7,16–18], the parameters of the IACA-DI model were defined through an empirical analysis of the robots' behaviour. In this work, it is intended to perform an optimisation process to identify values for these parameters, granting a better performance during the execution of the surveillance task. Considering the number of parameters of the IACA-DI model, which in most cases have real values, the number of possible combinations to determine the ideal values grows exponentially. Thus, applying a GA to find solutions in large search spaces should fit perfectly: we will describe here how the GA was defined and we will show achieved results in the next section.

Figure 2 illustrates the flowchart of the GA applied in this work and the genetic-code of the individuals. The GA applied is classical, with no additional changes in its structure. Thus, four main operations are defined in the GA structure: Evaluation, Selection, Crossover and Mutation. Evaluation of each individual is done through the application of its genetic-code as parameters of the IACA-DI model. Then, the IACA-DI model is executed in a defined number of time-steps and a performance score of the swarm is attributed to the individual who has the evaluated genetic-code. In addition, the GA uses an elitist percentage to always keep the best individual in the next generation. The genetic-code of the individuals is related to some of the main variables of the IACA-DI model: *evaporation rate* (Eq. 2), *simple probabilistic*, *elitist* and *inertial* percentages (used in the stochastic movement strategies (FSM State 2 - Fig. 1a)), and the constants *alpha*, *delta* and *eta* (Eq. 1). It is worthy to mention that the number of robots and the movement strategies sets were pre-established, taking into account the best results in our previous works [16,18].

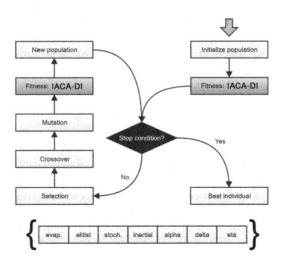

Fig. 2. GA flowchart. Evaluation of the individuals (fitness value) is performed through application of the IACA-DI model [16].

4   Experiments and Analysis

In this section, experiments related to the application of the proposed GA to the IACA-DI model will be presented and analysed. Considering that the parameters of the IACA-DI model were empirically defined in previous works [7, 16–18], through evolutionary computation, we intend to find parameters that optimise the results obtained by the model in the execution of the surveillance task.

Evaluation of each GA-individual is made through the application of the IACA-DI model. Each individual's genetic-code represents the parameters of the IACA-DI model. Thus, the higher the score that an individual (i.e., a robot configured accordingly) achieves performing the surveillance task, the better is its GA evaluation. Evaluation is made by computing task-points: in surveillance of indoor environments, a task point is achieved when all rooms have been visited by at least one robot, and then the count of visited rooms is restarted. On one hand, the effectiveness of this task is associated with having rooms to be cyclically visited, i.e., to reach task points. On the other hand, the efficiency consists in decreasing the time between two consecutive task-points, i.e., higher frequency implies that information about rooms' state is generally not outdated. While efficiency requires effectiveness, the latter does not imply the former.

Experiments were performed in three different environments of size (20×30) cells (E1 - Fig. 3a, E2 - Fig. 3b and E3 - Fig. 3c). According to previous works [7], in environments of such dimensions, a reasonable size for the swarm should be 3 robots (this would be the best trade-off between effectiveness, efficiency and cost, i.e., additional robots would not improve performance without yielding a high cost). Regarding the GA, each evaluation represents the mean of 30 executions (each one with 10.000 time steps) of the IACA-DI model. In addition, it was used 100 individuals in the population, stochastic tournament in selection, 80% of crossover, 2% of mutation and elitism to maintain the best individual.

Figure 4 illustrates the outcomes of the evolution of the GA: Fig. 4a illustrates overall results, and Figs. 4b, 4c and 4d the detailed evolution of the GA in the environment E1. In the detailed evolution charts, the x-axis represents the time evolution (generations) and the y-axis represents the performance (task-points) achieved by the IACA-DI model. Thus, the higher is a point in the chart, the greater is its performance. These charts have five different curves: (i) blue repre-

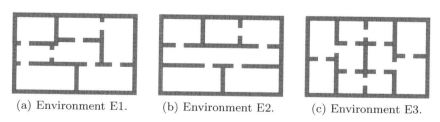

(a) Environment E1.   (b) Environment E2.   (c) Environment E3.

Fig. 3. Environments with (20×30) cells applied in the experiments: E1 - 7 rooms (Fig. (a)), E2 - 6 rooms (Fig. (b)); and E3 - 10 rooms (Fig. (c)).

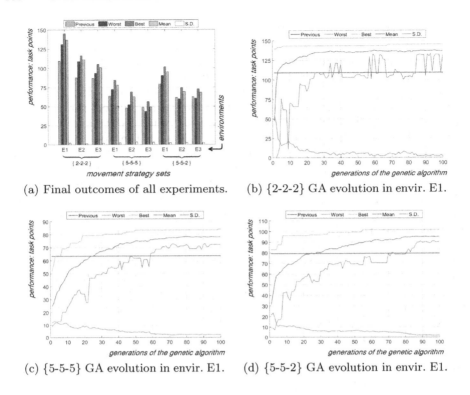

(a) Final outcomes of all experiments.   (b) {2-2-2} GA evolution in envir. E1.

(c) {5-5-5} GA evolution in envir. E1.   (d) {5-5-2} GA evolution in envir. E1.

Fig. 4. Performance of the GA evolution. Figure (a) illustrates overall results, and Figs. (b), (c) and (d) the detailed evolution in the envir. E1. (Color figure online)

sents the best performance achieved in previous works, i.e., where the IACA-DI model was calibrated just with empirical experiments; (ii) red the worst individual; (iii) yellow the best individual; (iv) purple the mean of the evaluation of a whole population; and, (v) green curve represents the Standard Deviation (SD). In Fig. 4a, the set $\{2, 2, 2\}$ represents three robots with deterministic strategy, the set $\{5, 5, 5\}$ three robots with inertial strategy and the set $\{5, 5, 2\}$ a heterogeneous swarm: $2/3$ composed by inertial strategy and $1/3$ by deterministic strategy (configurations based in previous works [17,18]).

In most of the experiments, it was created better individuals in the first generations compared to previous parameters: the manual calibration of the IACA-DI model was, therefore, far from being optimal. Since the GA uses an elitist technique to build future generations, the best individual of the next generation will never be worse than the current one, so the associated curve does not change negatively. Performance improvements of the best individual can be observed after several generations. For general comparison, considering the set of strategies $\{5$-5-$5\}$ in Fig. 4a, the performance of the best individual has increased from 63 to 83 task points in E1 (+32.12%), from 48 to 68 in E2 (+43.54%), and from 48 to 56 in E3 (+14.33%). On the other hand, the

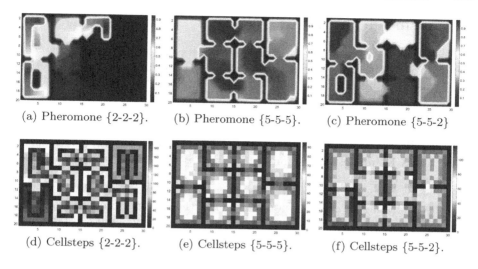

(a) Pheromone {2-2-2}.   (b) Pheromone {5-5-5}.   (c) Pheromone {5-5-2}

(d) Cellsteps {2-2-2}.   (e) Cellsteps {5-5-5}.   (f) Cellsteps {5-5-2}.

Fig. 5. Pheromone heatmaps and cellstep maps for environment E3, through the application of the genetic-code of the best individuals of the GA. (Color figure online)

other individuals can change their performance negatively: performance drops are associated with global search through mutations in the genetic-code. Let us consider Fig. 4c around generation twenty: despite elitism, every individual of the population has a probability to reproduce and, after generation twenty, a worse individual has appeared, causing a small fluctuation in the mean and in the S.D. of the whole population. Figure 4a shows, in all experiments, that it was possible to find a configuration for the parameters of the IACA-DI model that would allow to significantly increase its performance. The topology of the environment and the structure of connections among rooms, clearly have an influence on the performance achieved, in addition to the raw size.

Finally, the best individuals were evaluated using pheromone heatmaps and cellsteps maps. Pheromone heatmaps graphically show the pheromone concentration in the environment in a specific time step and the cellsteps maps represent the mean of times that the robots passed through each cell of the environment. In both experiments, warm colours represent high values and cold colours low values. Using the pheromone heatmaps, it is possible to analyse whether the pheromone concentration is well distributed and the cellsteps maps show whether the swarm is spreading throughout the environment in a uniform way. Figure 5 illustrates the experiments with heatmaps (Figs. 5a, 5b and 5c) and cellsteps (Figs. 5d, 5e and 5f). Considering an empirical analysis, it can be seen that the pheromone concentration is sufficient for the robots to perform their decision-making processes, i.e., the pheromone is well spread and it is not stagnant with either high or low concentration. However, considering the greedy characteristic of the deterministic strategy {2-2-2}, the evaporation rate β has had to be higher to increase the performance of the swarm. In turn, cellsteps maps have shown the same behaviour that was already observed in previous works [17].

5   Conclusion and Future Work

This work has investigated the application of genetic algorithms in the parameter optimisation of the IACA-DI model. Its goal is to coordinate swarms of robots in the execution of the surveillance, foraging or exploration tasks: previously, its parameters have been manually defined through empirical experiments. In this work, an evolutionary strategy, with a more specific methodology, was applied to automatically set these parameters closer to optimal values.

According to the results, it was possible to conclude that: (i) the parameters of the IACA-DI model were improved, making it possible to achieve a better performance (ranging from +14.33% to +43.54% in the analysed environments) compared to that with an empirical analysis; (ii) as expected, the GA has found that the deterministic choice strategy achieved the best performance considering task-points; (iii) experiments with pheromone heatmaps and cellsteps have shown similar behaviour to those found in previous works; (iv) the GA evolution is concentrated in the first 30–40 generations, with no particular improvements in the subsequent ones; and, (v) in this case, the application of an elitist selection was a good choice, since the search-space tend to be exponential.

Regarding future works, we intend to go deeper in the experiments with the GA and the IACA-DI model. More specifically, (i) to have a better understanding of the correlation between the parameters of the IACA-DI model; (ii) to perform experiments with swarms made up of more robots, and with larger environments with different topologies; (iii) to investigate an evaluation metric, where it takes into account task-points and homogeneity on the environment coverage, inhibiting the deterministic strategy bias; and, finally, (iv) to investigate a method to automatically define all parameters values of the IACA-DI model, considering, mainly, the sizes of environments and swarms.

Acknowledgments. Authors are grateful to FAPEMIG, CNPq and CAPES support and scholarships.

References

1. Bontzorlos, T., Sirakoulis, G.C.: Bioinspired algorithm for area surveillance using autonomous robots. Int. J. Parallel Emerg. Distrib. Syst. (IJPEDS) **32**(4), 368–385 (2017)
2. Brambilla, M., Ferrante, E., et al.: Swarm robotics: a review from the swarm engineering perspective. Swarm Intell. **7**(1), 1–41 (2013)
3. Byington, M.D., Bishop, B.E.: Cooperative robot swarm locomotion using genetic algorithms. In: SE Symposium on Systems Theory, pp. 252–256. IEEE (2008)
4. Calvo, R., Oliveira, J.R., Romero, R.A.F., Figueiredo, M.: A bioinspired coordination strategy for controlling of multiple robots in surveillance tasks. Int. J. Adv. Softw. **5**, 146–165 (2012)
5. Falleiros, E.L.S., Calvo, R., Ishii, R.P.: PheroSLAM: a collaborative and bioinspired multi-agent system based on monocular vision. In: Gervasi, O., et al. (eds.) ICCSA 2015. LNCS, vol. 9156, pp. 71–85. Springer, Cham (2015). https://doi.org/10.1007/978-3-319-21407-8_6

6. Lima, D.A., Oliveira, G.M.B.: A probabilistic cellular automata ant memory model for a swarm of foraging robots. In: International Conference on Control, Automation, Robotics and Vision, pp. 1–6. IEEE (2016)
7. Lima, D.A., Tinoco, C.R., Oliveira, G.M.B.: A cellular automata model with repulsive pheromone for swarm robotics in surveillance. In: El Yacoubi, S., Wąs, J., Bandini, S. (eds.) ACRI 2016. LNCS, vol. 9863, pp. 312–322. Springer, Cham (2016). https://doi.org/10.1007/978-3-319-44365-2_31
8. Lin, C.C., Chen, K.C., Chuang, W.J.: Motion planning using a memetic evolution algorithm for swarm robots. Int. J. Adv. Robot. Syst. **9**(1), 19 (2012)
9. Ludwig, L., Gini, M.: Robotic swarm dispersion using wireless intensity signals. In: Gini, M., Voyles, R. (eds.) Distributed Autonomous Robotic Systems, pp. 135–144. Springer, Tokyo (2006). https://doi.org/10.1007/4-431-35881-1_14
10. Nakano, R.C.S., Bandala, A., Faelden, G.E., et al.: A genetic algorithm approach to swarm centroid tracking in quadrotor unmanned aerial vehicles. In: International Conference on Humanoid, Nanotechnology, Information Technology, Communication and Control, Environment and Management (HNICEM), pp. 1–6. IEEE (2014)
11. Oliveira, G.M.B., Silva, R., Amaral, L., Martins, L.G.: An evolutionary-cooperative model based on cellular automata and genetic algorithms for the navigation of robots under formation control. In: Brazilian Conference on Intelligent Systems (BRACIS), pp. 426–431. IEEE (2018)
12. Pandey, A., Pandey, S., Parhi, D.R.: Mobile robot navigation and obstacle avoidance techniques: a review. Int. Rob. Auto J. **2**(3), 00022 (2017)
13. Rezk, N.M., Alkabani, Y., Bedor, H., Hammad, S.: A distributed genetic algorithm for swarm robots obstacle avoidance. In: 2014 9th International Conference on Computer Engineering & Systems (ICCES), pp. 170–174. IEEE (2014)
14. Saska, M., Vakula, J., Přeućil, L.: Swarms of micro aerial vehicles stabilized under a visual relative localization. In: International Conference on Robotics and Automation (ICRA), pp. 3570–3575. IEEE (2014)
15. Soysal, O., Bahçeci, E., Şahin, E.: Aggregation in swarm robotic systems: evolution and probabilistic control. Turk. J. Electr. Eng. Comput. Sci. **15**(2), 199–225 (2007)
16. Tinoco, C.R., Lima, D.A., Oliveira, G.M.B.: An improved model for swarm robotics in surveillance based on cellular automata and repulsive pheromone with discrete diffusion. Int. J. Parallel Emerg. Distrib. Syst. **34**, 53–77 (2017)
17. Tinoco, C.R., Oliveira, G.M.B.: Pheromone interactions in a cellular automata-based model for surveillance robots. In: Mauri, G., El Yacoubi, S., Dennunzio, A., Nishinari, K., Manzoni, L. (eds.) ACRI 2018. LNCS, vol. 11115, pp. 154–165. Springer, Cham (2018). https://doi.org/10.1007/978-3-319-99813-8_14
18. Tinoco, C.R., Oliveira, G.M.B.: Heterogeneous teams of robots using a coordinating model for surveillance task based on cellular automata and repulsive pheromone. In: Congress on Evolutionary Computation (CEC), pp. 747–754. IEEE (2019)
19. Vicmudo, M.P., Dadios, E.P., Vicerra, R.R.P.: Path planning of underwater swarm robots using genetic algorithm. In: International Conference on Humanoid, Nanotechnology, Information Technology, Communication and Control, Environment and Management, pp. 1–5. IEEE (2014)
20. Weyns, D., Omicini, A., Odell, J.: Environment as a first class abstraction in multiagent systems. Auton. Agents Multi Agent Syst. **14**(1), 5–30 (2007)
21. Zheng, Z., Tan, Y.: Group explosion strategy for searching multiple targets using swarm robotic. In: Congress on Evolutionary Computation, pp. 821–828. IEEE (2013)

Covering the Space with Sensor Tiles

Rolf Hoffmann[1]([✉]) and Franciszek Seredyński[2]

[1] Technische Universität Darmstadt, Darmstadt, Germany
`hoffmann@informatik.tu-darmstadt.de`
[2] Department of Mathematics and Natural Sciences, Cardinal Stefan Wyszynski University, Warsaw, Poland
`f.seredynski@uksw.edu.pl`

Abstract. The objective is to find Cellular Automata (CA) which are able to cover the 2D space by a minimum number of so-called "Sensor Tiles". A sensor tile consists of a central sensor pixel and 12 surrounding sensing pixels. Two probabilistic CA rules were designed that can perform this task. The first rule evolves very fast stable sub–optimal coverings, starting from a random configuration. The second rule finds several optimal or near-optimal coverings but needs much more time for their evolution.

Keywords: Covering problem · Wireless Sensor Network · Tilings · Matching templates · Probabilistic cellular automata · Asynchronous updating

1 Introduction

Our goal is to find a covering of the 2D space by so-called *sensor tiles* using CA. Our problem is one of the diverse covering problems [1] and it is related to the NP-complete *vertex cover problem* introduced by Hakimi [2] in 1965. A vertex cover is a set of nodes in a graph such that every edge of the graph has at least one end point in the set. A minimum cover is a vertex cover which has the smallest number of nodes for a given graph. Hakimi proposed a solution method based on Boolean functions, later integer linear programming [3], branch-and-bound, genetic algorithm, and local search [4] were used, among others. Other related problems are the *Location Set Covering Problem* [5] and the *Central Facilities Location Problem* [6]. These problems aim to find the locations for P facilities that can be reached within a weighted distance from demand points, minimizing the number of P, or minimizing the average distance, or maximizing the coverage. For covering problems there are a lot of applications, in economy, urban planning, engineering, etc.

Specifically, we have in mind *Wireless Sensor Networks* (WSN) as an application where a number of sensors are placed in an area, and the question is which of them should be currently active and able to monitor a part of an environment. The whole area should be covered (monitored) and the number of active sensors

© Springer Nature Switzerland AG 2021
T. M. Gwizdałła et al. (Eds.): ACRI 2020, LNCS 12599, pp. 156–168, 2021.
https://doi.org/10.1007/978-3-030-69480-7_16

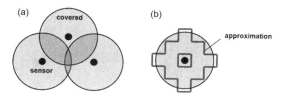

Fig. 1. (a) Sensors cover a certain area, (b) The circular range of a sensor is approximated by a discrete shape (in red). (Color figure online)

should be minimized in order to minimize the total energy consumption and prolong this way a lifetime of WSN. With low battery consumption the lifetime of WSN can be maximized by switching between optimal configurations of active sensors. This problem was already treated in many variants, e.g. [7,8].

We assume that sensors are regularly located in an area to be covered, available at any discrete location of a superimposed grid. The questions is how to turn them skillfully ON (active) or OFF (passive) to yield a sensor network with a minimum number of sensors, which we will call *min point pattern*. As shown in Fig. 1a, each active sensor (here also called *point*) senses a certain area in a circular range when battery is ON. Several sensors shall cover the whole space. A sensor with its range will be approximated by a discrete area (tile) (Fig. 1b).

The WSN covering problem is computationally expensive and near-optimal solutions can be found for instance with evolutionary algorithms [9]. We want to solve this problem by CA in a decentralized way. The problem of maximizing the lifetime of WSNs was already addressed in the CA context [10], but it turned out to be challenging using means such as Iterated Spatial Prisoner's Dilemma, the Second-Order CA or Learning Automata.

Here the idea is to treat the covering problem as a pattern formation problem, where *Parallel Substitution Algorithms* [11] served also as a source of inspiration. For the problem of forming a *Domino Pattern* we yielded already a good result by using a probabilistic CA rule [12]. There the number of dominoes was maximized by using overlapping tiles. We want to follow the same general approach, but now the problem is more difficult because the number of tiles has to be minimized.

In Sect. 2, the sensor tiling problem is described and optimal solutions are presented. In Sect. 3, two probabilistic CA rules are designed. In Sect. 4, the performance of the rules is evaluated, and conclusions are given in Sect. 5.

2   Optimal Covering with Sensor Tiles

2.1   The Problem and Its CA Modeling

Given an array of $N = (n \times n)$ cells, also called *field*. We assume that each cell contains a sensor which is either active or passive. The objective is to find a CA rule that can form a *Sensor Coverage Pattern* with a minimum number of active sensors that cover the whole area. An active sensor can cover (sense) a certain number of cells in its neighborhood. We can relate an active sensor with

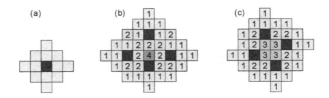

Fig. 2. (a) Sensor Tile. (b) Four tiles with max. overlap $v_{max} = 4$. (c) Four tiles with max. overlap $v_{max} = 3$.

its sensed cells to a *sensor tile* as shown in Fig. 2(a). A sensor tile is a discrete approximation of a real area sensed by an active sensor as depicted in Fig. 1(b). Note that sensor tiles are not automata cells, they are only used as a mean to find a cell rule and to define the covering of the space. We call the elements of a tile *pixels* in order to not confuse them with the cells of the space. A sensor tile consists of one center pixel (the *kernel* with the pixel value 1, in blue) and 12 surrounding pixels (the *hull* with value 0, in yellow).

Hull pixels of different tiles are allowed to overlap, but not with sensor points. This restriction is meaningful because we aim that the number of all active sensors is minimal and therefore the density of active sensor should be low.

We call the number of overlapping pixels at a certain site (x, y) "*overlap*" or "*cover level*" $v(x, y)$. Patterns with overlapping tiles are shown in Fig. 2(b, c). The cover level is depicted here by numbers and colors. In later shown figures only numbers or colors will be used.

The cell state is modeled as $q = s$ for the First Rule (see Sect. 3.1) and as $q = (s, h)$ for the Second Rule (Sect. 3.2). The state $s \in \{0, 1\}$ models an inactive/active sensor, and all sensor states build the pattern (a sensor configuration). $h \in \{0, 1, 2, 3, 4, 100\}$ stores the number of template hits, explained later in Sect. 3.2. We assume cyclic border conditions in order to simplify the problem. (Constant zero-boundaries with width 1 or 2 could also be used in order to keep sensor points within the borders).

2.2   Optimal Solutions

We call a coverage *valid*, if the sensor tiles cover the whole space without gaps (uncovered cells). There are valid coverages/patterns with a different number of active sensors, between a minimal and a maximal number (as you can see later in Fig. 3). We call a valid coverage with a minimal number of active sensors *min sensor pattern* (for short *min pattern*), and a coverage with a maximal number *max sensor pattern* (for short *max pattern*). In this paper we are interested in min sensor patterns, but max sensor patterns will also be considered. Note that there exist many equivalent sensor patterns taking into account the symmetries: translation, rotation, and reflection. When we speak of a pattern, we mean any representative in the class of equivalent patterns.

Using the CA rules described later, valid sensor patterns covering the whole space were found. They are listed in Table 1 for different field sizes. This table

Table 1. Valid sensor patterns (solutions) found for different field sizes. The table presents the number of sensor tiles, the maximum overlap in the set of solutions, and the density of sensors (point density). Notation for the max overlap values: $M(a)$ means $|v_{max} = M| = a$; $M(a, b, c)$ means $|v_{max} = M| = a, b, c$; $M(a..b)$ means $a \le |v_{max} = M| \le b$, and $M(+)$ means $|v_{max} = M| \ge 1$. On the right, three solutions with 7 tiles with different v_{max} are shown. Active sensors are shown in black, inactive in white.

Field Size N = n x n	Tiles L	Max. Overlap (for different solutions) v_{max}	Point Density R = L/N	Comment
3 x 3	1	2	1/9 = 0.111	only one solution
4 x 4	2	3(2), 4(2)	1/8 = 0.125	only two solutions
5 x 5	3	3(1)	3/25 = 0.12	
	5	3(everywhere)	1/5 = 0.2	equidistant
6 x 6	4	2(+), 3(2)	1/9 = 0.111	
	5	3(+)	5/36	
	6	3(+)	1/6 = 0.167	
7 x 7	5	2(+), 3(1), 4(4)	5/49 = 0.102	
	6	3(1 .. 5), 4(1)	6/49	
	7	2(everywhere)	1/7	equidistant
	7	3(+), 4(1 .. 2)	1/7	
	8	4(2..5)	8/49 = 0.163	
8 x 8	7	2(+), 3(2, 3, 10)	7/64 = 0.109	
	8	3(+), 4(1)	1/8	
	9	3(+), 4(1 .. 4)	9/64	
	10	3(+), 4(1 .. 4)	5/32 = 0.156	
9 x 9	8	2(+), 3(1 .. 4), 4(1)	8/81 = 0.099	
	9	2(+), 3(1 .. 7)	1/9	
	10	3(+), 4(1 .. 2)	10/81	
	11	3(+), 4(1 .. 2)	11/81	
	12	3(+), 4(1 .. 4)	12/81	
	13	3(+), 4(1 .. 4)	13/81 = 0.160	
10 x 10	9	2(+)	9/100 = 0.09	
	10	2(+), 3(1 .. 4)	1/10	
	11	3(1 .. 7)	11/100	
	12	3(+), 4(1)	3/25	
	13	3(+), 4(1 .. 3)	13/100	
	14	3(1), 4(1 .. 3)	7/50	
	15	3(+), 4(1 .. 4)	3/20	
	16	3(+), 4(1 .. 6)	4/25	
	17	3(+), 4(1, 2, 4, 8)	17/100	
	18	3(+)	9/50	
	20	3(everywhere)	1/5 = 0.2	equidistant
11 x 11	12	3(2 .. 6)	12/121 = 0.099	
	13 .. 21			
	22	3(+)	22/121 = 0.182	

presents the number L of sensor tiles, the maximum overlap v_{max} in the set of solutions, and the density $R(N) = L/N$ of sensors (point density). E.g. for $N = (7 \times 7)$, there are 5-tile patterns with (a) $|v_{max} = 2| \ge 1$ (several sites have overlap 2), (b) $|v_{max} = 3| = 1$ (only one site has overlap 3), (c) $|v_{max} = 4| = 4$ (four sites have overlap 4). The minimal point density for this example is $R_{min}(49) = 5/49 = 0.102$, and the maximal density is $R_{max}(49) = 8/49 = 0.163$. Recall that we search for min point patterns with a minimal point density.

Some min and max sensor patterns are shown in Fig. 3. The following min and max pattern were found (Table 1):

- (3×3) There is only one solution.
- (4×4) There are two solutions, each with two points. The maximal overlap level is 3 (appears twice) for the upper one ($|v_{max} = 3| = 2 \Leftrightarrow v_{max} = 3(2)$), and 4 for the lower one ($v_{max} = 4(2)$). There is no special min pattern.

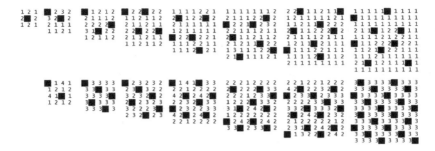

Fig. 3. Minimal sensor patterns (upper half), maximal sensor patterns (lower half). A black square represents a sensor point, and the numbers give the overlap level. Field sizes range from (3×3) to (10×10).

- (5×5) A min pattern with 3 and a max pattern with 5 points exist, but no pattern with 4 points. Note that there exists one cell with cover level of 3 in the min pattern, and there is no min pattern with $v_{max} = 2$ as we can find for $n = 6 .. 10$.
- $n = 6, 7, 8, 9, 10, 11$: There exist min/max patterns with 4/6, 5/8, 7/10, 8/13, 9/20, 12/22 points.

3 The Designed CA Rules

First, as a matter of principle, we have to decide (i) whether to use a *synchronous* or an *asynchronous* updating scheme, and (ii) whether to use a *deterministic* or a *probabilistic* rule. This makes four options: (1) synchronous updating & deterministic rule, (2) synchronous updating & probabilistic rule, (3) asynchronous updating & deterministic rule, and (4) asynchronous updating & probabilistic rule.

We have to keep in mind that we search for a CA rule that converges always or with a high probability to optimal or near-optimal patterns. From our previous work we have learned that it is very difficult or even impossible to design such a rule with the option (1), because we may have to avoid or dissolve conflicts, deadlocks, live-locks, and emerging oscillating, moving or clustering structures, as we know, e.g. from the *Game of Life*, in order to drive the pattern continuously to an optimum (not to get stuck in sub-optimal solution areas).

The remaining options (2–4) are related because the computation of a new configuration is stochastic. It seems that they can be transformed into each other to a certain extent.

Here we want to use option (4) because we have gained good results in solving another problem [12] in this way. Moreover, we don't need a clock for synchronization and buffering for the configuration, which is closer to the modeling of natural processes. In contrast to that former solved problem, we address here a more difficult problem where the number of tiles is minimized and not maximized.

3.1   The First Rule

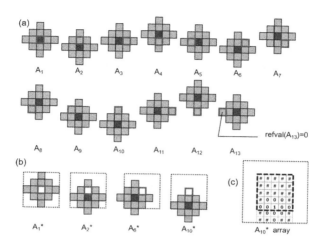

Fig. 4. (a) The 13 templates A_i of the sensor tile. The value $refval(A_i)$ of the reference pixel (marked in red) is used for cell updating in the case that all remaining template pixels (the neighborhood template) match with the corresponding cells of the current configuration. (b) The neighborhood templates A_i^*. The dotted box marks the (5×5)–window used for matching. The remaining neighborhood templates result from rotation of the shown ones. (c) A_{10}^* represented as an array reduced from (9×9) to (5×5). (Color figure online)

The idea is to modify the current configuration in a systematic way such that valid patterns appear and at last a min pattern. To do this, the CA configuration is searched for tile parts (specific local patterns) and if an almost correct tile part is found, it is corrected, otherwise some random noise is injected.

The tile parts are called *templates* A_i. They are systematically derived from the sensor tile (Fig. 4(a)). For each of the 13 tile pixels (so-called *derivation pixels*, marked in red) a template is defined by shifting the tile in a way that the derivation pixel appears in the center. Note that many of these templates are similar under various symmetries. A_3, A_4, A_5 are rotations of A_2; A_7, A_8, A_9 are rotations of A_6, and A_{11}, A_{12}, A_{13} are rotations of A_{10}.

We represent a *template* A_i is an array of size $(k \times k)$ of pixels, where $k = 2m - 1$ and $(m \times m)$ is the size of the tile, enlarged to a square box embedding it. Our tile is of size (5×5) including empty pixels, and the templates are larger because of shifting, maximal of size (9×9). The pixels within a template are identified by relative coordinates $(\Delta x, \Delta y)$. The center pixel at $(\Delta x, \Delta y) = (0, 0)$) is called *"reference pixel"*. Each template pixel carries a value $val(A_i, \Delta x, \Delta y) \in \{0, 1, \#\}$. The value of the reference pixel is called *"reference value"*, $refval(A_i) = val(A_i, 0, 0) \in \{0, 1\}$, which is equal to the value of the derivation pixel. The symbol # represents "Don't Care", meaning that a pixel with such a value is not used for matching (or does not exist (empty pixel), in another interpretation). Pixels with a value 0 or 1 are *valid* pixels, their values are equal to the values derived from the original tile. Some templates can be embedded into arrays smaller than $(k \times k)$ when they have Don't Cares at their borders.

We need also to define the term *"neighborhood template"* that is later used in the matching procedure. The neighborhood template A_i^* is the template A_i in which the reference value is set to #, in order to exclude the reference pixel from the matching process. The cell processing scheme is:

- At time-step t a *new* configuration is formed by updating N cells in a random order. For each time-step a new random permutation is used. The new configuration is complete after N cell updates (Each cell is updated once during this period) and it defines the *next* configuration at time–step $t + 1$.
- The rule is applied asynchronously. The new cell state $s' = f(s, B^*)$ is computed and immediately updated without buffering. B^* denotes the states of the neighbors within a local window, where the center cell $s(x, y)$ is excluded (for matching).

The following rule is applied:

$$
s'(x, y) = \begin{cases} refval(A_i) & \text{if } \exists A_i^* \text{ that matches with } CA\text{–}Neighbors(x, y) \; (a) \\ & \textbf{otherwise} \\ random \in \{0, 1\} & \text{with probability } \pi_0 \hspace{1.5cm} (b1) \\ s(x, y) & \text{with probability } 1 - \pi_0 \hspace{1cm} (b2) \end{cases}
$$

The neighborhood templates A_i^* are tested against the corresponding cell neighbors $B^*(x, y)$ in the current (5×5)–window at position (x, y). Thereby the marked reference position $(\Delta x, \Delta y) = (0, 0)$ of a neighborhood template is aligned with the center of the window. Note that we use for testing a window of size (5×5) which is smaller than the full size (9×9) of the neighborhood templates. Therefore, some valid pixels outside the (5×5)–window are not tested (e.g. the bottom 4 yellow pixels of A_{13}^* in Fig. 4(b)). The implementation with these incomplete neighborhood templates worked very well, but further investigations are necessary for proving to which extent they can be incomplete.

If all values of a neighborhood template A_i^* match then we register a hit that is stored only temporarily. There can be several hits equal to the cover level. If we have at least one hit, the sensor state of the current cell $s(x, y)$ is set to the reference value $refval(A_i)$, and then we create or validate a correct tile part in the pattern configuration. Otherwise, with probability π_0, the sensor state is set randomly to either 0 or 1, or remains unchanged with probability $1 - \pi_0$. There can be no conflicts, because the reference value is the same (uniquely derived from the tile) if there are several hits. (Examples: If A_0^* matches, there is one hit only and the reference value is 1. If $A_{10}^*, A_{11}^*, A_{12}^*, A_{13}^*$ match, we get 4 hits with reference values 0). As no conflicts can arise, the sequence of testing the templates does not matter, and one could skip further tests after a first hit.

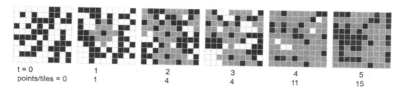

| t = 0 | 1 | 2 | 3 | 4 | 5 |
| points/tiles = 0 | 1 | 4 | 4 | 11 | 15 |

Fig. 5. A (10×10) simulation sequence yielding a stable pattern with 15 points, using the First Rule. Colors: blue (active sensor), white (not covered by a tile), yellow (cover level 1), light green (cover level 2), green (cover level 3). (Color figure online)

It is important to note that this rule obeys the criterion of stability, which means that a valid pattern without gaps (uncovered cells) is *stable* because we have matching hits at every site. Otherwise, some random noise is injected in order to drive the evolution to the aimed pattern.

10,000 runs were performed on (10×10)–fields with random initial configurations and a time-limit of 200 iterations, with $\pi_0 = 1.0$. The CA system converges quickly to a stable sub–optimal sensor pattern after 16.83 time–steps on average. (The evolution is slower for $\pi_0 < 1$.) These patterns contain 12–20 points and all cover the space as required. The number of evolved patterns with a certain number of points are:

points	9	10	11	12	13	14	15	16	17	18	20
number	0	0	0	14	369	2398	4647	2281	220	62	9

Most often the patterns contained 15 points. We see in Fig. 5 how fast a stable pattern with 15 points can evolve. The probability to find a near-minimal point pattern with 12 points was quite low (occurrence of 0.14% for this experiment with 10,000 runs). During this run no patterns with 9 (minimum), 10 or 11 points appeared, but a few max patterns. We can conclude that min sensor patterns are very rare in the whole set of all valid patterns covering the space. So now we want to improve our rule in order to evolve min patterns with a high probability.

3.2   The Second, Improved Rule

The purpose of this enhancement is to improve the rule in such a way that the number of points reaches a minimum. Whereas the first rule works with the state $q = s$ only, now the state is extended by the number of hits h, thus the full state $q = (s, h)$ is used. Now all neighborhood templates are tested and all hits are stored for every site (x, y). The number of hits $h(x, y)$ is:

- 0, if no neighborhood template matches or there is a gap,
- 1, if it results from one neighborhood template match where the reference value is zero (yellow colored),
- 2–4, if it results from the overlap at the same site (x, y) of 2–4 neighborhood template matches with reference values zero, that means that 2–4 tiles (yellow hull pixels) are overlapping,

- 100, if it results from the neighborhood template A_1^* match where the reference value is 1 (blue). Recall that blue pixels are not allowed to overlap. The number 100 was chosen in order to differentiate such hits from the other.

The hit number $h(x, y)$ holds the actual value after matching with all the neighborhood templates. Because of the random sequential updating scheme, the h-values in the (x, y)–neighborhood may not be up-to-date and can carry old values from the former configuration at time-step $t - 1$. Nevertheless, the h-values correspond mainly to the cover levels v, especially when the pattern becomes more stable. This inaccuracy introduces some additional small noise which can even speed-up the evolution. And when the pattern becomes stable, the hit number is equal to the cover level, $\forall(x, y) : h(x, y) = v(x, y)$.

The idea is to minimize the overlap between tiles by destroying cell states with high overlap level ($h > 1$) through noise, allowing reordering with a lower number of points. In order to find a rule we need to study the min point patterns with respect to their overlap values and local situations. From Table 1 and Fig. 3 we can see that min patterns contain some cells with a max overlap $v_{max} = 2, 3$. (There is a special case with $n = 13$ or multiples of 13 where there exists a pattern with $v_{max} = 1$ that we will not be taken into consideration here.)

First the new state s' is computed according to the First Rule, and additionally the number of all hits $h(x, y)$ is computed and stored. Then the new state is modified to s'':

$$s''(x, y) = \begin{cases} random \in \{0,1\} & \text{with probability } \pi_4 \text{ if } h(x, y) = 4 \\ random \in \{0,1\} & \text{with probability } \pi_3 \text{ if } C_1 \text{ or } C_2 \text{ or } C_3 \\ s'(x, y) & \textbf{otherwise,} \end{cases}$$

where
$C_1 = (hits3x3(x, y) > 14)$,
$C_2 = (hits3x3(x, y) > 13) \text{ and } (Active3x3(x, y) > 0)$,
$C_3 = (hits3x3(x, y) = 12) \text{ and } (Active3x3(x, y) = 0) \text{ and } (h(x, y) = 3)$

The conditions $C_{1..3}$ add additional noise in order to drive the evolution to the optimum when the local hit density is above a certain level. It was quite difficult to find these conditions through many trial and error simulations taken into account the local patterns in (3×3)–windows of valid optimal and near-optimal solutions. It would be interesting to find better conditions through further research. The ultimate goal is to find a rule that drives always to a *stable optimal* solution not excluding any solution from the set of all possible solutions.

The function $hits3x3(x, y)$ computes the sum of the hits of inactive cells in a local (3×3)–window with its center at (x, y), where active sensor cells and the center are discarded. The function $Active3x3(x, y)$ computes the sum of active cells in a (3×3)–window.

Now, for this improved rule, it is not clear whether the stability criterion is still fulfilled because of the additional noise. In fact, it turned out that reached min pattern are often stable, although some non-min pattern can be stable, too.

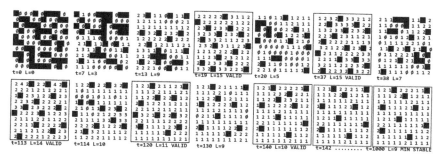

Fig. 6. Simulation of an evolution yielding a (10×10) min pattern with 9 points. Some valid point patterns at time-steps $t = 19, 37, 113, 120, 140, 142, 1000$ are shown. The final pattern is stable for $t \geq 142$.

Extensive simulations showed that noise injection under these additional conditions drive non-min patterns to min patterns. Unfortunately, at the moment, we cannot show that the evolution always ends up with a stable min pattern, because (a) we cannot prove that all reached valid non-min patterns are transients (meaning that then further noise will still be injected), and (b) that all reached min patterns are stable (meaning that then noise injection is always stopped).

A deeper analysis is a subject to further research. It remains an open question, whether a local CA rule can be found that always drives the evolution to a min point pattern, and preferably to any of all possible min pattern, not excluding solutions with a certain max. cover level or certain local sensor arrangements.

During a simulation, the number of complete tiles/points L is increasing, decreasing and fluctuating, and at the end the evolution is often driving towards a valid stable pattern, which often is a min pattern. Many experiments showed that optimal min patterns can successfully be found with the Second Rule if (a) the maximal number of time-steps T_{Limit} is chosen large enough and/or (b) several runs with random initial states are performed.

4   Simulation and Performance Evaluation

4.1   Performance for Field Size (10×10)

The improved rule was tested 10,000 times on 10×10 fields with random initial states ($s \in 0, 1$), for $T_{Limit} = 1,000$ time–steps, with $\pi_4 = 0.1$, $\pi_3 = 0.9$, and $\pi_0 = 0.1$ (yielding best results). For each run, several parameters were recorded, such as the time-stamp for reaching the greatest or smallest number of points in valid patterns. The number of patterns with the smallest reached number of points were:

```
points    9    10    11    12    13    14..20
number   56   362  3121  6178   283        0.
```

We can see that now optimal min patterns were reached in 56 out of 10,000 runs under this time limit. The other evolved patterns are close to the minimum. Patterns with 12 points appeared most often. No patterns with more than 13 points evolved. Compared to the first rule, the second rule finds a pattern much closer to the optimum or even reaches it. From the stored data we can also see that rare min patterns need a relatively long time to evolve ($t_{average} = 524, t_{min/max} = 75/997$), whereas patterns with more points appear faster (e.g. for 12-point patterns: $t_{average} = 311, t_{min/max} = 21/1000$)). Figure 6 shows the evolution of a stable min pattern with 9 sensors. During the evolution, other valid transient patterns with a different number of complete tiles L appear (encircled in Fig. 6). The percentage of finding an optimal min pattern can be increased by increasing the time limit. As we can see in Table 2 the percentage increases from 0.56% to 29% for $T_{Limit} = 100,000$.

4.2   Performance for Other Field Sizes

The Improved Rule was also tested on other field sizes and a different number of runs and time limits (Table 2). For sizes up to (8×8) all runs yielded optimal min patterns. For fields larger than (8×8), min patterns were found among others. The rate of finding a min pattern depends on the number of runs and the time limit T_{Limit}. As example we consider a (10×10) field with the same number 10^7 of total generation computations, which yields $100 \times 10^7 = 10^9$ cell rule computations. We 29 min patterns using 10^2 runs with $T_{Limit} = 10^5$, 56 min patterns using 10^4 runs with $T_{Limit} = 10^3$. This example shows that it can be better to perform more shorter runs than less longer ones, a result which is also known from optimization techniques with genetic algorithm.

Table 2. Simulation for different time limits and number of runs. Percentage of found optimal min patterns, and time steps needed ($t_{average}, t_{min}, t_{max}$).

N = n x n	min points	runs	T Limit	found min patterns [%]	t average of found min pat.	t min	t max	T₁₀% 10% found	E = T₁₀%/N
3 x 3	1	100	200	100	33	0	129	1	0.11
4 x 4	2	100	300	100	34	1	178	2	0.13
5 x 5	3	100	500	100	63	8	288	18	0.72
6 x 6	4	100	1000	100	85	8	369	24	0.67
7 x 7	5	100	5 000	100	528	38	2 480	109	2.2
8 x 8	7	100	10 000	100	1 089	41	4 259	111	1.7
9 x 9	8	100	30 000	85	5 267	402	21 267	1 123	14
10 x 10	9	100	100 000	29	36 541	1 222	90 209	16 183	162
11 x 11	12	100	200 000	28	81 850	2 963	199 811	41 501	343

We define the computing effort per cell to evolve $0.1R$ min patterns during R runs within times $t \le T_{10\%}(N)$ as $E(T_{10\%}, N) = (T_{10\%}(N))/N$, where the maximal needed time $T_{10\%}(N)$ was extracted from simulation data. If $E(N) = const$ then the needed time would be in $O(N)$ to reach 10% min patterns within

R runs. In our experiments this effort increases super-linear with N for $N = 64, 81, 100, 121$ as shown in Table 2. Therefore, it is costly to compute optimal solutions for large N. But as the CA model is inherently parallel regarding N, we can reduce the computation time significantly on a parallel computer. For large N the algorithm is still applicable, though we will terminate it due to restricted computing resources when having found a near-optimal solution.

5 Conclusion

First we have studied what is the minimum and maximum of sensor points for valid patterns for different sizes. Then we designed two CA rules that can find non-optimal and optimal min sensor patterns. The first rule evolves very fast to stable valid patterns, with a peak number of points lying between minimum and maximum. The design principle behind is methodical and based on a set of templates derived from all pixels of the sensor tile. The second rule was designed especially to find min patterns, and it can do so, although the time to evolve an optimal min pattern can exceed the available processing capabilities. In further work the possible sensor locations could be restricted, the charge of batteries could be taken into account, or this approach could be related to the vertex cover problem in order to compare time complexity.

References

1. Snyder, L.V.: Covering problems. In: Foundations of Location Analysis, pp. 109–135. Springer, Boston (2011)
2. Hakimi, S.L.: Optimum distribution of switching centers in a communication network and some related graph theoretic problems. Oper. Res. **13**, 462–475 (1965)
3. Gomesa, F.C., Menesesb, C.N., Pardalosb, P.M., Vianaa, G.V.R.: Experimental analysis of approximation algorithms for the vertex cover and set covering problems. Comput. Oper. Res. **33**, 3520–3534 (2006)
4. Richter, S., Helmert, M., Gretton, C.: A stochastic local search approach to vertex cover. In: Hertzberg, J., Beetz, M., Englert, R. (eds.) KI 2007. LNCS (LNAI), vol. 4667, pp. 412–426. Springer, Heidelberg (2007). https://doi.org/10.1007/978-3-540-74565-5_31
5. Church, R.L., ReVelle, C.S.: Theoretical and computational links between the p-median, location set-covering, and the maximal covering location problem. Geograph. Anal. **8**(4), 406–415 (1976)
6. Mehrez, A.: Facility location problems, review, description, and analysis. Geogr. Res. Forum **8**, 113–129 (2016)
7. Thai, M.T., Wang, F., Du, D.H., Jia, X.: Coverage problems in wireless sensor networks: designs and analysis, Int. J. Sens. Netw. **3**(3), 191–200 (2008)
8. Aziz, N.A.A., Aziz, K.A., Ismail, W.Z.W.: Coverage strategies for wireless sensor networks. World Acad. Sci. Eng. Technol. **50**, 145–150 (2009)
9. Moh'd Alia, O., Al-Ajouri, A.: Maximizing wireless sensor network coverage with minimum cost using harmony search algorithm. IEEE Sens. J. **17**(3), 882–896 (2017)

10. Gąsior, J., Seredyński, F., Hoffmann, R.: Towards self-organizing sensor networks: game-theoretic ϵ-learning automata-based approach. In: Mauri, G., El Yacoubi, S., Dennunzio, A., Nishinari, K., Manzoni, L. (eds.) ACRI 2018. LNCS, vol. 11115, pp. 125–136. Springer, Cham (2018). https://doi.org/10.1007/978-3-319-99813-8_11
11. Achasova, S., Bandman, O., Markova, V., Piskunov, S.: Parallel Substitution Algorithm, Theory and Application. World Scientific, Singapore (1994)
12. Hoffmann, R., Désérable, D., Seredyński, F.: A probabilistic cellular automata rule forming domino patterns. In: Malyshkin, V. (ed.) PaCT 2019. LNCS, vol. 11657, pp. 334–344. Springer, Cham (2019). https://doi.org/10.1007/978-3-030-25636-4_26

Implementation of Cellular Automata Using Graphene Nanoribbons with Magnetic Contacts

Konstantinos Rallis, Savvas Moysidis, and Ioannis G. Karafyllidis[✉]

Department of Electrical and Computer Engineering,
Democritus University of Thrace, 67100 Xanthi, Greece
ykar@ee.duth.gr

Abstract. We propose a novel architecture for the implementation of Cellular Automata (CA). The novel architecture is based on graphene nanoribbons with magnetic contacts, which are used as building blocks. In this CA implementation, information processing is obtained through top-gates, back-gates and the angles and magnitudes of the polarizations of the magnetic contacts. We use tight-binding Hamiltonians and non-equilibrium Green's functions to model and simulate the operation of the building blocks of the proposed CA implementation. Interconnections are local and CA cell states can be represented using top-gate and back-gate potentials, and the angles and magnitudes of the contact polarizations. We also describe the CA evolution rules. Our results showed that this CA implementation is capable of both digital and analog information processing. Furthermore, it can be effectively used for neuromorphic and in-memory computing.

Keywords: CA implementation · Graphene nanoribbons · Nanoelectronics · Magnetic contacts

1 Introduction

Graphene is a relative novel 2D material with excellent electronic properties, including high electron mobility and sustainability of high currents [1]. Graphene is a very promising material for carbon-based nanoelectronic devices and circuits and this led to the fabrication and study of graphene transistors [2], graphene quantum point contacts [3], graphene p-n junctions [4] and graphene logic gates [5].

In all these devices and circuits, graphene nanoribbons with non-magnetic metallic contacts have been used and information has been represented using top-gate and back-gate potentials. However, experiments revealed two more parameters that determine the operation of graphene devices, the magnetic polarization angles and magnitudes of the ferromagnetic contacts, used as source and drain electrodes [6]. Therefore, information can be represented using four independent

© Springer Nature Switzerland AG 2021
T. M. Gwizdałła et al. (Eds.): ACRI 2020, LNCS 12599, pp. 169–176, 2021.
https://doi.org/10.1007/978-3-030-69480-7_17

parameters, namely top-gate potentials, back-gate potentials, and polarization angles and magnitudes, which control electron flow via their spin. The structure and nature of these graphene devices is suitable for local interconnections and local information processing which makes them promising elements for constructing cellular automata (CA) architectures with novel computation properties.

Here, we propose a novel implementation of CAs using graphene nanoribbon devices with magnetic contacts. We use tight-binding Hamiltonians and non-equilibrium Green's functions (NEGF), described analytically in [7] and [8], to model and simulate the operation of the building blocks of the proposed CA architecture, which are graphene devices with magnetic contacts connected in series in L-shaped forms [9]. The states of the CA cells are represented by the conductance of each cell, which can vary either discretely or continuously. The rule of the CA evolution is a function of the top-gate potentials, the back-gate potentials and the values of polarization angles and magnitudes of the contacts. Our results showed that this novel CA implementation has new and useful properties which can be exploited to construct CA architectures that are capable of digital and analog information processing, neuromorphic computing and in-memory computing.

2   Structure of the of Graphene Nanoribbon Device with Magnetic Contacts

The proposed graphene device, that will be used as a building block of the CA architecture, is shown in Fig. 1.

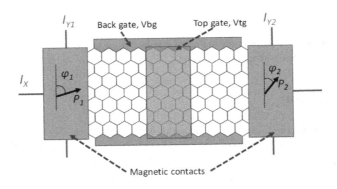

Fig. 1. Graphene device with magnetic contacts.

The graphene nanoribbon is placed on an insulating surface, usually silicon dioxide, and at the back of the insulator the back-gate electrode is developed. Since an insulator lies between the back-gate electrode and the graphene nanoribbon, no electron injection is possible, but the back-gate voltage, V_{bg}, affects the energy of the electrons transported through graphene. On top of the graphene nanoribbon the top-gate is placed and is separated from graphene with an insulating layer. The top-gate voltage, V_{tg}, cannot inject electrons, but affects transported electron energies locally. Buried in the insulating layer three metallic non-crossing conductors carry currents I_x, I_{y1} and I_{y2} that magnetize the magnetic contacts. The magnitudes and directions of these currents determine the direction and magnitude of the magnetic polarizations P_1 and P_2. In Fig. 1, P_1 and P_2 form angles ϕ_1 and ϕ_2 with the "y-axis". By varying the currents during the device operation, the magnitudes and angles of P_1 and P_2 vary in a controllable manner.

3 Operation and Properties of the of Graphene Nanoribbon Device with Magnetic Contacts

The operation of the graphene device is simulated using quantum mechanical methods, namely tight-binding Hamiltonians combined with the NEGF method, which are described analytically in [7] and [8], for the case of non-magnetic contacts. To include the effect of the magnetic contacts, the metallic contact self-energies Σ_1^m and Σ_2^m should also account for the projection of electron spins on the magnetic polarization vectors. To obtain this the self-energies become:

$$\Sigma_1^m = \Sigma_1 \otimes s_1 \tag{1}$$

$$\Sigma_2^m = \Sigma_2 \otimes s_2 \tag{2}$$

The spin projections s_1 and s_2 are given by:

$$s_1 = \tau \exp\left(ik_a\right)\left(I + P_{1,x}\sigma_x + P_{1,y}\sigma_y + P_{1,z}\sigma_z\right) \tag{3}$$

$$s_2 = \tau \exp\left(ik_a\right)\left(I + P_{2,x}\sigma_x + P_{2,y}\sigma_y + P_{2,z}\sigma_z\right) \tag{4}$$

I is the identity matrix and $P_{1,x}$ is the x component of the P_1 vector and so on for the other components. The electron wave vector is k_a and τ is the value of the overlap integral. The matrices σ_x, σ_y and σ_z are the Pauli spin matrices.

Figure 2 shows the conductance of the graphene device in its digital operation, which is obtained by setting the top gate potential equal to zero and the currents equal to zero, so that the contacts are not magnetized. Only electrons a few kT above and below the Fermi energy level are transported through the nanoribbon. The Fermi level is shown with the blue dotted line. The conductance, G, as a function of energy is quantized. In Fig. 2(a) the back-gate potential is also zero and the electrons that are transported face a conductance $(h/2q^2)G = 1$. The back-gate potential shifts the conductance up or down, depending on its value, and the transported electrons face different discrete conductance values. For example, in Fig. 2(b) the back-gate potential is set 0.25 V and the transported electrons now face a conductance $(h/2q^2)G = 3$. The quantization of

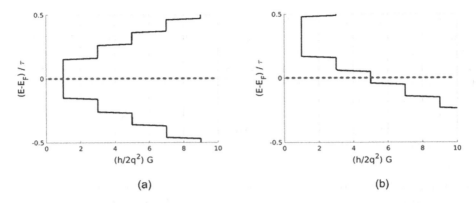

Fig. 2. Graphene device conductance in digital operation. The contacts are not magnetized. (a) $V_{tg} = 0.0$ V and $V_{bg} = 0.0$ V (b) $V_{tg} = 0.0$ V and $V_{bg} = 0.25$ V. The Fermi energy is denoted with a dotted blue line. (Color figure online)

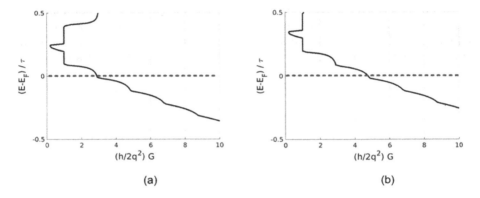

Fig. 3. Graphene device conductance in analog operation. The contacts are not magnetized. (a) $V_{tg} = 0.15$ V and $V_{bg} = 0.25$ V (b) $V_{tg} = 0.15$ V and $V_{bg} = 0.35$ V. The Fermi energy is denoted with a dotted blue line (Color figure online)

the conductance, combined with back-gate potential values, is used to obtain discrete values of the conductance that can be mapped to the CA cell states.

Non-zero values of the top-gate potential set the device in analog operation by smoothing the discrete conductance to an almost linear curve, as shown in Fig. 3 in which $V_{tg} = 0.15V$. In analog operation the currents are also set to zero so that the contacts are not magnetized. In Fig. 3(a) the back gate potential is $V_{bg} = 0.25V$ and electrons are transported through the nanoribbon with conductance $(h/2q^2)G = 2.82$. By varying the back-gate potentials the conductance curve is shifted up or down and the transported electron face a conductance that takes on continuous values. For example by setting $V_{bg} = 0.35V$, as shown in Fig. 3(b), the conductance curve is shifted upwards and the transported electrons face conductance$(h/2q^2)G = 4.67$.

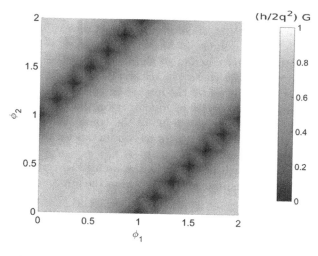

Fig. 4. Density plot of the graphene device conductance that shows the dependence of the conductance on the values of the contact magnetic polarization angles ϕ_1 and ϕ_2 (in rads)

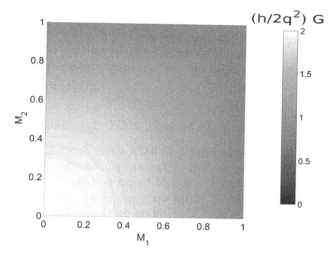

Fig. 5. Density plot of the graphene device conductance that shows the dependence of the conductance on the magnitudes of the magnetic polarizations of the contacts, M_1 and M_2 (normalized values)

Magnetization of the device contacts adds two more controlling parameters, namely the angles of the polarization vectors ϕ_1 and ϕ_2. These angles can be set to any value by adjusting the ratios of the magnetizing currents I_x/I_y. Figure 4 shows the dependence of the device conductance on the values of these two angles in a form of a density plot, where the value of the conductance is represented by a color and the correspondence of colors to conductance values is shown in the color bar on the right of the figure.

Two more controlling parameters of the device are the magnitudes of the magnetic polarizations of the contacts, M_1 and M_2. The values of M_1 and M_2 are determined by the magnitude of the magnetizing currents I_x and I_y. Figure 5 shows the dependence of the device conductance on the values of M_1 and M_2 in a form of a density plot, where the value of the conductance is represented by a color and the correspondence of colors to conductance values is shown in the color bar on the right of the figure.

In the next section we will describe the CA architecture that uses the device of Fig. 1 as a building block and we will describe the state and rule of the CA.

4   Implementation and Architecture of the Cellular Automata

Figure 6 shows the proposed CA architecture in which devices of Fig. 1 are used as building blocks. In this CA implementation a small grid of 12 devices is shown, but the CA can be scaled up by extending the architecture.

The CA cell is considered to be one graphene device connected locally to the neighbouring cells by sharing common metallic contacts, which can be magnetized or non-magnetized. We propose the state of the (i, j) CA cell, $C(i, j)$ to be the conductance of the graphene nanoribbon of this CA cell, which depends on and is a function of the potentials and the magnitudes and directions of the magnetic polarizations of the contacts:

$$C\left(i,j\right) = F\left(V_{tg}\left(i,j\right), V_{bg}\left(i,j\right), M_1\left(i,j\right), M_2\left(i,j\right), \varphi_1\left(i,j\right), \varphi_2\left(i,j\right)\right) \quad (5)$$

The user can define any function $F()$ as a CA state, depending on the problem she/he is dealing with. If one or more CA state parameters are not to be used, their values in the function of Eq. 5 should be set to zero.

Regarding the CA rule, which varies the conductance of the CA cells, a large spectrum of functions can be used, depending on the specificity of the problem at hand. Neighbouring CA cells share common metallic contacts, which can be magnetized. This provides the possibility of choosing and applying a variety local evolution rules. Top and back gate potentials can be applied independently in each CA cell. Furthermore, CA cells in the same architecture raw have common buried metallic conductors that carry the magnetizing current I_x and CA cells in the same architecture column have common buried metallic conductors that carry the magnetizing currents I_{y1} and I_{y2}. This fact provides the possibility of including in the CA neighbourhood, cells that are located in the same raw or column. The CA evolution rule that determines the state of a cell at the next time step $(t + 1)$ depends on the states at the previous time step (t) of the CA cells located in its neighbourhood, in the same column and in the same row, and is described as follows:

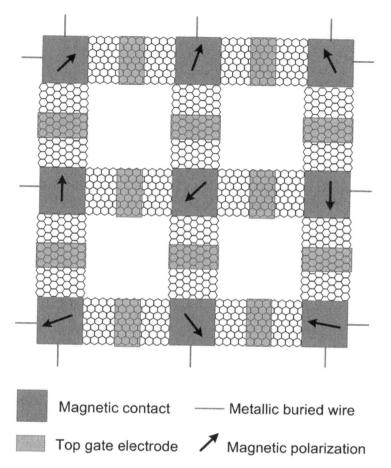

Fig. 6. CA architecture where devices of Fig. 1 are used as building blocks. Back-gates not shown.

$$C\left(i,j,t+1\right) = C\left(i,j,t\right) + \sum_{k,l} F_{neigh}\left(C\left(k,l,t\right)\right)$$
$$+ \sum_{k,\ l:Column} F_{column}\left(C\left(k,l,t\right)\right) + \sum_{k:Row,\ l} F_{row}\left(C\left(k,l,t\right)\right) \qquad (6)$$

In Eq. 6 the functions F_{neigh}, F_{column} and F_{row} represent the dependence of the evolution rule on the neighbouring cells, on the cells in the same column and on the cells in the same row.

The CA architecture of Fig. 6 can be used for both digital and analog computing. Furthermore, by considering the magnetic contacts as memory elements, the CA architecture can also be used for neuromorphic and in-memory computing, in which the top-gate and back-gate potentials are the computing inputs and/or variables.

5   Conclusions

We proposed an easy to fabricate graphene nanoribbon device with magnetic contacts and simulated its operation using exact quantum mechanical methods, namely tight-binding Hamiltonians and non-equilibrium Green's functions. We showed that this device is capable of both digital and analog computing. We proposed a new implementation of CAs in which an architecture is constructed using the graphene devices as building blocks. We described the CA cell state and the evolution rules that can be applied to this architecture. We argued that by considering the magnetic contacts as memory elements, the CA architecture can also be used for neuromorphic and in-memory computing.

Acknowledgement. This research is co-financed by Greece and the European Union (European Social Fund- ESF) through the Operational Programme Human Resources Development, Education and Lifelong Learning 2014–2020 in the context of the project "GRAPHENE NANOELECTRONIC AND QUANTUM CIRCUITS" (MIS 5049529).

References

1. Castro Neto, A.H., Guinea, F., Peres, N.M.R., Novoselov, K.S., Geim, A.K.: The electronic properties of graphene. Rev. Modern Phys. **81**, 109–162 (2009)
2. Schwierz, F.: Graphene transistors. Nat. Nanotechnol. **5**, 487–496 (2010)
3. Karafyllidis, I.G.: Current switching in graphene quantum point contacts. IEEE Trans. Nanotechnol. **13**, 820–824 (2014)
4. Nikiforidis, I., Karafyllidis, I.G., Dimitrakis, P.: Simulation and parametric analysis of graphene p-n junctions with two rectangular top-gates and a single back gate. J. Phys. D Appl. Phys. **51**, 075303 (2018)
5. Moysidis, S., Karafyllidis, I.G., Dimitrakis, P.: Graphene logic gates. IEEE Trans. Nanotechnol. **17**, 852–859 (2018)
6. Hill, E.W., Geim, A.K., Novoselov, K., Schedin, F., Blake, P.: Graphene spin valve devices. IEEE Trans. Magn. **42**, 2694–2696 (2006)
7. Datta, S.: Nanoscale device modeling: the Green's function method. Superlattices Microstruct. **28**, 253–278 (2000)
8. Datta, S.: Lesons from Nanoelectronics: A Perspective on Transport. World Scientific, Singapore (2012)
9. Moysidis, S., Karafyllidis, I.G.: Conductance of L-shaped and T-shaped graphene nanoribbons. Microelectron. J. **72**, 11–13 (2018)

A Customised Assessment Tool Based on Cellular Automata for the Visit-Ability of an Urban Environment

Irene Georgiadi[1], Giuseppe A. Trunfio[2], Ioakeim G. Georgoudas[1(✉)], and Georgios Ch. Sirakoulis[1(✉)]

[1] Department of Electrical and Computer Engineering,
Democritus University of Thrace, 671 00 Xanthi, Greece
{irgeorgi,igeorg,gsirak}@ee.duth.gr
[2] Department of Architecture, Planning and Design, University of Sassari,
Pal. Pou Salit, Piazza Duomo, 6 07041 Alghero, SS, Italy
trunfio@uniss.it

Abstract. This study copes with the problem of finding the optimal route that a pedestrian could follow in order to move into an urban environment taking into consideration various criteria and possible points of interest, either objective nor subjective. For this purpose, an appropriate computational model has been designed, based on Cellular Automata (CA) that responds taking into consideration the walkability of the urban area under study. The latter feature encompasses a variety of qualitative parameters in regard to the pedestrian mobility. Thus, this model aims at enforcing more sustainable transport approaches, such as walking. In order to evaluate the functionality of the proposed model, an initial application is carried out in the city of Xanthi, North-East Greece, in order to verify the plausibility and completeness of the proposed routes in different scenarios.

Keywords: Crowd modelling · Cellular Automata · Walkability · Dijkstra algorithm · Simulation

1 Introduction

The problem of finding the optimal route based on the specific needs, options and demands of a pedestrian is especially important in modern times. Nowadays, more people are choosing to move with their car even for short distances, which results in traffic congestion and increased air pollution. It also means eliminating economic cost of refueling and reduction of atmospheric emissions. Furthermore, walking is considered as a very effective type of physical exercise that improves health condition. Pedestrians, also interact with each other, thus increasing their social skills and improving their positive mood, reducing the number of traffic accidents as well.

Furthermore, the vast majority of research on transport planning focuses on motorized transport. The corresponding suggestions aim at alleviating traffic congestion usually by re-organising existing road infrastructure at the expense of the local environmental conditions. For instance, road broadening or new constructions could

© Springer Nature Switzerland AG 2021
T. M. Gwizdałła et al. (Eds.): ACRI 2020, LNCS 12599, pp. 177–187, 2021.
https://doi.org/10.1007/978-3-030-69480-7_18

possibly lead to urban sprawl, increased number of vehicles on the roads, thus more traffic noise and air pollution [1]. Thus, contemporary transport planning copes with more sustainable and environmentally friendly methods, such as walking [2]. A main drawback is that data collection is still inadequate and evaluation methods of walking as a transport mode are not very efficient [3]. To this direction, new concepts need to be defined rigorously, in order to help research to proceed effectively. The concept of walkability encompasses important quantitative and qualitative characteristics of walking in cities in order to facilitate transport planning. Though, there are still discrepancies in its definition [3, 4]. In all, the issue of moving in an urban environment can be considered as multi-parametric. Thus, developing a method that could propose the route (or indicate any suitable routes) that the pedestrian can follow in order to reach her/his destination by combining qualitatively different options of her/his own could be proven very useful. This method focuses on helping and prompting a person to move around the city, highlighting the city's points of interest, helping the person to evaluate alternative routes properly, combining multiple destinations appropriately and combining different routes, efficiently assigning any constraints. The proposed model aims at motivating people to choose walking as their main alternative of moving around. This work can also be regarded as a contribution to the urban informatics sector taking into consideration that it charecterises the environment by means of social media data in relevance to [5, 6].

This study deals with the problem of pedestrian movement within an urban environment in order to serve the need of visiting different places in that environment. An appropriate movement model is developed based on a parallel computational model, which enables the incorporation and elaboration of weights and parameters that could produce the proposed movements based on the options and demands of the user. This work extends the usability of the model proposed by Blecic et al. [7] by deploying the merits of Cellular Automata (CA) as an effective modeling platform that overcomes the difficulties that arise when trying to simulate a multi-parameterised system [8, 9]. Furthermore, the proposed tool offers a user-friendly customization environment for choosing a walking route in order to reach a destination, while visiting intermediate points of interest. In addition, the model is applied to the city of Xanthi, region of Thrace, North-East of Greece and it is verified by searching realistic routes within the historical center of the city.

In Sect. 2, the main designing and developing principles of the proposed model are described. In the next section, the response of the model is validated for various scenarios within a particular urban area in the city of Xanthi, Greece. The corresponding results are discussed as well. Finally, conclusions are drawn and future perspectives are mentioned in regard to the operational ability of the proposed model.

2   Model Description

The aim of this study is the development of a tool that could assess the visit-ability of an urban area by taking into consideration various destination options and other personal demands and preferences of a pedestrian. The model responds by proposing the most appropriate route, not necessarily the shortest one [10]. In the context of this study, we describe the degree to which a particular road is more preferable than another one, by using the term walkability, in accordance to [7]. Each road is evaluated according to this property and scored within a predetermined scale. A high value of walkability means that the road combines several features that make it more pedestrian-friendly, such as wide sidewalks, easy access, lack of traffic, small slope, places of interest etc.

As aforementioned, the simulation process of the proposed model is based on CA. For this reason, a grid is defined consisting of the cells that correspond to all parts of the city where the pedestrian could be found. The possible discrete situations in which a cell may be located are either zero (0) symbolizing non-existence of a road or one (1) symbolizing the existence of a road respectively. The Moore neighbourhood is applied to the model that consists of all the cells around the cell of reference. The radius of the neighbourhood is equal to one. Such an assumption introduces an error in the distance calculation for the diagonal cells. Yet, we approach more efficiently the Euclidean distance, which more realistically describes the space perception compared to the Manhattan distance that is the base of the von Neumann neighbourhood. In the proposed model, we assume that each cell knows only the state of the cells in its neighbourhood. Therefore, each cell may recognize whether there is a road around, but not the total length of the road or the exact route towards the desired destination. The process of finding the optimal path is performed gradually, through the evolution of the next generations of CA, until the point of interest or the final destination is reached.

Subsequently, the rule of the CA should be defined that will activate the cells of the neighbourhood and change the state of the considered cell. Dijkstra algorithm forms the backbone of the rule. The main goal of the Dijkstra algorithm is to find the minimum path between two distant nodes of a graph [11]. The CA rule searches the minimum distance between two cells in the grid alike. The inside process of both the Dijkstra algorithm and the CA rule is pretty much the same. The former starts from a node and finds the one that is closer to it, which is called discovered from then after. The process continues for all undiscovered nodes. The latter searches among all cells of its neighbourhood for a new cell that is closer to the target. Thus, we could claim that the CA rule adopts prominent structural features of the Dijkstra algorithm to define the next state of each cell in the CA grid. The rule continues to be applied to the CA until the destination cell is detected or all the cells in the grid are discovered.

Thus, the distance of each cell from the considered one is calculated by the following equation:

$$Distance = \sum_{k=1}^{p} 1 \qquad (1)$$

In Eq. (1), the *Distance* variable represents the distance between two cells. Parameter p defines the distance numbered in neighbourhoods between two cells. For example, for two cells in the same neighbourhood parameter p equals one, for those in the next neighbourhood parameter p equals two, etc. The distance is considered between each cell and the reference one. One (1) represents the length of the edges, that is, the distance between adjacent cells. The behavior of the pedestrian depends on many other factors apart from the minimum distance. This is realised by enriching Eq. (1)

with weighting coefficients in order to allow important factors to be taken into account in the process of exploring the optimal route Thus, Eq. (1) is modified in (2):

$$Distance = \sum_{k=1}^{p} 1 * n_k \tag{2}$$

Parameter n_k represents a cost factor, which is involved in the calculation of the distance and expresses whether this path gathers features that make it preferable to pedestrians. The range of accepted values varies from 0 to 1. Particularly, a path consisting of a sequence of CA cells that combine several desirable features has a low cost factor with values close to 0. This will make it more likely to be selected as a road against other neighbouring roads that have higher cost values. In order the value of parameter n_k to be calculated, all the factors that are considered to affect the attractiveness of the road must be defined. In the context of this study, twelve different factors are taken into consideration. The first one is cycling accessibility along the considered road. In addition, the length of the road in combination with the maximum speed and bi-directionality are particularly important road features. Whenever a road is characterized by a small number of moving cars and low speed limits, the risk of pedestrian accidents is significantly reduced. Moreover, large sidewalks where parking is forbidden are quite attractive for pedestrians. Roads that are well lit and provide shelter from the sun and/or rain create a sense of security. Sightseeing and places to rest are also promoted. On the other hand, sloping and uphill roads are less likely to be selected. All these attributes are combined into one size that determines the attractiveness of the road. It is called *profit factor S* and is derived, for each CA cell, from the following equation:

$$S_k = \sum_{j=1}^{n_a} \left(\left(\gamma_j a_{k,j}^r \right)^{\frac{1}{r}} \right) \tag{3}$$

Parameter n_a denotes the total number of the attributes of the path that are taken into account. Parameter $a(k, j)$ indicates the value of the j-th attribute at the k-th path. Parameter γ represents the weight of the j attribute. The sum of the weights of all attributes equals one ($\sum \gamma_j = 1$). Finally, factor r represents the flexibility among the attributes. Thus, cost factor n can be rewritten as follows:

$$n_k = 1 - S_k = 1 - \sum_{j=1}^{n_a} \left(\left(\gamma_j a_{k,j}^r \right)^{1/r} \right) \tag{4}$$

The values of parameter a for each attribute j of each path k are defined by the designer of the model. Inevitably, there is a strong subjective factor in these choices. For this reason, it would be useful an interaction to be introduced between the user of the model and the model itself that could affect the values of parameter a. This interaction could be formed as an option that would be provided to the user to post-evaluate the route suggestion made by the proposed model, according to his experience. The user's evaluation is defined between the values zero (0) and one (1), with the former corresponding to no satisfaction at all and the latter to complete satisfaction.

Therefore there is formed a factor that reduces the gain factor depending on the user's response and increases the cost factor, according to the following equation:

$$evaluation\_S_k = S_k * an, k \in path \tag{5}$$

Parameter *Evaluation_S_k* symbolizes the updated gain factor that takes into consideration the assessment of the pedestrian, whereas S_k represents the current value of the gain factor, *an* the response of the pedestrian, and k the corresponding path. Combining Eq. (4) and Eq. (5), then Eq. (6) is derived that describes the updated value of the cost factor for the *k-th* path, according to the response of the pedestrian:

$$evaluation_{n_k} = 1 - evaluation_{S_k}, \; k \in path \tag{6}$$

Obviously, *evaluation_S_k* can only get a value less than or equal to the value of the gain factor S_k (Eq. (5)). In such a frame, the updated gain factor *evaluation_S_k* of the road k cannot be assigned a greater value. In such a case, a route that proved to be more attractive to the pedestrian than it was originally assessed by the designer cannot be assigned a greater value of evaluation. In order to meet this need, the following behavior will be followed. Provided that the pedestrian's degree of evaluation reaches the maximum value of 1, then the pedestrian will be given the option to proceed to a second evaluation, *an2*. She/he will be asked to respond to what extent the proposed route exceeded her/his expectations. This behavior is defined by Eqs. (7) and (8).

$$evaluation\_n_k = n_k * (1 - an2), k \in path \tag{7}$$

$$evaluation\_S_k = 1 - evaluation\_S_k, k \in path \tag{8}$$

Parameter *evaluation_n_k* denotes the cost factor according to the assessment of the pedestrian, k represents the path that the pedestrian crossed, *n_k* denotes the cost factor for the current time, and *an2* the second response of the pedestrian. Accordingly, *evaluation_S_k* symbolizes the gain factor based on the response of the pedestrian. In the case of a second positive evaluation, Eqs. (7) and (8) outperform Eqs. (6) and (7).

Nevertheless, either positive or negative, the judgments of the pedestrians may be biased due to personal interest. In order the model to be protected from such behaviors, public opinion cannot be unreasonably adopted. A common practice is to use the arithmetic average of all submitted responses. Thus, they are Eqs. (9) and (10) that define the final value of the cost factor as soon as the evaluation of a pedestrian has been completed.

$$new\_n_k = \frac{sumVal_k * n_k + evaluation\_n_k}{sumVal_k + 1}, k \in path \tag{9}$$

$$new\_n_k = n_k, k \notin path \tag{10}$$

Provided that path k is included in the route that the pedestrian has already evaluated, then Eq. (9) is applied and parameter *new_n_k* symbolizes the updated value of coefficient n_k. Otherwise, the value of cost factor n_k remains the same (Eq. (10)).

Furthermore, parameter *sumVal* is defined as the sum of all submitted evaluations, whereas *evaluation_n_K* represents the cost factor according to the pedestrian, as calculated in Eqs. (6) or (7) respectively. Accordingly, the updated value of gain factor *new_S_k* related to the updated value of the cost factor *new_n_k* is provided by Eq. (11).

$$new\_S_k = 1 - new\_n_k \tag{11}$$

So far the basic mathematical principles of the model have been thoroughly described. Accordingly, the proposed system is designed that accepts personalised options and demands as input data and responds by outlining the route that the pedestrian could follow in order to reach her/his destination. With the aim of planning and then validating the model realistically, the city of Xanthi, region of Thrace, northeast Greece, was designated as a pedestrian area. The proper operation of the model needs an effective frame of inputting and processing data and outputting information correspondingly based on the road network of the city of Xanthi. This goal is succeeded by introducing a map image of a large part of the city of Xanthi in jpg format (Fig. 1(a)). In this image, roads are depicted in black on a continuous line. Thus, the underlying programmatic framework of the model is a two-dimensional array consisting of cells. The accepted state of each cell is either one (1) or zero (0) with the former representing the presence of a path in that cell and the latter the absence. Therefore the need arises to convert the information provided by the map into a two-dimensional (2-d) array consisting of units and zeros. One of the advantages of the Matlab programming language is that it provides several useful functions for image editing. Therefore, using the proper functions (*imread* and *im2bw*) the proposed system reads and converts the image into binary format and then inverts the colours so that the roads are denoted by 1 (black) and the rest of the area by 0 (white), thus producing the sub-serving 2-d array, named *Roads* (Fig. 1(b)).

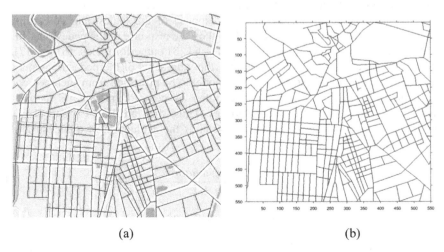

(a)   (b)

Fig. 1. (a) Map of a large part of the city of Xanthi that is provided as input to the proposed computational model (b) The corresponding binary image of the city of Xanthi city.

Furthermore, the system enables the pedestrian to enter data that meet her/his destinations of interest. The first option corresponds to the starting point and the other three to the points of interest she/he intends to visit. The model checks to confirm that the points given as inputs do not exceed the boundaries of the map. Otherwise, the user is required to return a valid point. Then the CA rule starts evolving based on the sub-serving framework that has been created, i.e. array *Roads*. The operation mode of the CA rule has been described above, but it should be noted that the CA rule acts as an approximating function that tries to find that point of an existing road that is closer to the point of interest and it is represented as a specific cell of the CA grid. Thus, array *Roads* that contains the road map is related to the CA.

Moreover, each road should be evaluated according to the set of attributes that the model supports (Table 1 in [7]). Algorithmically, this process takes place by intro-ducing a weighting factor for each of these attributes. In order to evaluate the degree of satisfaction of each feature for each road (parameter $\alpha_{k,j}$, Eq. (3)–(4)), each attribute is assigned to a separate array that is dimensionally equal to array *Roads*, i.e. equal to the underlying CA grid. Each cell is representing an intersection of roads and the model identifies the specific roads that surround each intersection. The CA rule starts from a cell that belongs to an intersection and tries to detect one neighbouring and unexplored cell that represents a part of a road, i.e. a path. Then another part of the road is identified and the process is completed when we reach another intersection-cell. The sequence of all explored cells, i.e. paths, from one intersection-cell to another corre-sponds to a detected road. This procedure is repeated for all other intersection-cells until all paths are found. The final stage is the introduction of the features for all roads. As soon as all paths that belong to the same road are joined together, then the degree that the road satisfies for each separate attribute is defined, according to Table 1 [7]. Based on these values and following Eqs. (3)–(5), the cost array n_k is calculated for each road and therefore for all the cells that form it.

3   Simulation Results

The initial scenario that is presented in this study, aims at confirming the proper operation of the model taking into consideration that there is no interaction between the model and the user as well as that the user fills in all requested data appropriately. According to the scenario, the pedestrian is standing at point (85, 33) of the Cartesian system of coordinates that is depicted in Fig. 1(b), whereas the points of interest are (45, 100), (120, 163) and (105, 205). In addition, it is assumed that the pedestrian requests the weighting factors method to be applied to the estimation of the optimal route, whereas the individualized evaluation method is skipped.

The tool that has been developed, initially presents the map of the city on the screen in order to facilitate the user to choose the points of interest. A few seconds later, the screen that displays the map switches off and the user is asked to define the point that she/he appears, responding to a question about her/his location as well. Finally, the user is asked whether she/her would like to evaluate the route before the process of optimal route estimation commences. As soon as the optimal route is computed, a message is displayed on the screen informing the user about the colour of the path on the map and the order of the destinations that she/he could follow in order to reach all desired destinations. After two seconds, the map of Xanthi appears with the colored path to cross (Fig. 2). This delay occurs so that the user is provided with the appropriate time to read the message and to be able to follow the path shown on the map. Five seconds later, the popup window that displays the map of Xanthi closes.

Another scenario aims at presenting the response of the model provided that the interaction between the model and the user is activated for the first time. In particular, the user assesses poorly the route proposed by the model. As a consequence, the model differentiates remarkably its response as soon as it is requested to provide a new proposal for the same destinations. As soon as the user submits her/his desired destinations the application asks her/him whether she/he would like to take into account other users' ratings. The answer is affirmative and the system informs the user that there are no ratings so far. The model continues with processing all input data and responds a few seconds later, by displaying a message on the screen that informs the user about the route that the model proposes. In particular, the user is proposed to move from the starting point (green) (10, 300) towards the cyan point (90, 350) and then the red point (90, 498) until she/he reaches the final yellow point (325, 385), following the red-coloured path (Fig. 3(a)). This response of the model is substantially based on the fundamental criterion of the minimum distance.

Fig. 2. The representation of the proposed route, according to the order that has been computed by the model.

Provided that the user has chosen to use the evaluation method, the model requests assessment of the proposed route. The rating ranges between 0 and 1. The user is 30% satisfied, thus she/he enters a value equal to 0.3 that corresponds to a relatively poor rating. Then the user requests the model to update its response for the same destinations and to take into consideration all submitted ratings. The model responds by proposing a noticeably diverse route, although the order of approaching the destinations remains the

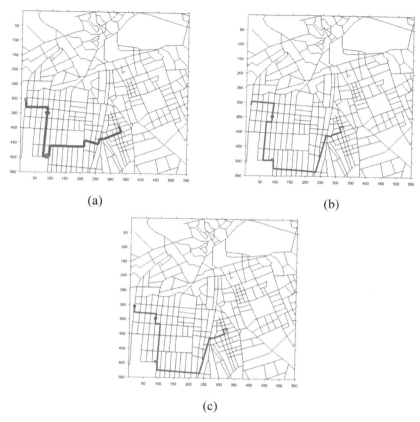

(a)

(b)

(c)

Fig. 3. (a) The response of the proposed route without any evaluation submission. (b) The response of the model for the same destinations when the evaluation option has been activated and only one (poor) rating has been submitted. (c) The response of the model as soon as a poor evaluation has been submitted after ten successive positive evaluations, in regard to the initial output of the model (depicted in Fig. (a)). (Color figure online)

same (Fig. 3(b)). Finally, the user is prompted to provide another evaluation. The main conclusion that can be drawn from the second scenario is that the output of the model is heavily influenced when there is only one submitted rating. In fact, a single evaluation greatly affects the weights of the system and thus the proposed route. Consequently, the poor evaluation at the end of the first response noticeably altered the cost factors n_k, thus affected the response of the system.

The third scenario investigates the behavior of the system in case that it receives a poor evaluation report after a large number of positive ones. After the very first evaluation that led the model to change its response from the one depicted in Fig. 3(a) to that illustrated in Fig. 3(b), the user repeatedly requests the model to propose a route for the same destination points, having activated the evaluation option as well. For each of the successive ten times that she/he is prompted to evaluate the output, the user submits the best available option, i.e. 1. Accordingly, the model responds identically, by proposing each time the same route, i.e. the one that is depicted in Fig. 3(b). This reaction, by itself is another proof of validity for the operation of the model; as long as the assessment is to the maximum, the model does not at least change its response. As soon as the user submits a poor evaluation value, i.e. 0.3, the model differentiates its response slightly. Figure 3(c) illustrates the corresponding route. It is obvious that this path differs from the initial one (Fig. 3(b)) but not at that extent, as in the previous scenario (change of response from Fig. 3(a) to Fig. 3(b)).

According to this scenario, the more stored ratings, the lower the impact of each individual rating on the final proposed route. Indeed, the overall cost factor is calculated on the basis of the arithmetic average of all cost factors that are formulated according to the corresponding evaluation Eq. (9). The more the assessments for each street section, the less the overall cost factor is affected by a single assessment.

4   Conclusions

There are many factors that influence pedestrian behavior in an urban environment. To develop a model that could approach such behaviours taking into account all the aforementioned factors is a difficult task by itself. From a mathematical point of view, it could be regarded as a multi-parameterized system that could be described by a set of partial differential equations that could hardly be solved. Thus, it is CA that could be regarded as an alternative method to approach an acceptable solution. In addition, experiments revealed three major categories that are considered to have an influence on pedestrian behavior; actual distance, attractive features of a road, and characteristics of a road in relation to its neighbours. In addition, the larger the number of submitted evaluations, the more reliable the model becomes.

Finally, there are various perspectives for further developing the proposed model. A useful idea could be to increase the features that are taken into account for the simulation of pedestrian behavior. In addition, the development of similar models for other cities could extend the options of visitors. Finally, transferring the operation of the model to an android platform would exceed its usability.

References

1. Sdoukopoulos, A., et al.: Development and implementation of walkability audits in Greek medium-sized cities: the case of the Serres' city centre. Transp. Res. Proc. 24, 337–344 (2017). https://doi.org/10.1016/j.trpro.2017.05.102
2. Vizzari, G., Crociani, L., Bandini, S.: An agent-based model for plausible wayfinding in pedestrian simulation. Eng. Appl. Artif. Intell. 87, 103241 (2020). https://doi.org/10.1016/j.engappai.2019.103241. ISSN 0952-1976
3. Dörrzapf, L., Kovács-Győri, A., Resch, B., Zeile, P.: Defining and assessing walkability: an concept for an integrated approach using surveys, biosensors and geospatial analysis. Urban Dev. Issues 62, 5–15 (2019). https://doi.org/10.2478/udi-2019-0008
4. Forsyth, A.: What is a walkable place? The walkability debate in urban design. Urban Design Int. 20(4), 274–292 (2015). https://doi.org/10.1057/udi.2015.22

5. Quercia, D., Schifanella, R., Aiello, L.M.: The shortest path to happiness: recommending beautiful, quiet, and happy routes in the city. In: 25th ACM Conference on Hypertext and Social Media, pp. 116–125 (2014). https://doi.org/10.1145/2631775.2631799
6. Berzi, C., Gorrini, A., Vizzari, G.: Mining the social media data for a bottom-up evaluation of walkability. In: Hamdar, S.H. (ed.) TGF 2017, pp. 167–175. Springer, Cham (2019). https://doi.org/10.1007/978-3-030-11440-4_20
7. Blecic, I., Cecchini, A., Trunfio, G.A.: Towards a design support system for urban walkability. In: ICCS 2015 International Conference on Computational Science (2015). Proc. Comput. Sci. **51**, 2157–2167. https://doi.org/10.1016/j.procs.2015.05.489)
8. Gerakakis, I., Gavriilidis, P., Dourvas, N.I., Georgoudas, I.G., Trunfio, G.A., Sirakoulis, G. Ch.: Accelerating fuzzy cellular automata for modeling crowd dynamics. J. Comput. Sci. **32**, 125–140 (2019). https://doi.org/10.1016/j.jocs.2018.10.007
9. Kontou, P., Georgoudas, I.G., Trunfio, G.A., Sirakoulis G.Ch.: Cellular automata modelling of the movement of people with disabilities during building evacuation. In: Proceedings of 26th Euromicro International Conference on Parallel, Distributed and Network-Based Processing (PDP), pp. 550–557. IEEE, Cambridge (2018). http://doi.ieeecomputersociety.org/10.1109/PDP2018.2018.00093
10. Adamatzky, A.: Computation of shortest path in cellular automata. Math. Comput. Modell. **23**(4), 105–113 (1996). https://doi.org/10.1016/0895-7177(96)00006-4
11. Dijkstra, E.W.: A note on two problems in connection with graphs. Numerische Math. **1**(1), 269–271 (1959). https://doi.org/10.1007/BF01386390

Time Discretization in Pedestrian Dynamics Simulations by Discrete-Continuous Model

Ekaterina Kirik$^{(\boxtimes)}$ ⓘ, Tat'yana Vitova ⓘ, and Andrey Malyshev ⓘ

Institute of Computational Modelling of the Siberian Branch of the Russian Academy of Sciences, Akademgorodok 50/44, Krasnoyarsk 660036, Russia
{kirik,vitova,amal}@icm.krasn.ru
http://3ksigma.ru

Abstract. A discretization of time in computer simulation of pedestrian movement is considered. Time step is very influencing on computational performance. But not only quick calculations is a criterion. The other one is a confidence to a simulation result. From both aspects, the discrete-continuous model SigmaEva is considered in the paper. It is shown that low and high time steps are not reasonable.

Keywords: Pedestrian simulation · Discrete-continuous model · Fundamental diagram · Flow rate · Time discretization

1 Introduction

Nowadays a using of computer simulations of pedestrian flows are already normal for applied tasks. Computer simulation helps to answer design questions to organize comfort conditions for people in mass events (musical, folklore, sport and other), safety question to provide evacuation under dangerous emergency (for example, fire) conditions [1–4]. One can find some modelling approaches: the social force model based on differential equations [5–7] (continuous approach) and cellular automation (CA) models were developed [8–11] (discrete approach). Discrete and continuous approaches are combined in models [12–15]. A discrete-continuous approach combines advantages of both approaches: people move in a continuous space, but there are only fixed number of directions where a person can move.

Applications are often not research activities, they demand quick solutions. So a tendency of model development is high performance algorithms (quick calculations). A confidence to a simulation result is on the other hand.

Numerical presentation of each model deals with a time discretization and, so called, time step Δt, which is a period of time after which new coordinates of particles are updated. For originally time-continuous models Δt determines number of calculations which are necessary to simulate the process from the beginning to the end and consequently Δt determines speed of simulations. For

© Springer Nature Switzerland AG 2021
T. M. Gwizdałła et al. (Eds.): ACRI 2020, LNCS 12599, pp. 188–197, 2021.
https://doi.org/10.1007/978-3-030-69480-7_19

discrete CA models shifts of each particle each time step are equal and do not depend on Δt, it depends on spatial discretization, all particle have got the same speed. For example, in [9,11,16,17] $\Delta t = 0.3$ s. In time and spatial continuous models each particle has got individual free movement speeds. Each time step a length of shift of each particle is determined by Δt and local density. Δt may vary from 0.001 [s] [18] to 2 [s] [19]. In [14] Δt depends on model parameters: particle's radius, a desired speed, an escape velocity.

In this article we investigate an influence of Δt on simulation results in the discrete-continuous model SigmaEva [15,20]. To compare results under different Δt we use a conjunction with fundamental diagram.

In the next section fundamental diagrams are discussed. Then we present the discrete-continuous model SigmaEva. In the fourth section results are presented. And we finish with a conclusion.

2   Fundamental Diagram

In terms of specific flow $J_s = \rho\, v(\rho)$ $[1/(ms)]$, fundamental diagrams look as follows. As the density ρ $[1/(m^2)]$ increases, the specific flow grows, attains its maximum, then decreases, Fig. 1. Speed $v(\rho)$ $[m/s]$ goes down with increasing ρ.

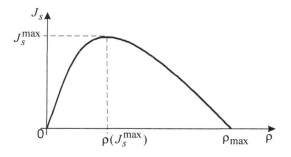

Fig. 1. Schematic behaviour of a specific flow.

Manifestation of fundamental diagram is implemented in the steady-state regime, when the time-spatial density is assumed to be constant and there are no conditions for transformations of the flow. People are assumed to be uniformly distributed over the entire area (e.g., in an extended corridor without narrowing) and move in one direction.

Various fundamental diagrams exist (for example, Fig. 2), and they are determined by many factors, including demographics [21], which have the same basic feature. In Fig. 2 the free movement speed is assumed $v^0 = 1.66$ [m/s].

In the paper there will considered fundamental diagrams by Kh [22] and WM [23] which are presented in the analytical form through velocity-density dependencies:

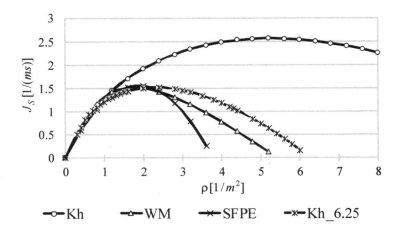

Fig. 2. Specific flows: WM [23], SFPE [24], Kh [22], $v^0 = 1.66$ [m/s].

$$v^{Kh}(\rho) = \begin{cases} v^0(1 - \frac{\ln \rho/\rho^0}{\ln \rho_{max}/\rho^0}), & \rho > \rho^0; \\ v^0, & \rho \le \rho^0, \end{cases} \tag{1}$$

$$v^{WM}(\rho) = \begin{cases} v^0, & \rho = 0; \\ v^0\left(1 - e^{-1.913\left(\frac{1}{\rho} - \frac{1}{\rho_{max}}\right)}\right), & \rho < \rho_{max}; \\ 0, & \rho \ge \rho_{max}. \end{cases} \tag{2}$$

The original forms of the velocity-density dependencies from [22] and [23] were transformed to input ρ_{max} in an explicit way and to make ρ_{max} a parameter [25]. There is critical value of the density ρ_0, under which a person can maintain desired speed (free movement speed) [22], for example, $\rho_0 = 0.51$ [$1/m^2$] for horizontal ways.

In Fig. 2 it was assumed that $\rho_{max} = 15$ [$1/m^2$] (curve Kh) and $\rho_{max} = 6.25$ [$1/m^2$] (curve $KhS\_6.25$) in (1), $\rho_{max} = 5.4$ [$1/m^2$] in (2).

3   Description of the Model

3.1   Space and Initial Conditions

A continuous modeling space $\Omega \in R^2$ is considered. A boarder $\partial\Omega$ (including open part $\partial\Omega'$ which is exit) is known.

A shape of each particle is a disk with diameter d_i, initial positions of particles are given insight Ω by coordinates of disks' centers $x_i(0) = (x_i^1(0), x_i^2(0))$, $i = \overline{1, N}$, N – number of particles (it is assumed that these are coordinates of body's mass center projection). Each particle is assigned with the free movement speed v_i^0 [m/s], the square of projection f_{0i} [m^2].

Each time step t each particle i may move in one of the predetermined directions $\overrightarrow{e_i}(t) \in \{\overrightarrow{e^\alpha}(t),\ \alpha = \overline{1,q}\}$, q – the number of directions (a model parameter). Particles that cross target line $(\partial\Omega')$ leave the modeling space.

It is assumed that a speed of each person is controlled in accordance with a local density and does not exceed the maximal value (the free movement speed).

3.2   Preliminary Calculations

To model directed movement a "map" that stores the information on the shortest distance to the nearest exit is used. The unit of this distance is meters, $[m]$. Such map is saved in static floor field S. This field increases radially from the exit; and it is zero in the exit(s) line(s). It does not change with time and is independent of the presence of the particles. To calculate the field S the Dijkstra's algorithm with 16-nodes pattern may be used, for instance. The idea to use the field S is imported from the floor field (FF) CA model [26].

3.3   Movement Equation

A person movement equation is derived from the finite-difference expression $v(t)\overrightarrow{e}(t) \approx \frac{\overrightarrow{x}(t) - \overrightarrow{x}(t-\Delta t)}{\Delta t}$ that is given by a velocity definition. This expression allows us to present new position of the particle as a function of a previous position and local particle's velocity. Thus for each time t coordinates of each particle i are given by the following formula:

$$\overrightarrow{x}_i(t) = \overrightarrow{x}_i(t - \Delta t) + v_i(t)\overrightarrow{e}_i(t)\Delta t,\ i = \overline{1,N}, \tag{3}$$

where $\overrightarrow{x}_i(t - \Delta t)$ is the coordinate in previous moment; $v_i(t)$, $[m/s]$ is the particle's current speed; $\overrightarrow{e}_i(t)$ is the unit direction vector, Δt, $[s]$ is the time step.

Unknown values in (3) for each time step for each particle are shift $v_i(t)\Delta t$ and direction $\overrightarrow{e}_i(t)$. In contrast with force-based models [5,6], the task of finding the velocity vector is divided in two parts. At first, the new direction is determined; then, value of possible shift is estimated in accordance to local density in the direction chosen. By this trick we omit the step of describing forces that act on persons in direct way, a numerical solution of N differential equations.

A probability approach is used to find a direction for the next step. A procedure to calculate probabilities to move in each direction is adopted from a previously presented stochastic cellular automata floor field model [10,27].

There are at least two ways to calculate shift $v_i(t)\Delta t$. They are considered below. A relaxation parameter Δt is a matter of investigation in the paper. Not only duration of simulation but dynamics of the model is dependant on Δt. Below we present a conjunction of the model and some fundamental diagrams in connection with different Δt.

3.4   Choosing the Movement Direction and Conflict Resolution

All predetermined directions for each particle for each time step are assigned with some probabilities to move, and direction is chosen according to the probability distribution obtained[1].

Probabilities in the model are not static and vary dynamically. The personal probabilities to move in each direction each time step depends on: a) the main driven force (given by a destination point), b) an interaction with other pedestrians, c) an interaction with an infrastructure (non movable obstacles). The highest probability[2] is given to a direction that has most preferable conditions for movement considering other particles and obstacles and a strategy of the peoples' movement (the shortest path and/or the shortest time).

We omit here exact formulas to calculate probability for particle i to move from this position to directions $\{\overrightarrow{e_i^1(t)}, ..., \overrightarrow{e_i^q(t)}\}$, decision rules to choose direction $\overrightarrow{e_i^{\hat{\alpha}}(t)}$. They are presented in [15,20]. Particles take new positions at the same time, i.e., as in CA models parallel update is used. In a case of conflicts in target positions on step t some procedure of conflict resolution is applied [15,20].

3.5   Shift Calculation

As it was shown above current person's speed is density dependent. We assume that only conditions in front of the person influence on speed. It is motivated by the front line effect (that is well pronounced while flow moves in open boundary conditions) in a dense people mass, when front line people move with free movement velocity, while middle part is waiting for a free space available for movement. It results in the diffusion of the flow. Ignoring this effect leads to a simulation being slower than the real process. Thus, only density $F_i(\hat{\alpha})$ in direction chosen $\overrightarrow{e_i(t)} = \overrightarrow{e_i^{\hat{\alpha}}(t)}$ is required to determine speed.

According to (1) to calculate new coordinates of the particle i we have to estimate shift $v_i(t)\Delta t$. There are at least two ways to do it.

One of them is to estimate a local density along movement direction, to substitute density to some speed-density dependence (for example, (1) or (2)) and then to calculate $v_i(t)\Delta t$ using some Δt, Fig. 3(left). If there are collisions with current positions of other particles the length of the shift is corrected, Fig. 3(right). Numerical procedures to estimate a local density is presented in [20].

The other one is pure geometrical way when the particle is moved along movement direction on distance $v_i^0 \Delta t$ or less taking into account current positions of other particle as it is shown in Fig. 3.

---

[1] In this discrete-continuous model we took inspiration from our previously presented stochastic CA FF model [10,27].

[2] Mainly with value > 0.9.

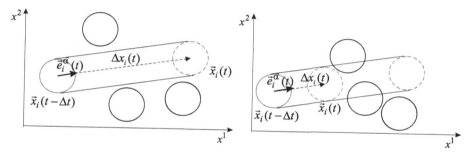

Fig. 3. Left: a position of the particle at moment t (red dashed line) under free conditions. Right: a position of the particle at moment t (blue dashed line) if there are other particles at moment $(t - \Delta t)$ along the track of the considered particle (right). (Color figure online)

4   Simulation Results

4.1   Case Study

We consider the simulation experiment under periodic boundary conditions. A straight corridor 50 m × 2 m in size with the control line in the right-hand side is the modeling area. People uniformly fill the entire area. It is known [28] that geometry influence on model dynamics, and straight corridor is chosen to exclude this influence. Periodic boundary conditions are necessary to compare simulation results with reference data which were obtained in similar conditions.

To reproduce the steady regime initial number of people N should be maintained [25]. It means that when a person reaches the control line (leaves the modeling area from the right-hand side), another person with the same parameters appears from the left (the inflow should tend to the outflow value).

Each person was assigned with a free movement speed of $v^0 = 1.66$ [m/s]. There were considered two cases when all persons were assigned with squares of projection, specifically $f_0 = 0.1$ [m²] and $f_0 = 0.125$ [m²].

We considered a set of numbers of people N_i, $i = \overline{1, m}$ involved in the simulation. The corresponding densities are estimated as $\rho_i = N_i/100, i = \overline{1, m}$, [1/m²]. As far as the shape of person's projection is a solid disc, the maximum number that can be placed in an area of 100 [m²] is 700 with $f_0 = 0.1$ [m²] and 625 with $f_0 = 0.125$ [m²], and the maximum density are $\rho_{max} = 7$ [1/m²] and $\rho_{max} = 6.25$ [1/m²] correspondingly.

There were considered a set of time steps $\Delta t = \{0.0625, 0.125, 0.25, 0.5\}$.

4.2 ΔT Versus Square of Projection

Time T required for $M = 1000$ people to cross the control line at the end of the corridor at given N_i is a quantity to be measured. In the stochastic model, the time should be averaged over a set of K runs under the same initial conditions.

To estimate the flow rate, the formula $J_i = M/T_i$, $[1/s]$ for each density $\rho = N_i/100$ is used, where $T_i = \sum_{j=1}^{K} T_{ij}/K$ is the average time over K runs required for M people to cross the control line. The corresponding specific flow is $J_{s_i} = M/T_i/2$ $[1/(ms)]$. This way of estimating the flow is similar to the method used in natural experiments to obtain real data.

A set of $K = 100$ runs for combination of parameters (f_0 and Δt) and $N_i, i = \overline{1,m}$ was performed and the average times were calculated: $T(\rho_i) = \sum_{j=1}^{500} T_j(\rho_i)/500$, $i = \overline{1,m}$, where $T_j(\rho_i)$ is the time required for $M = 1000$ people to cross the control line in one run at given ρ_i.

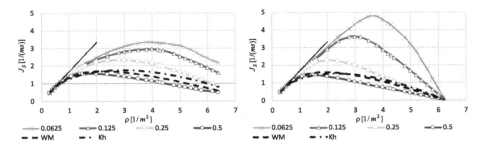

Fig. 4. Specific flow for simulated data for different Δt (geometrical way to calculate shift): $f_0 = 0.1$ $[m^2]$ (left); $f_0 = 0.125$ $[m^2]$ (right). WM—[23], Kh—[22] with $\rho_{max} = 7$ $[1/m^2]$ (left) and $\rho_{max} = 6.25$ $[1/m^2]$ (right). Straight line is given by $v^0 \cdot \rho$.

In Fig. 4 one can see simulated fundamental diagrams for different Δt for $f_0 = 0.1$ $[m^2]$ (left) and for $f_0 = 0.125$ $[m^2]$ (right). And reference data normalized to maximum density in the simulation experiment are presented. In Table 1 there are J_s^{max} and $\rho(J_s^{max})$ for all combinations of parameters considered. Geometrical way to calculate shift was used.

Table 1. J_s^{max}, $[1/m^2]$, $\rho(J_s^{max})$, $[1/m^2]$, for given Δt, f_0. Shift $v^0 \cdot \Delta t$, $[m]$, for 1.66 $[m/s]$.

Δt, $[s]$	f_0, $[m^2]$	J_s^{max}	$\rho(J_s^{max})$	f_0, $[m^2]$	J_s^{max}	$\rho(J_s^{max})$	$v^0 \cdot \Delta t$
0.0625	0.1	3.28	4.3	0.125	4.76	3.8	≈ 0.1
0.125	0.1	2.93	4	0.125	3.62	3	≈ 0.2
0.25	0.1	2.32	2.8	0.125	2.3	2	0.415
0.5	0.1	1.55	1.6	0.125	1.43	1.5	0.83

Straight line in Fig. 4 is given by production $v^0 \cdot \rho$. A conjunction of other lines with this line shows that free movement speed is maintained in the experiment.

One can see that up to ≈ 1 $[1/m^2]$ there is no influence of Δt, square of projection on model dynamics. Higher densities regulate current speed.

Figure 4 shows that low Δt give unrealistic dynamics of the model (in comparison with reference data). A reason of such dynamics is the following. Particles maintain speed v^0 making very small shift $v^0 \cdot \Delta t$, Table 1. Minimization of Δt tends to make movement of particles a continuous process. But real movement of people is more or less discrete from coordinates (position on the plane) point of view, because position of a person in the plane is changing discretely: new position of a person differs from previous position of length of the step. So for low densities a person tends to make step as long as possible but psychological effect (a keeping a comfort distance from others) is taking into account as well. Low Δt in the model considered do not allow to reproduce this phenomena.

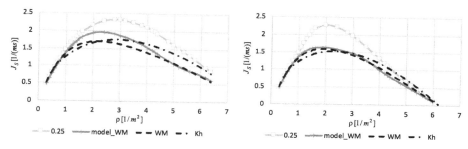

Fig. 5. Left: model_WM—specific flow for simulated data for $\Delta t = 0.25$, $f_0 = 0.1$ $[m^2]$, with (2) as an input data, WM—[23] with $\rho_{max} = 7.85$ $[1/m^2]$, Kh—[22] with $\rho_{max} = 7.85$ $[1/m^2]$, 0.25—curve from Fig. 4. Right: model_WM—specific flow for simulated data for $\Delta t = 0.25$, $f_0 = 0.125$ $[m^2]$, with (2) as an input data, WM—[23] $\rho_{max} = 6.25$ $[1/m^2]$, Kh—[22] with $\rho_{max} = 6.25$ $[1/m^2]$, 0.25—curve from Fig. 4.

The most pronounced conjunction with reference data are given by $\Delta t = 0.25$ and $\Delta t = 0.5$ for both squares of projection. From computational performance point of view they are more preferable as well.

Density in Fig. 4 is given in unit $[1/m^2]$. A difference between left and right graphs in Fig. 4 has a reason in different squares of projection and as a result different total square taken by particles in computational area.

High $\Delta t = 0.5$ [s] gives lower flow in comparison with both reference data.

$\Delta t = 0.25$ [s] gives divergence from reference data for middle densities. As we see a reason is a following. As far as geometrical way to calculate shift is used only geometrical possibility to make step is taking into account, no psychological effect is realized in this case. Consequently a reasonable way to regulate speed in the model is to estimate a local density along movement direction, to substitute density to some speed-density dependence (for example, (1) or (2)) and then to calculate $v_i(t)\Delta t$. As an example of this approach reference data and a simulated fundamental diagram is presented in Fig. 5. One can see considerably better convergence of the curves for middle densities. But divergence is not reduced totally. As we see the reason is in estimate of density:

a method used to estimate density gives lower density in average, the higher speed is obtained in this case, as a result more higher specific flow is obtained comparing with reference data. Figure 5 shows that density estimate applied is particles' square projection dependant as well.

5   Conclusion

In the paper the influence of computational parameter Δt which is responsible for computational performance of the simulation of pedestrian flow was considered. It is shown for the model presented that low Δt are not reasonable to consider. High Δt equals half a second gives specific flow lower then reference data. The best convergence with reference data was obtained for $\Delta t = 0.25$ [s]. The divergence given by geometrical way could be considered as a proof that fundamental diagrams includes psychological effect which is pronounced in a lower speed comparing with physically possible.

References

1. Kirik, E., Malyshev, A., Vitova, T., Popel, E., Kharlamov, E.: Pedestrian movement simulation for stadiums design. In: IOP Conference Series: Materials Science and Engineering, vol. 456, p. 012074 (2018)
2. Ronchi, E., Nieto Uriz, F., Criel, X., Reilly, P.: Modelling large-scale evacuation of music festivals. Case Stud. Fire Sa. **5**, 11–19 (2016)
3. Shimura, K., Khan, S.D., Bandini, S., Nishinari, K.: Simulation and evaluation of spiral movement of pedestrians: towards the Tawaf simulator. J. Cell. Autom. **11**(4), 275–284 (2016)
4. Mitsopoulou, M., Dourvas, N., Georgoudas, I.G., Sirakoulis, G.C.: Cellular automata model for crowd behavior management in airports. In: Wyrzykowski, R., Deelman, E., Dongarra, J., Karczewski, K. (eds.) PPAM 2019. LNCS, vol. 12044, pp. 445–456. Springer, Cham (2020). https://doi.org/10.1007/978-3-030-43222-5_39
5. Helbing, D., Farkas, I., Vicsek, T.: Simulating dynamical features of escape panic. Nature **407**, 487–490 (2000)
6. Chraibi, M., Seyfried, A., Schadschneider, A.: Generalized centrifugal-force model for pedestrian dynamics. Phys. Rev. E **82**, 046111 (2010)
7. Zeng, W., Nakamura, H., Chen, P.: A modified social force model for pedestrian behavior simulation at signalized crosswalks. Soc. Behav. Sci. **138**(14), 521–530 (2014)
8. Blue, V.J., Adler, J.L.: Cellular automata microsimulation for modeling bi-directional pedestrian walkways. Transp. Res. Part B **35**, 293–312 (2001)
9. Kirchner, A., Klupfel, H., Nishinari, K., Schadschneider, A., Schreckenberg, M.: Discretization effects and the influence of walking speed in cellular automata models for pedestrian dynamics. J. Stat. Mech: Theory Exp. **10**, 10011 (2004)
10. Kirik, E., Vitova, T.: On formal presentation of update rules, density estimate and using floor fields in CA FF pedestrian dynamics model SIgMA.CA. In: El Yacoubi, S., Wąs, J., Bandini, S. (eds.) ACRI 2016. LNCS, vol. 9863, pp. 435–445. Springer, Cham (2016). https://doi.org/10.1007/978-3-319-44365-2_43

11. Nishinari, K., Kirchner, A., Namazi, A., Schadschneider, A.: Extended floor field CA model for evacuation dynamics. IEICE Trans. Inf. Syst. **E87–D**, 726–732 (2004)
12. Seitz, M.J., Koster, G.: Natural discretization of pedestrian movement in continuous space. Phys. Rev. E **86**(4), 046108 (2012)
13. Zeng, Y., Song, W., Huo, F., Vizzari, G.: Modeling evacuation dynamics on stairs by an extended optimal steps model. Simul. Model. Pract. Theory **84**, 177–189 (2018)
14. Baglietto, G., Parisi, D.R.: Continuous-space automaton model for pedestrian dynamics. Phys. Rev. E **83**, 056117 (2011)
15. Kirik, E., Yurgel'yan, T., Malyshev, A.: On discrete-continuous stochastic floor field pedestrian dynamics model SIgMA.DC. In: Proceedings of the International conference "Emergency evacuation of people from buildings - EMEVAC", pp. 155–161. Belstudio, Warsaw (2011)
16. Kirchner, A., Schadschneider, A.: Simulation of evacuation processes using a bionics-inspried cellular automaton model for pedestrian dynamics. Phys. A **312**, 260–276 (2002)
17. Bandini, S., Rubagotti, F., Vizzari, G., Shimura, K.: A cellular automata based model for pedestrian and group dynamics: motivations and first experiments. In: Malyshkin, V. (ed.) PaCT 2011. LNCS, vol. 6873, pp. 125–139. Springer, Heidelberg (2011). https://doi.org/10.1007/978-3-642-23178-0_11
18. Helbing, D., Molnar, P.: Social force model for pedestrian dynamics. Phys. Rev. E **51**(5), 4282–4286 (1995)
19. Seyfried, A., Steffen, B., Lippert, T.: Basics of modelling the pedestrian flow. Phys. A **368**(1), 232–238 (2006)
20. Kirik, E., Malyshev, A., Popel, E.: Fundamental diagram as a model input: direct movement equation of pedestrian dynamics. In: Weidmann, U., Kirsch, U., Schreckenberg, M. (eds.) Pedestrian and Evacuation Dynamics 2012, pp. 691–702. Springer, Cham (2014). https://doi.org/10.1007/978-3-319-02447-9_58
21. Chattaraj, U., Seyfried, A., Chakroborty, P.: Comparison of pedestrian fundamental diagram across cultures. Adv. Complex Syst. **12**, 393–405 (2009)
22. Kholshevnikov, V.V., Shields, T.M., Boyce, K.E., Samoshin, D.A.: Recent developments in pedestrian flow theory and research in Russia. Fire Saf. J. **43**(2), 108–118 (2008)
23. Weidmann, U.: Transporttechnik der Fussgänger. Transporttechnische Eigenschaften des Fussgängerverkehrs (Literaturauswertung). IVT, Institut für Verkehrsplanung, Transporttechnik, Strassen-und Eisenbahnbau, Zürich (1992)
24. Nelson, H.E., Mowrer, F.W.: Emergency movement. The SFPE Handbook of Fire Protection Engineering, pp. 3–367 -3-380. National Fire Protection Association (2002)
25. Kirik, E., Vitova, T., Malyshev, A., Popel, E.: A conjunction of the discrete-continuous pedestrian dynamics model SigmaEva with fundamental diagrams. In: Wyrzykowski, R., Deelman, E., Dongarra, J., Karczewski, K. (eds.) PPAM 2019. LNCS, vol. 12044, pp. 457–466. Springer, Cham (2020). https://doi.org/10.1007/978-3-030-43222-5_40
26. Schadschneider, A., Seyfried, A.: Validation of CA models of pedestrian dynamics with fundamental diagrams. Cybern. Syst. **40**(5), 367–389 (2009)
27. Kirik, E., Yurgel'yan, T., Krouglov, D.: On realizing the shortest time strategy in a CA FF pedestrian dynamics model. Cybern. Syst. **42**(1), 1–15 (2011)
28. Kirik, E., Vitova, T., Malyshev, A.: Turns of different angles and discrete-continuous pedestrian dynamics model. Nat. Comput. **18**(4), 875–884 (2019)

DESERTICAS, a Software to Simulate Desertification Based on MEDALUS and Cellular Automata

Alassane Koné[1,2](✉), Allyx Fontaine[1](✉), Maud Loireau[2,3](✉),
Salifou Nouhou Jangorzo[4], and Samira El Yacoubi[2,3](✉)

[1] ESPACE-DEV, University Guyane, IRD, University Antilles, University Montpellier, University Réunion, Guyane, France
alassane.kone@ird.fr, allyx.fontaine@univ-guyane.fr
[2] IMAGES ESPACE-DEV, University Perpignan Via Domitia, Perpignan, France
yacoubi@univ-perp.fr
[3] ESPACE-DEV, IRD, University Montpellier, University Guyane, University Antilles, University Réunion, Montpellier, France
maud.loireau@ird.fr
[4] Université de Maradi, Maradi, Niger
njangorzo@gmail.com

Abstract. DESERTICAS is a cellular automata software specially designed for modelling and simulating the evolution of land degradation over time and space. It is based on coupling a continuous cellular automaton with the MEDALUS method that has been applied to assess the desertification phenomena on Mediterranean areas. Additionally, the built model will incorporate land use practices, exploitability and ownership factors. From an arbitrary initial configuration, DESERTICAS can predict the space-time evolution of land degradation towards the most advanced stage. The fully parameterized software will be applied to real data that are being processed for model validation.

Keywords: Cellular automata · MEDALUS · Desertification sensitivity index · Desertification software · Land degradation

1 Introduction

Contrary to widespread opinion, desertification is not the transformation of the land into desert neither the displacement of sand dunes [20]. According to United Nations Convention to Combat Desertification (UNCCD), desertification is defined as the degradation of soils, landscapes and terrestrial bio-productive systems in arid, semi-arid and sub-humid areas, resulting from several factors including climate change and human activities [20]. Desertification is an advanced, even a final step of land degradation process [8] and it contributes to create desert-like conditions [20]. The areas subject to desertification are dry areas and characterized by: low, infrequent, irregular and unpredictable

© Springer Nature Switzerland AG 2021
T. M. Gwizdałła et al. (Eds.): ACRI 2020, LNCS 12599, pp. 198–208, 2021.
https://doi.org/10.1007/978-3-030-69480-7_20

rainfall; large variations between day and night temperatures; soils with little organic matter and little water; a fauna and a flora adapted to climatic variations (drought, salty water and lack of water) [20].

Given the seriousness of the consequences of this phenomenon, the United Nations has defined strategies for the prevention and control of land degradation. In this context, several common and shared methodologies have been developed in order to assess, model and understand the desertification phenomena. MEDALUS (acronym for Mediterranean Desertification and Land Use) is one of the most popular project that was supported by Europe for this issue [4].

Based on MEDALUS approach, POWERSIM simulator [13] provides a temporal evolution of the desertification phenomenon but does not take into account microscopic and spatial changes of the soil degradation. Another software, LADA (Land Degradation Assessment in Drylands), that was developed by Food and Agriculture Organization of the United Nations (FAO), aimed at assessing and mapping land degradation at different spatial scales [14]. It is based on the assumption that the main causes of land degradation are due to human activities on the land. However, the assessment is made at a given time and does not integrate the dynamic aspect in the model.

In addition and using the GIS platform, the software SIEL was built in order to quantify and model spatially agricultural practices along with available natural resources [12]. However, the interactions between the different areas called activity centers is not integrated into the modeling process.

The main contribution of the present paper is to combine cellular automata approach to MEDALUS model in the built software DESERTICAS (DESERTIfication Cellular Automata Simulator) that aims to simulate the land degradation as a spatio-temporal phenomenon. Cellular automata (CA for short) are an idealization of real systems in which space, time and the physical quantities which determine the states are discrete. Since their inception by Stanislaw Ulam and John von Neumann in the late 1940s [9], they have been successfully used to model physical, environmental or engineering processes: population dynamics, solidification of crystals, image processing, etc. [2,19]. The main reason behind the use of CA models is their ability to describe a large variety of complex spatio-temporal phenomena based on a simple formalism. They have been successfully applied to simulate the propagation of several phenomena: fire, epidemics, pollution, etc. [7,17]. They will be coupled in this work with a MEDALUS assessment in order to describe the spatial expansion/contraction of the desert area. In addition to the used processes in MEDALUS method that are inherent to the land degradation, our designed model integrates other factors such as land use type, exploitability and ownership. The proposed model is fully parameterized and each parameter can be chosen by the user within a given range provided by MEDALUS model.

This paper is organized as follows: in the next section, a small introduction of the used notions in the built software is given. The developed model is described in Sect. 3 and the implementation steps including DESERTICAS presentation are given in Sect. 4. Section 5 is dedicated to the performed simulations and discussion. At the end, a conclusion is given with some perspectives.

2   Preliminaries

Our model is based on a continuous CA whose components will be defined according to the MEDALUS assessment extended by anthropogenic factors identified during field campaigns and through in-depth knowledge of the functioning of arid zones in the Sahel [11]. Let us start by briefly presenting the basic tools of the built software.

2.1   Cellular Automata

A CA is a discrete dynamical system that is formally defined by a tuple $(\mathcal{L}; \mathcal{S}; \mathcal{N}; f)$ [2,18]. The cellular space $\mathcal{L}$ is a d-dimensional lattice whose elements called cells are arranged depending on their shape and the space dimension d. Each cell state belonging to a discrete set $\mathcal{S}$ updates its value as a function of the current state of its neighborhood $\mathcal{N}_c$ according to a set of rules or transition function f. The most used neighbourhood types in a 2-dimensional CA are von Neumann and Moore for square cells or uniform one for hexagonal lattices. If the states of cell c at time t and $t+1$ are respectively denoted by s_c and s_c^+, the transition function is defined by Eq. (1):

$$f \colon \mathcal{S}^{n+1} \to \mathcal{S}$$
$$s_{\mathcal{N}_c} \mapsto ds_c^+ \tag{1}$$

where n is the number of neighbours except the cell.

A CA configuration or global state is defined by a function that attributes a state value in $\mathcal{S}$ to each cell in $\mathcal{L}$ at a given time. The global dynamics of the CA is defined by the function $\mathcal{F}$ that maps the configuration at time t to a new configuration at time $t+1$. If $\mathcal{S}^{\mathcal{L}}$ is the set of all the CA configurations defined on the lattice $\mathcal{L}$, s and s^+ two consecutive configurations, $\mathcal{F}$ is defined by:

$$\mathcal{F} \colon \mathcal{S}^{\mathcal{L}} \to \mathcal{S}^{\mathcal{L}}$$
$$s \mapsto \mathcal{F}(s) = s^+ \tag{2}$$

2.2   Introduction to MEDALUS

MEDALUS model has been developed by the commission of the European Union. It aims to assess land degradation by quantifying its factors grouped into four main types: soil, vegetation, climate and management factors [4].

Each factor is defined by its quality index (value between 1 and 2) [5].

$$ds = (l \times v \times w \times m)^{\frac{1}{4}} \tag{3}$$

The degree of land degradation, given by the desertification sensitivity index (ds), is defined as the geometric mean of soil (l), vegetation (v), climate (w) and management (m) quality indexes [4] (cf. Eq. (3)). The ds values are in the range $[1; 2]$ and its associated quality states are defined in Table 1.

Table 1. SDI states.

Class of weight	Desertification state
$I_5 = [1.78; 2]$	Very-degraded
$I_4 = [1.53; 1.78[$	Degraded
$I_3 = [1.38; 1.53[$	High
$I_2 = [1.22; 1.38[$	Moderate
$I_1 = [1; 1.22[$	Low

Table 2. Quality indexes of climate and management factors.

Class	Description	Index of climate	Index of management
1	High quality	$I_1^w = [1; 1.15[$	$I_1^m = [1; 1.25[$
2	Moderate quality	$I_2^w = [1.15; 1.81[$	$I_2^m = [1.25; 1.50[$
3	Low quality	$I_3^w = [1.81; 2]$	$I_3^m = [1.50; 2]$

3   Proposed Model

In this section, we describe the model for desertification phenomenon that is characterised by a space time evolution where the spread of desert area depends on the combination of degradation factors to be evaluated [4,10]. The model introduced in this work can be considered as the continuation and improvement of the model shown in a previous work of the authors [1]. Here, the coupling of CA and MEDALUS models is enhanced with additional factors in order to refine the dynamics of land states. The first novelty is to add the land type factor in the model. Six main types of land area, defined by their use, are considered: crop lands, forests, pasture areas comprising the cattle passages, residential areas and border areas such as roads and water streams. In our work, the land use type is denoted by p and will be represented by integers in the range $[1, 6]$. The second additional factor is exploitability denoted by e and takes 1 or 0 corresponding to exploited or unexploited land respectively. Land exploitation in DESERTICAS is subject to its ownership will or its agreement. If two areas have the same owner, they will be characterised by the same number. As shown in the results, the interaction between these new factors make desertification modelling more realistic.

The study area is represented by a **2-dimensional lattice** $\mathcal{L}$ divided into square cells. In the grid, each cell c is defined by its coordinates (i, j).

The state of each cell c at time t is given by a tuple $\xi(c) \in \mathcal{S}$ where $\xi(c) = (l_c, v_c, w_c, m_c, p_c, e_c, o_c)$ corresponding respectively to the indexes of the soil, vegetation, climate, management, land use type, exploitability and ownership. We denote by $\xi^+(c) = (l_c^+, v_c^+, w_c^+, m_c^+, p_c, e_c^+, o_c)$ the value of this variable for cell c at time $t + 1$. Therefore $\mathcal{S} = [1, 2]^4 \times [1, 6] \times \{0, 1\} \times \{1, 2, \ldots, k\}$, where k is the ownership identifier in the study area.

The neighborhood of a cell c is composed of the cell itself and its surrounding cells that are supposed to affect its evolution. In this paper, we consider the Moore neighbourhood of radius r defined as $\mathcal{N}_c = \{c_{i'j'} \in \mathcal{L}, max(|i - i'|, |j - j'|) \leq r\}$. As all cells in the neighbourhood have the same influence on the central cell c regardless of their position, they will be denoted by $c_i, 1 \leq i \leq n$ and $|\mathcal{N}_c| = n+1$ is the neighbourhood size. We extend the notation ξ to the neighborhood of the cell c by $\xi(\mathcal{N}_c) = (\xi(c), \xi(c_1), \xi(c_2), \ldots, \xi(c_n))$.

It is observed that the most important factors that have significant local influence in the evolution of land degradation are soil (l), vegetation (v), climate (w) and management (m). This will be characterised for a neighbor-hood $\mathcal{N}_c$ by four values computed as the geometric mean of these factors for all the neighbouring cells c_i, $i = 1, \cdots, n$ and gives for each $q \in \{l, v, w, m\}$,

$$q_{\mathcal{N}_c} = (q_{c_1} \times q_{c_2} \times \ldots \times q_{c_n})^{\frac{1}{n}} \tag{4}$$

Additionally, the overall evolution of each cell state will depend on the deser-tification sensitivity index ds (see Eq. 3) that is a real number given in the interval $[1; 2]$ as described in [1]. This will be updated according to the evolution of each factor l, v, w and m.

The transition rules used in DESERTICAS allow to update the state evo-lution of a cell c according to its state and the state of its neighborhood. The combination of all those components gives the degradation index of cell c [4]. However, extreme levels of the degradation factors, such as climate and man-agement, generate stress conditions in land and accelerated its degradation. The stress conditions of a cell c are applied when Properties 1 and 2 occur [1,16]. At least, the activity of the owner on a degraded cell is usually transferred in a cell having good condition. This happens when Property 3 is checked.

Property 1. The state of a cell c reaches the upper part of the range of *Degraded* state and its climate and management indexes are *High* i.e. $c \in D_1$:

$$D_1 = \{c \in \mathcal{L} \mid center(I_4) \leq s_c < upper(I_4) \text{ and } w_c \text{ or } m_c \text{ are } \textit{High}\} \tag{5}$$

where $center(I_i)$ and $upper(I_i)$ are respectively the center and upper bound of the interval I_i (see Table 1).

Property 2. The state of cell c reaches the upper part of the range of *High* state and its climate w_c and management m_c indexes reach the upper part of *High* range values i.e $c \in D_2$:

$$D_2 = \{c \in \mathcal{L} \mid center(I_3) \leq s_c < upper(I_3) \text{ and } center(I_3^w) \leq w_c \text{ or}$$
$$center(I_3^m) \leq m_c\} \tag{6}$$

where I_3^w and I_3^m are described in Table 2.

Property 3 [6,12]. Lands, initially unexploited, can be used by its owner by trans-ferring the activity from a *Degraded* land to a better quality land with the same characteristics and the same ownership. This transfer operation can only be done by the owner of this two lands or with his agreement and does not take into account the chosen neighborhood radius. The transfer operation is possible between two cells c and c', if $(c; c') \in D_3$:

$$D_3 = \{(c, c') \in \mathcal{L} \times \mathcal{L} \mid p_c \in [1; 2; 3], s_c < min(I_4) , e_c = 0 , e_{c'} = 1 , s_{c'} \in I_5 \tag{7}$$
$$p_c = p_{c'} \text{ and } o_c = o_{c'}\}$$

where I_4 and I_5 are described in Table 1.

To define the transition function, we first define the parameters α and a generic function g_α as follow. Let $\alpha = (\alpha_1; \alpha_2; \ldots; \alpha_9)$ be a tuple of factor powers such that $\alpha_i \in [0; 1]$ and $\sum_{i=1}^{9} \alpha_i = 1$. Let g_α be the α−weighted geometric mean defined by Eq. (8).

$$g_\alpha : \mathcal{S}^{n+1} \to [1; 2]$$
$$g_\alpha(\xi(\mathcal{N}_c)) = l_c^{\alpha_1} \times l_{\mathcal{N}_c}^{\alpha_2} \times v_c^{\alpha_3} \times v_{\mathcal{N}_c}^{\alpha_4} \times w_c^{\alpha_5} \times w_{\mathcal{N}_c}^{\alpha_6} \times m_c^{\alpha_7} \times m_{\mathcal{N}_c}^{\alpha_8} \times ds_c^{\alpha_9} \quad (8)$$

We now define the generic function h used in the transition function to take into account Properties 1, 2 and 3. Indeed, if the cell c reaches a *very degraded* state, it remains in its state ds_c. Indeed, desertification has irreversible character because if a disturbance changes the land from the vegetated state to the critical threshold of the degraded state, the removal of this disturbance will not return to the initial state [4, 15]. Moreover, in the stress conditions, a cell changes its state to one of superior states. Beside the particular conditions described previously, the state of a cell c is given by the combination of desertification factors [4]. For $x \in \{l, v, w, m\}$, we define

$$h_x : [0, 1]^9 \times \mathcal{S}^{n+1} \to [1; 2]$$
$$h_x(\alpha, \xi(\mathcal{N}_c)) = \begin{cases} x_c \; if \; ds_c \in I_5 \; (Irreversibility) \\ max(min(I_5); g_\alpha(\xi(\mathcal{N}_c))) \; if \; c \in D_1 \; or \; D_2 \; (Property \; 1 \; and \; 2) \\ (x_c \times x_{c'})^{\frac{1}{2}} \; if \; x = m \; and \; \exists! \; c' \in \mathcal{L}, \; (c; c') \in D_3 (Property \; 3) \\ g_\alpha(\xi(\mathcal{N}_c)) \; otherwise (Normal \; condition) \end{cases} \quad (9)$$

For a cell c, the transition function f computes in parallel each component of a cell c from its state and the states of its neighborhood. We have:

$$f : \mathcal{S}^{n+1} \to S$$
$$\xi_c^+ = (f_l(\xi(\mathcal{N}_c)), f_v(\xi(\mathcal{N}_c)), f_w(\xi(\mathcal{N}_c)), f_m(\xi(\mathcal{N}_c)), p_c, f_e(\xi(\mathcal{N}_c)), o_c)$$

$$\begin{aligned}
f_l(\xi(\mathcal{N}_c)) &= h_l((\alpha_{l1}; \alpha_{l2}; 0; 0; 0; 0; 0; 0; \alpha_{l9}), \xi(\mathcal{N}_c)), \\
f_v(\xi(\mathcal{N}_c)) &= h_v((\alpha_{v1}; 0; 0; \alpha_{v4}; 0; 0; 0; 0; \alpha_{v9}), \xi(\mathcal{N}_c)), \\
f_w(\xi(\mathcal{N}_c)) &= h_w((\alpha_{w1}; 0; \alpha_{w3}; 0; \alpha_{w5}; \alpha_{w6}; 0; 0; 0), \xi(\mathcal{N}_c)), \quad (10) \\
where \quad f_m(\xi(\mathcal{N}_c)) &= h_m((0; 0; 0; 0; 0; 0; \alpha_{m7}; \alpha_{m8}; 0), \xi(\mathcal{N}_c)),
\end{aligned}$$

$$f_e(\xi(\mathcal{N}_c)) = \begin{cases} 1 \; if \; \exists! \; c' \in \mathcal{L}, \; (c; c') \in D_3 \\ 0 \; if \; \exists! \; c' \in \mathcal{L}, \; (c'; c) \in D_3 \\ e_c \; if \; not \end{cases}$$

Thus, depending on the evolution of cell states, three kinds of processes can be described: degradation, regeneration and stability. A cell c is in the process of degradation if its states verify $ds_c < ds_c^+$. A cell c is in the process of regeneration if its states verify $ds_c > ds_c^+$. A cell c is in the process of stability or conservation if its states verify $ds_c = ds_c^+$.

4   Implementation

Written in Python, DESERTICAS is the software designed to model the phenomenon of land degradation based on our proposal. The interface is presented
in Fig. 1. It is divided into four parts.

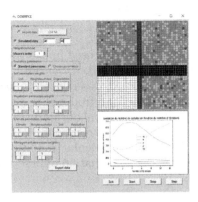

Fig. 1. DESERTICAS Graphical User Interface.

Data Importation. The first part is devoted to initialisation of the cell states
of the studied area. The user can import data from a CSV file by using
the button "CSV fill" or generate simulated data. The data relating to quality index of the four desertification factors, the land type, the exploitability and the ownership factors are generated or imported at the end of this
step. Let $l_c(0)$, $v_c(0)$, $w_c(0)$, $m_c(0)$, $p_c(0)$, $e_c(0)$ and $o_c(0)$ be respectively quality index of soil, vegetation, climate, the management, the land use type,
the exploitability and ownership factors of a cell c at initial time $t = 0$.
These initial chosen data in DESERTICAS implicitly initialize the state $\xi(c)$
to $\xi_0(c) = (l_c(0), v_c(0), w_c(0), m_c(0), p_c(0), e_c(0), o_c(0))$.

Neighborhood. The used neighborhood is Moore's order r with $r \in \{0; 1; 2; 3\}$.
Depending on the influence of the interactions between the desertification factors,
the neighborhood can be fixed to 0 if it is not considered in the evolution. The
neighborhood choice implicitly initializes the variables $\xi(\mathcal{N}_c)$ to $\xi_0(\mathcal{N}_c)$. The
desertification index $ds_c(0)$ is also set.

Tuple of Factor Coefficients α_q. The evolution of each factor index takes into
account the coefficient tuple α as defined in the transition function f in Eq. 10.
The coefficients α_i, $i \in \{1; 2; ...; 9\}$ are considered as integer and thereafter normalized by their sum. To make the interface readable, the tuples are divided
into: $\alpha_l = (\alpha_{l1}; \alpha_{l2}; \alpha_{l9})$, $\alpha_v = (\alpha_{v3}; \alpha_{v4}; \alpha_{v9})$, $\alpha_w = (\alpha_{w1}; \alpha_{w3}; \alpha_{w5}; \alpha_{w6})$ and
$\alpha_m = (\alpha_{m7}; \alpha_{m8})$. The default coefficients proposed by DESERTICAS are such

that all the factors have the same impact in the desertification process. That is to say: $\alpha_l = (1;1;1)$, $\alpha_v = (1;1;1)$, $\alpha_w = (1;1;1;1)$ and $\alpha_m = (1;1)$. However, thanks to a slide, users can choose their own coefficients to give more weight to some factors.

Result Display. The results are displayed through two canvas. The first one displays the evolution of the CA lattice and the second one presents the different curves of cell evolution according to their states at each time step. After importing data and choosing the parameters, the initial configuration of the grid will be displayed in the first canvas. The control buttons activate the evolution of the cells states on grid at each time step. It also allows to display simultaneously the grid configuration and the evolution curves of the cell states.

5   Results and Discussion

The three simulations presented in Fig. 2, extracted from DESERTICAS software, are obtained on the same initial configuration area. The size of the area is $W \times H = 40 \times 40$. This area is composed of four parts delimited by a street (in black) and a river (in blue). On the bottom left, we have a residential area (in white). On the three other parts, the state of each cell are random and they are represented by the following colors: orange for *verydegraded*, yellow for *degraded*, green for *high*, khaki for *moderate* and dark green for *low*. As we are studying more specifically arid zones, we assume that the climate has a high level. Another assumption is that on the right side of the river, there is a high human pressure characterised by a high management factor and on the up left side, there is a good management of the land.

A general observation is that the elementary processes of degradation (right side), regeneration (up left side) and conservation (bottom left side) occur simultaneously during the evolution. This comes from the fact that land factor states such as soil and vegetation are degraded or improved by the intensity of climate and human management factor and the management factor differs from left to right side.

We are first interested in the impact of the neighborhood. On Fig. 2(a) and (b), standard values for the coefficients α are used. The difference here is the choice of r to 1 and 2 respectively. We observe that the degradation process on the right side is emphasized when the neighborhood influencing the behavior of the cell is bigger. This can be explained by the fact that there is a general degradation aspect in the neighborhood: we observe few aggregated cells with low or moderate states, most of them are high or degraded.

In Fig. 2(a) and (c), we have the same neighborhood with $r = 1$ but the coefficients α differ. Those figures highlight the huge impact of the choice of the coefficients on the speed of the evolution of cell states. Choosing the right parameters gives a more realistic model for convergence. Setting all the coefficients to the same value for soil factors ($\alpha_l = (1;1;1)$) gives a bigger weight (equal to 2) to the external influences, *i.e.* neighborhood and global state than

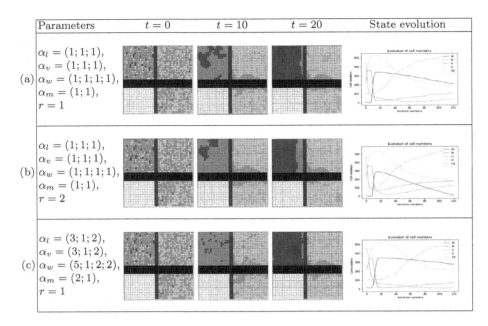

Fig. 2. Evolution of the same area with different parameters. (Color figure online)

the local state of the cell (see Eq. 8). Then the land factor will tend to an homogeneous value and the local aspect is neglected. The reasoning is the same for vegetation, climate and management. Refining factors can solve this problem of fast convergence by taking more into account the local characteristics. Hence, we tried different factors, and it appears that the one chosen in Fig. 2(c) are closer to reality according to geograph experts. The last column shows the evolution of the numbers of cells according to the interpretation of their states: *verydegraded* (DE), *degraded* (D), *high* (H), *moderate* (M) and *low* (W). The same tendency are observed in term of growth and decline. Early peaks that flatten out are explained by human practices that harmonize on the sub-areas. There is an increasing number of degraded cells explained by the arid climate and by half of the area with high human pressure. This phenomenon is similar to what can be observed in SIR model in epidemiology [3]. The difference is in the slope which are less steep in Fig. 2(c) what reinforces our interpretation about a slower convergence.

6   Conclusion

DESERTICAS is based on coupling CA approach, MEDALUS model and additional factors. Its purpose is to predict land evolution from the initial configuration according to a built-transition function. This function is based on the fundamental properties of land degradation process like factors combination, irreversible character, its impacts, etc. Also, this model is done according to a chosen neighborhood radius and coefficients assigned to the different factors. The coefficients represent the factors weights in weighted-geometric mean and allow to take into account the importance of these factors in the evolution process. The chosen parameters *i.e.* coefficients and the neighborhood allow to control cell degradation speed. Indeed, high coefficients associated to land factors allow to slow down the degradation process while identical coefficients to degradation factors accelerate the process until total extinction of cells (desertified). Also, a larger neighborhood allows to consider many cells of the CA grid in the given cell evolution and participates actively in the degradation speed growth. These different choices are made according to the user's knowledge of the desertification microscopic processes and the study area characteristics. That poses the adequacy and optimization problems rely on these parameters. As a perspective, the neighborhood radius and the weighted-geometric mean coefficients can be determined by an optimization method or artificial neural networks. Using, the second method of optimisation is conditioned by obtaining data from the earlier periods.

DESERTICAS is a decision support tool which can be used to control and protect the land against degradation. Unlike other existing desertification monitoring software, it allows to predict land degradation state in time and in space from an initial configuration.This is a notable advance in the strategies for fighting desertification through an annual monitoring.

In its current form, DESERTICAS is limited to the annual modeling of the land states under the effect of degradation factors. It does not include control actions aimed at curbing the harmful effects of its factors on the land quality state. As second perspective, actions can be integrated to follow the cells evolution and alert in high degradation level case. This actions will be guided by the control parameters of the model.

References

1. Koné, A., Fontaine, A., El Yacoubi, S.: Coupling cellular automata with medalus assessment for the desertification issue. In: The International Conference on Emerging Trends in Engineering & Technology (IConETech) (2020)
2. Chopard, B., Droz, M.: Cellular Automata Modeling of Physical Systems. Collection Ale'a-Saclay: Monographs and Texts in Statistical Physics, Cambridge (1998)
3. Cissé, B., El Yacoubi, S., Gourbière, S.: The spatial reproduction number in a cellular automaton model for vector-borne diseases applied to the transmission of chagas disease. Simulation **92**(02), 141–152 (2016)
4. Kosmas, C., Tsara, M., Moustakas, N., Karavitis, C.: Identification of indicators for desertification. Ann. Arid Zone **42**, 393–416 (2003)
5. Lahlaoi, H., Rhinane, H., Hilali, A., Lahssini, S., Moukrim, S.: Desertification assessment using medalus model in watershed oued el maleh, morocco. Geosciences **7**, 2–16 (2017)
6. D'Herbès, J.M., Fezzani, C.: Indicateurs écologiques roselt/oss: Une première approche méthodologique pour la surveillance de la biodiversité et des changements environnementaux. Collection ROSELT/OSS (2004)

7. Freire, J., Dacamara, C.: Using cellular automata to simulate wildfire propagation and to assist in fire prevention and fighting. Nat. Hazards Earth Syst. Sci. Discuss. **19**, 169–179 (2018)

8. Hill, J.: Land and soil degradation assessments in Mediterranean Europe. GMES-Project LADAMER (2003)

9. Von Neumann, J.: Theory of self-reproducing automata. In: Burks, A. (ed.) University of Illinois Press (1966)

10. Benslimane, M., Hamimed, A., Wael, E.Z., Abdelkader, K., Mederbal, K.: Analyse et suivi du phénomène de la désertification en algérie du nord. VertigO (2009)

11. Loireau M., et al.: Guide for the evaluation and monitoring of natural resource exploitation practices roselt/oss programme. ROSELT/OSS Collection (2005)

12. Loireau M., et al.: Local environmental information system to assess the risk of desertification: circumsaharan compared situations (roselt network). Science and planetary change/Drought (2007)

13. Rasmy, M., Gad, A., Abdelsalam, H., Siwailam, M.: A dynamic simulation model of desertification in Egypt. Egypt. J. Remote Sens. Space Sci. **13**, 101–111 (2010)

14. Nachtergaele, O.F., Licona-Manzur, C.: The land degradation assessment in drylands (LADA) project: reflections on indicators for land degradation assessment. In: Lee, C., Schaaf, T. (eds.) The Future of Drylands. Springer, Dordrecht (2008). https://doi.org/10.1007/978-1-4020-6970-3_33

15. Dódorico, P., Bhattachan, A., Davis, K.F., Ravi, S., Runyan, C.W.: Global desertification: drivers and feedbacks. Adv. Water Resour. **51**, 326–344 (2013)

16. Shoba, P., Ramakrishnan, S.S.: Modeling the contributing factors of desertification and evaluating their relationships to the soil degradation process through geomatic techniques. Solid Earth **7**, 341–354 (2013)

17. Slimi, R., El Yacoubi, S.: Spreadable cellular automata: modelling and simulations. Int. J. Syst. Sci. **05**, 507–520 (2009)

18. El Yacoubi, S., El Jai, A.: Cellular automata modelling and spreadability. Math. Comput. Modell. **36**, 1059–1074 (2002)

19. Wolfram, S.: Cellular Automata and Complexity. Addison-Wesley, Company, Science Mathematics Computing (1994)

20. secrétariat de la Convention des Nations unies sur la lutte contre la désertification (CNULD). Désertification: une synthèse visuelle. Centre international UNISFERA, July 2011

Double Diffusive Mixed Convection with Thermodiffusion Effect in a Driven Cavity by Lattice Boltzmann Method

Soufiene Bettaibi$^{(\boxtimes)}$ and Omar Jellouli

Laboratoire des Energies Renouvelable et Matériaux Avancés (LERMA),
Université Internationale de Rabat (UIR), Rocade Rabat-Salé,
11100 Rabat-Sala El Jadida, Morocco
bettaibisoufiene@gmail.com, jellouliomar@gmail.com

Abstract. We perform a numerical study of thermal diffusion effects on double-diffusive mixed convection in a lid-driven square cavity, differentially heated and salted. The fluid flow is solved by a multiple relaxation time (MRT) lattice Boltzmann method (LBM), whereas the temperature and concentration fields are computed by finite difference method (FDM). To assess numerical accuracy, the model (MRT-LBM coupled with FDM) are verified and validated using data from the literature. Besides reasonable agreement, satisfactory computational efficiency is also found. Thereafter, the model is applied for the thermal diffusion effect on a double-diffusive mixed convection in a cavity with moving lid. Results are obtained depending on various dimensionless parameters. It is found that upon increasing the Soret number, heat transfer is slightly enhanced whereas the thickness of the concentration boundary layer increases, thereby decreasing the mass transfer rate.

Keywords: Lattice Boltzmann method (LBM) · Finite difference method (FDM) · Thermodiffusion effect · Double diffusive mixed convection

1 Introduction

In the last few years an alternative numerical method has attracted much attention as a technique in fluid engineering. This method called Lattice Boltzmann Method (LBM) is a mesoscopic method. The fundamental idea behind LBM is to establish a simplified kinetic model to obey the corresponding macroscopic, i.e. Navier Stokes, equations. It has proved its capability to simulate a large variety of fluid flows [1–4]. The LBM has become a very successful alternative numerical method for computational fluid dynamics. Moreover, it is well suited for high-performance implementations on massively parallel processors, including graphics processing units [5]. The lattice Boltzmann method comes with two main collision models. One of the simplest and most widely used proposed by

© Springer Nature Switzerland AG 2021
T. M. Gwizdałła et al. (Eds.): ACRI 2020, LNCS 12599, pp. 209–221, 2021.
https://doi.org/10.1007/978-3-030-69480-7_21

Bhatnagar, Gross and Krook [6] called BGK model, is based on a single relaxation time (SRT) and proves very simple and efficient for simulating fluid flows. Up to now, the lattice Boltzmann equation with the BGK collision operator is still the most popular lattice Boltzmann method. Despite many advantages, the BGK model reveals some deficiencies due to numerical instabilities [7] and consequent difficulties to reach high Reynolds number flows. The second model called MRT operator [8] where each relaxation rate can be tuned independently, presents some advantages compared to the BGK model in terms of numerical stability. Because of this, the MRT-LBM has become increasingly popular in the recent years.

For solving thermal LBM model, several approaches have been proposed, which can be grouped into four categories: passive-scalar approach, multispeed-approach, double-population approach and hybrid approach. The multispeed approach consists in using only one distribution function for treating all thermo-hydrodynamic equations [9–11]. The passive scalar approach consists of treating temperature as the current along an extra-spatial dimension [12]. It is efficient, but being related to the four-dimensional lattices used in the earliest days of LBM research, it has somehow lost popularity The multi-speed model is most natural, but requires additional discrete speeds and is prone to numerical instabilities. The double population approach [13,14] makes use two independent functions for thermo-hydrodynamic equations. This model assumes that, the viscous dissipation and compression work can be neglected for incompressible fluids and the evolution of the temperature is given by the advection-diffusion Eq. [15,16]. This approach shows significant improvements in numerical stability, but to the cost of introducing an additional distribution function to simulate a passive scalar. The hybrid approach [16] used in this article, consists of leaving LBM only for the flow solution, while the energy equation is solved by a different numerical method, typically finite-differences or finite-volumes.

For this reason, in our work the LBM-MRT model is used for velocity field, on the one hand, and finite differences for temperature and concentration fields, on the other hand.

Thermosolutal buoyancy-driven flow in confined cavities represents a fundamental problem, with many engineering applications, such as pollutant transport, nuclear reactor cooling, cooling of electronic systems, to name but a few. Double-diffusive heat and mass transfer problems can be classified as problems involving natural convection, forced convection and combination of both, often referred to as mixed convection [17–22].

Diffusion of heat due to a mass concentration gradients (Dufour effect) and diffusion of matter induced by temperature gradients (Soret effect) are the subject of intensive research, due to the broad range of application in technology and engineering. These include mixture between gases, oil-reservoirs, isotope separation and many others [23–29].

For all the above cited works, the authors have used several configurations to study both the double-diffusive natural and mixed convection problems. Moreover, they applied different numerical methods to solve the basic thermo-fluid equations. Comparatively less attention has been given to the problem of a double-diffusive mixed convection with Soret effect in a driven cavity. From this point of view and to the best of the authors knowledge, no attention has been paid to explore the thermal diffusion effect (Soret effect) on a double-diffusive mixed convection in a cavity with moving lid, using the lattice Boltzmann method (LBM).

In this paper we present a numerical model for double-diffusive mixed convection with Soret effect in a lid-driven cavity. This model uses the Lattice Boltzmann method with multiple relaxation time for collision operator to simulate mass and momentum conservation and finite differences to compute the temperature and concentration fields. We also attempt to provide benchmark quality results on CPU time which can be compared with the existing data.

2 Mathematical Model

2.1 Definition of the Problem

The physical model under consideration is presented in Fig. (1). The two-dimensional lid-driven cavity has height H and width L (Aspect ratio $Ar = \frac{H}{L}$), the vertical side walls are thermally insulated and the top wall moves at a constant velocity $U_0 = 0.1$. The bottom and top walls are maintained at two different but uniform temperatures and concentrations such that the top wall has the temperature

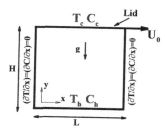

Fig. 1. Geometry of the enclosure and coordinate system.

T_c and concentration C_c, while the bottom wall has the temperature T_h and concentration C_h, respectively, where $T_h > T_c$ and $C_h > C_c$.

The thermophysical properties of the fluid are assumed to be constant except for the density variation in the buoyancy term according to the Boussinesq approximation:

$$\rho = \rho_0 \left(1 - \beta_T \left(T - T_m\right) - \beta_S \left(C - C_m\right)\right)$$

where ρ_0 is the fluid density at the reference temperature $T_m = \left(\frac{T_h + T_c}{2}\right)$ and concentration $C_m = \left(\frac{C_h + C_c}{2}\right)$, β_T and β_S are the thermal and mass expansion coefficients, respectively.

To solve the problem of double-diffusive mixed convection with Soret effect in a lid-driven cavity we assume: a Newtonian incompressible fluid, the Boussinesq approximation for buoyancy, viscous heating and compression work are neglected and no source term inside the cavity.

Based on these assumptions, the dimensional governing equations of mass and momentum are solved by the MRT lattice Boltzmann Method (MRT-LBM) while energy and species equations are solved by Finite Difference Method (FDM).

The non dimensional terms used in this work like thermal Grashof number, the solutal Grashof number, the buoyancy ratio, the Richardson number, the Reynolds number, the Prandtl number, the Schmidt number and the Soret number are defined, respectively, by:

$$G_{RT} = g\beta_T \left(\frac{(T_h - T_c) H^3}{\nu^2} \right); \ G_{RS} = g\beta_S \left(\frac{(C_h - C_c) H^3}{\nu^2} \right)$$

$$N = \frac{\beta_S (C_h - C_c)}{\beta_T (T_h - T_c)} = \frac{G_{RS}}{G_{RT}}$$

$$Ri = \frac{G_{RT}}{Re^2}; \qquad Re = \frac{U_0 . H}{\nu}; \qquad Pr = \frac{\nu}{\alpha}; \qquad Sc = \frac{\nu}{D}$$

$$Sr = \frac{D.K_T (T_h - T_c)}{T_m \nu (C_h - C_c)}$$

The average Nusselt and Sherwood numbers, defined by temperature and concentration gradients at walls, are calculated via:

$$Nu_{av} = -\frac{1}{T_h - T_c} \int_0^H \left(\frac{\partial T}{\partial y} \right)_{wall} dx$$

$$Sh_{av} = -\frac{1}{C_h - C_c} \int_0^H \left(\frac{\partial C}{\partial y} \right)_{wall} dx$$

The dimensionless variables governing this problem are U the x-component velocity and V the y-component velocity.

The following dimensionless quantities are given by:

$$U^* = \frac{U}{U_0} \qquad V^* = \frac{V}{U_0} \qquad \theta = \frac{T - T_c}{T_h - T_c} \qquad t^* = \frac{tU_0}{H} \qquad \Theta = \frac{C - C_c}{C_h - C_c}$$

2.2   MRT-LBM Hybrid Model for Fluid Flow

Within this approach, fluid is described by a particle distribution function which evolves in discrete space and time (a $D_d Q_q$ lattice; d dimensions and q velocities) following two steps: propagation and collision. Hence, the lattice Boltzmann equation is expressed as:

$$f_i (\overrightarrow{x} + \overrightarrow{e_i}, t + 1) - f_i (\overrightarrow{x}, t) = \Omega_i \tag{1}$$

where f_i is the probability of finding a particle at lattice node $\overrightarrow{x}$, at the time t, moving with velocity $\overrightarrow{e_i}$ ($i = 0, \ldots q - 1$) and Ω_i is the collision operator. Note that the time step is made unit by convention.

The Lattice Boltzmann equation with multiple relaxation time (MRT) can be expressed as:

$$f_i (\overrightarrow{x} + \overrightarrow{e_i} \Delta t, t + \Delta t) = f_i (\overrightarrow{x}, t) - M^{-1} S_{ij} \left[m_j - m_{ij}^{eq} (\overrightarrow{x}, t) \right] \tag{2}$$

M is a transform matrix projecting the discrete distribution function f into moment space $|m\rangle = M.|f\rangle$, m_j^{eq} is the equilibrium moment.

The physical meaning of the moments is as follows:

$$|m\rangle = \left(\rho\; e\; j_x\; j_y\; \epsilon\; q_x\; q_y\; p_{xx}\; p_{xy} \right)^\top \tag{3}$$

where ρ is the density, e is the energy, j_x and j_y the x and y components of momentum (mass flux) and ϵ is defined as the kinetic energy, q_x and q_y are the x and y components of the energy flux. In addition, p_{xx} and p_{xy} correspond to the diagonal and off-diagonal components of the viscous stress tensor, and $\top$ denotes the transpose operator.

The macroscopic fluid variables, density ρ and velocity $\overrightarrow{u}$ are obtained from the moments of the distribution functions as follows:

$$\rho = \sum_{i=0}^{q-1} f_i \qquad and \qquad \rho\overrightarrow{u} = \sum_{i=0}^{q-1} f_i \overrightarrow{e_i} \tag{4}$$

For the (D_2Q_9) lattices(Fig(2)), the nine discrete velocities $\overrightarrow{e_i}$ are defined as:

$$\begin{cases} \overrightarrow{e_i} = \overrightarrow{0} & i = 0 \\ \overrightarrow{e_i} = \left(\cos\left[(i-1)\frac{\pi}{2}\right], \sin\left[(i-1)\frac{\pi}{2}\right]\right)c & i = 1,2,3,4 \\ \overrightarrow{e_i} = \left(\cos\left[(2i-9)\frac{\pi}{4}\right], \sin\left[(2i-9)\frac{\pi}{4}\right]\right)c\sqrt{2} & i = 5,6,7,8 \end{cases} \tag{5}$$

Where ΔX and Δt are the lattice width and time step, respectively. It is chosen that $\Delta X = \Delta t$, thus $c = \frac{\Delta X}{\Delta t} = 1$ is the lattice speed.

With a (D_2Q_9) lattices, the transformation matrix M and the moment vector m are defined as:

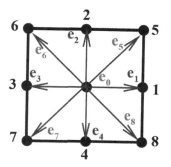

Fig. 2. Lattice structure for the D_2Q_9 model.

$$m = \begin{bmatrix} \rho \\ e \\ \epsilon \\ j_x \\ j_y \\ q_x \\ q_y \\ p_{xx} \\ p_{xy} \end{bmatrix} \begin{bmatrix} 1 & 1 & 1 & 1 & 1 & 1 & 1 & 1 & 1 \\ -4 & -1 & -1 & -1 & -1 & 2 & 2 & 2 & 2 \\ 4 & -2 & -2 & -2 & -2 & 1 & 1 & 1 & 1 \\ 0 & 1 & 0 & -1 & 0 & 1 & -1 & -1 & 1 \\ 0 & -2 & 0 & 2 & 0 & 1 & -1 & -1 & 1 \\ 0 & 0 & 1 & 0 & -1 & 1 & 1 & -1 & -1 \\ 0 & 0 & -2 & 0 & 2 & 1 & 1 & -1 & -1 \\ 0 & 1 & -1 & 1 & -1 & 0 & 0 & 0 & 0 \\ 0 & 0 & 0 & 0 & 0 & 1 & -1 & 1 & -1 \end{bmatrix} \begin{bmatrix} f_0 \\ f_1 \\ f_2 \\ f_3 \\ f_4 \\ f_5 \\ f_6 \\ f_7 \\ f_8 \end{bmatrix} = M.f \tag{6}$$

Where the equilibrium value of moments can be defined from the following equations:

$$\begin{cases} \rho^{eq} = \rho \\ e^{eq} = -2\rho + 3\left(u^2 + v^2\right) \\ \epsilon^{eq} = \rho - 3\left(u^2 + v^2\right) \\ j_x^{eq} = \rho u \\ j_y^{eq} = \rho v \end{cases} \quad and \quad \begin{cases} q_x^{eq} = -u \\ q_y^{eq} = -v \\ p_{xx}^{eq} = u^2 - v^2 \\ p_{xy}^{eq} = uv \end{cases} \quad (7)$$

The equilibrium density distribution function, which depends on the local fluid velocity and density is given by:

$$f_i^{eq} = w_i \rho \left[1 + \frac{3\overrightarrow{e_i}.\overrightarrow{u}}{c^2} + \frac{9\left(\overrightarrow{e_i}.\overrightarrow{u}\right)^2}{2c^4} - \frac{3\overrightarrow{u}.\overrightarrow{u}}{2c^2}\right] \qquad i = 0 \rightarrow 8 \qquad (8)$$

Where w_i is the weighting factor defined as:

$$\begin{cases} w_i = \frac{4}{9} & i = 0 \\ w_i = \frac{1}{9} & i = 1, 2, 3, 4 \\ w_i = \frac{1}{36} & i = 5, 6, 7, 8 \end{cases} \qquad (9)$$

The diagonal relaxation matrix can be written as:

$$S = diag\left[S_0, S_1, S_2, S_3, S_4, S_5, S_6, S_7, S_8\right] \qquad (10)$$

In the present work, we assume $S_0 = S_3 = S_5 = 0$ for both the mass and momentum conservation before and after collision. We also consider $S_7 = S_8 = \frac{1}{\tau}$ due to fact that the viscosity formulation is the same as SRT model. In the present simulation $S_1 = 1.64$, $S_2 = 1.2$ and $S_4 = S_6 = 8 \times \frac{(2-S_7)}{(8-S_7)}$.

It should be noted that in the LBM the kinematic viscosity ν is related to the relaxation time by the following relation:

$$\nu = (\tau - 0.5)\, c_s^2 \Delta t \qquad (11)$$

Where $c_s = \frac{c}{\sqrt{3}}$ is the speed of sound. For the (D_2Q_9) lattices the viscosity is positive which requires the choice of $\tau > 0.5$.

2.3   Finite Difference Method (FDM) for Temperature and Concentration Fields

Equation (4) is discretized by the Finite Difference Method (FDM) using the Taylor series expansion of the second order. To improve the stability of the hybrid model used in this article, Lallemand and Luo [16] suggest using a discretization in accordance with discretization speeds. They proposed the following discretization for the derivatives with $(\Delta x = \Delta t = 1)$:

For more clarity, in the following the variable (Φ) designates the temperature (T) or the concentration (C). Therefore, the equations for both scalars $(T$ and $C)$ can be written as:

$$\frac{\partial \Phi}{\partial x} = \left(\Phi_{i+1,j} - \Phi_{i-1,j} - \frac{1}{4}\left[\Phi_{i+1,j+1} - \Phi_{i-1,j+1} + \Phi_{i+1,j-1} - \Phi_{i-1,j-1}\right]\right) \quad (12)$$

$$\frac{\partial \Phi}{\partial y} = \left(\Phi_{i,j+1} - \Phi_{i,j-1} - \frac{1}{4} \left[\Phi_{i+1,j+1} - \Phi_{i-1,j+1} + \Phi_{i+1,j-1} - \Phi_{i-1,j-1} \right] \right) \quad (13)$$

And for Laplacian:

$$\nabla^2 \Phi = \left([\Phi_{i+1,j} + \Phi_{i,j+1} + \Phi_{i-1,j}] \right.$$
$$\left. - \frac{1}{2} [\Phi_{i+1,j+1} + \Phi_{i-1,j+1} + \Phi_{i-1,j-1} + \Phi_{i+1,j-1}] - 6\Phi_{i,j} \right) \quad (14)$$

For the time derivative, we use an explicit difference scheme. Then for the solution is conditionally stable:

$$\frac{\partial \Phi}{\partial t} = \left(\Phi_{i,j}^{n+1} - \Phi_{i,j}^{n} \right) \quad (15)$$

Substituting the Eqs. (12–15) to Eq. (4) or (5):

$$\begin{aligned}
\Phi_{i,j}^{n+1} = & \; \Phi_{i,j}^{n} \left(1 - 6\alpha \right) + \Phi_{i+1,j}^{n} \left(-u + 2\alpha \right) + \Phi_{i-1,j}^{n} \left(u + 2\alpha \right) \\
& + \Phi_{i,j+1}^{n} \left(-v + 2\alpha \right) + \Phi_{i,j-1}^{n} \left(v + 2\alpha \right) \\
& + \Phi_{i+1,j+1}^{n} \left(\tfrac{1}{4}u + \tfrac{1}{4}v - \tfrac{1}{2}\alpha \right) \\
& + \Phi_{i-1,j+1}^{n} \left(-\tfrac{1}{4}u + \tfrac{1}{4}v - \tfrac{1}{2}\alpha \right) \\
& + \Phi_{i+1,j-1}^{n} \left(\tfrac{1}{4}u - \tfrac{1}{4}v - \tfrac{1}{2}\alpha \right) \\
& + \Phi_{i-1,j-1}^{n} \left(-\tfrac{1}{4}u - \tfrac{1}{4}v - \tfrac{1}{2}\alpha \right)
\end{aligned} \quad (16)$$

The coefficient that accompanies $(\Phi_{i,j})$ in the above equation plays an important role for explicit schemes. These schemes are conditionally stable and then lead to constraints on the time step and space step choices. One of the required stability conditions for the current scheme is taken when the thermal diffusivity and viscosity are related to Prandtl number and limited by:

$$(1 - 6\alpha) \geq 0 \Rightarrow \alpha = \frac{\nu}{Pr} \leq \frac{1}{6}$$

On the other hand, the stability conditions of the scheme relative to the mass diffusivity and viscosity are related to Lewis number and limited by:

$$(1 - 6D) \geq 0 \Rightarrow D = \frac{\nu}{Le} \leq \frac{1}{6}$$

2.4 Boundary Conditions

In the present work, we consider two types of boundary conditions. We apply the Dirichlet boundary conditions (fixed temperature and concentration) at horizontal walls while the vertical walls are adiabatic, defined by:

$$U = V = 0, \quad \theta = \Theta = 1 \quad \text{at} \quad Y = 0, \quad 0 \leq X \leq 1$$
$$U = 0.1, \quad V = 0, \quad \theta = \Theta = 0 \quad \text{at} \quad Y = 1, \quad 0 \leq X \leq 1$$
$$U = V = 0, \quad \frac{\partial \theta}{\partial X} = \frac{\partial \Theta}{\partial X} = 0 \quad \text{at} \quad X = 0, \quad 0 \leq Y \leq 1$$
$$U = V = 0, \quad \frac{\partial \theta}{\partial X} = \frac{\partial \Theta}{\partial X} = 0 \quad \text{at} \quad X = 1, \quad 0 \leq Y \leq 1$$

The no slip boundary condition is imposed at all walls. This type of boundary condition in the LBM is achieved half-way between the boundary nodes [17]. As a result, an extrapolation is needed on boundary nodes to enforce the correct thermal boundary conditions.

The following expressions were used to impose the temperature (the same procedure for the concentration):

$$T_{i,0} = \frac{8}{3}T_{wall} - 2T_{i,1} + \frac{1}{3}T_{i,2} \tag{17}$$

For adiabatic boundary conditions at the walls:

$$T_{0,j} = \frac{21}{23}T_{1,j} + \frac{3}{23}T_{2,j} + \frac{1}{23}T_{3,j} \tag{18}$$

3   Model Validation

In order to check the validity of the proposed model, Table 1, reports a comparison of our numerical results with those of Ben Cheikh et al. [30] in terms of CPU time and number of steps for different grid sizes and for Rayleigh number $Ra = 10^5$. These authors used a finite volume multigrid method and compared two different schemes namely, the accelerated finite volume full multigrid method (AFMG) and the red and black successive overrelaxation scheme (RBSOR) inorder to study convective flow in a square differentially heated cavity, the top and bottom walls are thermally insulated whereas the west and east walls are maintained isothermally at constant and temperatures T_h (hot) and T_c (cold), respectively. It is to be noted that the CPU time performances obtained on a dual-1.73 GHz processor. From this table it is seen that the present model is more efficient in CPU than the two schemes used for comparison and shows also an interesting gain concerning in time step-size. Of course these data should be taken as a semi-quantitative indication, a more detailed comparison requiring the consideration of many parameters, including code optimization and related issues which are beyond the scope of this paper.

Concerning the double-diffusive mixed convection without Soret effect, a grid-dependence study was carried out by setting $Pr = 1$, $Le = 2$, $Re = 500$ and $G_{RT} = G_{RS} = 100$ ($N = 1$). Five uniform node resolutions, 31^2, 51^2, 61^2, 71^2 and 81^2 were examined.

In Fig. (3a–3b) we compare our results for the steady state velocity and temperature profiles along the mid-section of the cavity in the Y-direction, with the results of Al-Amiri et al. [21] obtained using stream function vorticity formulation. As shown from these figures, reasonable results are obtained using node a 81^2 grid resolution.

Thus, the present model is verified and validated with different numerical methods in the literature. The different comparisons indicate the effectiveness and accuracy of the proposed model. Next, the model is applied to the

Table 1. Comparison of CPU times and number of steps with Ref. [30] for different grid sizes, for $Ra = 10^5$.

Grid size	Method	Steps	CPU[s]	CPU[s]/Steps
32 * 32	Present	67500	19	0.00028
	AFMG [30]	5000	26	0.0052
	RBSOR [30]		33	0.0066
64 * 64	Present	113800	139	0.00122
	AFMG [30]	10000	209	0.021
	RBSOR [30]		450	0.045
128 * 128	Present	128400	640	0.00498
	AFMG [30]	20000	2300	0.115
	RBSOR [30]		18057	0.903
256 * 256	Present	460400	09455	0.02053
	AFMG [30]	40000	15595	0.390
	RBSOR [30]		632000	15.80

thermosolutal mixed convection with Soret effect in a cavity with moving top wall. We also endeavour to provide benchmark results to be compared with the existing data.

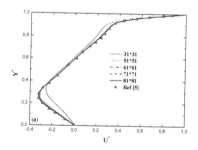 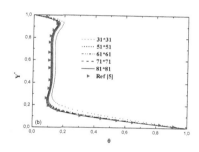

Fig. 3. Grid independence test for $G_{RS} = G_{RT} = 10^2$ ($N = 1$), $Le = 2$ and $Re = 500$, (a) U-Velocity and (b) Temperature.

4 Results of Thermosolutal Mixed Convection with Soret Effect

In this section we study the numerical procedure of MRT-LBM coupled with FDM for thermosolutal mixed convection with Soret effect in a lid-driven square cavity. The fluid velocity is determined by D_2Q_9 MRT-LBM model while the temperature and concentration fields are computed by FDM. The effects of various parameters such as the Soret number Sr, the buoyancy number N on the flow structure and the heat and mass transfer as well as the average Nusselt and Sherwood numbers are calculated. The Schmidt number $Sc = 5$, the Prandtl number $Pr = 0.71$, the Reynolds number $Re = 316$ and the Richardson number is fixed at $Ri = 0.1$.

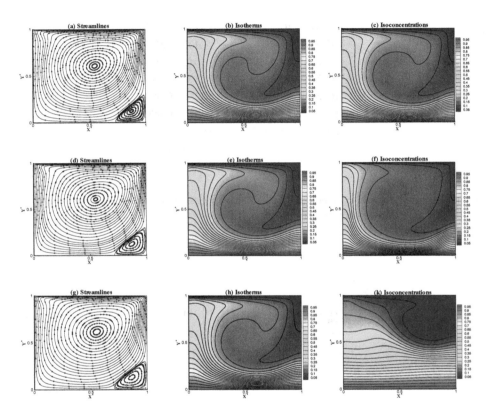

Fig. 4. Computed streamlines, isotherms and isoconcentrations: (a, d and c) for $Sr = 1$, (d, e and f) for $Sr = 0.5$, (g, h and k) for $Sr = 0$.

Effect of Soret Number Sr. In this subsection, numerical results are obtained for the thermal and solutal Grashof numbers fixed at $G_{RT} = G_{RS} = 10^5$ ($N = 1$), while the Soret number is changed in the range $Sr = 0, 0.5$ and 1. The results are reported in terms of streamlines, isotherms and isoconcentrations, respectively.

For $Sr = 0$, the problem reduces to a pure thermosolutal mixed convection. Fig(4a-4c) show the streamlines, isotherms and isoconcentrations predicted by the present hybrid lattice-Boltzmann finite difference simulation. As shown from

Fig. (4a), a primary circulation clockwise vortex occupies the whole volume of the cavity, with a secondary counterclockwise vortex that is formed near the bottom corners, due to the dominant effect of mechanically driven top lid to the entire cavity. The distribution of isotherms and isoconcentrations depicted in Fig. (4b–4c) show that there are steep temperature and concentration gradients in the vertical direction, near the bottom wall. By increasing the Soret number to $Sr = 0.5$ (Fig. (4d–4f)) and $Sr = 1$ (Fig. (4g–4k)), the flow patterns are characterized by a primary recirculating clockwise vortex, that occupies the bulk of the square cavity with a secondary counterclockwise vortex near the bottom corner, are the results of negative pressure gradient generated by the primary circulating fluid. In addition, steep temperature gradients are clustered in the vertical direction of the interior region and near the bottom wall. It is to be noted that, in this case, by increasing the Soret number, no significant effect is observed in terms of both streamlines and isotherms. Due to the significant dependence of the Sherwood number on the Soret number, we note a dramatic variation in the mass contours with thinner mass boundary layer forming along the wall (see Fig. (4f, 4k)). This is due to the increase in diffusivity upon increasing the values of the Soret number.

Table 2. Effect of Soret number Sr on the average Nusselt and Sherwood numbers for $G_{RT} = G_{RS} = 10^5$, $Re = 316$, $Sc = 5$ and $Ri = 0.1$.

Sr	Nu_{av}	Sh_{av}	CPU [s]	Steps
0	3.743	7.049	881.5	384500
0.5	3.809	5.773	815.4	353800
1	3.886	4.450	645	286200

This is also demonstrated from date in Table 2, in which we calculated the average Nusselt and Sherwood numbers for three values of the Soret number. One can note that, by increasing the Soret number from $Sr = 0$ to $Sr = 1$, the heat transfer represented by the Nusselt number is slightly increased. On the other hand, if the Soret parameter is increased, the thickness of the concentration boundary layer increases, thereby decreasing the mass transfer rate represented by the average Sherwood number.

Conclusion

In this paper we employ the lattice Boltzmann method with multiple relaxation time (MRT-LBM), coupled with the finite difference method (FDM) to simulate thermo-hydrodynamics. The fluid flow is computed by D_2Q_9 MRT model while the temperature and concentration fields are solved by FDM. The 2-D square differentially heated cavity and double-diffusive mixed convection without Soret effect was considered as validation test. Satisfactory agreement has been obtained, compared with different numerical methods in the current literature. The results show that the present model can yield benchmark quality results. The employed model has then applied to a thermosolutal mixed convection with Soret effect in a cavity with moving top wall. Results show that the heat transfer represented by the average Nusselt number is slightly enhanced upon increasing the Soret number. Whereas, the mass transfer represented by the average Sherwood number is decreased by further augmenting the Soret number.

As a perspective of this work, this new model will be extended to three-dimensional problems. It could be also tested with a parallel implementation using graphics processing unit (GPU) and especially in the combined mode problems which are computationally very expensive. Work along this direction is underway.

References

1. Succi, S.: The Lattice Boltzmann - For Fluid Dynamics and Beyond, 288p. Oxford University Press, Oxford (2001)
2. Benzi, R., Succi, S., Vergassola, M.: The lattice Boltzmann equation: theory and applications. Phys. Rep. **22**, 145–197 (1992)
3. Wolf-Gladrow, D.A.: Lattice-Gas Cellular Automata and Lattice Boltzmann Models: An Introduction, p. 308p. Springer, Berlin (2000). https://doi.org/10.1007/b72010
4. Filippova, O., Hanel, D.: A novel BGK approach for low Mach number combustion. J. Comput. Phys. **158**, 139–160 (2000)
5. Kuznik, F., Obrecht, C., Rusaouen, G., Roux, J.J.: LBM based flow simulation using GPU computing processor. Comput. Math. Appl. **59**, 2380–2392 (2010)
6. Bhatnagar, P., Gross, E., Krook, M.: A model for collision processes in gases. I. Small amplitude processes in charged and neutral one-component systems. Phys. Rev. **94**, 511–525 (1954)
7. Lallemand, P., Luo, L.-S.: Theory of the lattice Boltzmann method: acoustic and thermal properties in two and three dimensions. Phys. Rev. E **68**(3 Pt 2), 036706 (2003). Epub 2003 Sep 23
8. d'Humières, D., Ginzburg, I., Krafczyk, M., Lallemand, P., Luo, L.: Multiple-relaxation-timel attice Boltzmann models in three dimensions. Philos. Trans. R. Soc. Math. Phys. Eng. Sci. 437–451 (2002)
9. Chen, Y., Ohashi, H., Akiyama, M.A.: Thermal lattice Bhatnagar-Gross-Krook model without nonlinear deviations in macrodynamic equations. Phys. Rev. E **50**, 2776–2783 (1994)
10. Pavlo, P., Vahala, G., Vahala, L., Soe, M.: Linear stability analysis of thermo-lattice Boltzmann models. J. Comput. Phys **139**, 79–91 (1998)
11. McNamara, G.R., Garca, A.L., Alder, B.J.: A hydrodynamically correct thermal lattice Boltzmann model. J. Stat. Phys. **97**, 1111–1121 (1997)
12. Massaioli, F., Benzi, R., Succi, S.: Exponential tails in two-dimensional Rayleigh-Bénard convection. Europhys. Lett. **21**, 305–310 (1993)
13. Mezrhab, A., Moussaoui, M.A., Jami, M., Naji, H., Bouzidi, M.: Double MRT thermal lattice Boltzmann method for simulating convective flows. Phys. Lett. A **374**, 3499–3507 (2010)

14. Kuznik, F., Rusaouen, G.: Numerical prediction of natural convection occurring in building components: a double-population lattice Boltzmann method. Numer. Heat Tr. A-Appl. **52**, 315–335 (2007)
15. Kuznik, F., Vareilles, J., Rusaouen, G., Krauss, G.: A double-population lattice Boltzmann method with non-uniform mesh for the simulation of natural convection in a square cavity. Int. J. Heat Fluid Flow **28**, 862–870 (2007)
16. Lallemand, P., Luo, L.-S.: Hybrid finite-difference thermal lattice Boltzmann equation. Int. J. Mod. Phys. B. **17**, 41–47 (2003)
17. Béghein, C., Haghighat, F., Allard, F.: Numerical study of double diffusive natural convection in a square cavity. Int. J. Heat Mass Transf. **35**, 833–846 (1992)
18. Morega, A., Nishimura, T.: Double diffusive convection by Chebyshev collocation method. Technol. Rep. Univ. **5**, 259–276 (1996)
19. Makayssi, T., Lamsaadi, M., Naimi, M., Hasnaoui, M., Raji, A., Bahlaoui, A.: Natural double diffusive convection in a shallow horizontal rectangular cavity uniformly heated and salted from the side and filled with non-Newtonian power-law fluids: the cooperating case. Energy Convers. Manag. **49**, 2016–2025 (2008)
20. Alleborn, N., Raszillier, H., Durst, F.: Lid-driven cavity with heat and mass transport. In. J. Heat Mass Transf. **42**, 833–853 (1999)
21. All-Amiri, A.M., Khanafer, K.M., Pop, I.: Numerical simulation of combined thermal and mass transport in a square lid-driven cavity. In. J. Ther. Sci. **46**, 622–671 (2007)
22. Teamah, M.A., El-Maghlany, W.M.: Numerical simulation of double-diffusive mixed convective flow in rectangular enclosure with insulated moving lid. Int. J. Ther. Sci. **49**, 1625–1638 (2010)
23. Mansour, A., Amahmid, A., Hasnaoui, M., Bourich, M.: Soret effect on double diffusive multiple solutions in a square porous cavity subject to cross gradients of temperature and concentration. Int. Comm. Heat Mass Transfer **31**, 431–440 (2004)
24. Bennacer, R., Mahidjiba, A., Vasseur, P., Beji, H., Duval, R.: The Soret effect on convection in a horizontal porous domain under cross-temperature and concentration gradients. Int. J. Numer. Methods Heat. Fluid. Flow **13**, 199–215 (2003)
25. Rebai, L.K., Mojtabi, A., Safi, M.J., Mohamad, A.A.: Numerical study of thermosolutal convection with soret effect in a square cavity. Int. J. Numer. Methods Heat. Fluid. Flow **18**, 561–574 (2008)
26. Bahloul, A., Boutana, N., Vasseur, P.: Double-diffusive and Soret-induced convection in a shallow horizontal porous layer. J. Fluid Mech. **491**, 325–352 (2003)
27. Khadiri, A., Amahmid, A., Hasnaoui, M., Rtibi, A.: Soret effect on double-diffusive convection in a square porous cavity heated and salted from below. Numer. Heat Transf. A **57**, 848–868 (2010)
28. Joly, F., Vasseur, P., Labrosse, G.: Soret-driven thermosolutal convection in a vertical enclosure. Int. Comm. Heat Mass Transfer **27**, 755–764 (2000)
29. Tsai, R., Huang, J.S.: Numerical study of Soret and dufour effects on heat and mass transfer from natural convection flow over a vertical porous medium with variable wall heat fluxes. Comput. Mater. Sci. **47**, 23–30 (2009)
30. Nader Ben Cheikh: Rrahim Ben Beya, Taieb Lili, Benchmark solution for time-dependent natural convection flows with an accelerated full-multigrid method. Num. Heat. transfer. prat B **52**, 131–151 (2007)

Logical Gates on Gliders in Restricted Space Domain Cellular Automata

Alexander Makarenko[1(✉)] and Jordan Brajon[2]

[1] Institute of Applied System Analysis at National Technical
Universities of Ukraine, Igor Sykorski Kiev Polytechnic Institute, Kyiv, Ukraine
makalex51@gmail.com
[2] HD Rain, Paris, France
jordan.brajon605@gmail.com

Abstract. The new approach for logical operations implementations in cellular automata is proposed. For the implementation of logical gates the propagation of the gliders of cellular automata in bounded domain is considered. Special laws for collisions of gliders with domain walls and internal obstacles in domain are displayed. Logical gate XOR construction, examples of computations and some discussion are described. Comparison with usual approach is given.

Keywords: Cellular automata · Gliders · Restricted domains · Logical gates

1 Introduction

Cellular automata recently have many fields for theoretical investigations and applications [1–4]. One of the most interesting topics is related to the theoretical problems of computation and automata theory [2, 5]. The part of the problem is computation by collisions [6]. Implementation of logical gates in such case is one of the key tools. There are investigations on implementation logical gates on gliders [6, 7]. But such implementations have some drawback.

Consider a standard case of the implementation of logical operations with two inputs and one output. This requires two generators of the sequence of gliders. These sequences correspond to inputs of a logical operation. At the collision of the glider sequences, a new glider sequence is formed. The new glider sequence is interpreted as the values 0 or 1 in the logical operation [2, 5, 7].

It was theoretically shown that with the such constructions it is possible to implement the algorithms allowed by the Turing machine [2, 5, 7]. However, in the practical implementation of this approach, certain difficulties arise. First, initially the entire structure is built on the basis of an infinite space of cells. Second, the location of the glider sequence generators must be carefully selected. Another disadvantage is that when emulating long algorithms, all cell values are usually calculated.

So it is useful to search the other ways of logical gates emulations. In given paper we propose the new way for design of implementation of logical gates on the base of cellular automata. Our previous investigations [8] followed us to the idea of using the cellular automata in restricted domains for implementation the logical gates.

T. M. Gwizdałła et al. (Eds.): ACRI 2020, LNCS 12599, pp. 222–225, 2021.
https://doi.org/10.1007/978-3-030-69480-7_22

In our the problem arose of choosing rules for cellular automata near borders and internal obstacles. Among all the variety, the rules were chosen to the analogy of the reflection of a light beam from a reflecting surface.

In the second section we remember the elementary knowledge on gliders. The third section devoted the description of some ideas on using gliders in restricted domain. Construction of logical gate XOR, example of computations and some discussion are proposed in Sect. 4.

2 Basics in the Game of Life

Many are working on the game of life [1–9]. Some of them are studying variants: the addition of a probability [10], the modification of the rule of local evolution [11], applying the local transition rule asynchronously [12], non-homogeneous cellular automata rule [13]. We will also be interested in a variant of the game of life, as we will see later.

2.1 Special Pattern: Gliders

The reader will get more information on the patterns and on the game of life in general in [1–5, 7] and in [9]. In the papers [7, 9] we are interested on the one very important patterns in cellular automata - namely glider. It is important that in classics the geometry of cells set usually is infinite plane.

For our goals the most interesting is the interaction of two gliders. We call it a collision. After a collision, two gliders can disappear entirely or reveal certain configurations such as still life or oscillators or even give birth to a new glider. Like in [8], we add a third frozen state that will represent the irregularities (obstacles) of our initially two-dimensional cell space.

3 Motivation and Approach

In this part we will give some examples of the rules which we have chosen.

3.1 Rules Obtained

We found a local rule involving only the evolution of 24 configurations allowing a glider moving down and right to bounce from above on a horizontal wall. We obtain a rule of evolution of 96 of 12 610 possible configurations.

The purpose of this part is to present the logical gates that have been implemented from game of life through considering restricted domain.

3.2   XOR Gate

The XOR gate is a logical gate with two inputs labeled as A et B. The output value is 1 if and there one and only one input value equal to 1. The associated Boolean operation is ⊕: A ⊕ B. Here we consider XOR operation.

3.3   Implementation of Logic Gates in a Restricted Domain

Generally the logic gates set up here geometrically have two ducts at the top (repre- senting the two inputs). A glider in the conduit means that the entry is at 1 otherwise it is at 0 (see example showed on the Fig. 1). And a conduit down represents the exit. The external boundaries of the domain for cellular automata are rectangular. The bright lines correspond to internal walls. The width of the walls is equal to one cell. Inputs A and B at top of the picture are open for introducing single glider. Logical gates have been realized as computer programs in MATLAB. Below we give the results of computer simulation.

3.4   XOR Gate Implementation

The XOR gate has two inputs A and B (duct top left and top right on Fig. 1). At the initial moment and when A = 0 and B = 0 the inputs are empty. The evolution of XOR logic gate is given on Fig. 1 (when A = 1 et B = 0).

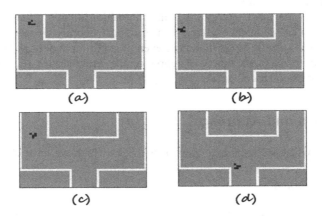

Fig. 1. XOR logic gate when $A = 1$ et $B = 0$: (a) $t = 0$, (b) $t = 15$, (c) $t = 30$, (d) $t = 100$

3.5   Comparison of Classical and New Implementation of Gate

Proposed in this paper approach for logical operations implementation is more intu- itive, more visual and simpler. The classical case requires the computations in domain with at least more than 100 × 100 cells. In our approach less than 25 × 25 cells are necessary for XOR implementation.

4   Conclusion

The proposed results provide a significant improvement in what has been done so far. Indeed, the consideration of a variant of the game of life in the restricted space domains allowed us to introduce new local rules near obstacles and walls. It is then possible to implement logic gates much more intuitive and much easier to use than the logic gates that have been created so far.

The main advantages of proposed approach are the next. First is the economy of computational resources. The second advantage is standard construction for elementary realizations of logical gates. This allows in principle realize each of the algorithms by using such standard elements. This study therefore provides an innovative result as it also opens up new and interesting perspectives.

References

1. Illiachinski, A.: Cellular Automata. A Discrete Universe. World Scientific Publishing, Singapore (2001)
2. Wolfram, S.: New Kind of Science. Wolfram Media Inc., Champaign (2002)
3. Chopard, B., Droz, M.: Cellular Automata Modeling of Physical Systems. Cambridge University Press, Cambridge (1998)
4. Adamatszky, A. (ed.): Collision-Based Computing. Springer, London (2002). https://doi.org/10.1007/978-1-4471-0129-1
5. Cook, M.: Universality in elementary cellular automata. Complex Syst. **15**, 1–40 (2004)
6. Adamatzky, A., Durand-Lose, J.: Collision-based computing. In: Rozenberg, G., Bäck, T., Kok, J.N. (eds.) Handbook of Natural Computing, pp. 1949–1978. Springer, Heidelberg (2012). https://doi.org/10.1007/978-3-540-92910-9_58
7. Rennard, J.P.: Implementation of logical functions in the game of life. In: Adamatzky, A. (ed.) Collision-Based Computing, pp. 491–512. Springer, London (2002). https://doi.org/10.1007/978-1-4471-0129-1_17
8. Faccetti, L., Makarenko, A.: 'Game of Life' with modifications: non-regular space, different rules and many hierarchical levels. Int. J. Inf. Content Process. **4**(1), 21–50 (2017)
9. Delahaye, J.P.: L'sutomata des chifferes. Pour la Science **394**, 80–85 (2010)
10. Goldengorin, B., Makarenko, A., Smelyanec, N.: Some applications and prospects of cellular automata in traffic problems. In: El Yacoubi, S., Chopard, B., Bandini, S. (eds.) ACRI 2006. LNCS, vol. 4173, pp. 532–537. Springer, Heidelberg (2006). https://doi.org/10.1007/11861201_61
11. Sipper, M.: Co-evolving non-uniform cellular automata to perform computation. Physica D **92**, 193–208 (1990)
12. Fates, N.: A Guided Tour of Asynchronous Cellular Automata, pp. 1–33. arXiv:1406.0792v2 (2014)
13. Dennunzio, A., Formenti, E., Provillard, J.: Non-uniform cellular automata: classes, dynamics and decidability. Inf. Comput. **215**, 32–34 (2012)

Modeling Carbon Dioxide Dispersion Indoors

A Cell-DEVS Experiment

Hoda Khalil$^{(\boxtimes)}$ (ID) and Gabriel Wainer (ID)

Carleton University, Ottawa, ON K1S 5B6, Canada
hodakhalil@cmail.carleton.ca, gwainer@sce.carleton.ca

Abstract. Carbon dioxide concentration in closed spaces is an indication of air quality and a means of measuring the number of occupants for controlling energy consumption. However, the dispersion of the gas and the accuracy of the concentration measurements as logged by carbon dioxide sensors are highly sensitive to the configuration of the closed space. Conducting case by case studies for each closed space is neither practical nor cost-effective. We hereby propose a formal model using cellular discrete-event system specifications for studying carbon dioxide dispersion indoors and for analyzing the effect of different configurations on the sensors measurements of the concentration. We present a case study of the model and compare the simulation results to ground truth data collected from two physical systems of two computer laboratories. The results demonstrate that the proposed model can be used to study carbon dioxide dispersion and the change of sensors' readings in closed spaces based on the configurations of the space.

Keywords: Modeling · Simulation · Cell-DEVS · Sustainability

1 Introduction

One reason for the substantial research effort in measuring CO_2 levels indoors is to maintain an acceptable level of air quality which in turn impacts the wellbeing of the space occupants [1]. Another reason is detecting the number of occupants to automatically control the environment (e.g. adjust heating and air conditioning) and consequently reduce energy consumption without compromising the occupants' comfort [2]. Although CO_2 sensors have advantages over many other kinds of ambient sensors (e.g. they are affordable and nonintrusive), CO_2 sensors are overly sensitive to configuration. The accuracy of CO_2 sensors differs case by case depending on several factors such as heating, ventilation, and air conditioning (HVAC) settings. Although researchers have conducted experiments on CO_2 sensors' accuracy for indoor occupants' detection [3], more research is required to measure the effect of the different configurations of closed spaces on the measurements recorded by CO_2 sensors. Observing the effects of such parameters on the indoor CO_2 level and the readings of CO_2 sensors is the motivation for this research. Real-life experiments for measuring the effect of room configuration are impractical, time-consuming, and sometimes impossible. This motivates us to use modeling and simulation (M&S) to perform the required

© Springer Nature Switzerland AG 2021
T. M. Gwizdałła et al. (Eds.): ACRI 2020, LNCS 12599, pp. 226–236, 2021.
https://doi.org/10.1007/978-3-030-69480-7_23

experiments for the objective of developing a robust general model that can be adapted to any closed space. This model can be reused, while adjusting the different required parameters (e.g. dimensions and windows locations), to measure their effect on the logged CO_2 concentration.

We use cellular discrete-event system specifications (Cell-DEVS) to model CO_2 behavior in closed spaces. Cell-DEVS is a "modification" of cellular automata (CA) modeling that has several advantages over other modeling techniques (Sect. 2.2). This makes it suitable for modeling complex systems. In previous work [4], we presented a simple 2-D toy model to demo the effect of placing the sensor in two different positions on the recorded CO_2 concentration. In this paper, we develop an advanced 3-D model with possible variable parameters (e.g. windows, furniture layout, and different arrival and departure times of occupants) and multiple occupants. We implement a case study model of a computer laboratory that physically exists at Carleton University and we use it to calibrate the model. We base the calibration on the ground truth data collected from the physical laboratory. Then, we validate the model by comparing the simulation results to a set of ground truth data collected from the sensors installed in another laboratory on a different floor in the same building.

We first explain essential background information to position the presented work (Sect. 2) and present examples from the literature of modeling CO_2 behavior indoors (Sect. 3). Then, we introduce the experimental setup. Previously, we used the CD++ simulator, while in this work we use an improved simulator (Cadmium) (Sect. 4). Then we present two versions of the model that are replicas of real-life laboratories: one for calibration and the other for validation (Sect. 5). We compare the simulation results to the ground truth data and discuss them (Sect. 6). Finally, we present the conclusion and propose future possible improvements (Sect. 7).

2 Background

In this section, we provide background information that is necessary for understanding the research problem and the experimentation process. In Sect. 2.1, we explore sensor-based occupant detection, while in Sect. 2.2 we offer basic information about the M&S methodology we use, and we emphasize its advantages.

2.1 Sensor-Based Occupants Detection

Automatically sensing occupants and adjusting the building systems based on the number of occupants have become paramount for saving energy. The use of sensors to detect occupants in closed spaces has been addressed in many theoretical and experimental work. Researchers have proposed ways of detecting the presence of occupants including cameras, computer applications, and sensor fusion. They have used different kinds of sensors for occupancy detection such as passive infrared (PIR) sensors, electromagnetic sensors (EM), image sensors, and CO_2 sensors. Each type of sensor has its advantages and disadvantages. We focus on CO_2 sensors for their proven advantages and since there is potential for improving their performance [3–5]. CO_2 sensors are sensitive to factors such as the level of HVAC, dimensions (width, length, and height), locations of the ventilation port, the presence of open windows and doors, and the location where the sensor is installed. Testing each physical closed room to know how its configuration parameters affect the readings of an installed sensor is an impractical time-consuming approach. Hence, we propose M&S as a solution.

2.2 Methodology

With M&S, we can achieve the goal of understanding the dynamics of CO_2 dispersion less expensively and more practically. We model CO_2 dispersion using Cell-DEVS which solves some of the shortcomings of CA by combining it with discrete-event system specifications (DEVS) [6]. Cell-DEVS defines a grid of cells where each cell is specified as a DEVS model. The next state of each cell is defined based on the current state of that cell and the states of the neighboring cells. Cell-DEVS has been used extensively to model social and environmental complex systems [7–9]. One advantage of Cell-DEVS, and its supporting tools, is the improved execution time. This is attributed to the fact that Cell-DEVS provides asynchronous execution to model the asynchronous nature of complex systems [6]. Also, Cell-DEVS formalism offers ways to define complex timing conditions. Besides, there is an extensive set of tools available for translating the formalism into an executable model. This facilitates validating the conceptual model against the physical system and allows for verifying the simulation.

A Cell-DEVS model can be formalized as follows: GCC = $(X_{list}, Y_{list}, I, X, Y, \eta, N, \{t_1, \ldots, t_n\}, C, B, Z)$, where X_{list} is the list of external input couplings (i.e. input values to the cell that couples it with its defined neighbors), Y_{list} is the list of external output couplings, I is the set of states, X is the external input events set, Y is the external output events set, η is the neighborhood size, N is the neighborhood set, $\{t_1, \ldots, t_n\}$ is the number of cells in each dimension, C is the cell space, B defines the border cells, and Z is a translation function that defines internal and external coupling.

3   Literature Review

In this section, we review some research efforts for modeling CO_2 dispersion in closed spaces while considering occupants. In their work, researchers have raised the issue of the importance of considering the location of CO_2 sensors and other configuration parameters in the modeled space, but no clear solution has been provided. Instead, a case by case solution for modeling is suggested.

Batog and Badura [10] present a model of a bedroom that contains big solid surfaces (e.g. bed and wardrobe) and one occupant. The authors perform two simulations: one with the possibility of CO_2 escaping through gaps around the windows and doors, and the other without such gaps. The occupant is assumed to spend eight hours sleeping in the room. The result of the simulations proves that the strategic placement of CO_2 sensors is important for accurate measurement. In particular, the authors do not recommend placing CO_2 sensors in corners nor near windows or doors. They also recommend that the height at which the sensor is installed should be above the level of the bed for the specific environment they model [10].

Pantazaras et al. [11] propose a method for tailoring models for specific spaces. The model takes into consideration the CO_2 concentration, ventilation, and multiple occupants. This is used to predict CO_2 concentration levels in the room. The model is only effective for short term predictions of CO_2 concentration levels [11].

A study that is not focused on CO_2 modeling but rather on the dispersion of hazardous gasses in closed spaces is presented by Makmul [12]. The study uses CA to model the influence of the spread of gas on the behavior of pedestrians. Makmul's objective is to aid designers in building safe public spaces that are practical during evacuations. The authors offer an experiment on a specific model of a closed space with two exits. The used model is a 2-D model that does not consider indoor space height [12].

To the contrary to previous research that deals with the problem in a case by case manner and considers a small subset of the configuration parameters, we offer a generic model of CO_2 dispersion using well-established formalism that is supported by tools. It is worth noting that the objective of this research is not to estimate the number of occupants in the room based on CO_2 levels, but rather to provide a mechanism for studying the effect of the space settings on the measurement and the dispersion behavior of CO_2. The presented solution reaches this objective while considering different configurations in the space where the CO_2 sensor is to be installed; a problem that was raised by researchers in the field of occupants' detection [3, 5, 11].

4 Experimental Setup

In previous work [8], we used CD++ (a toolkit that implements DEVS and Cell-DEVS theoretical concepts) to implement and simulate the model [13]. For the model presented in this paper, we use a newer Cell-DEVS simulator. Cell-DEVS Cadmium is a cross-platform header-only C++ library that can be used to implement and simulate Cell-DEVS models. A model simulated using Cadmium is defined in a header (.hpp) file and coded in C++. The simulator allows defining a general category of models using the programming language (C++) while reading specific configuration details for each model from a JavaScript Object Notation (JSON) file that is parsed by the simulator. On the one hand, we have implemented one general model in C++ for CO_2 dispersion and the breathing of occupants. On the other hand, the JSON file describes different initial configurations per cell. Each cell represents a specific segment of the physical space. The JSON file also specifies the dimensions of the room, the shape of the cells' neighborhood, and other configuration parameters. For visualizing the simulation results, we use Advanced Real-time Simulation Laboratory (ARSLab) DEVSWeb Viewer [14].

The general model we are presenting considers the dimensions of the closed space, ambient CO_2 concentration, size and location of CO_2 sinks (i.e. windows, doors, and ventilation ports), possible locations where occupants may exist, the breathing rate of occupants based on their activity level, concentration increase due to breathing occupants, and dimensions of the room. The model assumes ambient outdoor CO_2 concentration of 400 particles per minute (ppm) based on the American Society of Heating, Refrigerating and Air-Conditioning Engineers (ASHRAE) standards [15]. However, this value can be adjusted as a parameter specified for each JSON scenario. Human breathing is calculated based on the fact that humans breathe every five seconds, and the produced CO_2 in every breath (exhaling and inhaling) is a parameter that depends on the activity level [16]. The general model has seven types of cells: (1) walls and obstacles that do not allow CO_2 diffusion, (2) air cells whose CO_2 concentration is dependent on the concentration values in their neighborhoods, (3) CO_2 sources with a periodic increase in the CO_2 level added at an interval to mimic breathing in addition to the CO_2 diffused from the neighborhood, (4) open doors that diffuse CO_2 to the rest of the building with a fixed indoor background CO_2 level, (5) open windows that are also CO_2 sinks with a fixed outdoor background CO_2, (6) vents that diffuse gas through HVAC system with a reduced constant CO_2 level, and (7) workstation cells that act as normal air cells when not occupied and as CO_2 sources when occupied. The CO_2 diffusion is calculated by averaging the concentration level in the Moore neighborhood of each cell. This means that to get the concentration of each cell, the concentrations in either 27 or 9 cells are averaged in the cases of 3-D and 2-D models, respectively.

5 Case Study

In this section, we present a case study for two computer laboratories at Carleton University. We use the first physical system to calibrate the parameters of the model and the second to validate the calibrated model.

5.1 Calibration Model

The general model has flexible parameters, some of which are not available in the set of ground truth data that we have. For example, although the exact number of attendees in the lab is available, the arrival time of each person at the computer workstation they have used is not available. Also, the exact CO_2 concentration in the vents is not available. Thus, we had the space to change this data to calibrate the model to get simulation results that are as close as possible to the ground truth data. The parameters that we adjusted are the arrival and departure times of the occupants, the workstations that the occupants chose to use, ambient CO_2 concentration, and CO_2 concentration in the air pumped to the room through the ventilation ports. The exact steps to run the model, the code, and the parameter settings are available through the ARSLab repository [17].

The first computer laboratory we are modeling in this paper represents a $(9.5 \times 14.24 \times 3.25)$ m^3 closed space, with 48 workstations where students can sit to work on their computer assignments. The floor plan of the laboratory and the furniture layout are shown in Fig. 1. The ground truth data is based on the number of attendees for a 110-min tutorial that has taken place in the Winter term of the year 2019. Thirty nine students have attended the tutorial in addition to the teaching assistant (TA) who has been present throughout the tutorial. Students arrive and leave at different times along the period of the lab tutorial. The logged data (Fig. 3) for this period is based on one CO_2 sensor installed close to the door at 1.5 m height and logs the concentration level every 30 min. As the occupants arrive at the room, the readings of CO_2 concentration start to increase reaching the peak after the middle of the lab tutorial period when all students are present. The CO_2 starts to decrease again until all students leave the room (Fig. 3).

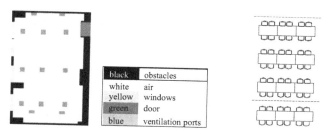

Fig. 1. Floor plan and furniture layout of the physical system of the calibration model (Color figure online)

The physical $9.5 \times 14.24 \times 3.25$ m^3 system is mapped to a $23 \times 35 \times 8$ cell^3 model. Table 1 shows how the physical system maps to the 3D model. Each cross-section of the room of 40 cm height maps to a 23×35 cell grid.

Table 1. Mapping the physical system to the 3D model

Cross-section (cm) (physical system)	0–40	40–80	80–120	120–160	120–200	200–240	240–280	280–320
Grid number (model)	0	1	2	3	4	5	6	7
Significance for simulation	Floor	Air	Air	Breathing	CO_2 sensors	Air	Air	Ceiling-vents

The 3-D Cell-DEVS model is formally specified as follows: CO_2 = <X_{list}, Y_{list}, Z_{list}, I, X, Y, Z, η, N, {t_1, t_2, t_3}, C, B, Z>, where X_{list} = Y_{list} = Z_{list} = {Ø}; I = type: {0, 1, 2, 3, 4, 5, 6} and conc: {float}; X = Y = Z = Ø; η = 27; N = {(0, 0, 0), (−1, 0, 0), (1, 0, 0), (0, 1, 0), (0, −1, 0), (−1, 1, 0), (1, 1, 0), (−1, −1, 0), (1, −1, 0), (0, 0, 1), (−1, 0, 1), (1, 0, 1), (0, 1, 1), (0, −1, 1), (−1, 1, 1), (1, 1, 1), (−1, −1, 1), (1, −1, 1), (0, 0, −1), (−1, 0, −1), (1, 0, −1), (0, 1, −1), (0, −1, −1), (−1, 1, −1), (1, 1, −1), (−1, −1, −1), (1, −1, −1)}; t_1 = 23; t_2 = 35; t_3 = 8; C = {C_{ijk} | i ∈ [0, 23[∧ j ∈ [0, 35[∧ k ∈ [0, 8[}; and B = {Ø} (unwrapped cell space).

For this case study, we specify a $40 \times 40 \times 40$ cm^3 cell size. Therefore, the physical system is translated to an approximated ($23 \times 35 \times 8$) cell model. To replicate the physical system, the CO_2 production for each occupant is calculated as follows based on two facts: (1) an average-sized person doing normal low-activity office work produces 0.31 L/minute/person of CO_2 [11] and (2) breathing occurs every 5 s on average. Therefore, an average person produces 0.02583 L of CO_2 per breath. Hence, every occupant breath increases the concentration of CO_2 in each occupied cell by:

$$\frac{0.02583}{cell\ volume} = \frac{0.02583 \times 1000}{40 \times 40 \times 40} \approx 0.000403 \tag{1}$$

It is worth noting that Eq. (1) gets calculated automatically based on the model parameters (i.e. cell volume and produced CO2 per breath specified in the input JSON settings file). We are including here how this calculation is done for the parameters we specify for the presented case study.

The simulation runs of 7,200 timesteps which is equivalent to two hours; each time step is one second. The session lasted for 110 min and we added five minutes before and after the session to get a better picture of the CO_2 level changes due to the arrival and departure of occupants. Figure 2(a) shows the simulation results at the beginning of the simulation where only one occupant is present (the TA), and during other timestamps as occupants start to arrive (Fig. 2(b) and Fig. 2(c)). CO_2 concentration is to the left of each figure (a, b, and c) and the occupants' locations are at the right. Occupants are represented as red squares and empty workstations are in grey. The two grids shown in the figure are layer 4 (left), which is the cross-section of the room representing the height at which the CO_2 sensor is installed (120–160 cm), and layer 3 (right) representing the height at which the seated occupants are breathing (80–120 cm). The legend below Fig. 2 maps the CO_2 concentration to the color used to visualize the simulation. Comparing the simulation results to the floor map of Fig. 1 shows how the area below the vents has less CO_2 concentration than other areas as the vents try to offset the CO_2 increase that occurs where the occupants are concentrated.

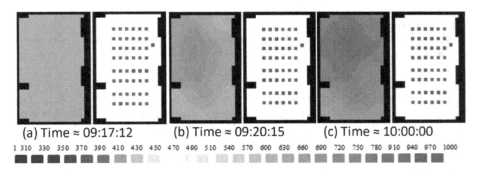

(a) Time ≈ 09:17:12   (b) Time ≈ 09:20:15   (c) Time ≈ 10:00:00

1 310 330 350 370 390 410 430 450 470 490 510 540 570 600 630 660 690 720 750 780 910 940 970 1000

Fig. 2. Simulation results during different timestamps (hh:mm:ss) (Color figure online)

Figure 4 is a plot of the simulation results. The figure shows that the simulation results after calibrating the model are similar to the ground truth data (Fig. 3).

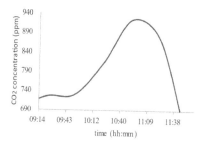

Fig. 3. Ground truth data plot

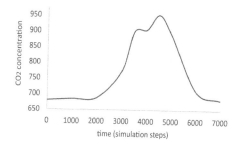

Fig. 4. Simulation results plot

Note that while the simulation results are logged every second, the ground truth data is logged every 15–30 min. This justifies a possible minor difference between the ground truth data and the simulation results. The plots of the simulation results are generated using Microsoft Excel© for ease of comparison. However, plots of the simulation results can be regenerated using the ARSLab charting tool [18].

5.2 Validation Model

In this section, we validate the rules used in the presented CO_2 model, using another room in the same building but on a different floor and with a different configuration. This physical system used for validation is another laboratory setting during a different time of the day, with only eleven occupants, a larger space, and no windows. The dimensions of this room are $15.8 \times 9 \times 3.25$ m^3. Figure 5 shows the floor plan of the room and the furniture layout. In the physical system, there is another lab session following this one and hence more students enter the room at the end of the laboratory, and we have tried to mimic this in the model. The CO_2 sensor is installed close to the door and logs the concentration level every 15 min. Figure 6 is a chart of the ground truth data of the CO_2 concentration during the studied period.

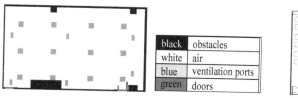

black	obstacles
white	air
blue	ventilation ports
green	doors

Fig. 5. Floor plan and furniture layout of the validation model

The formal model specification is the same as the one explained in Sect. 5.1 except for the following: $t_1 = 23$; $t_2 = 40$; and C = {C_{ijk} | i ∈ [0, 23[∧ j ∈ [0, 40[∧ k ∈ [0, 8[}. We have used the same ambient CO_2 concentration and ventilation concentration that have resulted from calibrating the model. We have executed the model for a simulation period equivalent to 7200 s (two hours) and Fig. 7 shows data collected from the simulation results. Comparing that simulation results (Fig. 7) to the data logged by the real sensors in the physical system (Fig. 6) demonstrates the resemblance between the model's data and the system's data. Simulation videos of the validation model and the original CO_2 model are available online through the ARSLab YouTube channel [19].

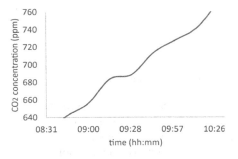
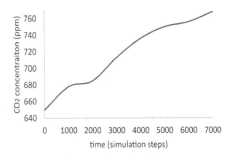

Fig. 6. Validation model ground truth data   **Fig. 7.** Validation model simulation results

6 Discussion

The model proposed is evinced successful at replicating the physical indoor space. However, as in any other experimental study, there are some threats to validity that are worthy of discussion. A minor validity threat is the existence of some approximations when converting the physical system into a model. Nevertheless, this does not affect the usability of the model as the model user is aware of it and can handle the slight approximations if needed. A second validity threat is that the current model assumes that the air in the room is at a steady-state and the CO_2 is diffused evenly in all directions. This is not usually the case due to the different types of HVAC and occupants breathing in different directions. Incorporating airflow in the room is a future feature that we are planning to add to the model. However, the model at the current state has successfully mimicked the physical system.

7 Conclusion

Motivated by the need for studying the effects of room configuration on recorded CO_2 concentration and the way CO_2 diffuses in closed areas, we present a generic model for indoor CO_2 diffusion. We have developed a generic Cell-DEVS model that accepts different room configurations as input parameters. We have calibrated the model using the settings of a real physical system of a computer laboratory at Carleton University. Then, we validated the model using another closed space in the same building during a different time and with different configurations. The simulation results resemble the physical systems as presented by the plot of CO_2 concentration in both the simulation and the physical system. The results suggest that the model is suitable for studying the spread of CO_2 indoors. The model can help to study the effect of placing sensors in different locations, the effect of changing the ventilation, increasing the number of occupants, changing the furniture layout, and many other configuration parameters. Future improvements to the model will target the flow field of the air in the room and conducting statistical analysis of the results of different case studies.

Acknowledgments. The authors would like to thank Thomas Roller for developing the supporting tools that convert floorplans to 3-D scenarios and chart the simulation results [18].

References

1. Al horr, Y., Arif, M., Katafygiotoua, M., Mazroei, A., Kaushik, A., Elsarrag, E.: Impact of indoor environmental quality on occupant well-being and comfort: a review of the literature. Int. J. Sustain. Built Environ. **5**(1), 1–11 (2016). https://doi.org/10.1016/j.ijsbe.2016.03.006
2. Jiang, A., Masooda, M.K., Soh, Y.C., Li, H.: Indoor occupancy estimation from carbon dioxide concentration. Energy Build. **131**, 132–141 (2016). https://doi.org/10.1016/j.enbuild.2016.09.002
3. Labeodan, T., Zeiler, W., Boxem, G., Zhao, Y.: Occupancy measurement in commercial office buildings for demand-driven control applications—a survey and detection system evaluation. Energy Build. **93**, 303–314 (2015). https://doi.org/10.1016/j.enbuild.2015.02.028
4. Khalil, H., Wainer, G., Dunnigan, Z.: Cell-DEVS models for CO_2 sensors locations in closed spaces. In: Bae K.-H., et al. (eds.) 2020 Winter Simulation Conference (WSC), Virtual (2020, in press)
5. Arief-Ang, I.B., Hamilton, M., Salim, F.D.: RUP: large room utilization prediction with carbon dioxide sensor. Pervasive Mob. Comput. **46**, 49–72 (2018). https://doi.org/10.1016/j.pmcj.2018.03.001
6. Wainer, G.: Discrete-event Modeling and Simulation: A Practitioner's Approach, 1st edn. CRC Press, Boca Raton (2009)
7. Wainer, G., Giambiasi, N.: Cell-DEVS/GDEVS for complex continuous systems. Simulation **81**(2), 137–151 (2005). https://doi.org/10.1177/0037549705052233
8. Khalil, H., Wainer, G.: Cell-DEVS for social phenomena modeling. IEEE Trans. Comput. Soc. Syst. **7**(3), 725–740 (2020). https://doi.org/10.1109/TCSS.2020.2982885
9. López, A., Wainer, G.: Improved cell-DEVS model definition in CD++. In: Sloot, P.M.A., Chopard, B., Hoekstra, A.G. (eds.) ACRI 2004. LNCS, vol. 3305, pp. 803–812. Springer, Heidelberg (2004). https://doi.org/10.1007/978-3-540-30479-1_83
10. Batog, P., Badura, M.: Dynamic of changes in carbon dioxide concentration in bedrooms. Proc. Eng. **57**, 175–182 (2013). https://doi.org/10.1016/j.proeng.2013.04.025
11. Pantazaras, A., Lee, S.E., Santamouris, M., Yang, J.: Predicting the CO_2 levels in buildings using deterministic and identified models. Energy Build. **127**, 774–785 (2016). https://doi.org/10.1016/j.enbuild.2016.06.029
12. Makmul, J.: Microscopic and macroscopic for pedestrian crowds. Dissertation, Mannheim University (2016)
13. Wainer, G.: CD++: a toolkit to develop DEVS models. Softw.: Pract. Exp. **32**(13), 1261–1306 (2002). https://doi.org/10.1002/spe.482
14. St-Aubin, B., Wainer, G.: ARSLab DEVS web viewer. https://staubibr.github.io/arslab-prd/app-simple/index.html. Accessed 17 Sept 2020
15. ASHRAE Standard 62.1 Ventilation for Acceptable Indoor Air Quality (2013). http://www.myiaire.com/product-docs/ultraDRY/ASHRAE62.1.pdf. Accessed 15 Aug 2020

16. Zuraimi, M.S., Pantazaras, A., Chaturvedi, K.A., Yang, J.J., Tham, K.W., Lee, S.E.: Predicting occupancy counts using physical and statistical CO_2-based modeling methodologies. Build. Environ. **123**, 517–528 (2017). https://doi.org/10.1016/j.buildenv.2017.07.027
17. CO_2 Spread Indoors. https://github.com/SimulationEverywhere-Models/Cell-DEVS-CO2_spread_indoor/blob/master/User%20Manual.txt. Accessed 18 Sept 2020
18. ARSLab CO_2 Charting. https://github.com/SimulationEverywhere-Models/Cell-DEVS-CO2_spread_indoor/tree/master/scripts/Cell-DEVS_co2-charting. Accessed 20 Sept 2020
19. ARSLab YouTube. https://www.youtube.com/watch?v=vD7fB2A5hNY. Accessed 20 Sept 2020

Disease Spreading Dynamics

Cell-DEVS Models for the Spread of COVID-19

Román Cárdenas[1,2(✉)] [iD], Kevin Henares[3] [iD],
Cristina Ruiz-Martín[2] [iD], and Gabriel Wainer[2] [iD]

[1] Universidad Politécnica de Madrid, Avenida Ramiro de Maeztu 7,
28040 Madrid, Spain
r.cardenas@upm.es
[2] Carleton University, 1125 Colonel by Drive, Ottawa, ON K1S 5B6, Canada
{cristinaruizmartin,gwainer}@sce.carleton.ca
[3] Complutense University of Madrid, Avenida de Séneca 2,
28040 Madrid, Spain
khenares@ucm.es

Abstract. Improved Susceptible-Infected-Recovered (SIR) models have been used to study the COVID-19 pandemic. Although they can predict epidemiology curves, spatial models cannot be easily built, and cannot model individual interactions. In this research, we show a definition of SIR-based models using the Cell-DEVS formalism (a combination of Cellular Automata and DEVS), showing how to deal with these issues. We validate the equivalence of a simple Cell-DEVS SIR model, and we present a SIIRS model, whose parameters are configured to imitate the spread of SARS-CoV-2 in South Korea. Such models may assist in the decision-making process for defining health policies, such as social distancing, to prevent an uncontrolled expansion of the virus.

Keywords: Cell-DEVS · Cellular models · Coronavirus · COVID-19 · Pandemics

1 Introduction

Current studies of COVID-19 [1, 2] include theory and methods of infectious disease dynamics. These methods are based on mathematical models that show how the disease spreads. The original Susceptible-Infected-Recovered (SIR) model [3] has been subsequently adapted to study the spread of diseases with a variety of new equations. Some recent extensions represent exposed individuals [4], latency of the disease, and the effect of quarantines [5], as well as the effects of isolation and contact tracing [6].

Several of the advanced models are based on formal mathematical methods, such as network dynamics, ordinary differential equations, finite equation theory, and others. Although these theoretical studies on infectious diseases are useful, they are difficult to apply in practice. Specifically, they have shortcomings for defining contact processes, the behavior of the individuals and the spatial dimension in the model. Cellular automata (CA) allows to develop models that overcome the above-mentioned shortcomings.

© Springer Nature Switzerland AG 2021
T. M. Gwizdałła et al. (Eds.): ACRI 2020, LNCS 12599, pp. 239–249, 2021.
https://doi.org/10.1007/978-3-030-69480-7_24

Although CA has been successfully applied to develop disease spread models, its discrete-time nature considers time as isomorphic to the natural numbers set $\mathbb{N}$ (i.e., time advances at constant steps). Therefore, all cell states that are supposed to happen between timesteps must be either neglected or delayed matching the simulation timestep. CA are not trivial to integrate with other models defined in other formalisms, as well as defining advanced timing conditions for each cell. The Cell-DEVS formalism [7] solves these issues by combining CA and the Discrete EVent System Specifications (DEVS) [8] to describe n-dimensional cell spaces as discrete-event models.

Here we illustrate the application of Cell-DEVS to build spatial models of spread of COVID-19. In Sect. 2, we present related work and introduce Cell-DEVS. Section 3 describes two models for pandemics and illustrates how to build them in Cell-DEVS. Section 4 shows the results of simulations performed under these models.

2   Background

Mathematical models of infectious diseases have been studied since the XVIII century, when Bernoulli proposed a model to analyze the effect of vaccination on the spread of smallpox [9]. In 1927, Kermack and McKendrick published what is considered to be the first modern mathematical model for pandemics [3]. This model classified the population into three different groups: susceptible (S), who can get infected with the disease (I), and then can recover (R). The success of the SIR model led to several improved. For instance, the Susceptible-Exposed-Infected-Recovered (SEIR) models [4] added a new class of infected individuals that cannot transmit the disease: the Exposed (E), which eventually become infected. SIRD models [10] include dying (D) individuals, and SIS models [11] include infected individuals that after overcoming the disease can be susceptible to it again. There are numerous combinations of these methods (e.g., SEIIR, SIRS, SEIRS, SIRDS, or SEIRDS), in which the number of individuals moving from one class to another is described using differential equations.

For the COVID-19 outbreak, numerous mathematical models used SIR-based models of prediction. For example, Danon et al. [1] used a SEIIR model for SARS-CoV-2 in England and Wales, tuning the coefficients of the corresponding differential equations according to estimates from the outbreak in China. Caccavo [2] showed a modified SIRD model that adequately describes the outbreaks of China and Italy by defining time-variant coefficients of the differential equations of the mathematical model.

2.1   SIR-Based Models Using Cellular Automata

The mathematical theory and methods of infectious disease dynamics do not include variable susceptibility of the population or the representation of spatial aspects of the spread of the disease. Using CA [12] for SIR-based models can address these issues effectively. For instance, [13] proposed a simple CA model that consider the effect of vaccination. In this model, the cells' population is inhomogeneous, and individuals can travel between neighbors on each time step. Alternatively, [14] presented a geographical CA corresponding to a SIRS model with multiple infection phases. Each phase implies a different probability of spreading the virus, and each infection state presents a variable chance of getting recovered. The cell space has irregular shapes with a varying dimension corresponding to a geographical location, length of the boundaries with the adjacent regions, and road links between two sections.

The SEIR CA model in [15] has probabilistic state transitions. Each cell represents an individual, and mobility is defined as a reciprocal change in neighboring cells. As each cell describes a single individual, the model was limited to small scenarios, and cannot be extrapolated to large cities with high population density, where the disease could affect the most. Finally, the SEIRDS model in [16] explores how the spread of infectious diseases is affected by population density, gender, and age structure. Infected individuals are not divided into subgroups based on the stage of the disease, and therefore the behavior of the pandemic is more predictable than in the models cited above.

2.2   The Cell-DEVS Formalism

The discrete-time nature of CA considers time as isomorphic to the natural numbers set $\mathbb{N}$, and any event between time steps must be either neglected or delayed to match the simulation time base. Furthermore, the synchronism of CA could lead to unnecessary processing. CA are also complex to integrate with other models defined using different systems specifications, and the definition of timing conditions for the cells is difficult.

Cell-DEVS [7] combines CA with Discrete EVent System Specifications (DEVS) [8] to describe n-dimensional cell spaces as discrete-event models. In Cell-DEVS, each cell represents a DEVS atomic model, and the cell space is defined as a DEVS coupled model that interconnects neighboring cells, as seen in Fig. 1 for a 2D Cell-DEVS.

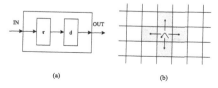

(a)   (b)

Fig. 1. Cell-DEVS model: (a) schematic of an atomic cell; (b) 2-dimensional Cell-DEVS

As shown in Fig. 1(a), when a cell receives an input, a local computing function τ is activated to compute the next state of the cell. If this is different from the current state, the change is transmitted to neighboring cells after a time delay d specified by a delay function D. Figure 1(b) shows that outputs from a cell (in the center) are received by the nearby cells using a von Neumann neighborhood. Cells are only active when they receive an external event or when they have a scheduled internal event. Otherwise, cells remain passive. As a result, this discrete-event approach only computes active cells, using a continuous time base (and time advances with events triggered by cells). Cell-DEVS models are equivalent to CA with explicit timing information. Cell-DEVS inherits modularity and hierarchical modeling from DEVS formalism, allowing cells to interact with other models, tools, data sets, and visualization mechanisms, making it easier and efficient to build complex cellular models.

CD++ [17, 18] is a simulator that allows defining models based on the Cell-DEVS and DEVS formal specifications. We define the local transition functions as follows:

```
rule: {PORT_ASSIGN} {NEW_STATE} DELAY {PRECONDITION}
```

When the PRECONDITION is satisfied, the state of the cell changes to the designated NEW_STATE. The PORT_ASSIGN values are transmitted to other components using different ports after waiting the required DELAY. If the PRECONDITION is false, the next rule in the list is evaluated until a rule is satisfied or there are no more rules available.

CD++ visualization engines ease in-depth analyses of the simulation traces for the models under study. The Cell-DEVS Web-viewer [19] allows us to easily visualize simulation results, display cells information and activity with ease.

3   Cell-DEVS Definition of SIR Models

In this section we present SIR Cell-DEVS models implemented in CD++.

3.1   Susceptible-Infected-Recovered (SIR) Model

The SIR model in this section is based on the model in [13] to simulate the spreading of epidemics in a 2D space. At time t, cell (i, j) has a number of individuals $N_{i,j}$, and it stores the ratio of individuals on each SIR group as follows: susceptible $S_{i,j}^t$, infected $I_{i,j}^t$, and recovered $R_{i,j}^t$. The model does not consider birth, immigration, or death: the population of each cell remains constant. At every timestep, a portion of cells' susceptible individuals becomes infected according to the following rule:

$$i_{i,j}^t = \min\left(S_{i,j}^{t-1}, S_{i,j}^{t-1} \cdot \sum_{(\alpha,\beta)\in V} c_{i,j}^{(\alpha,\beta)} \cdot m_{i,j}^{(\alpha,\beta)} \cdot \lambda \cdot \frac{N_{i+\alpha,j+\beta}}{N_{i,j}} \cdot I_{i+\alpha,j+\beta}^{t-1}\right) \quad (1)$$

The proportion of new infections $(i_{i,j}^t)$ depends on the ratio of infected individuals on the neighbors $(i+\alpha, j+\beta)\forall\alpha, \beta \in V$, as well as the density ratio between neighbors and the origin cell. It also depends on a connectivity factor $c_{i,j}^{(\alpha,\beta)}$ (the number of means of transportation between two cells), a mobility factor $m_{i,j}^{(\alpha,\beta)}$ (the probability of an individual in a cell $(i+\alpha, j+\beta)$ to move to cell (i, j)), and an infection rate λ. Additionally, a portion of the infected individuals $r_{i,j}^t$, recovers according to the recovery rate γ:

$$r_{i,j}^t = \gamma \cdot I_{i,j}^{t-1} \quad (2)$$

The complete behavior of the model is described as follows:

$$S_{i,j}^t = S_{i,j}^{t-1} - i_{i,j}^t; I_{i,j}^t = I_{i,j}^{t-1} + i_{i,j}^t - r_{i,j}^t; R_{i,j}^t = R_{i,j}^{t-1} + r_{i,j}^t \qquad (3)$$

To ensure that the amount of possible states is finite, the susceptible, infected, and recovered ratios are discretized as follows:

$$DS_{i,j}^t = \frac{\left[100 \cdot S_{i,j}^t\right]}{100}, DI_{i,j}^t = \frac{\left[100 \cdot I_{i,j}^t\right]}{100}, DR_{i,j}^t = 1 - DS_{i,j}^t - DI_{i,j}^t \qquad (4)$$

Code 1 shows the Cell-DEVS implementation of the model in CD++. We first define the size of the cell space, the type of delay (transport) and a von Neumann neighborhood. We also define state variables and the ports for each cell.

Code 1. Implementation of the Cell-DEVS SIR model in CD++

```
type: cell              width: 50      height: 50     delay: transport
neighbors: (-1,0) (0,-1) (0,0) (0,1) (1,0)
statevariables: population virulence connection movement i_sus i_infec i_rec
neighborports: initial infec rec pop sus

[sir-rules]
...
rule: {~pop := $population; ~infec:= $i_infec; ~sus:= $i_sus; ~rec:= $i_rec;}
{$i_sus:= round(((0,0)~sus - #(i_effect))*100)/100; $i_infec:= round(((1-#(recov-
ery))*(0,0)~infec+(0,0)~sus-$i_sus)*100)/100; $i_rec:= 1 - $i_sus - $i_infec;}
     1     { (0,0)~initial != -1 }
```

The keyword statevariables defines all the variables in the cell: population ($N_{i,j}$), virulence (λ), connection (c), movement (m), i_sus (DI), i_infec (DI) and i_rec (DR). The cell's ports used to transmit information to the neighboring cells are defined using the keyword neighborports followed by their names: initial, infec, rec, pop, sus. The transition rule uses the values of the state variables and the inputs received from neighbors. The rule presented represents a part of Eqs. (4) and (5). If the cell is not in the initial state ((0,0)~initial!=-1), we update the proportion of susceptible, infected, and recovered individuals. For example, the proportion of recovered individuals ($i_rec) is calculated as in Eq. (4). After the delay (1 time unit), the population of the cell and the proportions of S, I, and R are transmitted using the cell ports. Code 2 shows a macro used in the model.

Code 2. Implementation of the macros for the SIR model in Cell-DEVS.

```
#BeginMacro(i_effect)
min((0,0)~sus, (0,0)~sus*$virulence*((0,0)~infec+$connection*$movement/(0,0)~pop*
   ( (1,0)~pop * (1,0)~infec + (-1,0)~pop * (-1,0)~infec +
     (0,1)~pop * (0,1)~infec + (0,-1)~pop * (0,-1)~infec)))
```

This macro is used to calculate the proportion of new infected individuals according to Eq. (1) using the Von Newman neighborhood.

3.2   Susceptible-Infected-Recovered-Susceptible Model

The model in this section, based on the model in [14], defines a Cell-DEVS representation of a SIRS model. As in the previous case, each cell (i, j) has a fixed, heterogeneous population $N_{i,j}$ divided into three groups: S, I, R. Once infected, individuals remain ill from 1 to T_I days, after which they are immune for T_R days, after which they become susceptible again. The infected group can be divided into subsets depending on the percentage of individuals that have been infected during p consecutive days. Recovered individuals are classified based on how many days they have been immune:

$$I_{i,j}^t = \left\{ I_{i,j}^t(p) | p \in \{1, \ldots, T_I\} \right\}, \ R_{i,j}^t = \left\{ R_{i,j}^t(r) | r \in \{1, \ldots, T_R\} \right\}, \tag{5}$$

The ratio of individuals that become infected at time t ($i_{i,j}^t$) is described in Eq. (6). The proportion of new infections depends on the ratio of infected individuals in the neighboring cells and the population density ratio between neighboring cells and the origin. This model also considers a connectivity factor $c_{i,j}^{(\alpha,\beta)}$, a mobility factor $m_{i,j}^{(\alpha,\beta)}$, and an infection rate $\lambda(p)$. In this model, the infection rate varies with the stage of the illness (low in the first days of the infection, and high in the last days.

$$i_{i,j}^t = \min \left(S_{i,j}^{t-1}, S_{i,j}^{t-1} \cdot \sum_{\substack{(\alpha, \beta) \in V \\ p \in \{1, \ldots, T_I\}}} c_{i,j}^{(\alpha,\beta)} \cdot m_{i,j}^{(\alpha,\beta)} \cdot \lambda(p) \cdot \frac{N_{i+\alpha,j+\beta}}{N_{i,j}} \cdot I_{i+\alpha,j+\beta}^{t-1}(p) \right) \tag{6}$$

We also need to consider that the set of individuals in the last day of immunity, $R_{i,j}^{t-1}(r)$, become susceptible again. Hence:

$$S_{i,j}^t = S_{i,j}^{t-1} - i_{i,j}^t + R_{i,j}^{t-1}(r) \tag{7}$$

In each infected state $I_{i,j}^t(p)$, the recovery rate function ($\gamma(p)$) represents the probability for infected individuals to overpass the disease after being infected during p consecutive days. As the maximum allowed days of the disease is T_I, we set $\gamma(T_I) = 1$. Thus, the proportion of people infected for p consecutive days is equal to the proportion of people that have been ill during $p - 1$ days in a row and did not recover:

$$I_{i,j}^t(p) = \begin{cases} i_{i,j}^t, & \text{if } p = 1 \\ (1 - \gamma(p - 1)) \cdot I_{i,j}^{t-1}(p - 1), & \text{if } 1 < p \leq T_I \end{cases} \tag{8}$$

The first recovered state ($R_{i,j}^t(1)$) is the sum of the last infected state and the recovered individuals of the other infected states. The following recovered states simply takes the value of the previous recovered states.

$$R_{i,j}^t(r) = \begin{cases} \sum_{p \in \{1,...,T_i\}} \gamma(p) \cdot I_{i,j}^{t-1}(p), & \text{if } r = 1 \\ R_{i,j}^{t-1}(r-1), & \text{if } 1 < r \le T_R \end{cases} \quad (9)$$

The SIRS model was defined using CD++ as a Cell-DEVS model similar to the SIR model explained in Sect. 3.1. This new version includes different state variables and ports, and new local transition rules to calculate the new state of the cells. In Code 3, we include a part of the rules used to represents Eqs. (7–9).

Code 3. Implementation of the rules for the SIR model in Cell-DEVS.

```
rule: {~pop:=$population; ~sus_0:=$i_sus_0; ~inf_1:=$i_inf_1; ~inf_2:= $i_inf_2;
    ... ~rec_24:= $i_rec_24; ~rec_25:=$i_rec_25; ~rec_26:= $i_rec_26; ...}
    { $i_rec_28:= $i_rec_27; $i_rec_27:= $i_rec_26;
        $i_rec_23:= $i_inf_22 + #(local_recovered);
            $i_inf_22:= round((1 - $recovered_rate) * $i_inf_21*100)/100;
    ...

        $i_inf_2:= round((1 - $recovered_rate) * $i_inf_1*100)/100;
        $i_inf_1:= #(internal_infected) + #(external_infected);
        $i_sus_0:= 1-$i_inf_1-...-$i_inf_22-$i_rec_23 -...- $i_rec_28;}
    1 { (0,0)~initial != -1}
```

If the cell is not in the initial state, we calculate the proportion of individuals on each state of the disease. In this case, there are susceptible individuals ($i_sus_0), infected individuals on different phases of the disease (e.g., $inf_1 represents the proportion of individuals in the first day of infection) and recovered individuals with different immunity time left (e.g., $i_rec_28 represents the proportion of individuals in the last day of the immunity). The proportion of infected individuals in the second day of the disease ($inf_2) is calculated as the proportion of infected individuals the on the first day of disease minus the ratio of individuals who recovered (1-$recovered_rate) *$i_inf_1 as in Eq. (8). Then, the value is discretized to two significant digits. The rules to calculate the rest of the state variables are defined similarly. After a delay, (i.e., 1 time unit), the population of the cell and the proportion of R, I and S individuals are transmitted using the ports of the cell.

4 Case Studies

In this section, we present results of simulations using the two Cell-DEVS models described above. All models showed in this section represent a 50×50 space with a range 1 von Neumann neighborhood. The time units used correspond to one day.

4.1 SIR Model Simulation Results

The basic SIR allows exploring critical factors such as the infection and recovery rates. In this section we show that the results in [13] can be reproduced using our Cell-DEVS version of the model, using the same parameters than in the original model. The population of every cell $N_{i,j}$, is 100 individuals. Initially, only the cell in the middle contains infected individuals. The proportion of infected individuals of this cell, $I_{25,25}^0$ is 0.3. The remaining people in the cell are susceptible to infection ($S_{25,25}^0 = 0.7$ and

$R^0_{25,25} = 0$). The infection rate λ is 0.6, the recovery rate γ is 0.4, and the connectivity factor $c^{(\alpha,\beta)}_{i,j}$ is 1. The mobility factor is 1 for the cell itself, and 0.5 for the rest of the neighbors.

Figure 2 shows the percentage of infected individuals per cell. Cells in light grey correspond to areas with no infected individuals, while dark grey and black cells correspond to areas with a significant ratio of the population infected.

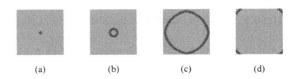

(a)   (b)   (c)   (d)

Fig. 2. Infected rate reported by simulations at day (a) 5, (b) 11, (c) 42, and (d) 60.

At day 5, shown in Fig. 2(a), only a few cells of the center of the cell space reported infection cases. As time advances, nearby cells get infected, whereas previous cells with cases start to get immunity, increasing the percentage of recovered individuals. The peak number of cases occurs the 42nd day, displayed in Fig. 2(c).

Figure 3 shows the evolution of the percentage of population that is susceptible (red dashed line), infected (blue line), and recovered (green dash-dot line). At time 0, almost all the individuals are susceptible (except a 0.012% of the population that is ill from the beginning, all in cell (25, 25)). As time advances, more people become infected, significantly reducing the percentage of susceptible individuals, and increasing the number of infected ones. The increment of infected individuals is less pronounced, as every day a 40% of sick people recover. At the end, 100% of the population has recovered. These results are the same than those presented in [13].

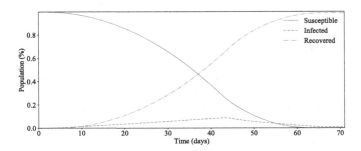

Fig. 3. Evolution of the susceptible, infected, and recovered individuals. (Color figure online)

4.2   SIRS Model Simulation Results

The SIRS model provides a finer grain parametrization, allowing the representation of more complex epidemics. It establishes a fixed number of days for the infected and recovered phases, and it allows to define different infection and recovery rates for each infected state. This makes possible to reflect government measures and changes in the population behavior. We show an example of these kind of dynamic scenarios. We use this model to mimic an approximate behavior of the spread of the SARS-CoV-2 in South Korea using real data for defining infection and recovery rates [20].

We configure a 50 × 50 grid, with a population of $N_{i,j}$ = 100 individuals per cell. We set the connectivity factor in 1 and the mobility factor to 0.6 for the neighboring cells. Again, we use the cell in the middle to trigger the epidemic ($I_{25,25}$ = 0.3, $S_{25,25}$ = 0.7, $R_{25,25}$ = 0). We set the infection phase length T_I to 22 days. The individuals experience the first symptoms in the 4th day and isolate themselves in the 8th day. Until this event, we establish a fixed infection rate λ of 0.15. The rest of the period they are considered isolated, and their λ is reduced to 0.01. The recovery rate γ is set to 0.07 for all the infected states. For this disease, we consider an immunity period of six days since there is not validated data for COVID-19. Figure 4 show the evolution of this spread.

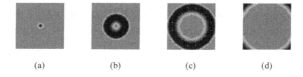

(a)   (b)   (c)   (d)

Fig. 4. Infected rate reported by simulations at day (a) 10, (b) 50, (c) 90, and (d) 140.

Here, light grey cells correspond to areas with no infected individuals. For the rest of them, the darker the background color is, the more non-susceptible (i.e., infected and recovered) individuals are present in the cell. As time goes by, the recovered individuals finish their immunity and becomes susceptible again.

Figure 5 shows how these non-susceptible ratios evolve. The infected population grows at a constant rate until day 93. After this moment, all the individuals have been exposed to the disease, so the infected ratio starts to decrease. As the proportion of infections decreases, the susceptible population increases again, reaching the maximum level of susceptible population at the end of the simulation. The recovered proportion remains low due to the short recovery period length of the scenario under study.

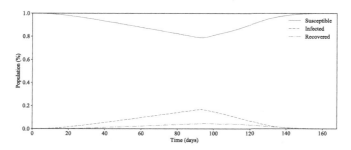

Fig. 5. Evolution of the susceptible, infected, and recovered individuals.

5 Conclusions

We presented a Cell-DEVS definition to simulate and study the spread of disease, focusing on the COVID-19 pandemic. We adapted the model in [13] to validate our approach, which was easily adapted to follow the specifications presented in [14], and we configured the simulation parameters using data from the spread of SARS-CoV-2 in South Korea [20].

In Cell-DEVS models, cells are only active when one or more cells in the neighborhood set notify a state change or any other external event is scheduled. Otherwise, cells stay passive, without requiring any extra computation. Compared with CA, where all cells are active in every simulation step, our approach saves computation time.

Another advantage of Cell-DEVS is its event-triggered time base. Time advances in a continuous timeline when events happen. Thus, the time advance is not fixed into a simulation step. This feature allows defining models where different cells' states have different time spams. We proved that we could define Cell-DEVS models equivalent to any CA with more accurate timing information with no additional effort.

As future work, we will define a SIRDS model that considers the death rate of the pandemic. Furthermore, model parameters such as connectivity or mobility factors will depend also on the different infection phases. With this model, we will be able to define a more precise model that considers more scenarios with complex government policies, such as limiting people mobility depending on the presence of symptoms, or the enforcement of using masks.

The implementations of the models are available at https://github.com/SimulationEverywhere-Models/COVID-Cell-DEVS-ACRI2020, and a number of simulation scenarios, including the ones presented here, can be found at https://bit.ly/3aiDM4j.

References

1. Danon, L., Brooks-Pollock, E., Bailey, M., Keeling, M.: A spatial model of CoVID-19 transmission in England and Wales: early spread and peak timing. MedRxiv (2020)
2. Caccavo, D.: Chinese and Italian COVID-19 outbreaks can be correctly described by a modified SIRD model. MedRxiv (2020)
3. Kermack, W.O., McKendrick, A.: A contribution to the mathematical theory of epidemics. Proc. R. Soc. Lond. Ser. A **115**(772), 700–721 (1927)
4. Li, M.Y., Muldowney, J.S.: Global stability for the SEIR model in epidemiology. Math. Biosci. **125**(2), 155–164 (1995)
5. Hou, C., et al.: The effectiveness of the quarantine of Wuhan city against the Corona Virus Disease 2019 (COVID-19): well-mixed SEIR model analysis. J. Med. Virol. **92**(7), 841–848 (2020)
6. Hellewell, J., et al.: Feasibility of controlling COVID-19 outbreaks by isolation of cases and contacts. Lancet Glob. Health **8**(4), e488–e496 (2020)
7. Wainer, G.A.: An introduction to cellular automata models with cell-DEVS. In: 2019 Winter Simulation Conference (WSC), National Harbor, MD, USA, pp. 1534–1548 (2019)

8. Zeigler, B.P., Praehofer, H., Kim, T.G.: Theory of Modeling and Simulation. Integrating Discrete Event and Continuous Complex Dynamic Systems, 2nd edn. Academic Press (2000)
9. Bernoulli, D.: Essai d'une nouvelle analyse de la mortalité causée par la petite vérole. Mémoires de Mathématiques et de Physique, pp. 1–45 (1760)
10. Matadi, M.B.: The SIRD epidemical model. Far East J. Appl. Math. **1**(89), 1–14 (2014)
11. Castillo-Chavez, C., Yakubu, A.A.: Discrete-time SIS models with complex dynamics. Nonlinear Anal. Theory Methods Appl. **47**(7), 4753–4762 (2001)
12. Wolfram, S.: Statistical mechanics of Cellular Automata. Rev. Mod. Phys. **55**(3), 601–644 (1983)
13. Hoya White, S., Martín del Rey, A., Rodríguez Sánchez, G.: Modeling epidemics using cellular automata. Appl. Math. Comput. **186**(1), 193–202 (2007)
14. Zhong, S.B., Huang, Q.Y., Song, D.J.: Simulation of the spread of infectious diseases in a geographical environment. Sci. China, Ser. D Earth Sci. **52**(4), 550–561 (2009). https://doi.org/10.1007/s11430-009-0044-9
15. López, L., Giovanini, L., Burguener, G.: Addressing population heterogeneity and distribution in epidemics models using a cellular automata approach. BMC Res. Notes **7**, 234 (2014)
16. Bin, S., Sun, G., Chen, C.C.: Spread of infectious disease modeling and analysis of different factors on spread of infectious disease based on cellular automata. Int. J. Environ. Res. Public Health **16**(23), 4683 (2019)
17. Wainer, G.A.: CD++: a toolkit to develop DEVS models. Softw. Pract. Exp. **32**(13), 1261–1306 (2002)
18. López, A., Wainer, G.: Improved cell-DEVS model definition in CD++. In: Sloot, P.M.A., Chopard, B., Hoekstra, A.G. (eds.) ACRI 2004. LNCS, vol. 3305, pp. 803–812. Springer, Heidelberg (2004). https://doi.org/10.1007/978-3-540-30479-1_83
19. Hesham, O., St-Aubin, B.: Cell-DEVS Simulation Viewer. http://cell-devs.sce.carleton.ca/intranet/webviewer/. Accessed 15 May 2020
20. Kim, S., Seo, Y.B., Jung, E.: Prediction of COVID-19 transmission dynamics using a mathematical model considering behavior changes in Korea. Epidm Health **42**, e2020026 (2020)

The Disease Spreading Analysis on the Grouped Network

Tomasz M. Gwizdałła$^{(\boxtimes)}$ and Katarzyna Lepa

Faculty of Physics and Applied Informatics, University of Łódź,
Pomorska 149/153, 90-236 Łódź, Poland
{tomasz.gwizdalla,katarzyna.lepa}@uni.lodz.pl

Abstract. The numerical studies of disease spreading processes are almost one-century old. The mainstream of these analyses is based on the ordinary differential equations which enable to estimate, especially, the epidemic curves for some assumed values of parameters describing the aggregate probabilities of passing through different phases if illness. In our paper, we present some results which can be obtained for the more individualized model, based on the analysis of direct interactions between the members of the community. We use the concepts of the SEIR model but we apply the different mechanisms to study the process of transfer of illness based on the representation of the community as the scale-free network. We can obtain the typical epidemic curves, study their spread, and also analyze the epidemic process in the internal groups of the community.

1 Introduction

The recent events related to the broad spread of the SARS-Cov-2 virus and caused by it COVID-19 illness caused the increase of interest in the techniques of numerical modeling of such processes. Due to the etiology of this illness, researchers started to study it with the same methods as usually used for other viral illnesses. The previous experience was concentrated mainly on influenza outbreaks and the techniques used for the study are related mainly to several techniques, just to mention a few: differential equation approach [1,2], Cellular Automata-based approach [3,4], the structured approaches [5,6].

Our model belongs to the third, which seems least numerous groups. In the paper, we propose to structure the community according to the scale-free network, which enables us to include a lot of modifications. Here we concentrate on only selected problems. They are the shape of epidemic curves for different methods of social graph creation, the effect of the "patient zero" location selection, the size effect, and the influence of illness on groups of different sizes.

2 Model

The crucial ideas related to the modeling of disease spreading phenomena are now about a hundred years old. In the paper written by Kermack, McKendrick,

© Springer Nature Switzerland AG 2021
T. M. Gwizdałła et al. (Eds.): ACRI 2020, LNCS 12599, pp. 250–260, 2021.
https://doi.org/10.1007/978-3-030-69480-7_25

and Walker [1], authors introduced the division of a population into different groups when considering the relation to the epidemic process. These groups were then not assigned names which are typical for contemporary studies, but the necessity to distinguish particular groups was clear. Currently, these groups are usually represented by acronym SEIR (with possible modifications), and, following this acronym, we use the abbreviation SEIR for the family of models enabling the study of the epidemic process.

We can show several typical approaches leading to the reproduction of the epidemic process. The most popular is the analysis of the comprehensive behavior of entire groups within the frame of a set of Ordinary Differential Equations (ODE). The typical set is constructed as, for example:

$$
\begin{aligned}
\frac{dS}{dt} &= \mu(N - S) - \beta\frac{I}{N}S \\
\frac{dE}{dt} &= \beta\frac{I}{N}S - (\mu + \delta)E \\
\frac{dI}{dt} &= \delta E - (\mu + \gamma)I \\
\frac{dR}{dt} &= \gamma I - \mu R
\end{aligned}
\tag{1}
$$

The detailed form of the upper equations as well as the detailed meaning of particular constants depends on the assumption of the model, but generally, we can say that all ODE-based approaches produce the results which are somehow averaged over the possible realizations of a real epidemic. It is very hard to take into account the stochastic effects which are often crucial for the spread of illness when considering the direct form of Eq. 1. Sometimes, the attempts to introduce the seasonal [2] or stochastic [7] external force are here observed. Most of Cellular Automata-based models are based on the attempt to determine the number of people in individual states located in individual cells [3,4]. Thus, we usually obtain the aggregate results in the cell grid covering the entire study area. The probabilistic effect comes here from the different values of possible communication rates for different pairs of cells.

In our paper, we are going to present the analysis of the model, based on the direct interaction of agents. The basic assumption is that the transfer of illness is performed as an effect of the direct interaction between two agents: the one who can infect and the one who can be infected. This assumption leads to the necessity to define, as the parameters of the model, the three factors:

- a set of states in which individuals may occur
- a graph of connections between individuals which describes the possibility of transfer of illness
- parameters describing the possibility of infection in a single act

As a set of states, we use the typical SEIR model. It means that every person can be in one of the four states:

- **S** (Susceptible) - individuals who have not been sick so far, they can get sick as a result of contact with a sick person;

- **E** (Exposed) - individuals who are already infected but they cannot transmit the disease to other people;
- **I** (Infectious) - individuals in the phase of the disease when they can transmit the disease;
- **R** (Recovered) - individuals who passed the disease.

The values typical for the particular illness are the values corresponding to the time of duration of phases **E** and **I**. Certainly, these times are not unambiguous, in reality, we should discuss some intervals and distributions. Here, we assume however that they are described by well-defined numbers. For the simplicity of calculations, we neglected several effects that can occur during the real epidemic. We neglect the mortality and birth rates. Since we consider relatively short times, these factors do not impact significantly the final result and we do not need to consider them. We do not take into account the possibility of reinfection. All individuals who pass the infection are moved to state **R**. We assume that they are permanently immune, so they stay in the state **R**.

The choice of the form of the graph describing the existing relations can be implemented in many ways. The simplest, when considering the Cellular Automata-related approach would be the assignment of individuals to the positions in the n-dimensional grid. The topology of such networks and the possible neighborhoods (Moore or von Neumann) define the potential number of interactions. We would follow the graph-related approach when the possible existence of link (interaction) between nodes (individuals) is defined by some graph-creation procedure. The graph should then reproduce the structure of the community. Such methodology started from the famous Erdos and Renyi paper [8] and through the Watts-Strogatz small-world concept [9] reached the preferential Barabasi-Albert network [10].

In our paper, we follow the Barabasi-Albert approach. The basic property of this model is that unlike most models when initially the nodes are created and then the connections between them are established according to some algorithm, in the BA technique we add parallelly nodes and edges. Technically, in the beginning, a small graph, containing just several nodes is created. The connections between them can be set in different ways, the simplest one is to build a complete graph with three nodes. The preferential character of the method is reflected in the procedure of further adding of vertices. The probability that the new node will be added as a neighbor to the i-th one is given by probability:

$$P(k) = \frac{k_i}{\sum k_j} \tag{2}$$

where k_i is the degree of i-th node and $\sum k_j$ is a doubled number of existing connections. Among the properties of this procedure, we can show some especially interesting for reflecting the human communities. We can easily introduce natural processes like mortality or births by just removing or adding new nodes. The network, created with this scheme is also scale-free. The connections distribution in the community has a power-law character which is typical for a lot of processes taking place in the real world. We can also include some processes enabling to take into account the specific processes like area or group affiliation.

The final point is to define the procedure describing the disease transfer. Usually, this process is described by some aggregate coefficient, like in formula 1. Let us divide the presentation of this element of the model into two parts. Firstly, we show its capabilities, then we enlist the simplified choice for this paper. The crucial observation is that the disease transfer is the process depending on the parameters characterizing the disease as well as the individuals taking part in this process. When considering the disease-related parameter we should take into account especially the duration of the infectious phase as well as possible differences of the infectivity in different phases of the same period. We can also consider the health of particular individuals. The current COVID-19 pandemic shows that some people are more susceptible than other ones. There exists e.g. the presumption that vaccination against tuberculosis can give some disease resistance and cause either individual or even herd immunity. The presented concepts show that we have a lot of possibilities of modeling the infection process and, in general, it can be described by sophisticated statistical distributions.

In the paper, we simplify the approach described above. This is mainly since we want to avoid the study of too many effects which can impact the final result. That is why we limit our description of disease transfer to just two parameters. They are p_M and p_I. Their interpretation is as follows. p_M is the probability that two individuals, who are connected in our graph, can meet during a one-time step. This value alone is the form of averaging over all contacts of particular individuals. p_I is the probability of infection in a single act. We can also consider the meetings between individuals as described by some distribution of time lengths and have to connect it with the infectivity of a particular illness. By averaging over all cases we can obtain a single number and we assume that p_I reflects this number.

The model has been introduced in [11] where the detailed discussion of some validation procedures and results for differences between two kinds of viruses are presented.

3   Results

The data used in the modeling shown in the paper are some mix of real and artificial ones. We consider two types of diseases and adjust values of periods, spent by individuals in particular phases, to the real values reported for these diseases. The first on is influenza, for which $t_E = 2\,days$ and $t_I = 4\,days$ is typically used (see eg. [4]). t_E and t_I means the duration of Exposed and Infectious phases respectively. As the second case, we choose COVID-19. This second disease is now certainly strongly studied and disputed. The values reported can differ one from another and we are, indeed, still in the stage of rather collecting data than to have a well-grounded database. Therefore, we decided to use the maximum value suggested by several papers (see eg. [12]). Finally, for COVID-19 we adopted the values $t_E = 0\,days$ and $t_I = 14\,days$. It means also that

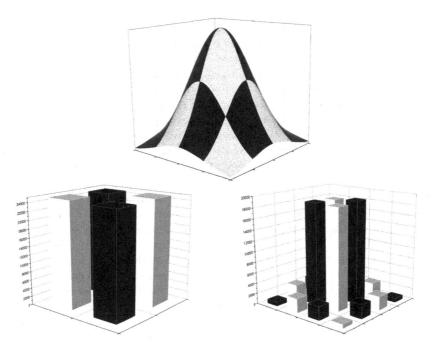

Fig. 1. The distribution of inhabitants in different parts of city. In the upper plot the ideal, symmentric gaussian distribution with the contours of considered areas marked. The lower plots show the relative number of individuals in different groups when divided into 4 or 16 groups.

our model for COVID-19 corresponds to the SIR model (Susceptible-Infected-Recovered), where the Exposed phase is absent. In all calculations, we assume also the lack of any intervention in the epidemic process.

The simulation is performed for two sizes of graphs (10000, 100000). This makes possible to continue our study concerning the size effect of disease spreading models [13]. We add also the effect of grouping. To do this, we construct the city with the "ideal" concentric distribution of inhabitants in its particular sectors. We assume that the probability density of finding the individual in the distance r from the geometric city center is given by the gaussian-like distribution $p(r) \propto \exp(-r^2)$. This distribution is presented in the Fig. 1 with the division into 16 symmetrically distributed areas. Individuals belonging to the same area form the group. We consider two divisions: into four groups and 16 groups. These divisions lead certainly to four approximately equally numerous groups for the first division and distinctly different groups for the second one. In detail, we have 4 highly numerous groups in the center ($\approx$20% each), 8 medium numerous at edges ($\approx$2.7%), and 4 very small at corners ($\approx$0.8%). For every simulation run, we sample separately the distribution of individuals. The lower plots show slight differences in the height of bars corresponding to different areas/groups.

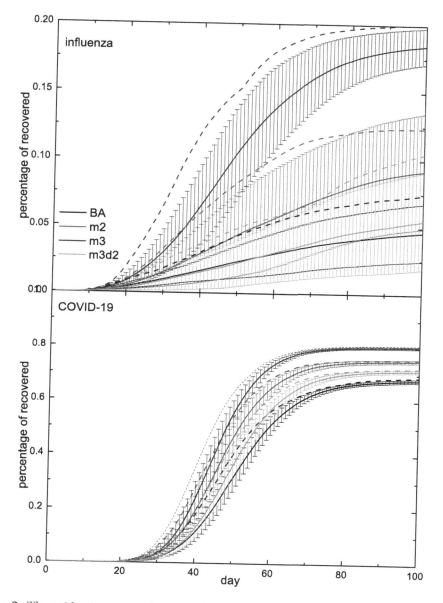

Fig. 2. The epidemic curves, shown as the number of Recovered for different diseases (upper and lower plot) and graph creation methods (the color of lines - same on both plots) for the number of individuals equal 100000 and for division into 4 equinumerous groups. The middle, solid lines correspond to the average percentage, the ribbon of bars shows the standard deviations. The dashed line corresponds to the case with the highest number of sick.

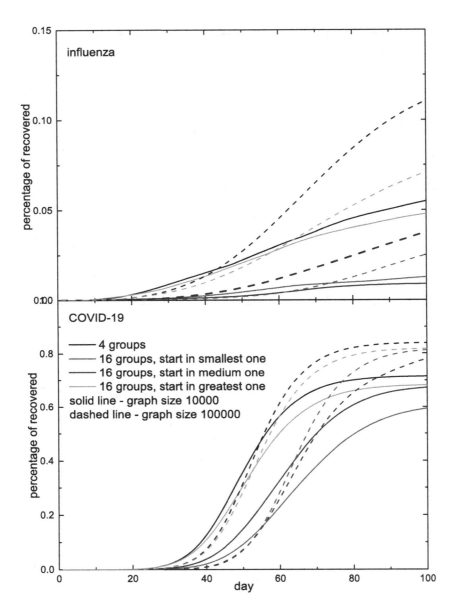

Fig. 3. The epidemic curves for different diseases, different community sizes and different divisions into groups.

Table 1. The final percentage of Recovered for different types of calculations, described in the headers of particular parts of the table. The numbers in parentheses are the percentages of sick in particular groups: in the largest, medium and smallest ones respectively.

Graph model	4 groups	16 groups, start in the smallest one	16 groups, start in the medium one	16 groups, start in the greatest one
Influenza, graph size 10000				
BA	0.047	0.032 (0.038, 0.017, 0.039)	0.023 (0.027, 0.011, 0.039)	0.03 (0.036, 0.016, 0.029)
m2	0.117	0.041 (0.05, 0.018, 0.051)	0.035 (0.043, 0.017, 0.038)	0.077 (0.094, 0.035, 0.059)
m3	0.17	0.097 (0.12, 0.037, 0.072)	0.077 (0.095, 0.033, 0.047)	0.162 (0.199, 0.066, 0.12)
m3d2	0.073	0.012 (0.015, 0.004, 0.02)	0.025 (0.032, 0.007, 0.013)	0.037 (0.046, 0.012, 0.018)
Influenza, graph size 100000				
BA	0.07	0.042 (0.051, 0.022, 0.041)	0.043 (0.051, 0.022, 0.039)	0.056 (0.067, 0.029, 0.055)
m2	0.155	0.05 (0.061, 0.023, 0.046)	0.106 (0.129, 0.049, 0.089)	0.135 (0.164, 0.062, 0.112)
m3	0.235	0.131 (0.161, 0.054, 0.097)	0.166 (0.205, 0.069, 0.128)	0.204 (0.251, 0.084, 0.152)
m3d2	0.109	0.022 (0.028, 0.007, 0.015)	0.024 (0.03, 0.008, 0.016)	0.072 (0.091, 0.025, 0.044)
COVID-19, graph size 10000				
BA	0.676	0.671 (0.805, 0.346, 0.651)	0.666 (0.801, 0.336, 0.631)	0.673 (0.81, 0.342, 0.595)
m2	0.749	0.731 (0.885, 0.351, 0.653)	0.735 (0.89, 0.351, 0.644)	0.736 (0.891, 0.355, 0.6)
m3	0.803	0.777 (0.945, 0.36, 0.59)	0.704 (0.856, 0.326, 0.56)	0.779 (0.946, 0.365, 0.665)
m3d2	0.718	0.534 (0.657, 0.22, 0.378)	0.667 (0.824, 0.27, 0.453)	0.675 (0.831, 0.281, 0.509)
COVID-19, graph size 100000				
BA	0.795	0.788 (0.947, 0.401, 0.717)	0.791 (0.951, 0.4, 0.727)	0.794 (0.954, 0.404, 0.737)
m2	0.84	0.828 (0.999, 0.41, 0.742)	0.832 (0.999, 0.412, 0.745)	0.832 (0.999, 0.411, 0.715)
m3	0.873	0.86 (0.999, 0.415, 0.754)	0.861 (0.999, 0.417, 0.759)	0.861 (0.999, 0.416, 0.747)
m3d2	0.838	0.794 (0.967, 0.364, 0.65)	0.811 (0.987, 0.374, 0.672)	0.819 (0.995, 0.38, 0.683)

When creating the interaction network, we use the typical Barabasi-Albert scheme, starting from three connected individuals. We introduce, however, the change related to the fact that it is more likely to create the connection between individuals (nodes) belonging to the same group than between those from different groups. We decided to enable the modification of probability given by Eq. 2 by performing some additional operations. Finally, we use four mechanisms of determining the probabilities (in the below formulas index *same* means nodes from the same groups, $diff$ - from different ones):

- **BA** - the pure BA model
- **m2** - $P_{same}(k) = min(1, \ 2 * \frac{k_i}{\sum k_j})$, P_{diff} - without change
- **m3** - $P_{same}(k) = min(1, \ 3 * \frac{k_i}{\sum k_j})$, P_{diff} - without change
- **m3d2** - $P_{same}(k) = min(1, \ 3 * \frac{k_i}{\sum k_j})$, $P_{different\,groups}(k) = 0.5 * \frac{k_i}{\sum k_j}$

The values of multipliers are taken completely arbitrary and they certainly lead to the change of slope of the power-law distribution of the number of neighbors. They do not change however the character of distributions. This arbitrary selection enables to study the effect of social links inside groups.

Finally, we have to assume the values of p_M and p_I. Since there exists no real data which makes it possible to estimate them, we assumed $p_M = 0.1$ and $p_I = 0.25$. We think that these values are indeed overestimated but they allow to study the effect. The very important factor supporting the use of them in the model is that it is very easy to modify them. It can be made when we find them too large or we want to introduce some particular effects like for instance well-known from recent times social isolation. Every result shown in upcoming figures and tables is the average over 10 runs.

In Fig. 2 we show the exemplary epidemic curves for both diseases and for 4 models of graph creation. We show also the spread of results around the average value. For influenza-type infection, the deviation can reach the value of $0.03-0.05$ what corresponds to the relative value up to about 70%. We can see also that for 100 time-steps, assuming that one time-step corresponds to one day, it is more than three months, the flu epidemic is still active. This is especially well visible when looking at the red curves corresponding to the m2 type of calculation. An interesting observation is that models BA and m3d2 lead to almost the same results. It means that this case should be in more detail studied by means of typical graph-related analysis concentrated on such properties like radius or diameter. For the COVID-based data, we can see the significantly smaller spread, the stabilization of the situation in the time of the simulation. There is also the expected effect of a significantly larger number of sick.

In Fig. 3 we show the influence of simulations' parameters on the epidemic curves for different divisions into groups. We use here m3d2 scheme. We can expect that such results can show us the influence of the social structure of the community on the epidemic process. We can observe also the presence of size effect, which is reflected in the significantly higher rate of sick for the larger community. It is interesting that this effect takes place in the scale-free network but we can observe the stabilization of obtained characteristics after passing some size of community [11]. We think also that this is the effect of the increase of the absolute number of links between nodes for such communities. We can show the same factor as responsible for the increase of the rate of sick individuals when "patient zero" is located in highly numerous groups either in the 4 group calculations or in the 16-group calculation in the one o the central groups. The relative differences are visibly smaller for COVID-19 related calculations but for this, more infective, the virus we can notice that the start in the lowly occupied group does not really depend on the size of this group. While the number of nodes in the smallest and medium groups differs by an order of magnitude, the results for them are similar.

The summary of results is presented in Table 1. Some form of test of our procedure is the similarity of values in the rows for the BA model of graph creation. The greater differences mean here the necessity to increase the number of simulation runs used in averaging. We can see that we have to do it, especially for influenza-type calculations. The most interesting result, in our opinion, is here the observation that for COVID-19 parameters, almost all individuals in large groups get sick.

4 Conclusions

We propose a model that enables the common consideration of different factors influencing the epidemic development in the given area. We think that thanks to the combination of analysis of social and medical processes at the level of individual interactions, we can create a realistic model that can reproduce the disease spreading. The features we would like to especially emphasize are as follows. The probabilistic character leads to the bundle of curves for particular input parameters, so we can show the particular behavior depending on the states in various intermediate phases. The reproduction of real social relationships gives the possibility of easy inclusion of different social processes, especially different forms of non-medical intervention. The individual character of disease transfer can be modeled in a lot of more or less complicated ways. We can also easily include, the typical for epidemics, seasonal processes.

References

1. Kermack, W.O., McKendrick, A., Walker, G.T.: A contribution to the mathematical theory of epidemics. Proc. R. Soc. Lond. **A115**, 700–721 (1927)
2. Nakamura, G., Martinez, A.: Hamiltonian dynamics of the SIS epidemic model with stochastic fluctuations. Sci. Rep. **9**, 1–9 (2019)
3. Sirakoulis, G., Karafyllidis, I., Thanailakis, A.: A cellular automaton model for the effects of population movement and vaccination on epidemic propagation. Ecol. Model. **133**, 209–223 (2000)
4. Holko, A., Mędrek, M., Pastuszak, Z., Phusavat, K.: Epidemiological modeling with a population density map-based cellular automata simulation system. Expert Syst. Appl. **48**, 1–8 (2016)

5. Ferguson, N., Cummings, D., Fraser, C., Cajka, J., Cooley, P., Burke, D.: Strategies for mitigating an influenza pandemic. Nature **442**, 448–452 (2006)
6. Ferguson, N., et al.: Impact of non-pharmaceutical interventions (NPIS) to reduce covid19 mortality and healthcare demand. Technical report, Imperial College London (2020)
7. Aron, J.L., Schwartz, I.B.: Seasonality and period-doubling bifurcations in an epidemic model. J. Theor. Biol. **110**, 665–679 (1984)
8. Erdös, P., Rényi, A.: On random graphs I. Publicationes Mathematicae Debrecen **6**, 290 (1959)
9. Watts, D.J., Strogatz, S.H.: Collective dynamics of 'small-world' networks. Nature **393**, 440–442 (1998)
10. Barabási, A.L., Albert, R.: Emergence of scaling in random networks. Science **286**, 509–512 (1999)
11. Gwizdałła, T.M.: Viral disease spreading in grouped population. Comput. Methods Programs Biomed. **197**, 105715 (2020)
12. Linton, N.M., et al.: Incubation period and other epidemiological characteristics of 2019 novel coronavirus infections with right truncation: a statistical analysis of publicly available case data. J. Clin. Med. **9**(2020), 538 (2019)
13. Orzechowska, J., Fordon, D., Gwizdałła, T.M.: Size effect in cellular automata based disease spreading model. In: Mauri, G., El Yacoubi, S., Dennunzio, A., Nishinari, K., Manzoni, L. (eds.) ACRI 2018. LNCS, vol. 11115, pp. 146–153. Springer, Cham (2018). https://doi.org/10.1007/978-3-319-99813-8_13

Epidemic Model with Restricted Circulation and Social Distancing on Some Network Topologies

Álvaro Junio Pereira Franco[(✉)] [ID]

Technological Center, Department of Informatics and Statistics,
Federal University of Santa Catarina, Florianópolis, SC, Brazil
alvaro.junio@ufsc.br

Abstract. A model to simulate the spreading of a disease on a network is proposed. The SIR model, a social distancing factor and network circulation restrictions are considered. We perform some experiments that give us an idea of how a disease spreads on different network topologies and social distancing factors.

Keywords: Epidemic models · Networks · Simulations

1 Introduction

Nowadays we are witnessing a pandemic. Control policies to lead this spreading are necessary. Some models which are used to simulate the dynamic of a disease, classify people in groups and they depend on the following scenario: 1. a person is subject to contract a disease even if he (she) was already cured; 2. a person is subject to contract a disease, however, if he (she) contracted it in the past and he (she) is now cured then he (she) cannot contract the disease again; 3. a healthy person can be immune or can be vaccinated, thus avoiding to contract a disease. This work focus on the second scenario, the SIR model. In this case, people can be *susceptible*, *infected* or *recovered*. Cellular automata models can also be used to study the spatial effects of an epidemic. White et al. [4] introduced a cellular automata model to simulate the epidemic spreading. Beauchemin et al. [2] used cellular automata to study the influenza A spreading. Here, we start our work applying the SIR model on a network.

The SIR model supposes, for each time t, a set of susceptible people S^t, infected people I^t and recovered people R^t. The people set maintains constant $N^t = S^t \cup I^t \cup R^t$. In this work, we concentrate the infections occurring in the contact of a susceptible person and an infected person. There is a *virulence rate* $v \in [0,1]$ that represents the potential infection of a contact. A *recovered rate* of infected people from the time t to $t+1$, $\varepsilon \in [0,1]$, is also considered. Next it is

This work was partially supported by Conselho Nacional de Desenvolvimento Científico e Tecnológico – CNPq (Proc. 423833/2018-9).

T. M. Gwizdałła et al. (Eds.): ACRI 2020, LNCS 12599, pp. 261–264, 2021.
https://doi.org/10.1007/978-3-030-69480-7_26

given a simple model to estimate the number of susceptible and infected people for each time t, $|I^t| = |I^{t-1}| - \varepsilon|I^{t-1}| + v|X^{t-1}|$, $|S^t| = |S^{t-1}| - v|X^{t-1}|$, $|R^t| = |R^{t-1}| + \varepsilon|I^{t-1}|$, where X^{t-1} is the set of people $p \in S^{t-1}$ that have encountered with some infected person. We use generalized automata networks [3] to simulate the spreading of a disease. These type of automata extend *cellular automata* mainly changing their topologies (network topology dependency). In this work, the network is used to represent the proximity among people. We consider a network G. The set of vertices adjacent to vertex i is denoted by $\chi(i)$. A real value in interval $[0, 1]$ is associated to each vertex i, and it represents the social distancing factor of vertex i. Additionally, a group of people is associated to each vertex (people from the same neighborhood, same city, etc). They can be susceptible, infected or recovered. A certain proportion from these people answer to social distancing. Two vertices are adjacents if the two people groups have some proximity. In this way, the generalized automata network can be used to simulate, for each time, the dynamic of susceptible, infected and recovered sets in each vertex. The group of people in a vertex i and on time t is denoted by the set $N_i^t = S_i^t \cup I_i^t \cup R_i^t$. The number of elements in the sets S_i^t, I_i^t and R^t can vary over time, however, there is no deletion in N_i^t.

A real value associated to each vertex is denoted by α_i^t, and it represents the social distancing factor of people in vertex i and time t. The social distancing factor partitions the sets of people in two sets: those people that answer to social distancing and those that do not answer (and could go out its vertex). Our experiments suppose that a person which does not answer social distancing, can stay in his (her) own vertex or can go through adjacent vertices.

We denote by $\dot{S}_i^t \subseteq S_i^t$ ($\ddot{S}_i^t \subseteq S_i^t$) the set of susceptible people in N_i^t that answer (do not answer) to social distancing. We define sets $\dot{I}_i^t$ ($\ddot{I}_i^t$) and $\dot{R}_i^t$ ($\ddot{R}_i^t$) in a similar way. We will assume that the social distancing factor of each vertex i on time t, α_i^t, is applied for susceptible people (and for the other groups) as the following $|\dot{S}_i^t| = \lfloor \alpha_i^t |S_i^t| \rfloor$ and $|\ddot{S}_i^t| = |S_i^t| - |\dot{S}_i^t|$. So, for each time t, the set of people from N_i^t that answer to social distancing $\dot{N}_i^t = \dot{S}_i^t \cup \dot{I}_i^t \cup \dot{R}_i^t$; and the set of people from N_i^t that do not answer to social distancing $\ddot{N}_i^t = \ddot{S}_i^t \cup \ddot{I}_i^t \cup \ddot{R}_i^t$. Next, we detail how the local rule treats the contact between people.

2   The Local Rule and the Contact Between People

We consider that few people that answer to social distancing can be infected. For the people that do not answer to social distancing, all the population can become infected. Therefore, for each vertex i, we can have people circling in i coming from the set N_i^t and from the set $\bigcup_{j \in \chi(i)} \ddot{N}_j^t$. We use a factor to represent the proportion of people which are circling in vertex i coming from vertex $j \in \chi(i)$ for each time t, here denoted by $\beta_{j \to i}^t$. The experiments performed by this work consider $\beta_{i \to j}^t = \frac{1}{\chi(i)+1}$ for all vertex i, vertex $j \in \chi(i)$ and time t. So, the proportion of people that go out each vertex is *equally distributed* among the vertex itself and its adjacents. Last section, we denote by X^t the set of susceptible people that encountered an infected person on time t. Now, we consider the distancing factor in it. Denoted by $\dot{X}_i^t$ ($\ddot{X}_i^t$) the set of people from $p \in \dot{S}_i^t$ ($p \in \ddot{S}_i^t$) that encountered an infected person in vertex i (in adjacent vertices of i). The set of people $p \in S_i^t$ that encountered infected people is denoted by $X_i^t = \dot{X}_i^t \cup \ddot{X}_i^t$. Thereby, the model is updated to $|I_i^t| = |I_i^{t-1}| - \varepsilon|I_i^{t-1}| + v(|\dot{X}_i^{t-1}| + |\ddot{X}_i^{t-1}|), |S_i^t| = |S_i^{t-1}| - v(|\dot{X}_i^{t-1}| + |\ddot{X}_i^{t-1}|), |R_i^t| = |R_i^{t-1}| + \varepsilon|I_i^{t-1}|$. Next, we analyze the *expected value* of $\mathbb{E}[|\dot{X}_i^{t-1}|]$ and $\mathbb{E}[|\ddot{X}_i^{t-1}|]$. The probability to occur an event Y is denoted by $\mathbb{P}\{Y\}$. The encounters of a person who answers to social distancing are restricted to the vertex that he (she) belongs. Let $\dot{Y}_{pi}^t$ ($\ddot{Y}_{pi \to i}^t, \ddot{Y}_{pi \to j}^t$) be an indicator random variable which is equal to 1 if a susceptible person $p \in \dot{S}_i^t$ ($p \in \ddot{S}_i^t$) meets an infected person (in vertex i, in vertex $j \in \chi(i)$); and it is equal to 0 otherwise. We can show that $\mathbb{E}[|\dot{X}_i^t|] = \dot{S}_i^t \mathbb{P}\{\dot{Y}_{pi}^t\}$ ($\mathbb{E}[|\ddot{X}_i^t|] = \ddot{S}_i^t \mathbb{P}\{\ddot{Y}_{pi \to i}^t\} + \sum_{j \in \chi(i)} T_j \mathbb{P}\{\ddot{Y}_{pi \to j}^t\}$), where $\dot{S}_i^t$ ($\ddot{S}_i^t$) is the set of susceptible people from $\dot{S}_i^t$ ($\ddot{S}_i^t$) circling in vertex i (and T_j is the number of susceptible people from i circling in $j \in \chi(i)$). The probabilities are all equal to the number of infected people circling in a vertex divided by the total people circling in such vertex. Now, let us rewrite the model in function of the expected values. It is important to note that we can work with lower and upper bounds for them. These bounds can always be integer numbers (as long as they are initially integers). Given $|I_i^{t-1}|, |S_i^{t-1}|, |R_i^{t-1}|$, and given constants ε and v, the model is update to (the symbol $=:$ means *by definition*): $\mathbb{E}[|I_i^t|] = |I_i^{t-1}| - \varepsilon|I_i^{t-1}| + v(\mathbb{E}[|\dot{X}_i^{t-1}|] + \mathbb{E}[|\ddot{X}_i^{t-1}|]) \geq |I_i^{t-1}| - \lceil \varepsilon|I_i^{t-1}| \rceil + \lfloor v(\mathbb{E}[|\dot{X}_i^{t-1}|] + \mathbb{E}[|\ddot{X}_i^{t-1}|]) \rfloor =: |I_i^t|; \mathbb{E}[|S_i^t|] = |S_i^{t-1}| - v(\mathbb{E}[|\dot{X}_i^{t-1}|] + \mathbb{E}[|\ddot{X}_i^{t-1}|]) \leq |S_i^{t-1}| - \lfloor v(\mathbb{E}[|\dot{X}_i^{t-1}|] + \mathbb{E}[|\ddot{X}_i^{t-1}|]) \rfloor =: |S_i^t|$; and $\mathbb{E}[|R_i^t|] = |R_i^{t-1}| + \varepsilon|I_i^{t-1}| \leq |R_i^{t-1}| + \lceil \varepsilon|I_i^{t-1}| \rceil =: |R_i^t|$. The previous model uses *floor* and *ceiling* functions. Observe that, if $|I_i^{t-1}|, |S_i^{t-1}|$ and $|R_i^{t-1}|$ are integer number then $|I_i^t|, |S_i^t|$ and $|R_i^t|$ will also be. The expected value of infected (susceptible, recovered) people of vertex i and on time t is at least (at most, at most) $|I_i^t|$ ($|S_i^t|, |R_i^{t-1}|$). Next, we describe some experimental results.

3   SIR Model Simulations: Results and Analysis

In this section we describe the experiments performed on different *network topologies*. For us, network topology is the way how the network connections are organized and how they define a structure (if any). Our motivation for these experimental analysis is that the topologies analyzed and real world topologies can have similarity. For a case of extreme necessity, some topology could be applied in practice and in a emergency way, changing temporarily the usual network connections. The topologies analyzed were the following: *cyclical* (the degree of each vertex is equal to 2), *complete* (each vertex has an edge for each other), and *grid*. Next, we show some characteristic graphics for the SIR model ($t \times n$, where t represents a day from 0 up to 200 and n represents the number of susceptible, infected or recovered people). The simulation considers networks with 100 vertices and each vertex i has $N_i^t = 3000$ people. Initially, each graph has 400 infected in a unique vertex that can be any one for cyclical and complete cases (by symmetry) and for the grid case, the bottom left vertex was chosen. All other people are initially susceptible and there is no recovered people. To obtain the SIR graphics for complete topology, we have had to increase the number of infected people (see next). The daily recovered and virulence rates are respectively $\varepsilon = \frac{29}{200}$ and $v = \frac{91}{200}$. Such rates have been recently used and they are related to the COVID-19 disease (see, for example, in [1]). The first simulations did not consider social distancing ($\alpha_i^t = 0$ for all i and all t). We can see the results in left graphics in Fig. 1. The other graphics do consider social distancing which was or constant in $\alpha_i^t = \frac{2}{5}$ for all i and all t (top middle and bottom right graphics) or periodical (the remaining graphics). We can compare the results for grid looking at to the top graphics. We clearly note the gain that social distancing can provide. For complete topology, we can compare the left and middle bottom graphics. The bottom left graphic did not consider social distancing and the number of infected people is 500. The bottom middle graphic consider periodical social distancing an it has 1000 initially infected. Observe the low number of infected people, almost constant over time and with a long plateau for the cyclical topology. We conclude this paper informing that a longer and more complete version of this work is being prepared to further publication.

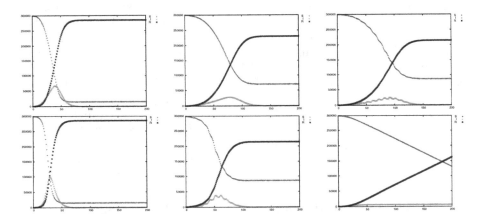

Fig. 1. On the top: The grid topology no social distancing, 40% social distancing, and periodical social distancing. On the bottom: The complete topology no social distancing and periodical social distancing; and cyclical topology 40% social distancing.

References

1. Bastos, S.B., Cajueiro, D.O.: Modeling and forecasting the Covid-19 pandemic in Brazil. arXiv preprint arXiv:2003.14288 (2020)
2. Beauchemin, C., Samuel, J., Tuszynski, J.: A simple cellular automaton model for influenza A viral infections. J. Theor. Biol. **232**(2), 223–234 (2005)
3. Tomassini, M.: Generalized automata networks. In: El Yacoubi, S., Chopard, B., Bandini, S. (eds.) ACRI 2006. LNCS, vol. 4173, pp. 14–28. Springer, Heidelberg (2006). https://doi.org/10.1007/11861201_5
4. White, S.H., Del Rey, A.M., Sánchez, G.R.: Modeling epidemics using cellular automata. Appl. Math. Comput. **186**(1), 193–202 (2007)

Preliminaries on a Stochastic Cellular Automaton Based Framework for Studying the Population Dynamics of COVID-19

Isaías Lima[2]($\boxtimes$) and Pedro Paulo Balbi[1,2]

[1] Faculdade de Computação e Informática, Universidade Presbiteriana Mackenzie, São Paulo, SP, Brazil
[2] Pós-Graduação em Engenharia Elétrica e Computação, Universidade Presbiteriana Mackenzie, São Paulo, SP, Brazil
isaiahlima18@gmail.com

Abstract. The propagation of infectious diseases through social interactions can be mitigated when health measures aim to reduce or remove the results of these interactions. This is the scenario of ongoing COVID-19 pandemic adopted quarantine policies, from social distancing to lockdown, and of immunization programs. When a sufficient number of interactions is suppressed, the spread of an infectious disease is ended achieving herd immunity, defined as the indirect protection given by immune individuals to susceptible individuals. Here we describe the preliminaries of a stochastic cellular automaton based framework designed to emulate the spread of SARS-CoV-2 in a population of static individuals interacting only via Moore neighbourhood of radius one, with a view to analyze the impact of initially immune individuals on the dynamics of COVID-19. This impact was measured comparing a progression of initial immunity ratio from 0 to 90% of the population with the number of susceptible individuals not contaminated, the peak value of active cases, the total number of deaths and the emulated pandemic duration in days. A herd immunity threshold of 60% was obtained from this procedure, which is in tune with the estimates of the currently available medical literature. Nevertheless, more accurate results demand more research efforts including better analysing the model probabilities of propagation and duration.

Keywords: Stochastic cellular automata · COVID-19 · SARS-CoV-2 · Infectious disease dynamics · Herd immunity

1 Introduction

Coronavirus Disease 19 (COVID-19) is a contagious disease that can be transmitted through social contact, with symptoms like fever, body aches and shortness of breath, caused by the Severe Acute Respiratory Syndrome-Corona-Virus (SARS-CoV-2) [3]. During the ongoing COVID-19 pandemic, individuals have

T. M. Gwizdałła et al. (Eds.): ACRI 2020, LNCS 12599, pp. 265–273, 2021.
https://doi.org/10.1007/978-3-030-69480-7_27

been presenting four types of dynamics regarding the effects and duration of the disease, as described in the recent literature, such as [4,6,7,13]. In these descriptions, the individuals can be classified as: **No Symptoms**, representing the ones who do not experience the disease effects but still can contaminate others through social contact; **Mild/Moderate Symptoms**, who present the disease effects partially, quickly becoming immune, while still contaminating others though social contact; **Severe Symptoms**, who end up needing hospitalisation and have a moderate death risk; and **Critical Symptoms**, those who need to stay in an Intensive Care Unit (ICU) with ventilation, with higher death risk.

Because in order to reduce the transmission of the SARS-CoV-2 public health measures involved different levels of quarantine, from social distancing to lockdown, several industries were affected, as well stock-markets, which responded strongly to the pandemic [3]. An important question is when these restrictions can be lifted without causing a second wave of infection, which implies the understanding of when and if herd immunity can be achieved [2]. Herd immunity is defined as an indirect individual protection from infection conferred by a sufficiently large proportion of immune individuals in a society, reducing the contamination ratio, or the average number of individuals contaminated by one ill person, to values under 1 [11].

In epidemiological studies, it is desirable to develop and parameterise mathematical models in order to predict and define control strategies and understand the impact of immune individuals on the dynamics of a disease [9]. Here, a computational model based on a stochastic cellular automaton (CA) is proposed to better understand the COVID-19 dynamics and respective herd immunity.

Cellular automata are discrete dynamical systems defined by a regular grid of cells, each one defined by a finite number of discrete states. The dynamics of a CA are defined locally, since each cell changes its state based on its own present state and those of its neighbouring cells. This principle is simple, but a CA can present arbitrary global complex behaviours. In addition, a stochastic CA defines its next state considering also a given probability distribution.

This article is organised as follow: in Sect. 2, we discuss and describe a stochastic CA implementation in order to model the dynamics of COVID-19 in a given population and a methodology to evaluate and understand the possibility of a herd immunity to appear in the population. In Sect. 3, we present the results of this evaluation. In Sect. 4, we discuss the results and propose future improvements to the model.

2   Model

Computational epidemiology models can include CAs [8,9,12] in order to simulate epidemic spreading.

Consider a closed population, without migrations, with $n \times n$ individuals, where each one has contact only with its direct neighbours, only interacting socially with them. Consider also that one of these individuals (**patient zero**) is contaminated with SARS-CoV-2, gets COVID-19, therefore being capable of following one of the four dynamics mentioned before (**No Symptoms**,

Mild/Moderate Symptoms, Severe Symptoms or **Critical Symptoms**).
According to Fig. 1, which describes these four dynamics based on [4, 6, 7], each
one shows up in a specific portion of a population: for example, 55% of the
contaminated individuals follow the **Mild/Moderate Symptoms** dynamics,
meaning that, if someone gets COVID-19, there is a 55% probability of the
person to present moderate symptoms.

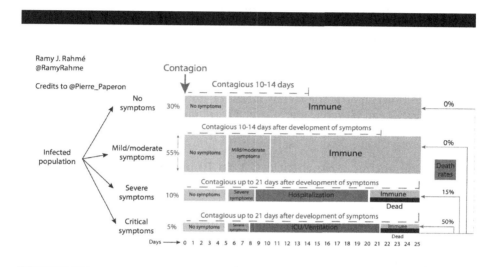

Fig. 1. Timeline, progression and mortality by severity of COVID-19, due to [10], after
[4, 6, 7, 13]. This chart provides the overall scheme for the framework explored in the
present work, with the actual values being just references of the disease at the time it
was crafted.

In the given population of $n \times n$ individuals, if one has COVID-19, in addition
to presenting the respective symptoms with a given probability the person has
a chance of contaminating the neighbourhood, so the same neighbourhood of
one individual defines the chances of being contaminated. As the neighbours of
a member of the population get contaminated by SARS-CoV-2, the probability
of this member to be contaminated gets higher and higher. In this case we
can observe that two probabilities define the behaviour of an individual: the
chance of getting ill and the possible dynamics the person will follow after getting
contaminated.

Other probabilities affect the behaviour of the members of this population.
For example, if one presents no symptoms, SARS-CoV-2 will be incubated for
around five days and the person will become immune but contagious afterwards.
This first period of incubation makes this individual already contagious since
first day of contamination. Around 10 days later he or she will cease to be

contagious and will not represent a risk for his or her neighbours. These durations of each state of the **No Symptoms** dynamics will not be deterministic, since the incubation period can take more or less days to be completed. Also the probability of an individual with no symptoms contaminating others is higher than the probability of an individual in hospitalisation. On the other hand, an hospitalised individual has a probability of dying because of the severity of the COVID-19 symptoms.

After some time, the whole population will be contaminated and submitted to the effects of COVID-19. Some individuals will become immune, others will eventually die and others will not even get sick at all. Going back to the beginning of the contamination proccess, if the population is initially immune, due to a vaccine, social isolation, or any other precautionary attitude, could the global dynamics of the population during the contamination evolve differently?

This question can be addressed by means of stochastic CAs [8,12]. The states defined by Fig. 1 can represent the states of a cell inside a CA of $n \times n$ cells, with a fix boundary condition, assuming *No Interaction* state for missing neighbours.

2.1   Implementing a Stochastic CA to Represent COVID-19 Dynamics

In a $n \times n$ stochastic CA implementing the dynamic described above, some states can be defined, **following the model described in Fig. 1 as a basis for the behaviour of the CA**:

0. **Susceptible:** capable of being contaminated;
1. **No Symptoms:** free of symptoms during the incubation period;
2. **Moderate Symptoms:** presenting moderate symptoms;
3. **Severe Symptoms:** presenting severe symptoms;
4. **Critical Symptoms:** presenting critical symptoms;
5. **Hospitalisation:** the period of hospitalisation after presenting severe symptoms;
6. **ICU/Ventilation:** the period of hospitalisation with ventilation after presenting critical symptoms;
7. **Contagious Without Symptoms:** immune to the disease, but capable of contaminating neighbours;
8. **Contagious Moderate Symptoms:** immune to the disease, but capable of contaminating neighbours after presenting moderate symptoms;
9. **Contagious Severe Symptoms:** immune to the disease, but capable of contaminating neighbours after hospitalisation;
10. **Contagious Critical Symptoms:** immune to the disease, but capable of contaminating neighbours after hospitalisation with ventilation;
11. **Dead:** those who died and are removed from the population, therefore no longer interacting;
12. **Immune:** immune to the disease and incapable of contaminating neighbours.

In terms of a SIR model (with its **Susceptible, Infected** and **Removed** states), our *Susceptible* state is SIR's **Susceptible**, the present *Immune* and *Dead* states can collectively be regarded as **Removed**, and the remaining states correspond to **Infected**. A SEIR (Susceptible, Exposed, Infected and Removed) model is not suitable in this case since the incubation period of SARS-CoV-2 makes an individual contagious since the very first day of infection.

First, it is important to define that each state has a contamination probability: for example, a cell with *Contagious Without Symptoms* state has 100% probability of contaminating the neighbourhood, considering that one individual in this situation would not notice having COVID-19 and would keep having social interactions with others normally. The contamination probability is defined as follow: for *Susceptible*, *Dead* and *Immune* individuals it will be considered to be inexistent; for *Hospitalisation* and *ICU/Ventilation* will be 10%; and for the other states it will be considered 100%.

Second, it is necessary to define and describe the state transition rules for the states. For states like *Susceptible*, the transition is defined by a probability of contamination given by the states of its neighbourhood. For other states, the transition is defined not by its neighbours, but by a duration. In this case, each day will be represented as a time step in the CA. Since this duration is not deterministic, a uniform distribution can be applied within ±20% of the duration to define the number of time steps a cell stays in the respective state.

The state transitions are described as follows:

- If a cell is in *Susceptible* state, the next state will be *No Symptoms*, according to the average probability of contamination given by each one of its neighbours in a **Moore neighbourhood** with $radius = 1$;
- The *No Symptoms* state has a duration of about five days, according to Fig. 1. The next possible states are *Contagious Without Symptoms* with 30% probability, *Moderate Symptoms* with 55% probability, *Severe Symptoms* with 10% probability, and *Moderate Symptoms* with 5%. So, after the respective stochastic duration of the *No Symptoms* state, any cell will have these probabilities of chaging to one of the corresponding states;
- The transitions of *Hospitalisation*, *ICU/Ventilation*, *Contagious Without Symptoms*, *Contagious Moderate Symptoms*, *Contagious Severe Symptoms* and *Contagious Critical Symptoms* sates are defined only by the duration of the previous states and can be understood with Fig. 1;
- The state transition to *Immune* is also defined by the duration of the previous states if the cell has the states *Contagious Without Symptoms* to *Contagious Critical Symptoms*;
- Finally, the state transition to *Dead* is aditionally defined by a death probability which is applied for cells in *Hospitalisation* state (15%) and *ICU/Ventilation* (50%) state.

With those state transitions defined, a stochastic CA can be implemented and run, stopping when a steady-state global state is achieved. This steady-state can be defined as a global configuration whose cells are only in the *Susceptible*, *Dead* or *Immune* states. The starting configuration, or time step zero, can be defined as one made up by a single cell in the *No Symptoms* state and all the others in the *Susceptible* state.

Some information could be obtained from this stochastic CA, such like:

- The dynamics of the number of cells with *Susceptible* state along the time steps, representing how many individuals are not infected;
- The dynamics of the number of cells with *Dead* state along the time steps, represeting how many individuals died;
- The dynamics of the number of cells with other states along the time steps, represeting how many individuals are currently infected.

With a stochastic CA implemented to emulate COVID-19 in the proposed population, the question about the impact of initially immune individuals in the global behaviour can then be investigated in terms of understandind what could be the necessary herd immunity to impact the dynamics as desired.

2.2   Analysing Herd Immunity

Using the COVID-19 stochastic CA model proposed above, the impact of initially immune individuals can be studied by changing the initial global state of the lattice. Besides initialising the CA with one contaminated cell and all the others as susceptible, randomly distributed immune cells can replace some of the susceptible cells.

Accordingly, firstly, an initial $n \times n$ grid with cells in the *Susceptible* state is created; then, one single cell is randomly chosen and reassigned to *No Symptoms* state (patient zero); finally, a randomly chosen percentage (m) of the remaining cells are reassigned to the *Immune* state. Since the CA is stochastic, a number of 10 simulations should be performed, each one executing the required amount of time steps until convergence of the predefined global configuration; along the way, the following should be monitored (to be later averaged out of the 10 simulations):

- The number of susceptible cells which did not have their state changed;
- The peak amount of cells actively infected;
- The final amount of immune cells;
- The total number of dead cells after convergence;
- The necessary number of time steps to converge.

Finally, the value of m may be increased between zero and 90%, with steps of 5%, allowing to check the variation of each output in terms of the number of initially immune cells. This procedure should be able to support the analysis of a possible herd immunity in the proposed population.

3   Results

The proposed procedure was run, monitoring the average outputs described earlier. Considering the average of 10 simulations for each value of initially immune individuals between zero and 90%, with steps of 5%, a total number of 190 simulations of the model were obtained, on a grid of $100 \times 100 = 10000$ cells with a fix boundary condition, assuming *No Interaction* state for missing neighbours. The implementation was written in Mathematica's native Wolfram language.

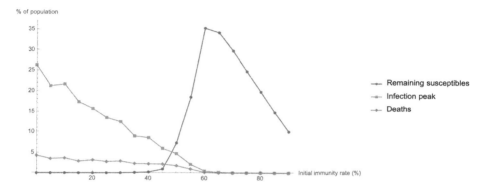

Fig. 2. Population configurations by the proportion of initially immune cells.

Figure 2 displays the impact of initially immune individuals on the dynamic of the population. First, we can observe this impact on the remaining cells in *Susceptible* state, or the impact on the number of individuals who were not contaminated during the propagation of the SARS-CoV-2. In a first moment, it is possible to infer that the more immune individuals initially in the population, the less susceptible individuals it has, but this linear relation is predominant only after an initial proportion of immunity of 65%. Before this value, the final amount of susceptibles is under 1% of the population and starts increasing around 45% of immunity. Second, we notice the impact of initially immune individuals on the infection peak, or the maximum number of active cases. The peak appears to have a negative linear correlation with the immunity ratio until this proportion achieves 65%, where it remains under 1% of the population. Third, the impact of the immunity ratio on the total amount of deaths. This behaviour is similar to the variation of the infection peak, but less linear.

Figure 3 gives an idea of the duration of the COVID-19 pandemic in the proposed population, as impacted by the immunity ratio. Apparently, ratios under 55% display a positive correlation, or a tendency of the pandemic to take longer time periods to end as the population increases its initial immunity. In other words, the remaining susceptible individuals do not receive any protection against contamination, but SARS-CoV-2 takes a longer time to spread. For ratios

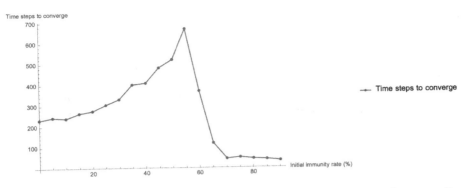

Fig. 3. Variation of the number of steps necessary to converge the CA by the proportion of initially immune cells.

over 55%, the pandemic takes less and less time to end, meaning that more individuals are not contaminated in the proccess.

The general picture indicates that there is a big change of their dynamics around 60% of immunity ratio.

4   Concluding Remarks

The proposed COVID-19 stochastic CA model allowed preliminary tests on building a framework to analyse the dynamics of the disease in a given population. More precisely, we performed an initial study on the impact of initially immune individuals in the dynamics of SARS-CoV-2 propagation in a population of static individuals interacting socially only with their neighbours in a Moore neighbourhood of radius one. Different levels of initial immunity rates, from zero to 90%, were evaluated, and the dynamics presented a threshold around 60% of immunity.

The model parameterisation regarding the contamination probabilities and the duration of each state was somewhat arbitrary, so that herd immunity results obtained should be revisited for proper confidence; nevertheless, it is surprising and encouraging that the 60% value that came out the experiments are definitely in tune with the current literature [1,5]. An explanation could be that the whole stochastic CA based architecture we defined may be endowed of a high degree of robustness to the its parameter values. But definite conclusion demands more evaluation, so that forthcoming research efforts should include better analysing the model probabilities of propagation and duration. And this is the direction we are taking.

Acknowledgements. This work was supported by research grants provided to P.P.B. by CAPES (STIC-AmSud CoDANet project, number 88881.197456/2018-01) and by CNPq-PQ 305199/2019-6. We also thank Ramy J. Rahmé for providing us with the chart in Fig. 1, which is an improved version of the one he originally posted in March

2020 in Tweeter, which, in turn, is an improved version of another chart due to Pierre Paperon, that had just been published in LinkedIn.

References

1. Aguas, R., et al.: Herd immunity thresholds for SARS-CoV-2 estimated from unfolding epidemics, July 2020
2. Britton, T., Ball, F., Trapman, P.: A mathematical model reveals the influence of population heterogeneity on herd immunity to SARS-CoV-2. Science **369**(6505), 846–849 (2020)
3. Ezhilan, M., Suresh, I., Nesakumar, N.: SARS-CoV, MERS-CoV and SARS-CoV-2: a diagnostic challenge. Measurement **168**, 108335 (2021)
4. Ferguson, N., et al.: Report 9: impact of non-pharmaceutical interventions (NPIS) to reduce COVID-19 mortality and healthcare demand (2020)
5. Jones, F.: The uncertainties about herd immunity, September 2020. https://revis tapesquisa.fapesp.br/as-incertezas-sobre-a-imunidade-coletiva. FAPESP Research (in Portuguese)
6. Lauer, S.A., et al.: The incubation period of coronavirus disease 2019 (COVID-19) from publicly reported confirmed cases: estimation and application. Ann. Intern. Med. **172**(9), 577–582 (2020). PMID: 32150748
7. Liu, Y., et al.: Viral dynamics in mild and severe cases of COVID-19. Lancet Infect. Dis. **20**(6), 656–657 (2020)
8. Mikler, A.R., Venkatachalam, S., Abbas, K.: Modeling infectious diseases using global stochastic cellular automata. J. Biol. Syst. **13**(04), 421–439 (2005)
9. Monteiro, L.H.A., Gandini, D.M., Schimit, P.H.T.: The influence of immune individuals in disease spread evaluated by cellular automaton and genetic algorithm. Comput. Methods Programs Biomed. **196**, 105707 (2020)
10. Rahmé, R.J.: COVID19 Chart: Timeline, Progression and Mortality by Severity (2020)
11. Randolph, H.E., Barreiro, L.B.: Herd immunity: understanding COVID-19. Immunity **52**(5), 737–741 (2020)
12. Hoya White, S., Martín del Rey, A., Rodríguez Sánchez, G.: Modeling epidemics using cellular automata. Appl. Math. Comput. **186**(1), 193–202 (2007)
13. Wölfel, R., et al.: Virological assessment of hospitalized patients with COVID-2019. Nature **581**(7809), 465–469 (2020)

Author Index

Printed in the United States
By Bookmasters